THE JOURNEY
OF SURVIVORS

THE JOURNEY OF SURVIVORS

70,000-Year History of Indian Sub-Continent

SUBHRASHIS ADHIKARI

PARTRIDGE

To order additional copies of this book, contact
Partridge India
000 800 10062 62
orders.india@partridgepublishing.com

www.partridgepublishing.com/india

CONTENTS

LIST OF FIGURES

Dedicated to all those who love history:
including the left wing, the right wing, and
my favorite crispy fried chicken wing.

ABBREVIATIONS

AAP	Aam Aadmi Party
AIML	All-India Muslim League
BCE	Before Common Era
BJP	Bharatiya Janata Party
CE	Common Era
CPI(M)	Communist Party of India (Maoist)
DMK	Dravida Munnetra Kazhagam
EIC	(British) East India Company
HSRA	Hindustan Social Republican Association
IMF	International Monetary Fund
INC	Indian National Congress
IPKF	Indian Peace Keeping Force
ISVC	Indus Saraswati Valley Civilization
LTTE	Liberation Tigers of Tamil Eelam
Mya	Million Years Ago
NDA	National Democratic Alliance
OBC	Other Backward Classes
RTC	Round Table Conference

SC	Schedule Caste
ST	Schedule Tribes
TV	Television
UCC	Union Carbide Corporation
UPA	United Progressive Alliance
USA	United States of America

ACKNOWLEDGEMENT

This book would not have been possible without the support of my lovely wife, Ranjini, and even lovelier daughter, Hridhima. Writing this book took a lot of time that belonged to them. The time sometimes included weekends and vacations. This book is a result of their love, understanding, and patience. Thanks for not throwing me out of the house. I would also like to thank my parents, in-laws, my brother, and his family for their support and encouragement. Thanks to all the friends, colleagues, and readers of my blog for the stimulating debates.

This book would not have been readable without my friend and editor of this book, Madhubanti Bose (Maddy). Maddy took the pain of going through each and every word I wrote and correct the pitiable grammar and spelling, which included mistakes like 'thrown' instead of 'throne'. No wonder she once wrote in a comment, "Sometimes you frustrate and fascinate me in equal measure." Not just English, she also corrected the errors of facts and judgments. Thanks, Maddy, for all the personal time that you took out for this book, and your failed attempt at improving my English.

This book would not have been presentable without the beautifully drawn cover page by my favorite artist Sandipan Dutta (Sandy). Sandy happily took up the challenge the first day I requested him. After lots of ideas and brainstorming, we ended up with this concept that portrayed the diversity of India and 'the journey' that this book is about. Thanks, Sandy, for the perfect job. You are a great artist. No one could have done it better.

Last, but not the least, I would like to thank the Partridge team for their support and help in publishing this book. My special thanks to Mary Oxley for her support that made my life easy.

PREFACE

It has been a challenge writing about the history of India in English. Neither am I good in English nor am I an expert in history. I am just a geologist who is interested in India's past. I hope that my lack of English writing skills is partially overshadowed by the information this book has to offer. I had to depend on the books and articles written by experts to write this book. The mythological stories and the input from guides we took at various tourist places also came as a big help. Experts write only on the subject of their expertise, and no one can be an expert in the entire history of India. While trying to understand my country, I never got hold of any one book that sums up the entire 70,000-year-long journey of India and her people. Most books deal with ancient, medieval, or modern India separately, and very few with all three. And then again, modern India mostly ends with India's independence. This book attempts to fill that gap. Being an outsider, I could put together the entire history of India without going into too much technical details. I wrote this book from a layman's perspective and hope that those who are interested in Indian history will find it useful.

History contains facts, mythologies, and some fiction. No sharp boundaries exist among these three end members. Facts are often written down with added fiction, which, with time, becomes a myth. History depends on old writings, folklores, and myths to interpolate the possible truth in between the scantly known facts that archaeologists sometimes dig up. The known history changes as more facts get revealed. History is, thus, prone to interpreter's bias. The British made a lot of contribution in unraveling the history of India. Quite naturally, Indian history was recorded from a colonial perspective. Later, to neutralize the bias, a nationalistic version of Indian history was born. Often, the two versions of history clashed with each other. History is also biased towards those who won battles and were alive to write about it. History of India, like everywhere else, got mingled with politics. The right and the left wing—each has its own version. I have tried my best to keep a neutral viewpoint. But even then, the history that I write is my version. It is a humble request to the readers to have an open mind while reading this book as nothing is an absolute fact. Enjoy the past filled with possibilities.

This book is chronologically divided into 13 chapters that deal with the long journey we commenced 70,000 years ago. The first chapter will give a brief introduction about our knowledge of prehistoric India. Chapter 2 to chapter 5 deals with our journey from hunters and gatherers to empire builders. In chapter 6, we reach our peak. Chapters 7 and 8 deal with our evolution with the rise of the Middle East. In chapters 9 and 10, we fall prey to imperialistic ambitions and fight back. Chapter 11 deals with India after independence. Every chapter has the date range corresponding to the period of history it belongs to.

While reading this book, one can either go sequentially through all the chapters or look at the 'Summary Table of Important Events in Indian History' at the end of the book and selected a chapter based on the dates of the event. The book has relivant references numbered within '[##]'. The reference for the corresponding number can be found at the end of the book.

For other countries, winning has been necessary for survival. But for us, survival has been winning. Kingdoms rose and fell, invaders invaded, flourished and perished; but we continued to survive. One thing that we have learned through the struggles is that survival is not about planning or being organized. That might help you win battles, but to survive, you need to stay alive each and every moment, helped by your intuitions. Indians were never good with chess. But when Anand defeated the highly organized Russian chess players, he did that through intuition and not through the tried-and-tested formula of rigorous planning and strategy. He showed the world a new way of winning chess: the Indian way. When the opponent is strong, planning seldom helps. Instead, we take one step at a time, surviving every moment. We survived the Greeks, the Huns, the Afghans, the Mughals, and the Europeans. Not many can claim of surviving such an onslaught. But we did it one invader at a time. We did it by the process of assimilation, not annihilation. It is obvious in the way we walk or drive our cars—one opportunity at a time. Probably that is why we love cricket so much. It is played one ball at a time.

As we traveled on the beautiful path called India, various travellers joined us. Sometimes we welcomed them, and at other times, we resisted. As more people joined, there were clashes and fights. There were times when we became friends and times when we were foes. There was chaos—chaos that became our identity. Chaos was the necessary evil for each group to survive together yet separately. But the journey continued. Let us begin the journey—our journey—the journey of survivors.

INTRODUCTION

India has always had a strange way with her conquerors.
In defeat, She beckons them in, then slowly seduces,
assimilates and transforms them.

—William Dalyrmple, *White Mughals: Love and*
Betrayal in Eighteenth-Century India

Variety Is the Spice of Life

Millions of years ago, long before the dawn of humans, a dramatic union between the Eurasian and Indian tectonic plates resulted in the birth of the mighty Himalayas. From Himalayas descended the great rivers of Indus, Saraswati, and Ganges, making Indian subcontinent rich and fertile. The fertile subcontinent became the preferred home for the migrating human population from various parts of the globe. The Indian subcontinent, thus, became one of the most diverse countries the world has ever seen. While the subcontinent evolved as new cultures merged with the old, relics of the past somehow managed to linger on. The uniqueness of such a society lies in its non-uniqueness. Some of these complexities are difficult for an outsider to understand. Working in a multinational company, I have interacted with many expats. While they were excited to learn about this new culture that is thousands of years old, India also frustrated them. The dirt scattered around, the lack of public etiquette, the crazy driving, the bureaucracy, and the hierarchy perplexed them. Since I grew up in this culture, I never realized the difference until one British gentleman asked me why so many Indians behave this way. There began my quest to apprehend this strange land to which I wasn't a stranger. To understand this mysterious land, one has to know its past. Only then can we truly appreciate its beauty, and only then can we comprehend its problems. The key to the solution of many of India's problems lies in its past, which is what this book will attempt to unravel.

Numerous attempts have been made to simplify the complex diversity of Indians by putting them into different pigeonholes. For long, there existed a racist classification scheme for the people of the Indian subcontinent, a legacy of the British Raj. Recently, an equally biased classification trying to fit the 'out of India' theory has been promoted. It is time we understand our diversity in a better and nonpartisan way. The diversity of Indians is evident in the study done by Indian Genome Variation Initiative funded by the government of India between 2003 and 2008 [1]. Genetic studies have not only proved the diversity but also showed that no mixing of genes happened in the last 10,000 years. This piece of evidence was the key in disproving the Aryan invasion theory. However, Arrian, the ancient Greek writer, noted difference between the looks of northern and southern Indians thousands of years ago. He wrote,

"The southern Indians resemble the Ethiopians a good deal, and, are black of countenance, and their hair black also, only they are not as snub-nosed or so woolly-haired as the Ethiopians; but the northern Indians are most like the Egyptians in appearance." The difference is because of migration of different groups that happened much before 10,000 years ago. Despite some difference in morphologies, there is not much, if at all, genetic difference.

People of the Indian subcontinent have often been morphologically divided into four broad groups: Caucasoid, Mongoloid, Austrics, and Negrito. Linguistically, they can be divided into Aryan, Dravidian, Tibeto-Burman, and Austroasiatic. It is important to mention here that word *arya*, as used in ancient Indo-Iranian texts, has nothing to do with race as many would like to believe. It denoted group of people who spoke in Aryan language. These languages (Aryan and Dravidian) developed much later compared to the time of migration of the different groups into India. There is no perfect correlation between the groups classified based on linguistics and morphology. This indicates a cultural effect of interaction among different groups over a long period of time.

Negritos are the broad-headed people from Africa. Around 70,000 years ago, they became the earliest-known modern humans to colonize the subcontinent. From here, some of them moved to Southeast Asia and Australia. These hunters and gatherers were facinated by the sea and always remained close to the coast. This event was thus named the Great Coastal Migration. They were probably the first sailors as they colonized islands like Andaman, Papua Guinea, and possibly Australia [2]. These early migrating group still exist in India as the Jarawas, Onges, Sentelenese, the Great Andamanis, Irulas, Kodars, Paniyans, Kurumbas, Baigas, and Birhors [3]. The population of the Baiga of central India and the Birhor of eastern India share not only many cultural, linguistic, physical, and genetic features with the Australian aboriginals but also a perfectly matching DNA [4]. We probably owe our sailing skills to them. Thousands of years later, their successors would again come to the subcontinent. But this time, they would not come as free men but as slaves of the Islamic kings. They would be known as Sheedi and live in modern Pakistan.

Protoaustraloids or Austrics were the next batch to migrate into the Indian subcontinent 40,000 years ago. They would then travel to Myanmar and the Southeast Asian islands. Austrics were farmers who cultivated rice and vegetables and made sugar from sugarcanes [3]. We might owe a lot of our agricultural skills to these people. Belonging to this group are Santhal, Munda, Lotha, Kol, Oraon, and Korku tribes. There are some authors [5] who relate the Australian aboriginals with Austrics instead of Negroids. Most of the people who linguistically fall into Dravidian and Austroasiatic groups are Austrics. They might have migrated from around the Mediterranean region [3], but the theory is debatable.

Mongoloids are a distinct group of people characterized by yellowish-brown skin colour, straight black hair, dark eyes with pronounced epicanthic folds, and prominent cheekbones [6]. They migrated from Southeast Asia and China and settled in and around the Himalayas. The Mughals who ruled India in the Middle Ages were distant relatives of the Mongoloid people of Mongolia (the place from where the group takes its name). The third phase of Mongoloids, albeit a very minor one, happened during the British rule when the Chinese workers landed in Kolkata. Many Chinese even received military training on

Indian soil during the world wars. Some of their population still survives in Tangra, the best place for lovers of Chinese food in Kolkata, and perhaps India.

Caucasians are Indo-European group of people. Numerous migrations of Caucasians have happened in and out of the Indian subcontinent through its western borders. There had been a lot of cultural intermixing between the Greeks and Indians during the time of Alexander. Post the fall of Mauryan Empire, there was a brief Indo-Greek kingdom in India. It was followed by Indo-Scythian and Indo-Kushans. Christianity found its foot on Indian soil in the first century with Saint Thomas's landing in Kerala. This happened much before Christianity spread to many parts of Europe. The White Huns (Hephthalites) came and settled in India as Rajputs, Gujars and Jats in around fifth century. Newer Caucasoid groups came again as Parsee and Jews when the Islamic rulers forced them out of their territory. The trend of migration continued with the Islamic and European conquests.

Different groups of people entered and re-entered the subcontinent over a period of 70,000 years. Sometimes they got friendly and mixed with one another, at other times they fought with one another, and many times they formed an alliance just to survive. While happy memories fade easily, the scars of battles remain. Studies provide strong evidence that we all have migrated to the subcontinent at some point of time. But what is more intriguing is the fact that even after so many phases of invasions, none of the communities have been totally erased. That's the peculiarity of India and Indians. We all have left our marks, and we have all survived. We all have contributed individually to the growth of this wonderful land, and now we must unite for the growth of this country. When we enjoy the samosa, we must not forget that the concept of samosa was brought to India by the Islamic invaders, and the potatoes (along with chillies and tomatos) stuffed inside it by the Europeans from Peru, and the spices that make it so yummy came from Southeast Asia. While reading this book, one must remember that variety is the spice of life, and we would have missed the spice without all the intermixing. The vibrant colorful India is a legacy of that diversity. We can either choose to remember the bitter fractions of our past and fight or celebrate the uniqueness of our non-uniqueness. Our great diversity gives us this magnificent opportunity to show the world how to live together in peace and harmony. Our unity can make not just India but the world a much better place. The choice lies with us.

Prehistoric India (70,000 to 5000 BCE)

*It [India] is not only a country and something
geographical, but the home and the youth of the soul,
the everywhere and nowhere, the oneness of all times.*

—Herman Hesse, *Herman Hesse: A Collection of
Criticism by Fudith Sielemann*

The Flintstones

Our civilization is a product of geological miracles. We survived against all odds and are soon to become the most populated country in the world. Our ancestors could have been wiped out 65 million years ago along with the dinosaurs. Or better still, we could both have survived! Jurassic Park wouldn't have been the best circumstances for a 'brain with little brawn' species to evolve and flourish. Had South and North American tectonic plates not collided to alter the ocean currents, and had Africa not been torn apart to create the Great African Rift Valley, Eastern Africa would have remained humid. In that happy environment, our lazy ancestors would have never put in the effort to walk upright, and there would have been no us! What if Indian plate did not rush to collide head-on with Eurasia? Without the Himalayas, born out of the collision, there would have been no fertile land for creation of the Indian civilization. After surviving all those chanced episodes, we were almost wiped out around 70,000 years ago by the Toba eruption.

Numerous Paleolithic sites [7] have been found in India as identified from the stone tools (shown in figure 1). Unfortunately, no human skeletons have yet been recovered. The dating of most of the sites is disputed. A site in Uttarbaini in Jammu was dated as 2.8 ± 0.5 million years old [8]. Similar findings have been made in Potwar plateau of Pakistan Punjab. The only fossil to have survived 500,000 years in the subcontinent is, not surprisingly, that of a woman. Indian women have the tenacity to survive against all odds. She was named Narmada 'man'. Guess those who found it did not look deep enough. As with most ladies, the age of this particular lady is also debatable. There is also no consensus about the fact that she is a *Homo sapien*. Few of these original 'Indians' survived the Toba eruption that took place 70,000 years ago. The deadly eruption created a ten-year-long winter. It resulted in an ecological disaster that destroyed most of the vegetation. The long and harsh winter decreased the human population of the world to just 3,000-10,000 individuals. All human beings alive today are descendants from those small numbers of individuals, as proven by genetic studies. In fact, every person alive in this world today can be traced back to a single female who lived 140,000 years ago and to a single male living 90,000 years ago.

Some of the 'original' Indians did manage to survive the Toba eruption. Similar stone tools have been unearthed below and above the Toba ash from few places in southern India. But they did not survive for long as our ancestors were on their way. Soon after the Toba catastrophe, the first notable flush of migration took place from Africa. It was called the great coastal migration. This more sophisticated group of *Homo sapiens* replaced the 'original' Indians. Since then, many more hopped in. The best evidence of these early Indians is preserved in Bhimbetka caves (figure 1) that have more than a dozen rock shelters. The first evidence of these ancient caves was found way back in 1888. They were mistaken for Buddhist caves as every other ancient Indian discoveries of the time. They were accidentally discovered again by Dr V S Wakankar while he was traveling by train to Bhopal. He realized that he was looking at something prehistoric. The caves contain one of the oldest rock engravings in the world [9]. The caves also have preserved cave paintings of different times superimposed on one another. Some claim a continuous occupation of these caves from 100,000 BCE to as recent as 1000 CE [10]. The people who stayed there were predominantly hunters and gatherers. The paintings revealed their love for hunting, music, and dancing. Later drawing depicts Puranic gods like Ganesha, Shiva Linga, Nandi, Swastika, and Trishula. Similar cave paintings have been found in many places scattered aroung India. Interestingly, some of the old rock paintings in Chhattisgarh resemble aliens and UFOs seen in Hollywood movies.

There are tribes present in various parts of India who are still untouched by modernization. There are around thirteen tribal languages spoken by more than half a million (1991 survey) tribal people. Their lifestyle throws light on the society our ancestors lived in. The Negrito race of Andaman is one such 'pure' race that has remained largely unchanged since the great coastal migration. They live in the forest and depend on hunting, fishing, and gathering. The tribals still use primitive bows, arrows, and spears to hunt. They love pig meat but hate birds or deer. Honey is their favorite. They hardly wear any clothes but are fascinated about their ornaments. They have not yet invented pottery and use hollowed wood as containers. They are the last of the people who still live like the firsts. They love to dance and sing. There are no coded laws, but order is maintained by few leaders. Loss of self-esteem in the clan is the most severe form of punishment, and it works pretty fine [11].

As the ice age melted away and earth became more hospitable, people started getting organized into groups and settled down in a fertile land. Human beings started to tweak the rules of nature. In nature, the big fish eats small fish, and the fittest survive. Humans created a world where even the weak could survive. They named this world 'civilization'. In the new world they were making, unity was strength. Civilization needed a tool—an idea—to bind people together. The idea came in the form of society and religion. Some among the clans claimed to be closer to god and declared themselves priests. Some of these priests specialized in healing the sick, some in predicting the future, while others at changing it. The first temples (dolmens) were created out of stones and menhirs, relics of which can be still traced in various parts of India. Each group/clan had one or more heads, usually a wise and elderly person.

Polygamy was common at that time. There are some tribes in the Himalayas (Laddakh) even today where a woman can marry many husbands. And then, there are many tribes where a man can take many wives. Divorces and widow marriages were common. While there might be rules about choosing mates, premarital sex was neither uncommon nor unsocial. There are customs that still exist among various tribes where young men and women dance together in the evenings as past-time. It helps them choose the most eligible mate. Some of the dancing rituals are painted in the caves of Bhimbetka. During marriage, in most tribes, the groom had to pay dowry to his father-in-law as he was going to take away a working member. To pay the money, some even worked under the father-in-law until he earned enough to ask for the bride's hand.

As the earth got warmer, some of the hunters and gatherers turned to a quasi-sedentary agricultural lifestyle. The transition was not a sudden revolution that happened around 10,000 years ago. It was a gradual change occurring over thousands of years. Evidence of early transition has been reported from north-central India [12]. Some believe that women took the lead to bring about the change. They were the ones who gathered seeds while men went to hunt. They were the ones who planted the seeds they gathered. Were they sowing the seeds of their own downfall? Agriculture created a civilization that slowly snatched women of their rights. Closed mind and orthodoxy are by-products of civilization.

Our ancestors tamed the wild and laid the foundation of our modern civilization. The early tillers practiced shifting-agriculture. It is still practiced by some tribes of Northeastern India, Odisha, and Madhya Pradesh. The community controlled certain measure of land and put some of it under cultivation every year. At the end of winter, a portion of land was chosen and marked for cultivation. Cutting the trees and shrubs cleared the land. They were then allowed to dry under the sun. The dried woods were burnt before the rains. The fire killed the weeds and insects while the ashes made the soil fertile. Holes were made in the ground with sticks. Seeds were sowed and covered back with mud. Then came the rain, and the seeds started to sprout. There were grand rituals after the harvest when the crops were divided among different families. Such harvest festivals are still held in different parts of India. The land was then left to recover for years, and they moved on to a new land to cultivate. Even though the farmland kept moving, the clans seldom moved for generations [11]. Along with agriculture, they started domesticating livestock. The first evidence of domestication is found from the Middle East dated as 11,000 years old. It probably started in India during similar times. Ships, goats, cattle, and pigs were common animals that were domesticated.

The quasi-sedentary lifestyle gave people ample time for art and craft. From that was born the artisans. The different customs of priests, farmers, and artisans marked the beginning of the first crude caste system. This advanced form of civilization grew in a limited area. Most people around the world continued with their hunting-and-gathering lifestyle. Mother Goddess, like Lajja Gauri, was the most common goddess of the prehistoric era. Lajja Gauri is a fertility goddess who sits in a squatting position with legs open as if she is about to give birth. She often has a lotus in place of the head depicting blooming youth.

According to Jared Diamond, the spread of food production through a long east–west axis like Europe to Asia was easy. The same was difficult along the long north–south axis of America or Africa as climate changed quickly over short distances across different latitudes. A single innovation in one place rapidly spread along the east–west axis. It helped in development of trading, technologies, pottery, metallurgy, writing etc. in Eurasia. Genetic diversity is the greatest along this axis of Eurasia as compared to the north-south axis of native America or Africa. This easy diffusion acted as a catalyst in the progress of human civilization in Eurasia while other continents failed to catch up [2]. Among these people, there were few who had the advantage of big rivers and raw materials. In the next chapter, we will walk with our ancestors as they create the first cities of the world with their newfound materialism.

The Legend of Indus (5000 to 2000 BCE)

*India, the cradle of human race, the birthplace of human
speech, the mother of history, the grandmother of legend,
and the great grandmother of tradition.*

—Mark Twain, *Following the Equator*

2.1   The Great Find

B etween the years 1829 and 1831, two British
military men independently traveled the vast
expanse of northwest India. One of them was James
Lewis who ran away from the British regiment, changed
his name, and became American Charles Masson. The
other was Alexander Burnes, a key player in the 'Great
Game' between Russia and Great Britain. Burnes traveled
to northwest India, Kabul, and Central Asia in search of
political information. Both these gentlemen chanced upon
many old mounds, including the one in Harappa. They

described the ruins without realizing its significance. At that time, for the Europeans, Indian history began with the invasion of Alexander the Great.

In 1856, British engineers were building railway lines through Harappa when they found lots of old bricks. They used those unclaimed bricks to build the railways without realizing what they were destroying. Years later, in 1872, another gentleman with the name Alexander unearthed some ruins from the village of Harappa. He called it a Buddhist city. Alexander Cunningham discovered and described many Harappan seals. But he still could not realize their true significance. Four more decades passed by without much progress until an Italian named Tessitori fell in love with India. He came to this new land to explore. Tessitori unearthed what he thought was a prehistoric site in Kalibangan. By that time, Max Muller had already stretched the Indian history back by few centuries before Alexander's invasion. Even though Muller never visited India, he learned Sanskrit and interpreted the ancient Indian texts. To his delight, he found a common link between Sanskrit and the European languages. There was a sharp contrast of Indo-European languages with the Dravidian languages of South India. The latter was not found anywhere else in the world, apart from a small village in Pakistan and few tribes in North India. His simple explanation was migration of Indo-European Aryans from west into India. They displaced the native Dravidians farther south. That also explained the mysterious Indian caste system. The Brahmins, who wrote the ancient texts in Aryan language, were considered as the invading Aryans. The people of lower caste were interpreted as the enslaved non-Aryans, which included Dravidians. The Sanskrit word *dasa* was literally translated to *slaves*. It was a fascinating story. All it required was some evidence to back it up. Tessitori's discovery was a step towards that.

The commencement of World War I meant that the discovery of the new archeological sites was postponed further. Excavation regained momentum in 1921–22 under a gentleman named John Marshall. Rai Bahadur Daya Ram Sahni and Madho Sarup Vats discovered Harappa during this new exploration phase. It was followed by discovery of Mohenjo-Daro. It was only in 1924 that the sites got their true recognition. John Marshall announced to the world the discovery of an ancient civilization, at par with the discoveries of Mesopotamia and Egypt. The new civilization, being on the bank of Indus River, was called as Indus Valley civilization. Soon after the announcement, people started finding similarity of the script and seals of Indus Valley civilization with that of the other old civilizations. It pushed back the history of Indian civilization to 3500 BCE [13].

This brought up a new challenge, though. How would the Aryan invasion theory fit with a preexisting Indian civilization? Two observations settled the matter. Firstly, the script of Indus Valley civilization did not appear to be Indo-European. Secondly, there was no evidence yet of presence of horses and chariots, both very common to the Aryans. The natives of Indus Valley civilization were thus considered by European historians to be different from the Aryans who wrote the Vedas. From reading the Vedas, it appeared that the people who wrote them were nomadic unlike the people of well-settled Indus Valley civilization. The Vedic people also attacked walled cities like those of Harappa and Mohenjo-Daro. The problem was that both Indus Valley civilization natives and the

Vedic Aryans lived in the same area along the fertile belt of Indus and Saraswati. Considering them to be separate, as believed then, the only possible explanation was that one group replaced the other. The wars mentioned in Vedic texts justified Aryan invasion. Since the Aryans still exist in form of Indian 'Hindus', they must have invaded and replaced the natives of Indus Valley civilization, who were now assumed to be Dravidians. It fitted perfectly with Max Muller's theory. Presence of Dravidian-speaking Brahui community in Pakistan's Sindh and Baluchistan helped the cause. Recent studies, however, show that the Brahui people migrated from South India as recently as 100 CE. More than history, the story made perfect political sense to the ruling European class. It helped in building a bridge between the influential upper-class Indians and British, making it easier to manipulate the Indians. One must not forget that the British were just taking advantage of the weakness that was already there in our society.

With further research, however, people started to doubt the Aryan invasion theory. No evidence of violent invasion has yet been found. Artifacts collected from Indus Valley civilization sites have a lot of similarity to modern India (of both north and south), like the Shiva linga, swastika, shell bangles, cubical dice, vase with painting of the story of thirsty crow, toy wheels, and even possible horse bones [14]. All this points towards continuation of the culture of Indus Valley civilization into modern India. The final nail in the coffin of the Aryan invasion theory came from the genetic studies. Previous genetic studies were biased by small number of samples. The results were force-fitted to Aryan invasion theory. Recent studies, having adequate samples, tell a different story.

The unique genetic marker Haplogroup U (a type of mitochondrial DNA or mtDNA shared by common ancestors) is present in both Europeans and Indians. Studies show that these two groups shared a common ancestry as predicted by Aryan invasion theory. However, the studies also showed that the separation between these two groups took place more than 10,000 years ago. There is no record of 'Aryan invasion' in our DNA. There is no differentiation of gene type on the basis of caste, tribe, region, or religion. Haplogroup U, which is common in the Caucasians and North Indians, is also present in the tribes of eastern India. Most interestingly, the M-group (earlier considered as the marker for Aryans) occurred in high frequency among all Indians irrespective of caste, tribes, or the language they speak [15]. In fact, it can be said with some confidence that the M-group has actually spread out of India. If there is a mixing between the Indians living in north and south India, it happened before 10,000 years ago, much before the proposed Aryan invasion.

In 1947, India not only got independence but was also partitioned into India and Pakistan. While the major Indus Valley civilization sites went to Pakistan, India was not ready to give away it's precious past. After a long debate, the finds of Indus Valley civilization that were kept in museums all across India were divided equally between the two nations. In a way, not only India but also the Indus Valley civilization was partitioned. Loss of the Indus Valley civilization sites meant that there was an extra effort put in by independent India to hunt for similar sites in her own territory. The efforts met with success. More Indus Valley civilization sites were found along what has been interpreted as the bed of the long-lost Saraswati River, than on the banks of Indus. The results are not surprising as there were not much effort put on the other side of the border to unearth these ancient sites. One should not, however, undermine the importance of Saraswati River. It would be more appropriate to call this ancient civilization as Indus-Saraswati Valley civilization (ISVC). Slowly but surely, the mystery of the great ancient civilization was unveiled.

2.2   The Mystery Unveiled

The dry coldness of the ice age that had forced humanity into the caves for ages was melting. Out of the caves, into the land, human beings warmed up to new challenges. The east–west axis from Turkey to India has been the cradle of civilization. Archeological sites uncovered in Israel and Uzbekistan are pushing back the date of human civilization. The find of Gobekli Tepe has changed the perception about our past [16]. This grand temple was built 11,000 years ago in Turkey. It establishes the complex architectural thinking capability of the ancient people. The earliest evidences of civilization in India have been unearthed from Rakhigarh, Mehrgarh, Balochistan and Lahurdewa [17]. They date back to the Neolithic period (9,000 to 4,500 years ago). These proto-cities marked the beginning of the legend of Indus.

Farming and animal domestication started when the climate became humid [18]. It also marked the beginning of the villages, or the early cities (or proto-cities). Before the discovery of Rakhigarhi, the proto-ISVC was thought to have developed in the west, in and around Mehrgarh. It was commonly believed that the cities spread eastwards into Indus Valley and then Saraswati Valley. Recent excavations challenged that interpretation. Current studies show that the early civilization was distributed over a wider area from Ganga Valley to Iran. It was a period that coincided well with the increase in the intensity of SW monsoon. Wheat and barley were the first cereals to be cultivated [19]. Fixed agricultural land resulted in the establishment of permanent villages and towns. Systematic storage of food is evident from the excavated food repository compartments. Along with cultivation of plants, domestication of animals also began. The increasing occurrence, corresponding with decreasing body size of animals like sheep, is a clear evidence of domestication [8]. With surplus of products compared to consumption, people of proto-ISVC began trading. Metals and gemstones have been found in the sites that are not indigenous to the Indus and Saraswati Valley plain. They had to be transported from faraway lands like Afghanistan, Iran, and coastal areas. Artifacts made in the valley have been found in faraway places too. Interaction and trading with other cultures was a common practice of the time. Different cultures were getting inextricably mixed for the first time in history. Different tribes were no more a threat, but an oppourtunity. The influence of trading by people of ISVC included North Afghanistan, Turkmenistan, Iran, Bahrain, Failaka, Oman, and Mesopotamia [13, 20].

Organized burial sites have been excavated from Mehrgarh and Rakhigarh. Many persons have been buried with food and jewelry, showing their faith in life after death. It is similar to other ancient cultures around the globe. Increase in the population of ISVC with time resulted in space constraints in the burial sites. Bones of old corpses were dug out and buried in a smaller place to make way for new corpses [8]. Similar 'second burial' can be seen even today in places like Taiwan. The space constraint probably led to the development of cremation. Earliest evidence of cremation is found from the H-site of ISVC dated to around 3,700 years before present. Cremation became a common practice all over India much later.

While rains created the villages of proto-ISVC, it was the lack of it that turned the villages into big cites. As the rains decreased and northern India became drier, the people of ISVC required innovation to survive. The innovation resulted in the creation of irrigation canals, dams, and large ponds to quench the thirst of ever-growing population. Large urban centers were developed that were surrounded by smaller settlements. These were the places of opportunities, and people started to migrate from neighbouring villages. The cities rapidly grew in size. Emergence of the elite is evident from types of jewelry obtained from Kunal [20]. Social status is also evident from the differences in the types of graves between the rich and not-so-rich people. There were special residential sites probably meant for very important persons. Unlike the Egyptians, however, there was no evidence of grand structures or any central religion. Nor is there any evidence of large-scale army or any significant wars. That is quite amazing considering that, at its peak, ISVC was the largest Bronze Age civilization in the world (figure 2).

The conversion from a busy hunting-and-gathering lifestyle to a more sedentary lifestyle gave people more time for art and crafts. While the people of ISVC moved ahead, the rest of India maintained hunting-and-gathering lifestyle. Few groups showed evidence of agriculture and animal domestication. This latter group set up the early republic villages in India. These villages remained unchanged for thousands of years till industrialization. They were not isolated groups. They interacted and traded with one another. Each village had its own culture and rules but dependent on one another for survival.

Though each site of ISVC is a bit different, they all have many common elements. All cities grew up along a river, not necessarily Indus or Saraswati. The cities were well organized, having planned roads, good drainage systems, fortified walls, and houses made of standard-sized bricks. Few of the earliest-known flush-ilets in the world have been found from ISVC sites. All houses had toilets, quite contrary to modern India. These toilets were connected to a common sewerage pipe. Some houses also had tandoor oven. The people of ISVC might have been the first ones to enjoy the delicious kababs and tandoori dishes. There were standard weights and linear measurement scale. Metal alloys of pure copper, tin, arsenic, lead, nickel, zinc etc. were very common. These metals were mostly mined from nearby Aravalli hills. Metallurgy started in India as early as 5,500 to 5,000 years ago.

The people of ISVC harvested wheat, barley, mustard, peas, rice, millets, cotton, walnuts, pulses etc. Domestic animals comprised of cattle, buffaloes, sheep, goats, pigs, camels, elephants, dogs, and cats [20]. The people of ISVC developed their own script, one of the four earliest-known scripts in the world. Unfortunately, the script has not been convincingly deciphered yet. Scripts were essential in maintaining trading records with other civilizations. Similar scripts have been found in Sumeria, showing the importance of script in trading. Just like Sanskrit was later restricted to the Brahmins, it might be possible that the ISVC script was also restricted. Maybe only the traders knew it, and the language died with the traders. Or maybe not. Remarkably, similar script have been found at Vaishali in Bihar dating to just 600 BCE. Did the language survive as the people of ISVC moved towards east?

The common deities of ISVC were the Mother Goddess, a Yogi with a pair of horns interpreted as proto-Shiva (Pashupati), fire god as deciphered from the fire altars, praying to banyan trees as evident from the seals and animals like cattle. Cattles were important part of the ancient society. They not only helped in agriculture but also provided milk and dairy products. Dried cow dung was used as fuel, and even the cow urine was considered to have medicinal values. Cows thus became equivalent to wealth and slowly became sacred. Hindu symbols like the swastika have been unearthed from ISVC (similar sign has been found from other ancient places not related to India). The holy baths of Harappa replicate the traditional Hindu sacred bath spots. Cremation of the dead, akin to Hindu death ritual, already existed at the last phases of the civilization. Many scholars believe that the skeletal biology of the peoples of Harappa match with that of present-day Indians. The people of ISVC did not use horse as predominantly, probably because they traded via sea route. There are pieces of evidence of chariots used for internal transport. One ISVC site has been uncovered that some archaeologists claim to contain horse bones. Interestingly, the Vedas mention about Saraswati River, a holy river that some claim to have dried up while ISVC was still flourishing around 1900 BCE [21]. Some late ISCV sites are built over the dried bed of (interpreted) Saraswati River. In Rig Veda, Saraswati was an energetic river that was flowing in her full glory. Her beauty mesmerized the Vedic poets. It is on the banks of Saraswati River that the Vedic minds were churned, from which came out their knowledge and wisdom. Saraswati thus became the goddess of knowledge and the consort of Brahma, the creator. The river died because of tectonic movements in the Himalayas, but her spirit became eternal. If Saraswati River existed during early Vedic time and ISVC continued after the river dried up, both these people have to be contemporaneous. It contradicts the theory that the Vedic people displaced the people of ISVC. A study done by James Shaffer in 1993 confirms that there has been no foreign invasion of ISVC [21]. So what happened to ISVC?

No civilization can grow forever. There comes a time when it gets saturated. Rapid urbanization and growing population made the ISVC unstable. The cities started to get decentralized. The western sites were abandoned, and the population started to move towards east. They had to interact with the people living in Ganges plain, incorporating their culture, pottery, and language. The people of ISVC were forced to return to a more stable agricultural lifestyle after their bold experiment with urbane lifestyle. They diffused with the rest of India, but their journey continued. Chakrabarti [18] wrote:

"One has to admit that the Harrapans eventually came to be rather thinly stretched on the ground and the weakening of their political fabric was almost inevitable. They were swallowed up, as it were, by the much less advanced pre-agricultural groups of inner India."

4

The Vedic People (2000 to 1000 BCE)

Who verily knows and who can here declare it, whence it was born and whence comes this creation?

—Rig Veda 10.129

3.1 Yama's Abode

Different Indo-Iranian tribes migrated in and out of India between 2000 and 1000 BCE. Each of them had different cultures, but they were genetically linked. These people composed the oldest-known scriptures of Indian civilization: the Vedas. Vedas are the window to the mind of our ancestors. *Veda* can mean *wisdom, knowledge,* or *vision.* There are four Vedas: Rig Veda, Yajur Veda, Sama Veda, and Atharva Veda. These ancient scriptures were orally transmitted for centuries and composed over many generations, making it difficult to date them. Rig Veda is the oldest of all the Vedas and is often dated to 1400 BC.

The Vedas consist of chants (*Samhitas*), rituals (*Aryanyakas* and *Brahmanas*), and philosophies (*Upanishads*). While this book has no scope to deal with the Vedas in details, it will touch upon two key characters in Vedas and one important battle. That will probably give enough clues to who these people were.

The first character is that of Yama (or Yam Raj), the god of death. According to Hindu mythology, Yama and his sister Yami were the first persons on earth. Yami wanted to have a child with Yama, which the latter refused. Yama died without having a child. As per Vedic faith, a childless person is trapped in the land of dead forever. Yama, the great king, was the first mortal to die. Being the first, he got the role of evaluating the life of those to follow. He then became a god, the guardian of the south, and the guide of the dead souls. He, it is believed, is the one who decides our fate after our death. The 'good' are rewarded and the 'bad' punished. 'Good' are the ones who follow *dharma* (duty), which is the Vedic way of life. The 'bad' are the ones who disobey. We need rules that define 'good' to maintain order in the society and to maintain the social order. The order puts the Brahmins (priests) on the top of the chain, followed by the Kshatriya (warriors), with weakest at the bottom. Without rules, the weak will protest. Without rules, there will be revolt and chaos. Without rules, there will be no civilization. But first, some sacrifices were required to build a civilization.

> First the Angirases won themselves vital power, whose fires were kindled through good deeds and sacrifice. The men together found the Pani's hoarded wealth, the cattle, and the wealth in horses and in kine.

Atharvan first by sacrifices laid the paths then,
guardian of the Law, sprang up the loving Sun.
Usana Kavya straight was hither drove the kine.
Let us with offerings honor Yama's deathless birth.
(01.038.04/05 Rig Veda [22])

Angirases, the leader of a Vedic tribe, created power
and wealth by good deeds and sacrifice. Down the line
was born the son of sun god, the king of golden era, the
deathless Yama. The name of the great king is also found
in ancient Iranian text of Avesta. Similarities in the names
contained in Vedas and Avesta are evidence of a period of
common cultural development between the tribes of India
and Iran. According to the Iranian legends, Yama (known
as Jamshid in Iran) was the fourth and greatest king of all
times. During his regime, the world prospered. It was Yama
who divided people into four castes: priests, warriors,
farmers, and artisans. It was Yama who created laws for
his great ancient civilization of Jambudweep (ancient name
of the land of India, Mount Meru being at its center).

According to Avesta, Ahura Mazda warned Jamshid
that a catastrophe is going to occur in the world and the
evil winters are about to fall. He advised Yama to construct
a boat and populate it with the fittest of men and women,
a pair of all animals and plants, and enough supply of food
and water. This story is similar to the Vedic story of Matsa
Avatar of Vishnu who warns Manu of the great flood. Manu,
like Yama, is also the son of sun god, a *Suryavanshi*. In this
story, a small fish asked Manu to save him from the big
fishes. Big fish eating small fish is the rule of the jungle, the
rule of hunters and gatherers. Manu took the fish and put it
into a pot. Protecting the weak marks the transformation
from the wild into a civilized world [23]. Safe in the pot,

without any predators, the fish slowly started to grow. Once it was large enough, it had to be shifted to a pond. The fish outgrew the pond. It was then taken to the sea. There also it kept growing until the clouds broke and rains poured in, starting the great flood. The fish, an avatar of Vishnu, then warned Manu and advised him to make the boat just like Ahura Mazda. Manu goes on to save the life on earth.

The story of the great flood is a very popular story all around the ancient world, and every civilization seems to have its own version. In Mesopotamia, *manu* means *boat* or *ark*. Some believe that the story spread from Mesopotamia through Indus Valley to India [24]. In German, Manu is the progenitor of mankind, from which the English word *man* originated. In the European version, it was Noah who plays the role of Manu, or Jamshid. Interestingly, *nau* (sounds similar to Noah) means *boat* in Sanskrit. The Chinese character that means *boat* is a combination of three letters: vessel/boat, eight, and mouth. It probably meant eight people (Noah's boat had eight people) on a boat [25]. Once the floods receded, a new era began. The new era was the golden era of the Indo-Iranians. The king of that era was Manu or Yama or Jamshid. Probably they all had same origin. According to the myths, Yama's golden era lasted for over a thousand years. Historically, the golden era could well mark the beginning of Indo-Iranian civilization. In this new civilization, what role did Asura/Ahura play?

3.2   Asura: The Good God

The Hittites Mitanni Treaty signed 3,400 years ago in Syria mentions Vedic deities like Mitra, Varuna, Indra, and

Nasatya (Ashvins). It is the oldest archaeological evidence of Rig Vedic gods [22]. It is fascinating that these Vedic people were spread out from the banks of Saraswati River to as far away as Syria. Like most other ancient people, our ancestors too prayed to gods for wealth, protection, happiness, fame, and power. There were offerings and ceremonies to bring the gods to one's favor. And like most ancient people, they too prayed to gods that represented nature like *Mitra/Surya* (sun), *Varuna* (water), *Indra* (rain and thunderstorm), *Soma* (moon), *Rudra* (storm), *Agni* (fire), *Vayu* (wind), and *Ashvins* (sunrise and sunset). While modern minds have become rigid in search of truth, the minds of our ancestors were open to infinite possibilities. We look at the world through binary lenses of right or wrong, truth or false, and good or bad while our ancestors saw the entire spectrum. Gods were a personification of nature. The colors that our ancestors put into the stories, which came down to us as mythologies, made them so strong that they survived orally for thousands of years. Beneath all the creative imaginations, all the colors, is a truth that still makes us ponder. The mythologies had gods (the lesser gods or demi gods as opposed to the 'Gods' or Trinity: Brahma, Vishnu, and Shiva)—the Devas—and they had the devils—the Asuras. Asuras, the enemy of Devas, were the image of everything that represents bad. Who were they? Where did they come from? And how did they become our enemy? Let us dig into Vedas for more answers.

> THOU art the King of all the Gods, O Indra: protect
> the men, O Asura, preserve us. (1.174.1 Rig Veda [22])

Who was this Asura who was at par with the gods like Indra? Why was Asura called the king of all gods, and why did our ancestors pray to him for preservation? We know from Puranas that both Asura and Devas were born of same parents. They spoke in the same language and followed similar religious customs. If we believe the texts, then we can assume that they shared common ancestors. Devas and Asuras even intermarried. Laxmi, the goddess of wealth, is a daughter of Asura king Puloman. She became the consort of Vishnu. It is because of her that the Asuras and Devas united and the ocean was churned (*samudra-manthan*). Her abode is within the earth, and it is from earth that we get all our wealth.

> Wise Asura, thou King of wide dominion, loosen the bonds of sins by us committed. (1.024.14 Rig Veda)

> He, strong of wing, hath lightened up the regions, deep-quivering Asura, the gentle Leader. (1.035.07 Rig Veda)

> May he, gold-handed Asura, kind Leader, come hither to us with his help and favor / Driving off Raksasas and Yatudhanas, the God is present, praised in hymns at evening. (1.035.10 Rig Veda)

> High glory hath the Asura, compact of strength, drawn on by two Bay Steeds: a Bull, a Car is he. (1.054.03 Rig Veda)

Surprise! Asura is a rich and powerful but gentle leader. He is not an enemy according to the early verses of Rig Veda. (The language of Rig Veda evolved with time, and linguists use that as a guide to determine relative age of the verses.) The Vedic people sought his favor and help. Early Rig Veda goes on to praise Asura even further:

> Even as he mounted up they all adorned him: self-luminous he travels clothed in splendor / That is the Bull's, the Asura's mighty figure: he, omniform, hath reached the eternal waters. (3.038.04 Rig Veda)

> This Bull's most gracious far-extended favor existed first of all in full abundance / By his support they are maintained in common who in the Asura's mansion dwell together. (10.031.06 Rig Veda)

> Served by the seven priests, he [Agni] shone forth from ancient time, when in his Mother's bosom, in her lap, he glowed / Giving delight each day he closeth not his eye, since from the Asura's body he was brought to life. (3.029.14 Rig Veda)

> Wise, with your Law and through the Asura's magic power ye guard the ordinances, Mitra-Varuna/ Ye by eternal Order govern all the world. Ye set the Sun in heaven as a refulgent car. (05.063.07 Rig Veda)

> As such we seek thee now, O Asura, thee most wise, craving thy bounty as our share / Thy sheltering defense is like a mighty cloak. So may thy glories reach to us. (08.079.06 Rig Veda)

Asura was associated with fire god, bull, and magic powers. Bull was an important symbol of ISVC, and fire is a sacred symbol of Zoroastrians of Iran who worship Ahura Mazda. Was the yogi with horn (*Pashupati*) found in an ISVC seal Ahura? Was there a common connection among the Iranians, Vedic Indians and the people of ISVC? At this moment, I am just speculating. The Iranians pronounce *sh* as *ha* and thus Asura as Ahura. According to Rig Veda, Asura is a rich king with a strong fort for defense. Asura had built forts and thus represented people who settled down. Many interpreters, in contrast, considered the Vedic people as semi-nomadic. Is Asura the missing link between the people of ISVC and the Aryans of India and Iran? Whoever these people were, the Vedic people wanted their share of wealth and protection. Were they asking too much?

> These Asuras have lost their powers of magic. But thou, O Varuna, if thou dost love me / O King, discerning truth and right from falsehood, come and be Lord and Ruler of my kingdom. (10.124.05 Rig Veda)

> That other, Asura, too was born of Heaven. Thou art, O Varuna, the King of all men / The chariot's Lord was well content, forbearing to anger Death by sin so great / This sin hath Sakaputa here committed. Heroes who fled to their dear friend he slayeth / When the Steed bringeth down your grace and favor in bodies dear and worshipful. (10.132.04 Rig Veda)

Was the Asura kingdom weakening? Does it mark the decline of ISVC? There was a definite rift between the Asuras and the Vedic people, a rift created or intensified during the reign of Sakaputa, probably after he killed some of the Vedic people. Thus began the epic enmity between the Devas and the Asuras.

> A sharpened weapon is the host of Maruts. Who, Indra, dares withstand thy bolt of thunder? Weaponless are the Asuras, the godless: scatter them with thy wheel, Impetuous Hero. (08.085.09 Rig Veda)

> As when the Gods came, after they had slaughtered the Asuras, keeping safe their Godlike nature. (10.157.04 Rig Veda)

> He [sun] rose, a light, that kills Vrtras and enemies, best slayer of the Dasyus, Asuras, and foes. (10.170.03 Rig Veda)

Since then, there have been many battles fought between the Devas and Asuras. Sometimes Asuras won while at other times the Devas were victorious. If we believe that Asura and Ahura are same, then the enemy of Vedic people was the god of the Zoroastrians of Iran. Interestingly, Daevas, which sounds like Devas, are the enemies of Zoroastrians. Daevas originally meant *the shining ones*. Later, Daevas became *younger gods* or *wrong gods*. The English word *devil* has its root in the word Daevas. That is not the only word having similiarity. The famous Vedic drink *Soma* is known as *Hoama* among the Zoroastrians. It has to be too much of a coincidence. There was most likely a common origin and a later split between the Iranian Ahura/Asura and Indian Deva/Daeva tribes. The split is often dated to 2000 BCE.

A priest named Zoroaster founded Zoroastrian religion. From the little we know about Zoroaster's life, he was born into Spitama clan and was probably a Vedic Brahmin priest. However, he rejected the pagan way of life and worshiped monotheist god Ahura Mazda. He also opposed the animal sacrifices, drinking of Soma, and the caste system. His ideas were not accepted quickly, and he had only one convert: his cousin. As expected, he got opposition from the local religious authorities. After 12 years, he left home and went westwards. King Vishtaspa accepted him and made Zoroastrianism the official religion of his kingdom. Zoroaster died in his late 70s [23], but his religion spread far and wide. The philosophy of the Devas spread east, and all their enemies became Asura. Ravana, a king from Sri Lanka, also became Asura even though he is not related to Iranians. The philosophy of Ahura spread west, and all their enemies (not just the Vedic tribes) became Daevas. In the Mauryan time, there was a place called Patala in the far-west corner of India at the mouth of River Indus. Beyond it lived the Asuras, the fire worshippers. Is it also a coincidence that in the Puranas, the land of Asura is called Patala?

If we shed our binary bias of good-bad and look through the eyes of our ancestors, we will see the boundaries of righteousness fade away. There are stories of Asura doing good deeds and Devas doing evil ones. Asuras and Devas balance each other, none being the supreme authority. During the golden era both Asuras and Devas were friends. When one dominates the other, the balance is broken. A mortal priest can curse even Indra, the king of Devas. The

extreme fluidity in the concepts of good and bad is wisdom
that our modern mind needs to realize. There is a small
tribe called Asuras in Chotanagpur, India. They are expert
iron smelters. Navaratri is widely celebrated in India as the
festival where Devas defeat the Asuras. Ravana is killed by
Lord Rama, avatar of Vishnu, and Mahishasura is killed
by Goddess Durga, consort of Shiva. The Asura tribes do
not celebrate this festival. Instead they mourn during
Navaratri. In this land of survivors, even the Asuras have
survived.

3.3   Battle of Ten Kings

The Vedic tribes grew in size and the intertribal
conflicts increased as they fought over common resources.
One of the big battles mentioned in Rig Veda is Dasarajna,
commonly known as the Battle of Ten Kings. In this famous
battle, the Puru tribe allied with nine other kings. These
kings belonged to tribes Alinas, Anu, Bhrigus (Indo-Aryans),
Bhalanas, Dasa (Dahae?), Druhyus (Gandharis), Mistaya
(Indo-Aryans), Parse (Persians?), and Panis (Parni?). They
fought with Trtsu-Bharata king Sudas (for the conceptual
map of the battle, see figure 3).

> With all-outstripping chariot-wheel, O Indra,
> thou far-famed, hast overthrown the twice ten
> Kings of men / With sixty thousand nine-and-
> ninety followers, who came in arms to fight with
> friendless Susravas. (01.153.9 Rig Veda [22])

Ten kings came with 60,990 men to fight Sudas, who
was alone. With one king against ten, it was supposed to

be a one-sided battle, just like the Pandavas facing the Kauravas in the epic *Mahabharata*.

> With Soma they brought Indra from a distance, Over Vaisanta, from the strong libation / Indra preferred Vasisthas to the Soma pressed by the son of Vayata, Pasadyumna / So, verily, with these he crossed the river, in company with these he slaughtered Bheda / Like thirsty men they looked to heaven, in battle with the Ten Kings, surrounded and imploring / Then Indra heard Vasistha as he praised him, and gave the Trtsus ample room and freedom / Like sticks and staves wherewith they drive the cattle, Stripped bare, the Bharatas were found defenseless: Vasistha then became their chief and leader: then widely were the Trtsus' clans extended. (07.033.2–6 Rig Veda [22])

One of the nine kings who allied with the Puru tribe was a Vedic king. He brought the holy Vedic ritual drink Soma from faraway land to please Indra. But Indra preferred priest Vasistha, who joined the weak and defenseless Trtsu-Bharata. Once Vasistha became their chief, Trtsu-Bharata became strong.

> Where heroes come together with their banners raised, in the encounter where is naught for us to love, Where all things that behold the light are terrified, there did ye comfort us, O Indra-Varuna / The boundaries of earth were seen all dark with dust: O Indra-Varuna, the shout went up to heaven / The enmities of the people compassed me about.

Ye heard my calling and ye came to me with help
/ With your resistless weapons, Indra-Varuna, ye
conquered Bheda and ye gave Sudas your aid / Ye
heard the prayers of these amid the cries of war:
effectual was the service of the Trtsus' priest / The
men of both the hosts invoked you in the fight,
Indra and Varuna, that they might win the wealth,
What time ye helped Sudas, with all the Trtsu folk,
when the Ten Kings had pressed him down in their
attack. (07.083.2–6 Rig Veda [22])

It was a fierce battle. The dust from the battlefield
engulfed the world in darkness, and the screams of the
mortals reached the heaven. Just when the ten kings
surrounded the Trtsu-Bharatas and all seemed lost, Indra
and Varuna came to their rescue.

What though the floods spread widely, Indra made
them shallow and easy for Sudas to traverse / He,
worthy of our praises, caused the Simyu, foe of
our hymn, to curse the rivers' fury / Eager for
spoil was Turvasa Purodas, fain to win wealth,
like fishes urged by hunger / The Bhrgus and the
Druhyus quickly listened: friend rescued friend
mid the two distant peoples / Together came
the Pakthas, the Bhalanas, the Alinas, the Sivas,
the Visanins / Yet to the Trtsus came the Arya's
Comrade, through love of spoil and heroes' war, to
lead them / Fools, in their folly fain to waste her
waters, they parted inexhaustible Parusni / Lord
of the Earth, he with his might repressed them:
still lay the herd and the affrighted herdsman /
As to their goal they sped to their destruction:

they sought Parusni; e'en the swift returned not /
Indra abandoned, to Sudas the manly, the swiftly
flying foes, unmanly babblers / They went like
kine unherded from the pasture, each clinging
to a friend as chance directed / They who drive
spotted steeds, sent down by Parusni, gave ear,
the Warriors and the harnessed horses. (07.18.5–9
Rig Veda [22])

Parusni River mentioned in the hymn has been
interpreted as River Ravi, on the bank of which was the
land of Bharata. When Sudas was crossing the river,
probably chased by his enemies, there was a big flood.
Sudas managed to cross the river with the help of Indra
while most of his enemies were drowned and washed away.
Sudas's men slaughtered the rest of the enemies. Bharata
tribe was victorious, probably creating the identity of
Bharat (alternate name for India that came into use much
later) for the first time.

Murthy compares *Mahabharata* with the Battle of Ten
Kings [27]. Both were battles in which the weaker side
fought and won against a stronger side. Sudas, a Bharata
king, has been compared to Yudhisthira, another Bharata
king, son of Dharma, eldest among the Pandvas. Arjuna,
son of Indra, was the chief fighter among the Pandavas,
and like Indra, he was the key to the outcome of the battle.
In the battle, Indra's close companion was Maruts just like
Bhima in Mahabharata who is son of Maruts. The twin
Ashvins were like Nakula and Sahadeva, son of Ashvins.
While Vasistha was the chief priest of Sudas, his decedent
Vyasa was the chief priest of Pandavas. Murthy goes on
to compare Varuna, the lord of water, with Krishna. The
great epic *Mahabharata* might have been inspired by the

Battle of Ten kings. A Chalukyan inscription dating to 635 mentioned that 3,735 years have passed since the great war. That would date the Battle of Mahabharata to 3102 BCE. Astronomers date the war to 3000 BCE based on the two eclipses that happened during the war within a span of 13 days. That would coincide with the time of ISVC. There is, however, no conclusive evidence about the date of the battle, if it at all took place.

3.4   India during Vedic Era

The early Vedic people were animal herders. They spread out and were assimilated into the tribes of Ganges plain. The herders settled down into numerous small chiefdoms, with their leaders referred to as *rajas*. The leaders were not decided by kinship—they were chosen. The elders (inevitably male) were immensely respected and had most powers, as evident from the Indian myths. Bhishma vowed celibacy for his father in *Mahabharata*, and Parasuram reluctantly killed his mother at the command of his father (though she was later resurrected). In contrast, the Greek myths had a common theme where their own sons killed fathers, like Uranus and Cronus. Such themes were very uncommon in ancient Indian myths. Fathers had the ultimate authority in a family. When the epics of *Ramayana* and *Mahabharata* were written, smaller kingdoms started to form. In such kingdoms, the eldest eligible son inherited the rule. Men, the once hunters, were the natural choice as soldiers. It is the men who took the throne. This increased the value of son in the society [24].

Despite being a patriarchal society, women enjoyed some freedom. Their status varied between different chiefdoms. Women broadly played three roles in the society. There were the family women whose role was mostly restricted to household works and children. There were few occasions when they acted as queen regnant. These women, if they were from aristocratic background, did receive education and other privileges. The second role women played were that of saints and philosophers. Brahmavadinis were women who never married and became experts in Vedas. Lopamudra, Vishwawara, Sikta, Ghosha, and Maitreyi were Brahmavadinis who composed hymns of Vedas. *Sadyodvahas* were women who studied Vedas till they got married. Women saints/nuns were also common among Buddhists and Jains. The third role women played were that of prostitutes and dancers. Organized prostitution was legal and common in the cities. There were *Rajdasis* who danced for the kings and *Devadasis* who danced for the temples. They enjoyed high status and respect in the society.

Sanskrit, an Aryan language, has words like *langala* taken from non-Aryan Munda community found farther east of India. It means *plough*, use of which goes back to pre-Harappan times [24]. These words have been used in old Sanskrit texts indicating early mixing between the two communities. The people of the Ganges were already expert in agriculture, from whom the Vedic people learned quite a bit. Plough is the symbol of Balarama, the god of agriculture. He is the elder brother of Krishna. Krishna, with his cattle's, probably represents animal husbandry. Both animal husbandry and agriculture were the main activities of that time. Agriculture meant extra crop, which in turn resulted in trading. Trading was done in exchange of cattle and sometimes gold. Trading brought money, money brought economic inequality, and inequality made society more complex. With the development of complex structures, the caste system became firmly established. The evidence of the hierarchy of the caste-based society comes from the following hymn in Rig Veda:

> When they divided Purusa how many portions did they make? / What do they call his mouth, his arms? What do they call his thighs and feet? / The Brahmin was his mouth, of both his arms was the Rajanya [Kshatriya] made / His thighs became the Vaisya, from his feet the Sudra was produced / The Moon was gendered from his mind, and from his eye the Sun had birth / Indra and Agni from his mouth were born, and Vayu from his breath / Forth from his navel came mid-air the sky was fashioned from his head / Earth from his feet, and from his car the regions. Thus they formed the worlds. (10.90.11–14 Rig Veda [22])

Brahmins (priests), who were required by both Kshatriyas and Vaishas, rose to the top of all castes. Being the only caste with access to the holy scriptures, Brahmins became the mouth. Kshatriyas were the warriors who represented the strength of arms. Vaisyas, the businessmen, were the thighs on which the society stood. Sudras were supposed to be born out of feet, which to many depicted their low status and was an insult. The critics ignore the verse that says that the earth was born of feet as well. Earth was very important to our ancestors. Feet keep the whole body stable, and without it, the system becomes immobile. Here, one needs to compare this verse with the Chinese myth. According to it, the 'black-haired commoners' were supposed to be born out of the various worms in the body. However, this Vedic verse did represent a social stratification in which Sudras were placed at the bottom.

Social classes are the foundation of any society. Like most ancient societies, Indians were also stratified into different classes. The various classes became castes over time. The benefits of a caste-based society were that it gave people purpose, reduced competition, and designated work for each and every individual. That gave stability to the society, making the country strong. Caste system was the main reason for India's growth in the ancient era, and it is because of such importance that it survived for thousands of years. However, it did come at the cost of freedom of choice. Over time, groups like Kshatriyas (warriors) and Brahmins (scholars, sages, and priests) had more demand and thus power in the society. On the other hand, the status of Sudras—people who served the other castes like labors, artisans, and craftsmen—declined. Vaishyas (farmers and merchants) were somewhere in between. Because of their wealth and challenge they often posed on the Brahminic order, Brahmins portrayed the Vaishas in negative light. Later, as the cities grew, people of non-Vedic tribes (maybe the ones mentioned as Raksasas, Yaksasas, Dasas, Nagas, and Mlecchas in the ancient texts) became part of the system. Since they originally did not belong to the Vedic Society, they were assimilated into the caste system based on their merits. Though majority of them got the status of Vaishya and Sudra, those who were good fighters became Kshatriyas [11]. The tribal people were not forced into the system. They joined because it provided them economic security while being able to maintain their own identity. The untouchables did not belong to any caste, and hence, they were outcastes. They are often called *Dalits*, meaning *broken.* In the ancient times, being made an outcaste was the most severe form of punishment. The outcastes were either people who were punished, lost their religion by defying the rules made by high caste Brahmins, or had a contagious disease and hence isolated. The tribals who scavenged for food or could not fit into any of the assigned castes might have also become outcastes. They got the dirty job of cremating or disposing the dead, cleaning toilets and sewages, and doing leatherwork. Dalit women have often been sexually exploited. They were barred from covering their upper body. There were places where tax was collected from Dalit women if they wanted to cover their bossom. The amount of tax was proportional to the size of their breast. A dalit woman from Travancore, named Nangeli, protested against the brutal system in nineteenth century. Instead of paying tax she cut her breasts and offered it to the tax collector. She died the same day due to excessive blood loss. Her sacrifice led to abolishment of breast-tax in Travancore. Her place in now called Mulachiparambu - land of the breasted women. The caste system still had some flexibility. There were cases of priests becoming Kshatriyas and Kshatriyas becoming priests, as we see in *Mahabharata*.

Towards the end of the Vedic era, the tribes became stable and well established. The tribes were organized as *gana-sangha* and were headed by the tribal chief called *raja*. Victory in conflicts increased the dominance of powerful tribes that will later become empires. Stability resulted in the growth of science and astronomy. An Indian Vedic priest named Baudhayana of Yajurveda School wrote many mathematical *sutras* (books). It included what we now know as the Pythagorean theorem and square root of two. People had time to question and think about their existence. The questions made way for the first Indian philosophical renaissance. Glimpses of the questions raised are found in the following hymn of Rig Veda:

> Then was not non-existent nor existent: there was no realm of air, no sky beyond it/
>
> What covered in, and where? And what gave shelter? Was water there, unfathomed depth of water?
>
> Death was not then, nor was there aught immortal: no sign was there, the day's and night's divider/
>
> That One Thing, breathless, breathed by its own nature: apart from it was nothing whatsoever/
>
> Darkness there was: at first concealed in dark knew this All was indiscriminated chaos/
>
> All that existed then was void and form less: by the great power of Warmth was born that Unit/
>
> Thereafter rose Desire in the beginning, Desire, the primal seed and germ of Spirit
>
> Sages who searched with their heart's thought discovered the existent's kinship in the non-existent/
>
> Transversely was their severing line extended: what was above it then, and what below it?

There were begetters, there were mighty forces, free action here and energy up yonder

Who verily knows and who can here declare it, whence it was born and whence comes this creation?

The Gods are later than this world's production. Who knows then whence it first came into being?

He, the first origin of this creation, whether he formed it all or did not form it,

Whose eye controls this world in highest heaven, he verily knows it, or perhaps he knows not. (10.129.1–7 Rig Veda [22])

Philosophical Renaissance (1000 to 300 BCE)

When there was neither kingdom, nor king;
there was neither governance, nor governor, the
people protected themselves by dharma.

—*Mahabharata* 12.59.14

4.1 Being God

Upanishads, also called Vedanta, are the concluding section of Vedas. It dates back to the axial age (~eighth century BCE) when traders were creating a revolution all around the globe. In India, the smaller tribes had formed sixteen distinct village republics called Mahajanapadas. It included Anga, Assaka (or Asmaka), Avanti, Chedi, Gandhara, Kashi, Kamboja, Kosala, Kuru, Magadha, Malla, Machcha (or Matsya), Panchala, Surasena, Vriji, and Vatsa (or Vamsa). These villages had one of the earliest democratic forms of governance in the world. They ran on the principles of *dharma*. Dharma means duties or laws, and duties were laid down for every individual based on his profession. Even the king did not hold imperialistic power. He had to abide by the *Rajdharma* that laid down the rights, privileges, and responsibilities of the king. According to *Mahabharata*, "though the king is invested with authority and power, true sovereignty belongs to dharma, not the king." By this time, kings were determined by kinship, but smaller elected groups called *sabhas* or *samitis* controlled their power. The king did not possess the land of the people, which meant the house and the field. The *dharma* of the king was to protect the people, in return for which he received taxes. This resulted in a strong society and weak state unlike China where the king enjoyed absolute power. Such strong society and weak state continues in India till this day.

While the world was busy building empires, Indians of the axial era were busy building philosophies. The older Vedic ritualistic philosophy was at its fag end, and the devotional Hindu religions were yet to take its full form. On one extreme were the spiritual Upanishadic philosophies (dvaita and avaita philosophies) that believed in soul, karma, and the cycle of birth and death. On the other extreme was the atheist philosophy like Charvaka which did not believe in karma, cycle of birth, or soul. Within that spectrum, we had the middle path of Buddhism and Mahavira's reformed Jainism. It was a philosophical renaissance, the first of its kind in India.

Upanisahads literally means *sitting at the feet of* (*up* [*at*], *pa* [feet], *nishat* [sit]). Disciples learned this higher knowledge as they sat at the feet of their gurus (teachers). There are more than 200 Upanishads composed over a wide range of time. The oldest ones are the principle

Upanishads. Rig Veda contains Aitareya Upanishad; Sama Veda contains Chandogya and Kena Upanishad; Krishna Yajur Veda contains Katha, Taittiriya, Svetasvatara, and Maitrayani Upanishad; Shukla Yajur Veda contains Isha and Brhadaranyaka Upanishad; and Atharva Veda contains Mandukya, Mundaka, and Prashna Upanishad. Each Upanisad belonged to different school of thoughts. Some of them were monistic (*avaita*) while others dualistic (*dvaita*).

Our ancestors believed in three worlds: the world of men obtained through son, the world of fathers obtained through rites, and the world of god obtained through knowledge. According to Upanishads, knowledge was the best of the three. Knowledge itself was of two types: the *para vidya* (higher knowledge), and *apara vidya* (lower knowledge) (Mundaka Upanishad 1.1.4–1.1.6). Lower knowledge includes the four Vedas, phonetics, rituals, grammar, etymology, metrics, and astrology. The higher knowledge is the knowledge of ultimate truth, or Brahmana (different from the Brahmin caste), which could be obtained through Upanishads. One can find a distinct shift in the mindset of people from the 'rituals' of Vedas to 'knowledge' of Upanishads. Rituals and sacrifices have now become inferior karma. Chandogya Upanishad compares those who involve in ritualistic sacrifices as dogs who chant, "Om! Let's eat. Om! Let's drink." According to Mundaka Upanishad (1.2.7–1.2.10), "the rituals and 18 sacrificial forms are inferior karma. The deluded, who delight in this as leading to good, fall again and again into old age and death. Abiding in the midst of ignorance, wise in their own esteem, they thinking that they are learned. But they are fools, afflicted with troubles, who go about like blind men led by one who is himself blind. These deluded men, regarding sacrifices and works of merit as most important, do not know any other good. Having enjoyed in the high place of heaven won by good deeds, their atman enter again this world or still lower one. The true knowledge is thus realizing the Brahmana."

Instead of praying to gods, Brahmana became the ultimate truth that one needs to realize. Brahmana has been described as that which is ungraspable and without any identity. It is *eternal, all-pervading, omnipresent, and exceeding subtle.* Brahmana is the source of all things including us and is nothing separate from us. It comprises the whole universe and the one beyond. Brhadaranyaka Upanishad says: "Brahmana is everything, everything was created from him. He who knows that he is Brahmana becomes so. A god who knows that becomes that, a man who knows that becomes that. Even god cannot prevail against men who know Brahmana. Those who worship god thinking that god is separate from them, are ignorant. They are like animals to gods. Just like animals serve them, they serve god." [28]

Those who are ignorant, they live in the material world of *Maya*. According to Svetasvatara Upanishad [4.10], the Pakriti (nature) is *Maya*: "The whole world is pervaded by beings that are part of Brahmana, the creator of Maya." Sorrow, happiness, good, bad, ego, sin, old age, death, hunger, caste, gender, and emotions are all part of *Maya*. Beyond the illusion of our material world of *Maya*, there is the absolute reality called Brahmana. Those who are devoted to one particular god can rejoice only in this world. Ultimate salvation comes through the realization of Brahmana [Maitri Upanishad, sec. 4.5–4.6].

In the dualistic (*dvaita*) philosophies, the Brahmana (supreme soul) is different from atman (individual soul) while in monistic (*avaita*) philosophies, they are one and the same. Our ego creates a sense of separation, making us believe that we are a different personality. That personality is just the body. The body dies, but the atman does not. If the atman is the ripple in a big pond, Brahmana is the pond made of all the drops of water of which ripples are a part.

> He who sees all beings as his own self and his own self in all beings, he does not feel any revulsion by reasons of such a view. (Chandogya Upanishad 6.10)

Atman has no caste or gender. Chandala, by performing sheer good deed, can become a higher caste in the next life. Chandogya Upanishad (7.26) reveals that everything springs from atman. It is free from sin, old age, death, sorrow, and hunger.

> Atman is neither born, nor does it die. Atman did not spring from anything, nothing sprang from it. It is the unborn, eternal, everlasting, ancient, and is not slain even when body is destroyed. Sitting he travels far, lying he goes everywhere. (Katha Upanishad 1.2.18–1.2.21)

The atman is often described as the lord of the chariot. The intellect is the charioteer, mind is the reins, the senses are horses, and the roads are sense objects. Beyond the senses are sense objects, beyond the object is mind, beyond mind is intellect, and beyond intellect is the atman. By realizing the atman, one realizes Brahmana. Upanishads reveal the path to realize the Brahmana and thus achieve *moksha* or liberation. "When 5 organs of knowledge are at rest together with the mind, and when intellect ceases functioning [calm], that state is the highest. It can be attained through yoga/ meditation. It is not an outward possessing but an inward discovery. When all desires that dwell in the heart are destroyed, then mortal becomes immortal"; and that is possible through real knowledge [28]. Only knowledge can help one distinguish truth from Maya.

Vedic way of life sets four key goals for an individual: *dharma*, *artha*, *kama*, and *moksha*. *Dharma* is to perform one's duties, *artha* is to gain wealth, *kama* is to have sex and continue the progeny, while *moksha* is to attain liberation. According to Swami Vivekananda, there are different types of people and thus different paths for achieving *moksha*. For emotional people, or the men of heart, there is the path of worship and devotion (bhakti yoga). For the intellectual people, men of head, there is the path of knowledge (gyaan yoga). For active men, both head and heart, there is the path of work (karma yoga). And for the eccentric men, there is the path of mysticism (tantra yoga). These are different paths that prepare one for the same final realization.

According to Swami Chinmayananda, there are five sheaths of Brahman/consciousness [29]. The outermost of the sheaths is called virat or the gross body. One who is controlled by his/her gross body is in the state of *annamaya* and is concerned mainly about food and other outer pleasures like the animals. This gross body can be brought under control by asana or physical exercise. Inside that is the more subtle body called *hiranyagarbha*. It is subdivided into the vital air, mental, and intellectual in the order gross to subtle. One who is controlled by the vital air is in the stage called *pranamaya* where he/she tries to stay alive by protecting and defending, like the hunters and gatherers. It is through *pranayam* (breathing exercise) that one controls their vital air. One who is controlled by his/her mind is in the third stage called *manomaya* when he/she figures out the desires and values of life, like 'civilized' humans. It is through *Dharana* that one withdraws the mind from outer objects and concentrate on *atman*. The next stage is *vijnanamaya* when one uses his/her intellect and becomes philosophical. It is through *dhyana* or meditation that one controls one's mind and intellect. The subtlest is the casual body or iswara. This final stage is of spiritual bliss known as the *anandamaya*. This is when you realize that you are Brahmana. It is the ultimate stage that is attained through *Samadhi*.

The crux of the Upanishads may be summarized in the following four lines:

> *"Tat tvam asi"* (Chhandogya Upanishad): That which is the subtlest of all is the self of all this.

> *"Ayam atman Brahman"* (Mandukya Upanishad): This atman/soul is Brahman

> *"Aham Brahmasmi"* (Brihadaranyaka Upanishad): I am consciousness.

> *"Prajnanam Brahman"* (Aitareya Upanishad): Consciousness is Brahman.

The entire philosophy of Upanishad stands on the concept of Brahmana, atman, and the cycle of life. Whether one believes in it or not, the philosophy is very appealing and is bound to inspire many for generations to come.

4.2   Seeing Is Believing

The West perceives India as the land of spirituality, and we have seen that spirituality was a very important part of India. However, the uniqueness of India does not lie in its spirituality but rather in the variety of its philosophies. Unfortunately, only the spiritual side of India has been popularized globally. Slowly, even we started to believe in that image of India. It meant that the atheist philosophies of Charvaka / Lokayata have been ignored and seen as anomalies. Considering Buddhist and Jain philosophies also as atheist philosophy, a large percentage of the population of India was atheist during axial era.

Brihaspati is often called as the founder of Charvaka philosophy. He is probably a historic figure, different from the one who taught the Devas and Asuras. Parts of his lost writings are found in the text Sarvasiddhantasamgraha:

> Chastity and other such ordinances are laid down by clever weaklings; gifts of gold and land, the pleasure of invitations to dinner, are devised by indigent people with stomachs lean with hunger. The building of temples, houses for water-supply, tanks, wells, resting places, and the like, pleases only travellers, not others. The Agnihotra rituals, the three Vedas, the triple staff, the ash-smearing, are the ways of gaining a livelihood for those who are lacking in intellect and energy. The wise should enjoy the pleasures of this world through the more appropriate available means of agriculture, tending cattle, trade, political administration, etc. [30]

The quote would not look out of place even in the 21st century. The protest against the caste system is nothing new; the fight started thousands of years ago. The atheist philosophies posed a direct challenge to the authority of the rulers and priests. We find it being criticized and threatened in most of the Vedic texts that had survived.

In Ramayana, Rama was challenged by Javali, a Charvaka. He tells Rama, "There exists no other world but this." Then he adds, "Follow what is within your experience and do not trouble yourself with what lies beyond the province of human experience." [31] Rama only reply was, "O Javali, I perceive with regret the action of my illustrious parent in permitting one of atheistic ideas, who has fallen from the path of rectitude enjoined in the Vedas, to remain in his court. Those who preach the heretical doctrine of the Charvaka School, are not only infidels, but have deviated from the path of truth. It is the duty of a monarch to deal with such persons as with outlaws, nor should men of understanding and learning stand in the presence of such atheists" [32].

Again, in *Mahabharata*, we see a Charvaka posing troubling questions to the king. When the victorious Pandavas were returning after the war, a Charvaka asked, "What have you gained by destroying your own people and murdering your elders? You should die." This made the Pandavas feel guilty. However, the other Brahmins declared that the Charvaka was a demon in disguise and not to be listened to. The Charvaka, along with his question, was burnt to ashes.

Ajita Kesakambali, contemporary of Buddha, records the earliest documented materialism in India. As per him, everything in this world is made of four elements (prithvi/earth, jal/water, agni/fire, and vayu/air). The fifth element, called *aakash* (ether), cannot be perceived and hence was not considered as real. Consciousness is also made of these elements, and soul is considered as nothing but a conscious body. Since soul is born with the body and also gets dissolved with the body, the reaping of the fruits of good or evil deeds in the next life is impossible. Notice the contrast with the philosophies of Upanishads. According to the Charvaka philosophy, there was no need for god or any form of creator. Everything is formed from the properties inherent in the elements. There is no heaven or hell other than the enjoyment of happiness that is heaven and suffering misery that is hell. Performing duties mentioned by Vedas for every caste is only for the benefit of the upper class. They have no bearing on afterlife, as there is none [33]. The Charvaks wanted to create a society out of logic and common sense and not on blind faith or fear of god.

4.3 The Awakened One

A man was born in Lumbini (Nepal) into a Shakya clan sometime between 2,600 and 2,400 years ago. His name was Gautama. A wealthy prince by birth, he realized while travelling around his kingdom that all his wealth was not going to prevent him from the miseries of illness, old age, and death. His status gave him power over his pupil but not over his own body or mind. When Gautama was 28 years old, there was a major clash between them and the neighboring village over the sharing of waters of Rohini. Gautama wanted to settle the dispute through peaceful means while majority wanted war. After voting, the council decided that their village would fight. Not surprisingly, this man did not take part in the fight. He was sentenced to exile for dishonoring his oath of obeying the decision of the majority. Even though Gautama was a son of the king, he was not above the republic. He renounced his wealth and power at the age of 29 years to become an ascetic after seeing the miseries of old age, disease, and death. Gautama was desperate for a solution. He met many sages, but none could satisfy his quest. Hungry, weak, and frustrated, he sat under a pipal tree in Bodh Gaya (Bihar) to meditate—to know the absolute truth. Under the tree, the once prince named Gautama transformed to Buddha, the awakened one. From there, he went to Sarnath, where he gave his first sermon.

The Lumbini excavation in Nepal (though debatable) has pushed back Buddha's date of birth by few centuries to 600 BCE [34]. Buddha was against the Vedic rituals, superstition, caste system, metaphysics, miracles, and priest crafts. Like Charvaka, the Buddhist philosophy was about logic, observation, and experience. There was no need of god. However, unlike Charvaka, the emphasis was on ethics and belief in rebirth and karma. The Buddhist teachings are about compassion and humbleness. There is a story where a businessman became irritated by the idleness of Buddha. He just sat in one place and meditated instead of going out and doing some real work. The angry businessman came towards Buddha and spat on him. The followers of Buddha were angry and wanted to avenge the insult, but since the guru was there, they did not move. Buddha, however, was not affected, and he went ahead with his meditation. The businessman went back to his home, surprised. He could not sleep throughout the night. Buddha's lack of reaction and anger left him confused and ashamed. The next day, he went to Buddha and asked for forgiveness. Buddha looked at him and said that since he did not do anything wrong there was no need for him to say sorry. The businessman was further amused and tried to explain that he did spat on him. Buddha calmly replied that the man who did that is no more because the man in front of him is a changed man.

Buddha taught orally, and most of his teachings were written down much later. The writings were definitely subjected to modification, alteration, and possibly some misinterpretation. The core Buddhist teachings are threefold: the four noble truths, the doctrine of dependent origination, and the noble eight-fold path. The four noble truths (*arya satya*) are *duhkha* (suffering), *duhkha-samudaya* (causes of suffering), *duhkha-nirodha* (cessation of suffering), and *duhkha-nirodha-gamini-pratipat* (there is a way leading to the end of suffering). The second important teaching of Buddhism was the doctrine of dependent origination (*Pratityasamutpada*). It tells us the cause of the suffering. We suffer from old age and death (*jara-marana*) only because we are reborn (*jati*). We are reborn because we have the want to be born (*bhava*). That, in turn, comes from our attachment to enjoyment (*upadana*). Our attachment comes from our craving (*trsna*) for contact (*sparsha*) with sense object. Our dependence on the sense organs comes from consciousness (*vijnana*), which depends on the karmas of past life. Sufferings come from the bad karmas, which, in turn, come from spiritual ignorance (*Avidya*). Thus, spiritual ignorance is the root cause of all sufferings. If there is suffering, then there is existence. *Nirvana* (nonexistence or liberation) is achieved by following the middle path [35]. The way to end the suffering is the eight-fold path. It constitutes *samyag-dristi* (right view), *samyag-samkalpa* (right intention), *samyag-vak* (right speech), *samyag-karmanta* (right action), *samyag-ajiva* (right livelihood), *samyag-vayama* (right effort), *samyag-smrti* (right thought), and *samyag-samadhi* (right concentration).

Later, Buddhism got separated into various schools. The two broader groups are Sravakayana/Hinayana and Mahayana. Hinayana is the older school that is closest to the original teachings of Buddha. It emphasizes Nirvana through individual himself without the need of divine help. Mahayana, on the other hand, considers Buddha himself as divine. Buddha became the absolute self (like the concept of Brahmana in Upanishads), which runs through all the individual selves. The ideal saint is a Bodhisattva, one who has attained nirvana. He is ready to suffer for the sins and miseries of the world so that everyone else can be liberated. This ultimate sacrifice echoes the sacrifice of Christ who would come much later. Interestingly, while Christ is said to perform miracle and bring dead back to life, Buddha refuses to do so as it was against nature. Mahayana appealed to the masses and helped in making Buddhism popular around the Asia.

The scripture *Mahaparinibbana Sutta* describes the last few months of Buddha's life. Buddha is said to have passed away in the small town of Kushinagar (in Malla, one of the sixteen Mahajanapadas). It was the capital of Kosala Kingdom and was built by King Kush, Lord Rama's son. Kushinaga thus became the fourth holy place for Buddhist. Lumbini (birthplace), Bodh Gaya (achieved enlightenment), and Sarnath (gave his first sermon) being the other three. Buddha was old and ill when he went to Kushinagar, and he knew that he was about to die. His quest for spirituality began when he went to search for the solution of these three sufferings. He realized that while no one can excape the three sufferings, one can make them insignificant. He said to his favourite disciple Ananda, "I am turning 80-years of age; and just as a worn-out cart, Ananda, can only with much additional care be made to move along." Buddha requested Ananda to prepare his final bed in between two *sala* trees, with his head towards the north. The great man spoke the final words to his disciples on the full moon night of Vaisakha month (April–May), "Decay is inherent in all component things! Work out your salvation with diligence." After some time, he passed away. The body was prepared for six days before final cremation. After cremation, his relics were collected and taken to Kushinagar by the king of Malla. He wanted to make a stupa. However, on the spread of the news of Buddha's death, other kings claimed part of the relics. It included King Ajarasatru of Rajagirha, the Lichchhavis of Vaishali, Sakyas of Kapilvastu, Bulis of Alakappa, Koliyas of Ramagrama, and the Mallas of Pava. There was almost a war among the kings for a piece of the man who spent his life for peace. The war was avoided only after the intervention of a wise Brahmin named Drona, who managed to distribute the relics to all the kings in fair proportion. The kings built stupas, within which the final remains of Buddha was kept. Buddha himself thus became god. Huge statues of Buddha, the god, were built at many places by his followers, quite contrary to the philosophy of Buddha who opposed idol worship. The irony was that in 1021, Sultan Mahmud of Ghazni, follower of Islam and a hater of idol worship, started breaking down the Buddha statues in Swat and Bajaur.

4.4 The Great Hero

Like Gautama, there was another prince born in Bihar at a similar time named Vardhamana. He too left his wealth and family to live the life of an ascetic. It shows how important spiritual awakening was at that time even for the rich and non-Brahmin youths. Vardhamana's journey to become Mahavira, the great hero/warrior, was tough. He wandered around hungry, weak, and even naked for 12 years before his enlightenment: *Kevala Jnana*. Many people wrongly attribute Mahavira as the founder of Jain religion. He was the 24th and the last of the Tirthankaras. He brought the last great reform to the religion. Parsva, the 23rd Tirthankara, is considered as the only other historical figure. Parsva usually has a serpent protecting him while Mahavira is depicted with a lion below. Parsva existed 300 years before Mahavira. He too was a king like Mahavira who renounced worldly pleasures at the age of 30 years. According to ancient text *Kalpa Sutra*, Parsva had 164,000 male followers, 327,000 female followers, 16,000 monks, and 38,000 nuns. Evidence for other Tirthankaras is scanty. Considering a gap of 150 years between Tirthankaras, Rishabha, the first Tirthankara, would be contemporary of ISVC. There are some historians who claim that to be true. The naked male idols in standing yogic posture, typical to Jains, excavated from ISVC could well represent Jain monks.

Like Buddhists, Jains also do not believe in God. They do believe in soul, rebirth, and karma. To them, the universe was neither created nor will it be destroyed. It is independent and self-sufficient, and it does not require god to govern it. Nonviolence and love were the virtues of the era. Such virtues were taught through moral stories about

Mahavira, just like the tales of Buddha. In one such story, there was an angry venomous cobra named Chandkaushik who terrorized the villagers. Once, Mahavira was going to a jungle to meditate. The villagers warned him about the serpent. Mahavira ignored the warnings and went ahead. When Chandkaushik saw Mahavira meditating in his territory, he became angry. He went towards him and spat his deadly venom towards Mahavira many times. It would have killed any mortal. Chandkaushik was surprised to see Mahavira unharmed and unmoved. Mahavira opened his eyes and said in a calm and compassionate voice, "Understand Chandkaushik, and realize where you are going." The affectionate eyes of the great saint calmed the serpent down. He had visions of his past life and realized that the monstrous serpent was not his true identity. Ashamed of his bad deeds, he went back into his hole and lived the rest of his life there in peaceful manner. He did not retaliate even when few angry villagers were hurting him by throwing stones. After death, he went to heaven. Peace and harmony come from the feeling of love and equality of all living beings.

According to Jain philosophy, the universe consists of living (*jiva* or soul) and nonliving (*ajiva*). They come in contact with each other, leading to production of energy. The energy creates the process of life and death. This can be ceased (i.e. the energy can be exhausted), leading to salvation. Jainism proposes seven fundamentals (*tattva*) [35]:

> *Jiva: Jiva* is the eternal soul, the conscience, the intelligence, and is different from the body. *Samsari* is the ordinary soul that through salvation can become the *Siddha/Mukta* or liberated soul.

Ajiva: *Ajiva* is the nonliving substance made up of *pudgala* (matter), *dharma*, *adharma*, *akasa* (space/ether), and *kala* (time).

Asrava: It is the influx of *karma* (action/work/deed) into the soul when the *jiva* and *ajiva* interact. *Karma* decides what happens to the living body. Good *karma* is *punya* and bad karma is *paap* (sin).

Bandha: It means bondage i.e. not free or liberated. *Karma* masks or binds the inherent perfection of *jiva*. *Jiva* cannot be liberated as long as *karma* enters the body.

Samvara: The stoppage of the influx of *karma*, good or bad, into the *jiva* is called *samvara*.

Nirjara: *Jiva* will be free only when the *karma* is shredded or burnt. Freedom can be achieved either by *Savipaka Nirjara* or *Avipaka Nirjara*. The former is the long natural process of *karma* becoming mature and separating from *jiva*. The latter is the shorter way where by means of ascetic process the *karma* can be forcefully separated from *jiva*.

Moksha: As the karma separates, the *jiva* becomes free and liberated. That state is called *Moksha*. *Moksha* can be attained through nonviolence (*ahimsa*), truth (*satya*), not accepting anything that is unwillingly offered (*Asteya*), celibacy (*Brahmacharya*), and non-possessiveness (*Aparigraha*) [35].

Jainism is divided into two sects: *Digambara* and *Shvetambara*. The highest *Digambara* monks do not wear clothes as it means attachment to desire for material things. This only applies to men. Women monks wear white and are called *Aryikas*. This means that women cannot attain full liberation and need to be born as men in the next life to be liberated. *Shvetambara* monks wear white clothes, and thus, both men and women can achieve liberation. They cover their mouth with a square white cloth (*muhapatti*) in order to prevent inhaling small insects or other airborne life forms. Jains eat vegetarian food collected from followers' houses and do not save edibles beyond the next meal. Water is not kept even for a single night. All eating and drinking has to be done between sunrise and sunset.

According to Jainism, knowledge is of two types: *Pramana*, or knowledge of things as it is, and *Naya*, or knowledge of things in its relation. Truth and reality is relative to how one perceives it. All objects are infinite while human perception is finite. It reminds us of the old Jain story of the blind men and the elephant. One man touched the tail of the elephant and mistakes it as rope, and another one touches the trunk and thinks that it is a pillar; the ear is mistaken as curtain and the body as wall. Every interpretation just by itself is wrong. Only when all the interpretations are looked at together they realize that it is an elephant. In a way, it warns its followers not to cling too much to any one philosophy, including their own. It urges people to be open and liberal to the viewpoint of others. Open mind and coexistence of a spectrum of philosophies was the strength of that era, a strength that has weakened over the years. The 'survivors', however, kept on evolving.

4.5   The Magic Surgeon

The northeast of India was yet to start building a civilization while the south was slowly condensing into one. Western India was already aging and was seeing competition from the mighty Persian Empire. The Persians had annexed and incorporated Afghanistan and Gandhara into their domain. The center of Indian civilization has now shifted from Sapta-Sindhu farther east into the Gangetic plain. That is where the first powerful kingdoms of India would take shape. Unfortunately, being in the floodplains on the foothills of active Himalayas, most of the archaeological sites are way below the ground to unearth. While Persian Empire was glorified because of its contact with the Greeks, Indian kingdoms of that time did not receive similar attention. The ignorance is also because of the reluctance of our ancestors to write down detailed history. There must have been powerful empires as even the mighty Persians dared not to cross the Indus. Alexander defeated the Persians but avoided direct combat with the eastern kingdoms of India.

The stability brought by powerful empires and the rich and fertile Gangetic plain led to the Indian Renaissance. The Upanishad philosophy made god redundant, the Charvaka proclaimed god does not exist, Buddhism had no need for god, and Jainism did not believe in god. God lost its significance in that era while spirituality gained importance. The orthodox Hindu philosophy, and along with it the Brahmins, was losing its ground. The people of the oppressed caste had an escape route through Buddhism and Jainism. No wonder the Brahmins would label this new era as the Kali Yug, or the era of darkness.

Apart from philosophy, trading was also important both within India and with foreign countries (Egypt, Greece, and Southeast Asia). The people of Greece did not know about India but used their products. They thought of Indians as east Ethiopians because of their darker skin color. Trading took place through roads, rivers, and sea. Trading roads in India were well maintained with places for shelter and hospitals on the side of the roads at regular intervals. India exported silk, muslins, cloths, cutlery, armor, brocades, embroideries, rugs, perfumes, drugs, ivory, jewelry, and gold. The wealth from trading led to the growth of science and literature. Educational institutions nurtured young minds. Takshashila University in Gandhara was one of the oldest universities in the world. The name means *the city of cut stone*. It is situated in modern Rawalpindi, Pakistan. The earliest ruins of the university dates back to 800 BCE. It is one of the oldest-known universities of the world. It was known for science, medicine, arts, grammar, astrology, and astronomy. Panini wrote his famous book on Sanskrit grammar in this university.

The Indian philosophy of infinity and cyclicity of life gave our early thinkers the vast concept of time and space unlike any other nation at that time. The concept of zero, minus, decimal, and infinity was probably already conceived by then. *Paramanus* (closest analog to atoms), the basic building blocks of the universe, are mentioned in Vaisheshika Sutra of Kanaad. It was written as early as in sixth century BCE. Jain text Suryapragnapti classifies numbers into three types and also describes five kinds of infinity. Indians, along with Egyptians, made substantial progress in surgeries. Sushruta wrote a book on medicine and surgery during sixth century BCE. He was from southern parts of India but spent most of his time in Varanasi. The book includes surgical techniques for tooth extraction, cataract operation, removal of prostate gland, vesicolithotomy, hernia surgery, caesarian section, management of hemorrhoids, fistulae, laparotomy, and the principles of fracture management. More importantly, the book includes details of plastic surgeries. Rhinoplasty was continued to be performed by local surgeons in India even in the 19th century based on his principles. British surgeons Thomas Cruso and James Findlay witnessed rhinoplasty performed live at a British residency in Poona. British officers, whose noses were cut by Tipu Sultan, came to a local Indian surgeon for treatment. Thomas and James were surprised by what they saw. They realized the potential of this magic surgery and went on to popularize the same in the west. On October 1794, in the issue of *Gentleman's Magazine* of London, they published the details of what they saw. This episode marks the beginning of modern plastic surgery. The basic concepts still remain the same as was in India over 2,500 years ago.

4.6   Adventures of Sikander

In 559 BCE, Cyrus became the king of Persia. He went on to become the ruler of the largest empire the world had yet seen. The vast stretch of land from Mediterranean in the west to Indus in the east was under his reign. At the same time was born another ambitious king who would grow up to rule India's most powerful state Magadha. His name was Bimbisara, and he belonged to Haryanka Dynasty. He annexed Anga kingdom in the east and was looking to control the entire Gangetic plain and, along with it, the river trade. His ambitions were in sharp contrast to that of his friend and guru Buddha. Rise of Bimbisara marked the end of the democratic states or the Mahajanapadas. The definition of *raja* changed from *the protector* to *the ruler*. Bimbisara started the beginning of the administrative system in India [24]. He was succeeded (492 BCE) by his even more ambitious son, Ajatashatru. Bimbisara was probably imprisoned and killed by his own son. In this, Kali Yug fathers were slowly losing their importance.

While Cyrus's successor Darius was eyeing Greece, Ajatashatru was chasing his father's dream. He annexed Kosala, Kashi, and the entire Ganges plain up to Chandigarh, gaining full access to the river trade. He built his fort near the bank of Ganges at Pataligrama. The city later became Pataliputra and now called Patna. Ajatashatru died in 461 BCE and was succeeded by Udayabhadra. His reign was followed by bloody successions as the three latter kings came to power after killing their fathers, the previous king. Killing one's own father went against the *dharma* of Indian society. People revolted against the atrocities of the greedy kings. Their viceroy replaced the Haryanka Dynasty in 413 BCE, starting the beginning of Sishunaga Dynasty. Once again, the Indian society overpowered the state. Half a century later, in 345 BCE, the Nandas displaced them. Nandas made history by being the earliest-known lower-caste Sudra to take the throne. History was also being made in the west. It was the time when the Persian Empire was falling again and a new ruler dreamt of taking control of the whole world.

Before moving west, let us go farther east to the powerful Vanga Empire (modern Bengal). With a vast shoreline favorable for development of ports, the empire became a powerful sea trader. They traded with Southeast Asia. According to Sri Lanka's ancient chronicles,

Sinhabahu, the king of Vanga (Bengal), punished his son Vijaya after the latter did some misdeeds. Vijaya, along with his 700 men, were sent to exile. They took a ship and sailed to Tambapani (Sri Lanka) around 544 BCE. It is said that he landed on the island in the day Buddha died. They settled down in this beautiful island and named it Sinhala, meaning *lion men* [36]. Vijaya established the first kingdom of Sri Lanka. Vijayan Dynasty ruled for a span of over 600 years. People of Vanga also established colonies in Malay Archipelago and Siam (in modern Thailand) as early as 2,500 years ago. Some Indians do take pride in the fact that they never colonized the world. Even Greek writers thought, "No Indian ever went outside his own country on a warlike expedition, so righteous were they." The pride is slightly misplaced. Ironically, it was a port on the same shores of Bengal through which the Europeans would come to colonize us.

Vanga was ruled by the powerful Gangaridai (heart of Ganges) Empire at the same time the Nanda Dynasty ruled Bihar [37]. According to the writings of Greek authors like Megasthenes and Ptolemy, Gangaridai was the most powerful empire in India at that time. They maintained an army of '20,000 horses, 200,000 infantry, 2,000 chariots and 4,000 elephants trained and equipped for war'. They might have meant the collective empire of Nanda and Gangahridai Dynasty. Ruins of the empire have been excavated from a small village called Berachampa, just ~35 kilometres from Kolkata.

In the west, Alexander III of Macedon [38] annexed the Persian Empire and the western fringes of India. He then eyed the riches of eastern India. There are lots of myths surrounding the legend of Macedon. Thousands of years ago, when the gods walked with the mortals, Indian saints unraveled the mystery of immortality. The magic was found in the juice of Soma plants, growing in the banks of the great Indus River. Alexander the Great, known locally as Sikander, came to know about it and wanted to find it so that he could rule the world eternally. In his voyage, he befriended a local person who was guiding him towards the secret and sacred place. After a point of time they parted ways to make the search quicker. One day, accidentally, a dried fish fell into a spring from the hand of Sikander's friend. To his surprise, the dead fish came back to life and swam away. Sikander's friend had found the fountain of life, also known as *Aab-i-Hayat*. He drank from the magical spring and told the soldiers to inform Sikander. By the time Sikander returned, the spring vanished along with his friend. Sikander's friend became a legend. His story can be traced back to the Gilgamesh epic, the Alexander romances, the Jewish legend of Elijah and Rabbi Joshua ben Levi, and even the Koran. He is known by many names. He is al-Khadir or Khwaja Khizr of Muslims, Uderolal or Jind Pir of Hindus, and Utnapishtim of the Gilgamesh epic. He is the immortal prophet whose abode is a green island in the Indus River. He roams along the banks of the river and helps people in trouble. He has white beard and rides on a palla fish.

In 326BC Sikander became the first invader to cross the Indus River. He allied with the king of Taksashila, Ambhi Kumar (Omphis of Greeks). That alliance was one of the reasons why Takshashila University survived Sikander's onslaught. Sikander's men saw the university, the 'like of which was not seen in Greece'. With help from Ambhi, Sikander built a bridge across Indus River. However, his confidence was shattered the moment he crossed into India. Sikander did manage to win against the resilient smaller Indian border tribes called Asvakas but only after a tough fight. The Asvaka women took up arms and fought alongside their men. They preferred a glorious death to a life of dishonor. Sikander was wounded in the fighting. The Macedonian army slaughtered the entire population of Massaga and Ora.

Sikander's soldiers were tired after the long and eventful journey away from home. They were now facing the most powerful empire they had encountered so far. With a small army, he easily defeated the mighty Persian Empire. However, he faced his toughest opponent in the form of Puru (Greek Porus), a ruler of a small Indian kingdom in the west. The huge Indian war elephants and their superior weapons, like the two-metre bow, made the army of Puru formidable despite their small numbers. Sikander's strength was his tactics and battle plan. His bold and unexpected move to cross the river at peak monsoon tilted the balance of the war in his favor. Puru's son died in the battle but not before wounding Sikander and killing his enemy's favorite horse. Sikander did manage to win the Battle of Hydaspes against Puru, but it left his army devastated. It was the costliest battle fought by Sikander's men. Sikander was impressed by the bravery of Puru and asked him how he should be treated. Puru replied, "As a king treats another king." The two great men became friends.

On the east of Ganges, India's most powerful kingdoms were ready to take on Sikander. According to the Greek authors, Sikander retreated, fearing a valiant attack from the joint forces of Nanda and Gangaridai Empire (figure 4). It was probably the biggest army in the world of that time [39]. Sikander's army was homesick and was in no mood to take on their biggest foe. Sikander had to return disappointed without fulfilling his dream of conquering the world. He succumbed to the wounds, which he suffered while returning, three years later in Babylon. Once, while in India, Sikander asked a group of Jain philosophers why they were ignoring the great conqueror. The philosophers replied, "King Alexander, every man can possess only so much of earth's surface as this we are standing on. You are but a human like rest of us. . . . You will soon be dead, and then you will own just as much of the earth as will suffice to bury you." For the Indians, Sikander's adventures were just a minor trouble at the borders. Sikander did not leave behind much impact on Indian culture and thus hardly finds any mention in the contemporaneous texts. However, he did left behind a part of his army. The Brokpa tribe, who now lives in Laddakh, claims to be the kin of Sikander's men. This tribe is only found in four villages: Dah, Hano, Darchik, and Garkon. Because they live in harsh terrain where no invasion has taken place, these blonde, red-haired, blue-eyed, and fair-skinned people have maintained their distinct genetic identity (which has only faint Greek link).

Rise of Empires (300 BCE to 300 CE)

Indians dye their beards various colors; some that they may appear white as the whitest, others dark blue; others have them red, others purple, and others green. Those who are of any rank have umbrellas held over them in the summer. They wear shoes of white leather, elaborately worked, and the soles of their shoes are many-colored and raised high, in order that they may appear taller.

—Nearchus (Officer in the army of Alexander)

5.1 Vendetta

The rule of the Nandas, a low caste, was a direct challenge to the Brahmins and their caste system. The Nandas must have come to power after an epic revolt, of which unfortunately we do not know much. We only hear the prejudiced story of the Brahmins who portray the Nandas as evil for obvious reasons. The last of the Nanda ruler was Dhana Nanda. His minister and advisor was the loyal Raksasas. Out of his pride, Dhana Nanda insulted a Brahmin named Vishnu Gupta. Furious and outraged, the Brahmin vowed vengeance. He was a professor of economics and political science at the ancient Takshashila University. Vishnu Gupta was as wise as he was shrewd. He never forgot an insult and was waiting for the right moment to fulfill his vengeance. Vishnu Gupta saw his opportunity in the form of a bright young boy.

Who was this young boy, and what was his actual name is a matter of a long debate. Vishakhadatta's Mudrarakshasa, written between fourth and eighth century, names the boy as *Nandanvaya*, a descendant of Nandas. Vishnu Gupta brainwashed the ambitious young prince to usurp the king. Dhana Nanda came to know about the plan and sent the boy into exile in the Himalayas, along with his eight rebel friends. In the Jain version, the boy's mother was from a community that kept peacocks, and hence, he was Mayura (Mayur meaning *peacock*). His father was a chieftain who was killed in a battle, and his mother was forced to go into hiding with him. Vishnu Gupta, quite accidentally, saw this boy and at once was impressed by his strength and intelligence. He knew that he could mold this perfect raw material into his weapon of vengeance. He kidnapped the boy and trained him to become the future monarch of India. Once the boy was ready, he attacked the Nandas. It was too early, and the powerful Nandas easily defeated him. Mayura, with his troops, ran away into the Himalayas.

It is from this point that the different versions of the story start to merge. Vishnu Gupta trained the young boy for many years, preparing him for the battle. The boy had now turned into a man named Chandragupta Mayura and Vishnu Gupta into a more intelligent and cunning

Chanakya. Chanakya was to Chandragupta what Aristotle was to Alexander. Chanakya managed an alliance with Parvateshwar, the king of the mountains. They, together with help from the Greeks, captured Pataliputra, and the mighty Nandas were forced into exile. Parvateshwar and Chandragupta divided not only the huge kingdom between them but also Nanda's daughters. While Chanakya was an advisor to Chandragupta, Rakshasa became the advisor of Parvateshwar. Nanda's daughter whom Parvateshwar married poisoned him to avenge her father. His son Malayaketu succeeded him. Rakshasha turned Malayaketu against Chandragupta to avenge Nanda's defeat. However, Chandragupta easily defeated young Malayaketu [40].

Chanakya got his sweet revenge, but it was not enough. He dreamt of freeing the western fringe of India from the Greeks and uniting the whole of India under one consolidated rule. With advice from Chanakya, Chandragupta attacked Alexander's successor. He succeeded in defeating them easily, thus becoming the ruler of an enormous land stretching from Bay of Bengal in the east to Indus River in the west. It was now that Chandragupta met his biggest foe, Seleucus I Nicator, the most able Macedonian satrap of Alexander. There was a fierce battle between Chandragupta and Seleucus. The battle ended in a peace treaty that was heavily biased towards Chandragupta. Seleucus had to give Chandragupta part of his empire, which included Afghanistan and Baluchistan. Chandragupta also married his daughter. In return, all Chandragupta lost were 500 war elephants, probably old. The elephants helped Seleucus expand his kingdom farther west. The alliance also resulted in cultural interactions between the Indians and the Greeks. There were exchanges of ambassadors between the two cultures, along with science, philosophy, and literature.

With his east and west flank secured, Chandragupta now eyed south. He crossed the Vindhyan Mountains and conquered the Deccan plateau. With the exception of Orissa (Kalinga), Tamil region, and the northeastern mountains, the rest of India was united under one rule: the Maurya Empire. Chandragupta ruled for 24 years. One of Chandragupta's wives, named Dhurdara, gave birth to a son. The story of the birth of the child is no ordinary one. Chanakya used to give Chandragupta small doses of poison every day to make him immune to poisoning attempts. During the last stages of her pregnancy, Dhurdara unknowingly ate the poisoned food meant for her husband. Not being used to the poison, she died immediately. In order to save the child, Chanakya cut her open. By the time the child was brought out, a small droplet of poisoned entered the child's blood leading to spots, or *bindu*, on his skin. The child survived and was named Bindusara.

Once Chandragupta gained all Chanakya ever wanted, he renounced everything. Bindusara was declared as the new king. It was Chanakya who guided how Chandragupta should live his life; however, it was Chandragupta who decided his own end. After giving up all earthly pleasures, much against Chanakya's wish, he went south in search of salvation. Chandragupta died as a Jain saint in Karnataka and probably by self-starvation in a cave at Sravana Belgola in Mysore [40]. Chanakya continued to guide the young Bindusara and strengthen the Maurya Empire.

5.2 Chanakya's Wisdom

Chanakya's character has a lot of similarity to that of Krishna. Both guided a weak side to victory with the help of their political intelligence. Both were inspired not by the lust for power but vengeance, and both did not shy away from using cunning tactics. It is interesting to compare Gandhi to Chanakya as well. Both gave India freedom from Western powers, and again both did not aspire to rule. While Chanakya made Chandragupta the king, Gandhi made Jawaharlal the prime minister. However, the tactics used by both these great men were drastically different. Gandhi's India was weak and hence the strategy of nonviolence while Chanakya's India was powerful enough to defend by sword. While Gandhi gave the world nonviolent way to freedom, Chanakya gave the world ruthless strategies of conquering.

We know about Chanakya from his books, especially *Arthasastra*. It is a treatise on economics and is one of the greatest political books of the ancient world. There is some debate whether Kautalya, who wrote *Arthasastra*, is Chanakya. Some historians think that Kautalya is different from Chanakya but wrote the book based on the teachings of Chanakya. The book, however, is a masterpiece. "Truly radical 'Machiavellianism,' in the popular sense of that word," said Max Weber, "is classically expressed in Indian literature in the Arthasastra of Kautilya: compared to it, Machiavelli's The Prince is harmless." [41] Chanakya was at times ruthless with his strategies, but it was the need of the hour. Some of the strategies he stated are valid even in today's world. The focus was not just on a strong empire but more importantly on a sustainable one. The key was to identify the risks from within and outside and eliminate them before the threat becomes significant.

Chanakya believed that for a king to succeed, the people he ruled must be happy. A good portion of the money that was gained by the king should be distributed amongst the pupils. People do not care who the king is. As long as they are happy, they will remain loyal. The king can enjoy a long and peaceful rule when his subjects are loyal to him. The leader should also provide law and order that protects people's money from thieves and officials. Hence, the king needs to provide fair justice. Punishment should act as deterrent to crime. It is a necessary evil required to protect the innocent and bring order in the kingdom. In *Mahabharata* (book XII), Bhishma teaches King Yudhishthira, "If the rod of force did not exist in this world, beings would be nasty and brutish to each other. Because they fear punishment they do not kill each other ... rod of force puts this world into a stable order, O king." While justice delayed is justice denied, the king should not torture his people for no reason. Chanakya warns, "It is a bad leader who tortures people, a good one keeps his people happy." [42]

In the opening stanzas of his book *Chanakyasutra*, he writes, "The root of happiness is morality, root of morality is wealth, root of wealth is enterprise." [42] Even though money does not bring happiness, poverty would not bring a happy state. It is through enterprise and trading that one makes a country wealthy. A wealthy country is a happy country. Not surprisingly, trading grew rapidly during Mauryan rule. Once people are happy, the next threat was from relatives and people who were lusting for power. He warned the king to observe the body language of everyone he interacted with no matter how close they were. Anyone who was not loyal or showed immoral character must be punished in a way that it becomes a lesson for others.

Chanakya taught that a king becomes great by his deeds and not by luck. "One trusting in fate," he believed, "being devoid of human endeavor, perishes. . . . The object slips away from the foolish person, who continuously consults the stars." Power lies in the present, and hence, he wrote, "We should not fret for what is past, nor should we be anxious about the future; men of discernment deal only with the present moment." [43] To secure the future, one needs good strategies. To build such strategies, one needs a group of wise, intelligent, and loyal people. Utmost care should be taken to ensure that the strategy is not leaked to the outside world. Secrecy was the key to the execution of a plan [42].

Once the interior of the country was secured, it was important to secure the borders. According to Chanakya, every nation acts to maximize power and self-interest. Hence, morality has no meaning while dealing with other nations. It is in sharp contrast to the importance he gave on morality while dealing with his own countrymen. Chanakya's foreign policies can be summed up in his favorite formula: 'saam, daam, dand, bhed'. Saam is to have a diplomatic discussion between the opposing parties and come to a peaceful agreement. If the first strategy failed, the next one was *daam*. *Daam* meant bribing the important members in the enemy camp and force the opposition ruler to his terms. If *daam* failed, it was time for *dand* or punishment. Punishment meant the threat of war. If the opponent was weaker, then either they become friends or were conquered by force: "The conqueror should march if superior in strength, otherwise stay quiet." Even if the opponent is of equal strength, one should avoid direct confrontation because when 'two clay pots are banged against each other both will break'. When battle was not an option, the last and the ultimate weapon was *bhed*. *Bhed* aimed at breaking the opponent from within. Chanakya created a web of secret agents in all neighboring countries. They became close friends of the enemy. Their task was not only to get information but also to find weaknesses of the opponent. The weaknesses were used to disunite the opponent. Chanakya describes four types of people who act against their king: the enraged, the frightened, the greedy, and the proud. The agents had to find these people in the enemy camp and slowly indoctrinate them to act against their king.

Chanakya spoke of three types of war: "there is open war, concealed war and silent war." Open war is obvious, and concealed war is guerrilla warfare. It was the concept of silent war that was the product of his crafty mind. In this kind of warfare, secret agents and spies assassinated important leaders in the enemy kingdom. The aim was not just to create divisions among key ministers but also spread propaganda and disinformation [41]. Chanakya is believed to have created a secret force of young and beautiful female assassins. It was relatively easy for them to become intimate with the leaders of the enemy and poison them. There were women agents who would act as if they were in love with a targeted leader. Then she would go to another leader and disclose her love for him. She would coax her new lover to kill the old one. Once the old leader was killed, she would disclose to the king that the murderer has killed her love. With one stone, she would kill two birds without any harm to herself. Once the powerful opponent is weakened by *bhed*, it was time to attack and bring down the wounded enemy. It was during this time of war that one needed allies. If the probable ally wanted to remain neutral, then Chanakya's spies would secretly create situations where the neutral nation would be forced to confront their neighboring nation.

Chanakya considered the neighboring states as the biggest threat while the neighboring state of the enemy must be an ally as "enemy's enemy is a friend." However, "war and peace are considered solely from the point of view of profit" and not out of goodwill or charity. Once the enemy was defeated, Chanakya opposed massacre of the opponent nation. Apart from the important leaders, the rest should be spared. The lower-ranked soldiers should be hired. A massacre will frighten the neighboring kingdoms and even his ministers. It would create more enemies. "He should not use towards them insults, injuries, contemptuous words or reproaches. And after promising them safety, he should favor them like a father" and gain more loyal subjects. The king "should adopt a similar character, dress, language and behavior [as the new subjects]. And he should show the same devotion in festivals in honor of deities of the [conquered] country, festive gatherings and sportive amusements." [44]

It is believed that Chanakya starved himself to death, like Chandragupta, after Bundusara insulted him. There was a plot against Chanakya by Subandhu, the minister of Bindusara. Subandhu told Bindusara that Chanakya was responsible for the death of his mother. He convinced the king that Chanakya should be punished. Bindusara believed the story and insulted Chanakya. This led Chanakya to take the drastic step. By the time Bindusara realized his mistake, it was too late. Subandhu was later executed. The shrewd strategies of Chanakya laid the foundation for Ashoka's innovative method of conquering the world by *dharma*. It is to that king, one of the greatest ever, to whom we will now turn to.

5.3 Conquering by Dharma

After being successful in Egypt and Mesopotamia, the craze to dig out the past infected the British in India. The main objective was to understand the past of the people they are ruling in order to rule them better. However, it was difficult to inhibit personal desires. Many of the archaeologists started to collect the antiques for themselves. Sometimes they stole idols from temples, angering the locals. It became an obsession that resulted in the discovery of a lost empire that was so far thought to be a myth. The writings of Greek authors and Buddhist texts told of a glorious Maurya Empire and a great ruler named Ashoka. Yet evidence was scanty. In 1915, archaeologists found a pillar inscription that gave the first clue. Soon many rock edicts and pillars were discovered from all around India. Sanchi, a Buddhist structure created by Ashoka the Great himself, was also discovered near Bhopal. After all the bits and pieces of the puzzle were put together, an amazing story was revealed.

Chandragupta ruled for 34 years before leaving his throne to his son, Bindusara. Bindusara, a Charvaka, consolidated the Maurya Empire and ruled for 28 years. His son Sumana was groomed as the future king. One day young Sumana slapped the bald head of his father's chief minister as a prank [45]. That small mistake would change not only his destiny but also that of the world. Radhagupta, the angry chief minister, realized that a man who does not respect others would never be an able king. He allied with other ministers and turned them against Sumana in favor of another son of the king named Ashoka. Ashoka was not Bindusara's favorite, and the feeling was probably mutual. Bindusara heard that Ashoka was conspiring to kill him and seize the throne. He sent him away from their capital Pataliputra to govern a faraway land in Ujjain. It was here that Ashoka fell in love with a merchant's daughter named Devi [46]. Devi was an adherent follower of Buddhism, and it is from her that Ashoka learned about the religion. She bore him a son named Mahendra around 285 BCE and a daughter named Sanghamitta three years later [40].

Meanwhile, there was a rebellion among the Taxilans. A sick Bindusara, on the advice of his chief minister, sent his able son Sumana to curb the rebel. However, his health was deteriorating. Bindusara immediately sent the news to Sumana and told him to return as fast as he can. Radhagupta's men purposefully delayed the news. It was Ashoka who got the news early and was able to come to Pataliputra before his brother. The king died soon after, and Ashoka declared himself as the new king. On hearing about the treachery of his brother, Sumana marched with his army to get back his throne. Radhagupta tricked him. An artificial elephant was created with an image of Ashoka riding on it. A hidden ditch was dug around it as a trap. On seeing Ashoka, Sumana attacked it will full force but fell into the ditch and was killed [45].

Radhagupta had his revenge, but little did he know that he had unleashed a monster. Ashoka went on to kill all his brothers who lusted for the throne. He only spared his younger brother Tissa. Ashoka made him his deputy. After eliminating all possible heirs, Ashoka was declared as the king in 270 BCE. Ashoka's cruelty was well known. His ruthless conquering of enemies for four years earned him the name of *Chand* (*cruel*) Ashoka. He is said to have hired an executioner named Chandagirika for his prison where he tortured the prisoners with the five great agonies [45]. It was considered as the most dreaded prison in India.

Ashoka married once more. This time, it was a dynastic arrangement with Asandhimitra. Ashoka continued to expand his empire after marriage. His lust for power finally brought him face-to-face with the small but resilient kingdom of Kalinga. Kalinga was asked to surrender, which they denied. It resulted in a bloody war that took over 150,000 lives [47]. It is said that the Daya River, passing through the battlefield, turned red after the war. Ashoka himself was shocked by the ruthless outcome of the battle. The strong effect that the war left on Ashoka can be understood from the writings from one of his rock edicts:

> Beloved-of-the-Gods, King Priyadarsi [that's what Ashoka liked to call himself], conquered the Kalingas eight-years after his coronation. One hundred and fifty thousand were deported, one hundred thousand were killed and many more died [from other causes]. After the Kalingas had been conquered, Beloved-of-the-Gods came to feel a strong inclination towards the Dhamma, a love for the Dhamma and for instruction in Dhamma. Now Beloved-of-the-Gods feels deep remorse for having conquered the Kalingas. (Rock Edict No. 13) [48]

The battle metamorphosed *Chand* (*cruel*) Ashoka into *Dharm* (*moral*) Ashoka. Ashoka met Nigrodha, the orphaned son of his brother Sumana whom he killed. Ashoka was surprised to see a calm Nigrodha who was not angry with his father's murderer. Nigrodha, now a Buddhist monk, inspired Ashoka to become a devoted Buddhist and adopt the path of nonviolence [46]. One must not forget the influence of Devi on Ashoka too. Ashoka did not convert to Buddhism overnight. It was a gradual process of transformation. Ashoka is said to have built 84,000 temples around his kingdom [49]. He also started to erect rock edicts and pillars to write message to his people (figure 5). It was his way of promoting his dharma, or *Dhamma* as it was called then. Dharma does not mean religion but morality. Even though he was a Buddhist, the rock edicts and inscriptions were tailor-made for the sentiments of the people. Ashoka pleaded to respect all things living. The edicts and inscriptions talk of friendship and peace. The way he ruled was unheard of anywhere around the world, making him one of the greatest kings. He helped develop not only his own kingdom but also that of his neighbors as evident from Rock Edict 2 below:

> Everywhere within Beloved-of-the-Gods, King Piyadasi's domain, and among the people beyond the borders, the Cholas, the Pandyas, the Satiyaputras, the Keralaputras, as far as Tamraparni and where the Greek king Antiochos rules, and among the kings who are neighbors of Antiochos, everywhere has Beloved-of-the-Gods, King Piyadasi, made provision for two types of medical treatment: medical treatment for humans and medical treatment for animals. Wherever medical herbs suitable for humans or animals are not available, I have had them imported and grown. Wherever medical roots or fruits are not

available I have had them imported and grown.
Along roads I have had wells dug and trees planted
for the benefit of humans and animals. [48]

While Chanakya warned that neighbors are enemies,
Ashoka made them his friend. One must not forget that
Ashoka was so powerful that his neighbors were afraid to
act against him, especially when he was not threatening
them. The example he had set in Kalinga was not forgotten.
For the first time, a single ruler united the whole of India
(including Pakistan and Afghanistan). He indirectly
controlled even the southern kingdoms of India, including
Sri Lanka. His influence went around 5,000 kilometres (600
yojanas) west of his border. It included Greco-Persian king
Antiochus II and Egyptian king Ptolemy III of whom he
mentions in his rock edicts. He was undoubtedly the most
powerful ruler in the world at that time. He used his power
to spread Buddhism by sending missionaries all around
Asia. It was because of the efforts of Ashoka that Buddhism
turned into one of the most popular religions around the
world, especially China. All this happened just because of
Sumana's prank.

The man who promoted the religion of peace spent
his last days in a not-so-peaceful manner. After his
wife Asandhimitra died, he remarried young queen
Tissahraccah [49]. She was anti-Buddhist and has been
portrayed in literature as the wicked stepmother. Ashoka
spend a lot of time with the bodhi tree instead of his young
wife. It is said that Tissahraccah became so jealous of the
holy tree that she poisoned it [49]. Ashoka managed to save
it, but his health deteriorated. When Kunala, Ashoka's son
and heir apparent, went to Takshashila as governor the
queen used her men to blind him. Secretly, she created

an anti-Buddhist community. The rebel group was mostly composed of Brahmins who revolted against the king's preferential treatment of Buddhists. When Ashoka came to know about Tissahraccah's treachery, he executed her. It did weaken the anti-Buddhist faction, but the damage was already done [46]. Years later, blind Kunala appeared with his wife in Ashoka's court in disguise. He pleased the king with his music. When the king wanted to reward him, he revealed his true identity. Kunala then asked his father to give him his rightful throne as a reward. Ashoka objected as a blind man can never be a king. Only after Kunala explained that he wanted the throne not for himself but for his son Samprati did Ashoka agree.

Into his 60s, Ashoka became more obsessed with Buddhism. Most of his state treasury was drained to create Buddhist temples and to send Buddhist missionaries around the world. Ashoka's grandson Dasaratha became the heir-apparent. On advice of councilors, Dasaratha banned donations from the state treasury to manage Ashoka's fantasies. Ashoka was left with no choice but to donate his personal belongings [45]. Soon, he was left with nothing. Four years since his wife tried to poison the bodhi tree, Ashoka the Great died an unhappy death. Dharma Ashoka was probably repaying the sins of Chand Ashoka.

5.4   End of Mauryans

The Indian Philosophical Renaissance of early axial age gave way to the great Maurya Empire. It was the largest monarchy in India, greater than the Mughals or the British Raj. From Afghanistan to Bengal, and from Kashmir to Deccan, all was covered under one central rule. The Mayurians indirectly governed even the southern kingdoms. The population under Mayurians was over 50 million. The capital Pataliputra was probably the largest city in the world at that time. Pataliputra was about twice the size of Rome under Emperor Marcus Aurelius. The city was 13 kilometres long and 2.5 kilometres wide. It had 570 towers and 64 gates and was surrounded by a moat 180 meters wide and 14 feet deep. Since stone was scarce in Bihar, the walls protecting the city were made of wood with slits for archers [41]. Numerous structures were built during Ashoka's rule, along with the rock edicts and the beautifully sculpted pillars. Sanchi is one such example. Such structures along with royal roads, trees, water and shelter along the road, and hospitals must have changed the Indian landscape.

Some historians portray Ashoka's rule as pro-Buddhist. Though his public messages show no such biasness, there are some inscriptions that suggest that he did not tolerate insults to Buddhism. According to Tibetan writer Taranatha, "a follower of Nirgrantha [Jain or Charvaka] painted a picture, showing Buddha prostrating himself at the feet of the Nirgrantha. Ashoka ordered to kill all Nirgantha's of [North Bengal]." [50] In one day 18,000 people lost their lives, quite contrary to the teachings of Buddha. Interestingly, Ashoka called himself as 'beloved of god', and Buddhist religion had no god. He definitely favored Buddhism personally and economically, but he did not impose it on his people. There was no record of forceful conversion. He believed that 'a person must not reverence to his own sect or disparage the beliefs of another without reason'. Probably that is why he punished, if at all, those who insulted the religion of someone else.

Maurya Empire did not last long. Nine (or ten?) monarchs ruled the Maurya Empire for 137 years. After Ashoka, the dynasty started to fall apart. Jalauka, one of Dasaratha's uncles, declared himself as the king of Kashmir. Another Mauryan prince Virasena created a separate kingdom in Gandhara. Kalinga broke away and became independent once again. The southern kingdoms too became independent. Dasaratha managed to hold on to the powerful center at Pataliputra. Puranas mention that Samprati did succeed Dasaratha as Ashoka promised. No imperial inscriptions were issued, or survived, after Dasaratha. There is not enough information about the latter rulers of the once-great dynasty. Brihadratha was the last king who was assassinated by his minister who went on to create the Shunga Dynasty. Some say that the Mauryan lineage survived and later constructed the Chittorgarh Fort in fourth century. Evidence, however, is scanty.

Ashoka donated a lot of money to the Buddhists, and that drained out the treasury. Moreover, there were a large number of soldiers who were not fighting anymore because of Ashoka's peaceful policies. But an enormous amount of money was required to maintain them. There must have been a lot of economic pressure on the kingdom. Trading was essential for keeping the balance in economy. Trading flourished till Ashoka's rule; however, it went on a decline during the reign of latter weaker kings. Vast empire with an empty treasury was a recipe for disaster. It weakened the unity of the empire. The highly centralized rule from Pataliputra added to the instability. Even wine was a state monopoly. Even though there were royal roads connecting the important cities, there must still be communication barriers from the center to the extreme ends of the empire.

It acted as a huge handicap for such a large empire. Slowly, the empire faded away from our memory. Barring few lines about the names of the Mauryan kings, the Hindu scriptures preferred to remain silent. Dust slowly covered the remains of the empire and thus was lost India's first experiment towards imperialism. The biggest city of the time is now under the densely populated city of Patna, and there is no way one can dig up the past to know more. Maybe it is better that it remains that way.

5.5   India under Mauryans

Much of the knowledge about India during Maurya Empire comes from the Greeks. Before Alexander, they hardly knew anything about India. During Maurya Empire, Greeks started to have direct interaction with Indians. Authors like Megasthenes (350–290 BCE), Arrian (86–160), and Ptolemy (90-168) wrote about the great nation in the East. While India itself has been divided into numerous smaller entities, the West always considered India as one land with Indus as its western border, Himalayas as its northern extreme, and bounded by sea in the south. Greeks considered India as a civilized country like them that was surrounded by barbarian tribes on all sides [51]. Indians considered these fringing tribes as demons and called them by names like Raksasas and Pisachas.

The Greek authors write about the great rivers of India, the largest being Indus and Ganges. These rivers, along with the double monsoons, made India fertile. Most of the land was under irrigation with two crops a year. Millets, wheat, rice, sesame, and bosporum were the major crops. While other nations ravage the soil during war and turn it to uncultivated lands, in India the farmlands were respected; and even during wars, the farmers were left alone. The unwritten law, that enemy's lands were never burnt or trees cut, prevented famines [51]. Plenty of gold, silver, copper, iron, and tin were mined, which were used as ornaments and weapons. The houses in the city were made of bricks. However, the ones in the river floodplain or in the coasts were made of wood. The only other great Indian kingdom at that time was on the east of Ganges. It was called the Gangaridai Empire. The Greek authors also mention a kingdom in the mountains called the Pandean nation, which was governed by women. A similar nation named Strirajya finds mention in *Mahabharata* and *Ramayana*. More about this mysterious nation will be discussed later.

Writing was already well developed during the rule of Ashoka. His inscriptions were written mostly in Brahmi — the script of common people. Panini wrote a book on Sanskrit grammar around 500 BCE, long before Ashoka. But Sanskrit was restricted to the Brahmin community and was not widespread. Most laws were not written but memorized at that time, and they were very strict. There were hardly any cases of theft in the entire country. All houses were left unguarded even though there were valuables kept inside the house. According to Greeks, the Indian law prohibited keeping of slaves with all citizens being free and having equal rights. There are some Indian texts that do mention about domestic slavery, which the Greeks might have overlooked as it was quite different from the slavery they knew. According to Indian laws, if the slave bears the child of the master, then she is free. Also, he/she could buy herself freedom. It might be possible that the Mauryans banned slavery. We know that Chanakya did not prefer to enslave the people captured in war; instead, he wanted to rule them like their own king.

There was a caste-based system for proper governance. Megasthenes interpreted seven castes (or may be classes) from what he observed. It included priests (Brahmins) and philosophers, farmers, herdsmen, traders/artisans, military, overseers, and councilors/assessors. Intercaste marriage or change of caste was not allowed; however, there were exceptions. Men from any caste could become a philosopher. The philosophers lived modest lives and were exempt from tax. They had moderate houses, slept on beds of rushes or deerskins. They abstained from animal food. These liberal philosophers mentioned by Greeks were probably Jains and Buddhists who did not adhere to the Brahmin caste system. Sarmanes were different from Brahmins. Most honored of the Sarmanes were the Hylobioi. They lived in the woods, ate wild fruits and plant leaves, and wore tree barks. They abstained from sexual intercourse and wine. Kings consulted them through messengers about causes of things and which god to pray through them. Next in honor were the physicians who studied nature of men. They had simple lives but did not live in fields. They ate rice and barley, which they got just by asking or people entertaining them as guests. They had knowledge in pharmacy, ointments, and plasters. There were also diviners and sorcerers who were experts in customs related to death. Brahmins who gave advice to the king, like Chanakya or Rakshasa, were the most powerful. According to the Greek authors, the Indians who lived up in the mountains prayed to Dionusos while majority of the ones living in the plain prayed to Herakles. Dionusos was probably Shiva and Herakles, Krishna. It seems like these were the main gods of those times. Not much is mentioned about Buddhists or Jains separately, probably because they did not look much different from the Hindu priests.

Indians were considered as slender, tall, and lighter than other men. They wore white clothes made of cotton. The undergarment, also made of cotton, reached below knee halfway down to the ankles. Upper garment was thrown partly over their shoulders and partly twist in fold around the head. Wealthy Indians wore earrings of ivory. They dyed their beards with different hues (red, purple, green) according to taste and used umbrellas to protect them from the sun. Shoes were made of white leather and were elaborately trimmed and had high soles. Indians exercised by applying friction to their body, the most common is rolling a smooth ebony roller or log of wood over their skin. They were fond of finery and ornaments. Their robes were worked in gold and embedded with precious stones. They also wore flowered garments made of fine muslin. The main Indian food was rice and curry. Greeks noticed a peculiar habit of the Indians. They did not have any fixed timing when they took food or when the entire family ate together. Indians ate whenever they felt hungry.

Indian women had mixed status. Manu Smriti advised men to control women: "Her father controls her childhood, her husband guards her in youth, and her sons guard her in old age. A woman is not fit for independence" (Manu Smriti 9.2–9.3). Such sentiments were very common around the world of that time. Women were the hidden half of history as men dominated the public arena. Aristotle believed that 'man is by nature superior to female, so man should rule and women should be ruled'. Demosthenes wrote, "We keep hetaerae for the sake of pleasure, female slaves for our daily care, and wives to give us legitimate children and to be the guardian of our household." Condition of women was not as bad as the writings depicted. Women remarriage was not uncommon. Arthasastra (3.2) says, "the property that a woman receives before marriage, she shall endow in the name of her son after remarriage. A barren widow who had been faithful to her husband shall have his property as long as she lives." Though limited, women had rights to property.

The Greek writers wrote that the Indian men married many women, 'hoping to find helpmates for pleasure and children'. They married without giving or taking dowries. When a woman attained a marriageable age, her father would announce a public competition in which prospective grooms would compete. Only the winner was allowed to marry the woman. Invitations were sometimes wisely sent only to favorable candidates. Sometimes the women had the right to choose from the competitors. Thus, marriage in India must have been a big event even then. This type of marriage was probably restricted to the rich people.

The wealthiest of Indians used elephants for transport. Next in honor were the chariots drawn by four horses. After that came the camel. Common men rode on horses. India also had the largest elephants trained for war. Indian soldiers were heavily armed. The foot soldiers carried huge bows that equaled in length to the man who carried it. Nothing could evade an Indian archer's shot [51]. On their left hands, they carried bucklers made of undressed oxhide, which were as long as their height. Some were equipped with javelins, and all with swords. Horsemen were equipped with two lances and shorter bucklers as compared to the foot soldiers.

Greek perception of India mostly came from their personal interaction in the capital Pataliputra and from what they heard from Indians, especially priests. There must have been a lot of diversity that the Greek authors failed to capture. We also hear from them about strange animals, demons, and giant ants that dug gold. The Indian philosophy, mythology, folk tales, and mathematics did influence the Greeks. The Greeks, in turn, left a lot of influence on India like the stone sculptures and astronomy. This two-way cultural interaction changed both the East and the West forever.

5.6   The Revenge of Kalinga

After the decline of Maurya Empire, the western part of India nosedived into chaos. Pusyamitra Sunga, general to the last Mauryan king, betrayed his master. No more did he want to follow the command of a feeble king. The glorious days of Maurya Empire were long gone. It was his time to rise. It was his duty to make things right. So in 185 BCE, the general killed his king and became the master of what was left of Chanakya's dream. Some historians have blamed Pusyamitra for persecution of Buddhists, which he may have done for political gains. During his rule, India went back to a decentralized political structure. He ruled for 36 years followed by his son Agnimitra. Kalidasa, one of the greatest poets ever, wrote *Malavikagnimitram* (try Maal-avi-ka-agni-mit-ram) during this era. The epic poem took inspiration from the love story between Prince Agnimitra and an exiled servant girl named Malavika. Agnimitra fell in love with her the moment he saw her painting. Mad in love, he tried to create various excuses to catch a glimpse of her. There were two problems. Firstly, Malavika was not of royal descent; and secondly, Agnimitra was already married. When his wife came to know of her husband's affair, she managed to get Malavika arrested. But fate had other plans. Investigations revealed that the servant girl had royal blood flowing through her veins. Malavika was released and finally united with Agnimitra.

Magadha and Pataliputra were under the Sunga Dynasty, which had ten kings and ruled for over 100 years. The dynasty ended just like it began. His minister Vasudeva Kanva assassinated the last king, Devabhuti. Vasudeva then took over the throne. Times were difficult. The Sungas had to fight the Indo-Greeks trying to invade from the west and the emerging Satavahana Dynasty in the south. But more importantly, an old enemy was rising from the ashes. Years ago, a devastating war left Kalinga shattered. Kalinga was down but not out. They lurked in silence under the shadows of the Mayurians, waiting for the wounds to heal, waiting for the right time to strike back. Ashoka had not only attacked them but had stolen their pride. Kharavela, the greatest king of Kalinga, was now ready to get it back.

We come to know about Kharavela from his Hathigumpha inscription [52] carved in the Elephant Cave of Udayagiri, Odissa. The inscription is dated to 157 BCE. Kharavela was linked to the ancient Chedi Dynasty and was a descendant of Mahameghavahana Dynasty. He became the king of Kalinga when he was 24 years old. In the first year as a king, he renovated Kalinga and consolidated his throne by pleasing his subjects. From the second year, he became aggressive and attacked the western regions, extending his empire. Festivals were held in the fourth year, celebrating his success. Soon after, a 300-year-old canal built by the Nandas was re-excavated to flow through their city. In the seventh year, he was blessed with a son. Next year, he attacked an Indo-Greek king, probably Demetrius, and captured Rajagriha. In memory of the famous victory, he built a grand palace for himself called Mahavijaya (Great Victory). By now, the Kalinga Empire was firmly established. Kharavela then looked south. He attacked and broke down the southern confederacy that had been troubling him for quite some time now. As he was already prosperous and powerful, it was finally the time for the ultimate revenge. With a powerful army, Kharavela marched into Magadha. His mighty elephants caused panic among the people of Magadha. He stormed into the king's palace and made the king of Sunga Dynasty bow to his feet. Tables were turned, and now it was time for Magadha to become the vassal of Kalinga. From there, he brought back the Jain idol that was once stolen from them by King Nanda.

With all the money that he had accumulated from his raids, he brought prosperity not only on himself but also upon the people he ruled. He built a grand city and spent lots of money on the welfare of his people. Trading through sea improved, especially with Southeast Asia. Councils were held of wise aesthetics and sages from far and wide. Though he seemed to favor Jainism, religious harmony was an important part of his rule. After his death, however, Kalinga went back to silence.

5.7   A Greek Hindu

A lonely stone column stands silent in the middle of nowhere in Vidisha, Madhya Pradesh. You might pass by it and easily miss it or even choose to ignore it until you know what is written on that apparently insignificant pillar. There are two inscriptions. The first one says:

This Garuda-standard was made by order of the Bhagavata. . . . Heliodoros, the son of Dion, a man of Takshashila, a Greek ambassador from King Antialkidas, to King Bhagabhadra, the son of the Princess from Benares, the savior, while prospering in the fourteenth year of his reign.

And the second one:

Three are the steps to immortality which . . . followed lead to heaven, [namely] self-control, self-denial and watchfulness. [53]

The pillar was erected by the order of the ambassador of Greek king Antialkidas from Takshashila named Heliodoros. He came to the prosperous Indian king named Bhagabhadra on his fourteenth year of reign. He was probably a Sunga king. There are two important things to note here. One is about Gandhara (parts of modern east Afghanistan starting from Kabul to west Pakistan Swat Valley). It was once a Hindu kingdom hosting one of the oldest universities in the world named Takshashila. It was captured by Cyrus and was appreciated as the richest kingdom under him. It was then Alexander's turn to snatch it from the Persians. Chandragupta got it back from the Greeks. The Greeks then recaptured it, only to be taken back by the Sakas. Soon, it would become a Buddhist kingdom recaptured by Hindu kings only to be conquered by the Arabs and Turks. The second interesting point is the collaboration between Indians and Greeks. It started during Chandragupta's reign and continued much after the decline of Maurya Empire. One reason for that is the mutual self-respect that they had for each other.

The Greek ambassador called himself Bhagavata Heliodoros, making him a follower of Lord Krishna. It was the beginning of the newly emerging Bhagavata sect, and Heliodoros was one of the earliest converts. The Greeks adapted to the Indian culture easily as the gods of both Greeks and Indians were very similar. The new devotional form of Hinduism was easier to be followed by the masses. It had the flexibility of allowing people from other religions to convert [24]. Conversion to Hinduism became difficult later. The interaction between the Greeks and Indians created a unique Indo-Greek culture.

Indo-Greeks ruled western part of India, including Gandhara and Punjab. Demetrius founded the kingdom in second century BCE. The most famous king of the dynasty was Menander, or Milinda of Buddhist text Milinda Panha. According to Strabo, the Greek geographer, Milinda conquered more tribes than Alexander. Milinda became a Buddhist after the Buddhist sage Nagasena defeated him in a debate. In one such discussion Milinda asked Nagasena, "How many years of seniority do you have?"

"Seven, Your Majesty," replied Nagasena.

"How can you say it is your seven? Is it you who are seven, or the number that is seven?"

Nagasena looked at a vessel of water in which the king's reflection was seen. He asked, "Are you the king or this reflection?"

"I am the king. The reflection exists because of me."

"Similarly, oh sire, the number is seven, not me. But the number exists because of me."

After many such debates, the king was impressed by Nagasena's reasoning. Milinda then asked the sage if he would have more discussions with him. To that, Nagasena replied, "If you discuss as a scholar, yes. If you discuss as a king, no." He clarified that when scholars discuss, there is a logical debate where the truth is unraveled. One of the two who debated is convicted of error. The loser acknowledges his mistake without any anger. In contrast, a king only puts forward his point. Those who differ are fined or punished. On hearing the difference, King Milinda agreed to discuss with Nagasena as a scholar. The king and the sage were engaged in long philosophical and spiritual discussion after which Milinda became a disciple of Nagasena. It was Asoka who introduced Buddhism to the Greeks, and now the religion was ready to spread across Asia. While Buddhism continued to increase its territory, the territory of the Indo-Greeks started to decrease after Milinda's death. Some writings say that the king left his kingdom after getting converted to Buddhism. He made his son the king. Other versions say that he died in a camp while on a campaign. Milinda was a popular king because of his justice and kindness. It is said that, like Buddha, many cities contended for possession of his ashes. Monuments containing his ashes were constructed in his name. After his death, it was the Indo-Scythians, or Sakas, who started to grow at the expense of Indo-Greeks.

At the same time, Qin Shi Huang unified China and established the Qin Dynasty in 221 BCE. He built the Great Wall of China to protect his people from the attacks of Hsiung-Nu, the ancestors of Huns. Qin Dynasty displaced the Hsiung-Nu tribe, creating a domino effect that pushed the Saka clan towards India. Sakas are originally Aryan tribes of Central Eurasia and Siberia who spoke Iranian language. They were distant relatives of the Vedic Indians. Interestingly, the Sakas are mentioned in *Ramayana* and *Mahabharata* as well. They allied with Kambojas, Pahlavas, Parada, Yavanas, and Tusharas at different times, fighting against the Indian kings. Some of the communities of Jats, Gujars, and Rajputs are considered to be descendants of the Sakas (and White Huns) [54]. Maues was the first Indo-Scythian king in India at around 100 BCE. The rule of Sakas continued into the classical era till another Indo-Iranian group, the Kushans, replaced them.

5.8   The Headless King

It is a UNESCO World Heritage Site. It has the finest examples of Indian art. It is sculpted out of the mighty Deccan basalts hidden amidst the dense forests, and it is 2,200 years old. It is hidden probably to protect itself from invaders, and invaders there were many. During these uncertain times, who build these magnificent caves of Ajanta? These were educational institutes of the Buddhist monks. It is generally agreed that they were sculpted during the rule of Satavahana Dynasty (Andhra Dynasty). Satavanas were feudatories to Ashoka. They became independent after the disintegration of the Maurya Empire. Satavanas felt the domino effect that started in China as the Sakas pushed them from northwest. They moved south, expanding their kingdom from Maharashtra to Andhra Pradesh. King Kharavela is said to have fought with the Satavanas and managed to keep them at bay. However, soon after Kharavela's death, the Satavanas gained control over central India. Later, they managed to push the Sakas (Western Satraps) back. Satavanas king Shalivahana is said to have begun the Shalivahana era after defeating the Sakas. That year marks the beginning of the widely used Saka calendar of India, starting 78 CE. It was because of Satavanas that the Indo-Iranian invaders never reached south of India. Satavanas were now the connecting link between the empires of northern and southern India. Unlike the centralized rule of the Mayurians, power was distributed throughout the hierarchy of officials during the rule of Satavanas. The king never took the imperial title [24]. Their rule carried over to the other side of the millennia into the classical age till the third century.

An interesting legend took shape in the same era. It was written later in 13th-century Korean chronicle named *Samguk Yusa*. The chronicle links the origin of one of the legendary queens of Korea to Ayodhya. Queen Huh was the wife of King Suro, the founder of Karak kingdom. According to the stories, Huh was born in Ayodhya, India. Her father, the king of Ayodhya, sent her on a ship to Korea after receiving orders from the god who appeared in his dream. Many of Koreans claim to be her descendants. After almost 2,000 years, the mayors of Ayodhya in India and Kim-Hae City in Korea signed a sister-city bond based on this legend.

The Satavanas were pushing the Sakas from the south and the Kushans from the north. Kushans spread from the Kabul Valley and were invading towards east. They were Zoroastrians who reached their peak under King Kanishka at around 127 CE. Kushans controlled the Silk Route, and now Kanishka also had control over the marine trade of India. His empire had diplomatic relationships with Romans, Sassanid Persia, and Han China [55]. He extended his kingdom up to Mathura in the east and Oxus in the west. The weakened Sakas (Western Satraps) became his vassal. After the Chinese general Pan-cha'o captured Pamir region, Kanishka's eastern frontier was threatened. As a solution, he sent an ambassador to the Chinese empire with a proposal of marrying one of the Chinese princesses.

Angered by the bold request, Pan-cha'o insulted and returned the ambassador. To avenge the insult, Kanishka attacked the Chinese but lost and had to pay annual tributes to the Chinese empire. Kanishka attacked again after Pan-cha'o's death. This time, he himself joined the camp with a much larger force. He was finally victorious and took control over the Pamir region. No more did he need to pay tribute to Chinese empire.

In India, Kanishka became a Buddhist, and Buddhism flourished during his reign. His character had a lot of parallel with Ashoka the Great. The Buddhist texts portray him as stupid and violent, doing evil deeds before his conversion to Buddhism [55]. After conversion, he became kind and gentle. He held the fourth Buddhist council in Kashmir [24]. There was a Brahmin named Matrceta who got converted to Buddhism after his debate with Arya Deva, a pupil of Nagasen. King Kanishka wanted to meet the famed sage Matrceta, but the latter could not visit him due to his old age. Instead, Matrceta wrote a letter to the king. He apologized for not being able to visit him. He advised the king about the dangers of the youths in his kingdom and asked him to make wise policies to protect them. He also requested the king to be kind towards animals and give up hunting. He wanted the king to be gentle like the moon instead of being fierce like the sun.

Kanishka was the first king to introduce Mahayana Buddhism to China. Lokaksema, a Kushans monk, translated the Buddhist texts into Chinese for the first time. The craze for translating Sanskrit Buddhist texts into Chinese led to the invention of printing in China [31]. Buddhist architecture flourished under Kanishka, as is evident from the discovery of Kanishka Stupa in Peshawar. The architecture had Greek influence, probably left over by Indo-Greek king Milinda. The Gandhara School of Art developed during this time. Kanishka built numerous large statues of Buddha and himself. One life-size statue of the great king has been found from Mathura while another statue was recovered from Kausambi. Both statues were headless. Interestingly, only the head was cut while the rest of the statue remained intact. Some say that it was made that way because Kanishka was a selfless warrior. The truth, however, is that the statues were vandalized, and this happened much before the Islamic invasions. According to a Bengali legend, it was the followers of a Deccan king killed by Kanishka who ruined the statues after their failed attempt to assasinate him.

The Kushans Empire started to decline with the invasion of Indo-Sassanids around the mid of third century. Indo-Sassanids were also Zoroastrians. Under the influence of their high-priest Kartir, they persecuted the non-Zoroastrians including Hindus, Buddhists, Christians, and Jews. It was probably the earliest event of state-sanctioned persecution in the name of religion in this part of the world. They would never be able to penetrate deep into Indian territories. By fourth century, a new power was rising in India to fill the void and confusion left over by the Maurya Empire. The uncertain times were to fade away, and another golden era was about to take shape.

5.9   Blood Silver

Trading through the sea was much cheaper than via land. India, owing to its long coastline, had a big advantage. Sea trading was not new to India. The first invaders who landed in India 60,000 years ago had already mastered the art of sailing. It is believed that the word *navigator* had its origin in the Sanskrit word *navgatih*, having the same meaning. The brave sailors from Sind inspired the character of Sinbad, the sailor of *Arabian Nights* fame. The people of ISVC traded with the Mesopotamians via sea route. The dockyard in Lothal, Gujarat, is one of the oldest in the world. Gujarat has been manufacturing boats for thousands of years. There were two types of boats. The smaller ones were made of single log meant for coastal route. The larger ones, which could be up to 75 tons, were for long-distance travel. Some of those ships had the capacity to hold up to 700 passengers. Indians traded spices, jewels, textiles, ivory, and animals including peacocks, elephants, and rhinoceros with Egyptian Jews, Greeks, Romans, and Southeast Asians [24]. According to Pliny, Roman writer of first century, Indians took away 50 million sesterces (Roman currency) every year from Rome [56]. The trade was so one sided that Rome once banned Indian traders. Lots of Roman coins have been unearthed from India. The trading with Romans was strong enough for the Romans to have built the Temple of Augustus in the Kerala coast. The huge inflow of money made the merchants prosperous. As per Maddison's calculations (based on scant data), India had the highest GDP in the world from first century up to tenth century [57].

Because of the active trading routes, many people sailed to India to escape execution. It is thought that the last pharaoh of Ancient Egypt, Cleopatra, planned to escape to India with her family when Octavian attacked them in 30 BCE. Unfortunately, she could never make it. However, many Jews and Christians did make it to India to take refuge. Among the ten lost tribes of Israel, one is believed by many to have arrived in India. People who claim to have descended from these original ancestors call themselves Bene Israel, and they live mainly in Mumbai. In 70 AD, after the Romans destroyed the Second Temple, the Jews revolted. To curb the revolt Romans persecuted the Jews, and many of them escaped to India. The Jews landed in Kerala, and the Indian kings gave them shelter [58].

According to the Indian Christian tradition, Christianity arrived in India when Saint Thomas landed in Kerala. We hear different myths about the great saint from songs and stories passed verbally down the generations. There are various legends about the man and his miracles. Saint Thomas is supposed to have arrived at Kerala in 52 CE along with many sailors, all of whom became his followers. The sailors were sick after a long and difficult journey. A local Jew took the Christian sailors to the rich Hindu Nair family for shelter. Their family physician cured them. Pleased by the hospitality of the Nairs, Saint Thomas gave them four silver coins. The coins were given to Saint Thomas by his guru, who was crucified and later resurrected. The coins were stained with the blood of Jesus Christ himself. Being a gift from the saint, the Nair family decided to keep it and not use it [59]. These silver coins were called *rakta velli*, or blood silver. Saint Thomas had since then built seven churches and performed many miracles in India. He became famous and converted many locals to Christianity before being martyred at the hand of neighbouring king. Most of the early converts were probably Jews and Brahmins. Centuries later, Saint Thomas is said to have become a Hindu deity worshiped as Thondachan, the grand ancestor. Thondachan is worshiped as a form of Shiva who is blind and deaf. It is an example of how Indians assimilated other cultures.

With time, the coins became legend, and the legend became a curse. In 16th century, the Portuguese landed in India. They were surprised to see Christians already present in this land. But these Christians did not follow their customs, and the Portuguese tried to Latinize them by force. When they heard about the legend of the coins smeared with the blood of Jesus, they wanted it for themselves. They tried to hunt it down, killing many Indians in the process. The Nair family managed to escape the persecution, and the coins survived the test of time. It is said that the Nair family still secretly protects the coins.

Age of Empires (300 to 1200 CE)

From here [Mathura, Uttar Pradesh] to south, all is
Madhyadesa [Middle Kingdom/Central India]. Its people
are rich. The inhabitants of Madhyadesa dress and eat
like people in China.

—Faxian

6.1 New Beginnings

India survived the various phases of invasion. Foreign powers gained ground in India and tried to rule her. India did not resist the storm. She allowed it to wither and then slowly absorbed it. The two regions in India where the foreign powers had least influence were the south and the northeast. In the south, a new dynasty came to power, displacing the early dynasties of the southern big trio: Cholas, Pandyas, and Cheras. This new dynasty was called Kalabhras, and they were Buddhist. Kalabhras rose after a revolt against the special favors given to the Brahmins. In central India, the Nagas (devoted to the serpent god) were gaining ground while farther up in Assam, we find the record of their first historical ruler: the Varman Dynasty. The ancient Lacchavi clan also became quite influential and was now ruling Nepal. As the foreign powers were weakening, a new empire was ready to take on the world, continuing the journey of the survivors.

The reign of Gupta Empire would come to be known as the golden era of India. Many believe that it was the only golden era India ever had, but I beg to differ. There could be at least five golden eras: first during the time of ISVC, second during the Renaissance up to Ashoka's reign, third during Gupta Empire, fourth under the Cholas, and the fifth during Akbar's time. The Rashtrakuta and Vijayanagara Empires were equally powerful. Though the Gupta Empire was not as huge as the empire of Ashoka, it was big enough to unite most of India. More importantly, it was more stable and probably more prosperous. The Gupta kings had not forgotten the Mayurians. *Mudrarakshasa*, the story of Chanakya and Chandragupta, was written during the Gupta rule. The Gupta kings even wrote their own inscriptions like Ashoka, and many were right beside the Ashokan inscriptions. The old Mauryan inscriptions were not destroyed. They acted as an inspiration because the motto of the Gupta Empire was similar to that of the Maurya Empire.

Shadow of doubt looms over the origin of one of the greatest empire India has ever seen. Many authors believe that the Guptas were originally from Bengal [60]. The surname Gupta is mostly associated with low-caste Vaishas. Vaishas were agriculturists, cattle raisers, and traders. It could well be that the Guptas were low-caste rulers, which was not something new in Indian history [61]. Buddhist Maurya Empire followed the Sudra Nanda Dynasty, and then the Vaisha Gupta Empire followed the foreign dynasties. To some Brahmins, these were the signs of Kali Yug. Quite contrary to what the Brahmins were portraying, India was regenerating herself in literature, science, arts, and astronomy.

Hinduism was evolving once more to accommodate the changes of time. The ritualistic Vedic religion metamorphosed to philosophic Upanishads, and now it was time for devotion. Devotion had a mass appeal, and the new philosophy, promoted by the Puranas, helped revive Hinduism in India. The Gupta Empire thus marked the revival of Hinduism, but at the same time, other religions like Buddhism and Jainism also flourished. Secularism has always been the strength of great rulers of India. Many Hindu gods found their way into Buddhist and Jain texts. Buddhism was so dominant at that time in India that even the Hindus had to accommodate Buddha in their own religion. Buddha was given the status of the ninth incarnation of Vishnu in Agni Purana. According to it, Buddha created a non-Vedic path purposefully to divert the mighty Asuras from the Vedic ways, so that they are taken to hell and Devas can regain power. Foreign rulers like Milinda and Kanishka came to rule India but later became influenced by Buddhism. It shows the strong presence of Buddhism in India. These stories of Puranas were probably reflecting those sentiments. However, most Hindu texts were silent about Buddhism, reflecting the tensions between the two groups. This peculiar behavior of accommodating even without accepting is very typical of India.

It is through the Buddhist texts, rather than Puranas, that we come to know about the beginnings of Gupta

Empire. I Tsing, a Chinese monk who visited India in 672 CE, wrote about Sri Gupta building a temple for Chinese pilgrims around mid of third century. The temple was 40 *yojanas* (1 *yogana* is 1 to 3 mi as calculated by different authors) east of Nalanda University. That would place it between Murshidabad and Malda (36). The early Gupta ruler belonged to Bengal. Sri Gupta was the first known ruler of the Gupta Dynasty. His son Ghatotkacha succeeded him. Both of them were probably feudatories to the Kushans. However, the first real founder of the imperial Gupta Empire was Chandra Gupta I, son of Ghatotkacha who reigned from 315 CE to 335 CE [62]. It is easy to confuse Chandra Gupta I with Chandragupta Maurya who lived 600 years before the Guptas. Chandragupta Maurya founded the Mauryan Dynasty and threw out the Greeks while Chandra Gupta I officially founded the Gupta Dynasty, which would grow to throw out the Kushans and other foreign rulers. Both these dynasties united major part of India under one rule. Chandra Gupta I was known as *Maharajadhiraja*, or the king of kings. He married the daughter of the leader of famous Lacchavi clan, a marriage alliance that made him more powerful [62]. There were many gold coins issued by him showing him with his wife, Kumara Devi. From the distribution of the coins, we can guess that his rule was restricted to the Ganges region. It would be his son, Samudra Gupta the Great, who would go on to unite most of India once again.

6.2 Conquests of the Great

Two rock inscriptions side by side, separated by over 500 years, mark the reign of two of India's greatest emperors. One promoted peace and harmony while the other glorified war. In one, there was the message of the grandson of Chandragupta. On the other, the message was from the son of Chandra Gupta I. The former used peace to conquer while the latter required conquering for peace. Ashoka's father, Bindusara, was against Ashoka as his successor. After Bindusara's death, there was a four-year war of succession in which Ashoka overpowered all his brothers and took the throne. Samudra Gupta, however, was his father's favorite. His father declared him as the successor, even though there were others older than him. After Chandra Gupta I's death, the angry brothers went on a war of succession. Samudra Gupta managed to return victorious, going on to becoming the ruler of rulers.

Samudra was a title taken by him after his conquests that extended his empire from one sea (samudra in Hindi means sea) to the other [62]. We come to know about his conquests from the Allahabad Inscriptions [63]. His war campaign started in central India with the conquering of the neighboring kingdoms of Achyuta, Nagasena, and the Kota Dynasty in and around Uttar Pradesh. After consolidating his kingdom, he went south. He marched into Madhya Pradesh, Vindhyans, and the Deccan. Samudra Gupta went farther south through the east coast into Godavari, Vizagapatam up to Kusthala of Tamil Naidu [64]. He probably conquered the lands of the west coast while returning. In many of the kingdoms he conquered, he reinstated the kings after the latter accepted to be his vassal (Figure 6).

With the south in Samudra Gaupta's domain, he was ready to take on the more powerful foes of the north. The violent and bloody war of extermination started with the defeat of Rudrasena I Vakataka of Vindhyans. Samudra

Gupta conquered Uttar Pradesh, Bihar, Assam, Himachal, Garwal, Kumayun, Nepal, Rajasthan, Haryana, Punjab, and Sind. He overthrew the Kushans and the Sakas of western India. These kings were too powerful to be shown mercy, so he destroyed them instead. Samudra Gupta knew best that the policy of kindness that he showed to the southern kingdoms would not work in the north. After all his conquests, he celebrated his victory with *Asvamedha* ritual [64]. In such a ritual, a horse was freed and was followed by the king and his army. All the land over which the horse passed came under the king's rule, if unchallenged. It was a kind of horse sacrifice, which meant that the king of kings, having conquered earth, has now conquered the heaven [62]. Samudra Gupta was a brave man who led from the front in all the battles. Interestingly, a man like him was also a poet who liked to play the veena. The bloody wars that united India led to a regime of peace, harmony, and prosperity.

Unlike the Mayurians, the Gupta Empire was highly decentralized with the king at the top of the hierarchy. This resulted in a stable and a highly efficient government. The capital of Gupta Empire was still Pataliputra (modern Patna), which, for over 600 years, had been the powerhouse of India. The entire territory was divided into provinces, each province with its own local leader. Agriculture was very important part of the economy; however, industry and trading also flourished. Art and science thrived during the Gupta Empire. Mathematics and astronomy reached its zenith. Hindu and Buddhist temples built during this period showed advanced form of architectural skills. Many important literatures were also written during this era. Samudra Gupta's son Chandra Gupta II maintained the peak of Gupta Empire, something that Ashoka's successors could not manage to do.

6.3 The Glory

Chandra Gupta II ruled from 380 CE to 415 CE. There is an interesting story about how Chandra Gupta II came to throne as written in Vishakadatta's *Natya-darpana*. Ramagupta took over the throne after his father Samudra Gupta's demise. It is evident from coins of that era that this part of the story might actually be true. The new king forcefully married the fiancée of Chandra Gupta II named Dhruvswamini. He then attacked the Sakas of western India but was defeated. The Saka king Rudrasimha III wanted Dhruvswamini in exchange of peace. The weak king agreed, much to the dislike of Chandra Gupta II. A furious Chandra decided to put his life at risk and save Dhruvswamini. He went to meet Rudrasimha, disguised as the queen, and killed him. After the assassination, the Saka kingdom of Gujarat fell apart and was taken over by the Gupta Empire. Chandra Gupta II came back and killed his coward brother. He married his love Dhruvswamini and became the much-deserved king. The marriage between Chandra Gupta II and Dhruvaswamini was indeed real as is apparent from some of the inscriptions. Marrying a widow wasn't considered a sin at that time. Dhruvaswamini bore him Prince Kumara Gupta I. Chandra Gupta II also married a Naga princess named Kuberanaga. It was a marriage for political alliance. Kuberanaga bore him a daughter named Prabhavati Gupta. Prabhavati was married to Rudrasena II of Vakataka Dynasty. It strengthened the latter's alliance with the Gupta Empire. According to the writings of poet Kalidasa, Chandra Gupta II conquered twenty-one kingdoms including Persians, Huns, Kambojas, Himachal, and Kashmir.

Chandra Gupta II, also known as Vikramaditya, had number of able ministers, many of whom are mentioned in his inscriptions. The king is said to have nine gems in his court, the famous being poet Kalidasa. *Abhijñānaśākuntalam*, the most popular Sanskrit play written by Kalidasa, is a love story of Shakuntala and King Dushyanta. Also in his court was Amara Sinha, a Sanskrit grammarian and poet, who was possibly a Buddhist. *Amarakosha*, a book on Sanskrit grammar, is his only book that survived. Chandra Gupta II built plenty of architectural marvels, like the Udayagiri caves of MP. Metallurgy reached its peak as is evident from the iron pillar made by him as a symbol of victory against Vahilakas. This piece of iron has not rusted or decomposed even after 1,600 years. It even survived a direct hit by Nadir Shah's artillery in eighteenth century. Quite ironically, the iron pillar now stands inside the complex of Qutub Minar, erected as a sign of victory of foreign invaders against Indian kings.

The Chinese Buddhist pilgrims started visiting India during Chandra Gupta II's reign. One of the first to visit India was Faxian, and his writing gives us a picture of India under the Guptas. According to Faxian, the Buddhism that was known in China was an impure version. He wanted to know the true Buddhism that had its origin in a faraway country called India. In his quest to understand true Buddhism and get a copy of the original texts, he, along with four other scholars, began the long and arduous journey towards the holy land of India. Faxian was already 60 years old when he began the 14-year-long journey that started in the year 399 [65].

Shan Shan, a country in China, was the first place where he met the followers of Hinayana Buddhism. This was the older version of Buddhism and probably spread very early to this region. Then he went through the Tartar countries into Karashahr, also known as Yanqi (from Agni, or fire). This is an ancient Buddhist city on the famous Silk Route where people followed Hinayana Buddhism. According to Faxian, people there dressed like the Chinese but studied Indian books and spoke Indian languages. It is interesting to know that Indian culture had spread so far away from its roots. In Kothan, they found tens of thousands of Buddhist monks who followed the Mahayana form of Buddhism. From there, they went to Kashgar, the land of Hinayana Buddhist monks who owned sacred relics like Buddha's spittoon and tooth. From Kashgar, after climbing the snowy peaks of the Himalayas, they reached Darel. Then they reached Udyana where they found the first people who spoke the language of central India, or the Middle Kingdom. The next stop was Takshashila and Peshawar where the Kushan king Kanishka built a mighty statue of Buddha that was over 120 meters high. This entire region was filled with the legends of Buddha. After the tedious journey all but two of Faxian's companions went back to China. One of the two companions who stayed back died of cold on their way to Afghanistan through the snowy peaks. Finally, after crossing the Indus River, Faxian and his only companion reached to the Middle Kingdom of India [65].

According to the writings of Faxian, the Middle Kingdom, or the kingdom under Chandra Gupta II, was rich and prosperous. Crime was rare, and the punishments were mild. There was no need of capital punishment, and the taxes were very low. The only worries for travellers were the wild elephants and lions. The cities were well connected through properly maintained roads that had places of shelter. Rooms with beds, mattresses, foods, and clothes were provided for the travellers. Brahminism was the dominant religion in this region. The charity houses maintained by Hindus gave shelter to people of all religion and castes (except the Chandalas or outcastes). The maximum number of days a traveller was allowed to stay in one place was limited. Faxian was impressed by the public medical facilities in Pataliputra (modern Patna). He wrote: "All the poor and destitute in the country . . . and all who are diseased, go to these houses, and are provided with every kind of help, and doctors examine their disease. They get the food and medicine which their cases require, and are made to feel at ease; and when they are better, they go away of themselves." [31]

Magadha had the largest cities and towns. People here were very rich and donated a lot in charity. There was free hospitals set up in the city for all. Faxian also mentions a festival where a heavily decorated five-storeyed four-wheel car was dragged through the road. It was a Hindu festival, but Buddhists were also invited. What Faxian saw was probably a Rath Yatra. The rath (chariot) carried big idol of god Jagganath. It was a big and popular festival. Huge crowds gathered to see it. There were occasions when people were crushed under the wheels of the gigantic chariot. The English word *juggernaut* (from Jagganath) originated from this festival. Faxian's only companion found central India so mesmerizing that he stayed back to seek salvation. All that Faxian had learned he wanted to take back to China and give his people the true knowledge of Buddhism. Hence, he continued his journey through Nalanda, Bodh Gaya, and Tamralipi. He gained more knowledge, copied many Buddhist texts, and drew pictures. From the port of Tamralipi, he sailed to Sinhala, from there to Java, and finally back to China after some dangerous adventures through the sea.

6.4   A Beautiful Mind

Symbols and astronomy were an important part of Vedic culture, meant mostly to please the gods. Astronomy was dependent on mathematics. Trading that flourished in India from ancient times made it necessary to develop easy calculating methods. This triggered the growth of mathematics and astronomy in India. The ISVC, as early as 3000 BCE, had east–west alignment of streets. The mysterious ring stone discovered from ISVC was probably used to track the path of sunlight through the year. Knowledge of basic geometry is evident from the systematic aspect ratios of the buildings of ISVC. More complex geometries are seen during Vedic era. Shulbasutras of 600–1000 BC dictated the methods of making fire altars having complex geometric shapes. Boudhayana's Shulbasutras also mention about the concept of Pythagoras theorem. It states that "the diagonal of a rectangle produces itself both areas [i.e. the square of the diagonal is same as the area] produced separately by its two sides." He calculated the square root of two to decimal places [67]. The first evidence of zero (though debatable) is often attributed to Pingalacharya's Chandasastra written around 200 BCE. Pingala also wrote about binary numerical system and Fibonacci numbers (*Matrameru*) [68]. Indians might not be the only ones to realize the concept of zero. The Babylonians have been using it since third century BCE, and even Mayans discovered it independently. But it was the Indians who used it extensively as a number and popularized it around the modern world. Unlike any other ancient civilization, Indians were unique in using large numbers like 10^{55} used in *Ramayana*. It was possible only because of the invention of decimal system.

Around 476 CE, towards the dying phases of Gupta Empire, a mathematician named Aryabhata was born. He grew up to become one of the most brilliant mathematicians of all times. Unfortunately, even our own scientists have misspelled his name as Aryabhatta while naming our satellites [66]. He was the head of Nalanda University, an ancient center for higher learning located near Patna. The entire complex of Nalanda was made of brick and had libraries, classrooms, and hostels. Students from all around the world, including Persia, China, Greece, and Tibet, came here to study before it was burnt down.

Aryabhata took Indian mathematics and astronomy to the next level. We come to know about him from his book *Aryabhata*. He knew that the earth is a sphere and not flat. He also declared that the stars do not revolve around the earth; it is the earth that rotates instead. He acknowledged that the moon eclipses the sun, and the great shadow of earth eclipses the moon. His challenge to the geocentric model did not face the resistance that Galileo faced more than 1,000 years later. Aryabhata measured the diameter of earth as 44,860 kilometres, just 12 per cent off from modern measurement. He also gave the approximate value of pi as 3.1416, wrote equations to find the area of triangle and circle, gave tables for sines, and solved linear equations like ax-by=c [67]. It was Aryabhata who showed that zero was not just a numeral but also an important concept and a symbol [69]. With all those contributions, he is rightly attributed as the father of Indian mathematics.

Varahamihira was another famous Indian mathematician/astronomer who was born during the Gupta Era. He lived in Ujjain from 505 CE to 587 CE. His work tells us about the lost Indian texts on mathematics/astronomy before the time of Aryabhata. Varahamihira's texts also mention about the Greek and Roman works. It is an evidence of cultural and scientific interaction between the two great civilizations. Varahamihira wrote, "The Greeks, though foreign, must be honored since they have shown tremendous interest in our science [Mlecchas hi Yavanas tesu samyak shastram kdamsthitam/ rsivat te'pi pujyante kim punar daivavid dvijah]" (Brihat-Samhita 2.15).

While Indian mathematics was rising, the Gupta Empire was declining. Chandra Gupta II was succeeded by his son Kumara Gupta I on the year 415. His vast empire was threatened by the growing power of Pusyamitra of central India and the invasions of White Huns from the west. Kumara Gupta I managed to keep both of them at bay. His victory over the troublemakers was celebrated by performing *Asvamedha (horse sacrifice)* like many other kings before him. Nalanda University was probably built during his reign. However, towards the end of his rule, the enemies were gaining ground. The task of restoring order was given to his son Skanda Gupta. Skanda Gupta took the throne in the year 455 and fought many fiery battles to re-establish the authority of Gupta Empire. By the time he avenged his enemies, his father was dead. He narrated the tales of his victory to his mother, whose 'eyes welled with tears of happiness' [62].

Skanda Gupta was the last of the great Gupta kings. He died in 467 CE, and the throne was passed on to his half-brother Puru Gupta. Puru Gupta was too old when he took the throne and was soon replaced by his son. There were many Gupta rulers who came to power after Puru Gupta, but the empire was shrinking. It was being slowly pushed towards the eastern fringes of India. The Huns (Hephthalites or White Huns) finally broke through the Indian defense after centuries of struggle. The solid resistance of India and China to the Huns made them invade Europe and had devastating effect on Rome [24]. The king of Huns, Tomarana, won the battle of Eran in 510 CE. Bhanu Gupta (the military lieutenant of Narasimha Gupta) and his feudatory Goparaja lost the battle, and along with it the control of Malwa. Tomarana's son Mihirakula further expanded his kingdom, restricting the Guptas just to Bengal. It was the White Huns who destroyed the Takshashila University almost a century after Nalanda University started. The Huns were gradually assimilated into the Indian caste system as Kshatriyas (warriors). Many Rajputs clans trace their origin to the White Huns, Sakas, and Kushans.

Along with arts and science that flourished during the Gupta era, there was considerable change in the religious philosophies. Buddhism started its gradual decline towards the end of Gupta rule. A new cult of Tantric Buddhism evolved from the dying Mahayana Buddhism. Hinduism itself was changing as various heterodox creeds like Saivism, Vaishnavism, Shakti Cult, along with the Brahminical Hinduism were integrated into one. Christians in the West were bringing in a new concept of Trinity: Father, Son, and Holy Spirit. Like them, Hinduism independently evolved its own concept of Trinity: Brahma, the creator of Maya; Vishnu, the sustainer of Maya, and Maheshwar/ Shiva, the destroyer of Maya. The concept of Trinity was a move towards monotheism by uniting all the different polytheist gods under the umbrella of three main Gods. Then the three were united under one supreme spirit: the Brahmana. While worldwide other monotheist religions were eliminating mother goddess, in Hinduism the old fertility goddess had found a new home. Gaja-Lakshmi was written in Puranas as the wife of Vishnu, Saraswati of Brahma, and Shakti of Shiva. Ganesh and Kartik, a popular Kushan god of war, became the son of Shiva and Shakti [70]. The Vedic yagna lost its popularity while the sacrifices survived in patches as part of the idol worship. Gods were no longer just a property of the Brahmins. The door to salvation was opened to common man.

6.5 The Poet King

If not for the unfortunate turn of events he would have become a poet and a dramatist. Fate, however, had something else planned for him. Harsha, the son of the king of Thaneshwar, grew up in a happy family along with his elder brother Rajya Vardhana and their much-loved younger sister named Rajyasri. Rajyasri was married to Grahavarmana, the king of Kanauj. Harsha was on a hunting trip when he had a nightmare. In his dream, a lioness jumped into the forest fire after seeing her partner engulfed by it, leaving behind her cubs. It was a bad omen. Few days later, he received the news of his father's severe illness. Harsha's mother, unable to bear the pain of her husband, performed *sati* (self-immolation) after donating all her wealth [71]. This was first textual evidence of *sati* in India. The king soon followed her. It is mentioned that the dead king was cremated on the banks of River Saraswati. Was the lost river still alive?

Sati originally meant *wife* just like *pati* meant *husband*. *Sati* finds no mention in ancient Indian texts. Brahmins later tried to manipulate and misinterpret old texts to justify *sati*. Even Manu Smriti, while describing the duties of a widow, does not mention of self-immolation. Rig Veda (10.18) asks young widows to resume normal life instead of grieving over dead husband. The self-immolation was not part of original Vedic custom and was probably introduced by the Saka clans. Traditionally, the Sakas buried alive the wives of the dead king along with the royal servants so that they could serve him even after his death. After the Sakas came to India, they started cremating the dead, inspired by the Indian ritual. The wives of the dead king jumped into the fire to be with the king in his afterlife. *Sati* was limited only to some warrior families, and the wife performed it out of her own choice. Some of the Rajput clans who had originated from the Sakas practiced a custom called Jauhar. Interestingly, *Saka* is another name of Jauhar. It was an honorable self-immolation of women when their husband had died in a war and the city was under siege. It was suicide to protect one's honor that was at a risk of being violated by the victorious enemies. Later, with frequent invasions of the Turks from the west, *jauhar* and *sati* became more common. It was a custom that has been promoted by the Brahmins for their own benefit. Interestingly, *Padma Purana* banned Brahmin women from performing *sati*.

On hearing the news of his father's demise, Rajya Vardhana had to abandon his fight with the White Huns and rush to the capital. He was crowned as the new king of Thaneshwar. Post-Gupta era, North India got divided into many small kingdoms, each wanting to grow beyond its borders. Devagupta, the king of Malwa, invaded Kanauj, killed Grahavarmana, and took Rajyasri as prisoner. The fate of their sister angered the two brothers. Rajya Vardhana, now the king of Thaneshwar, attacked Devagupta. Harsha was eager to join his brother, but Rajya told him to stay back and protect the capital. Rajya did not want to give too much importance to a weak king like Devagupta; he was more than enough to handle it. Rajya was right, and he won the battle against Devagupta easily. However, his luck ran out as he unexpectedly met the more powerful and shrewd king of Bengal on his way back [72].

According to Harsha's biography written by Bana, Shashank, the king of Gaur (Bengal), treacherously murdered Rajya Vardhana while pretending to be his ally. There is no historical evidence of the treachery. Shashank was a chieftain of the weakened Gupta Kings of Bengal. He defeated the Guptas and made his own kingdom, with its capital at Gaur. He was a powerful king and is often credited for creating the first separate political identity of Bengal. It is possible that he started the Bengali calendar as it began during his reign. His empire covered the entire Bengal, Bihar, and went up to Bhubaneswar [73]. Shashank was probably on a raid with his army when they stumbled upon Rajya Vardhana. Alternatively, it could be possible that Shashank allied with Devagupta against the Vardhanas. It would not be a surprise as they both faced threats from the growing power of Vardhana Dynasty. Rajya Vardhana died in the battle against Shashank.

Harsha Vardhana had no choice but to accept the crown. It came at the cost of the life of his mother, father, brother-in-law, and his own brother while his sister was rotting in the prison of Shashank. Harsha vowed revenge against all his enemies. The neighboring kings were warned to either become his vassal or get ready for annexation.

It was Shashank's head, however, that he wanted badly. Harsha allied with King Bhaskara Varman of Assam and marched against Shashank. A messenger informed Harsha that his sister has managed to escape from the clutches of Shashank and ran away into the forest of Vindhyan. Harsha ordered his army to march against Shashank while he went into the forest in search of his sister. In the forest, Harsha met a Buddhist monk who took him to Rajyasri. After Rajyasri managed to run away into the forest, she wanted to commit suicide. It was this monk who had saved her. She then decided to become his disciple. The monk also influenced Harsha to become a Buddhist. Harsha managed to get his sister, only remaining family, back. However, he was not able to defeat Shashank.

It is evident from the inscriptions and coins that Harsha was the most powerful emperor in North India. Shashank kept troubling him throughout his life. It was only after Shashank's natural death that Harsha managed to conquer Bengal. At his peak, Harsha's empire extended from Punjab and Gujarat to Bengal and Orissa, including the entire Indo-Gangetic plain north of the Narmada River (figure 7). Even though he was a king, he continued his passion of writing plays and poems. The famous ones written by the king are *Nagananda*, *Ratnavali*, and *Priyadarsika*. *Nagananda* was the most acclaimed of the three. It is a story of the sacrifice of Jimutavahana to save the Nagas (serpents). The story is a unique collaboration of Hindu and Buddhist faith. India had many kings greater than Harsha, and India also had many scholars better than Harsha. But Harsha's talent of using both the sword and the pen with equal grace made his greatness inimitable.

6.6   The Chinese Traveler

Much of what we know about India during the time of Harsha Vardhana is from the works of the most famous Chinese traveller to India, Xuanzang. Like Faxian, his main motto to come to India was to collect and record the original Buddhist works. Unlike Faxian, he was just 26 years old when he started his journey to India in the year 627. At that time, the Eastern Turks were fighting with the Tang Dynasty of China; and thus, foreign travel was banned in China. Xuanzang, desperate to come to India, managed to slip out of China illegally [65]. It was the same year when Prophet Mohammad was fighting the Battle of the Trench in Medina against the Jews and Arabs. It marked the beginning of the rise of Islam that would add a new twist to the twisted history of the world.

Xuanzang's travel was long and dangerous. He survived robbers, was lost in a desert without water for five days, and twelve of his companions died while crossing the snowy Hindu Kush. He met the Great Khan of Western Turk Dynasty (Turko-Mogul) in Uzbekistan, who shared good relationship with the Tang Dynasty. He went farther south into Samarkand, which was controlled by the Persians who were fighting against the Western Turks [74]. Xuanzang found many abandoned Buddhist temples there, probably built by the Kushans. In Afghanistan, he found plenty of Buddhist sites and relics. He met the first Hindus and Jains in Gandhara; however, it was not part of India anymore. India physically started in Laghman, at the easternmost corner of Afghanistan. The Buddhist and Hindu influence that Faxian saw while traveling to India had now been replaced by Turko-Mughal and Persian cultures.

India itself had also changed. Buddhism, although still active, was on the decline. The population of Udayana (Swat Valley), a once Buddhist-dominated land, had declined dramatically. Xuanzang had been looted by a band of fifty robbers in Faxian's 'safe India'. While traveling farther east from Ayodhya on the Ganges River, he and his companions were captured by river pirates. They wanted to sacrifice Xuanzang to Goddess Durga. The pirates were about to kill him when a massive storm engulfed them. Fearing that it was because of Xuanzang's spiritual powers, they ran away [74]. The increase in robbers and pirates depict the decline in the economic condition of Indians. Though there were still many rich people, the inequality had started to increase.

After visiting many important Buddhist sites, Xuanzang arrived at Magadha. The capital of the once-great city of Mayurians now lay in ruins. Magadha was still home to many great Mahayana monks. Both Buddhists and Brahmins taught at the Nalanda University. The teachings of Brahmin teachers were different from the Buddhist teachers. Buddhists themselves had eighteen different schools. The monks of different schools wore their robes in different styles. The students were taught meticulously with activities to make learning easier. Xuanzang learned a lot in Nalanda and considered it as the best university in the world. The money for maintenance of the university came from the taxes collected from people while the villagers provided food and milk. In the curriculum, the children were taught 'twelve chapters' till they were 7 years old. Then they were taught the 'five sciences'. The chief monk of the university admitted Xuanzang as his disciple. Xuanzang probably met Brahmagupta, the great Indian mathematician and astronomer, in Nalanda.

Brahmagupta was the first person to give the rules to compute zero. He made many discoveries in algebra and geometry. Aryabhata's round-earth model was still not widely accepted. Brahmagupta had to challenge the theory of flat earth again and proclaim that the earth was a sphere. People opposed by explaining that all objects would fall down if it were a sphere. Brahmagupta argued that all objects were indeed falling but towards the earth itself. The nature of earth is to attract objects towards it just like nature of water was to flow down. For the first time ever, we hear the concept of gravity long before the enlightening apple fell on Newton's head. But Brahmagupta was not as fearless as Aryabhata in challenging the orthodox system. Al-Beruni (tenth century Islamic scholar), while considering Brahmagupta as the best mathematician of his time, criticized him for favouring the religious orthodoxy by opposing Aryabhatta: "Why do you, after having spoken such [harsh] words [against Aryabhata and his followers], then begin to calculate the diameter of the moon in order to explain the eclipsing of the sun, and the diameter of the shadow of the earth in order to explain its eclipsing the moon? Why do you compute both eclipse in agreement with the theory of those heretics, and not according to the views of those with whom you think it is proper to agree?" [31]

Xuanzang also noticed the caste system, and he mentioned four divisions. The caste system he described was more rigid than the one described by Megasthenes. Intercaste marriage was not allowed, and women could marry only once. He considered the Indians as hasty, having irresolute temperament, but were of pure moral principles. The moral principles came from the fear of bad karma that could affect them in their next lives. If one committed a crime, the highest order of punishment was to be made an outcaste, i.e., thrown out of the community into the wild. The rituals for the performance of last rites also varied from place to place. Three of the most common ones were cremation, water burial where the corpse was floated into a stream, and cast away of the body in wilderness to be eaten by animals.

Xuanzang made friendship with Harsha, the king who had built numerous Buddhist stupas. When he visited Harsha, the king was holding a grand competition where scholars from various Buddhist schools came and debated their philosophies. Xuanzang won the competition and impressed the king. He helped Harsha establish diplomatic relations with China. Harsha sent missions to China, and in return, the Chinese emperor Tai Tsung of Tang Dynasty sent his own embassy to Harsha. From Harsha's kingdom, Xuanzang traveled to the kingdom of Pallava Dynasty in the south. Buddhism had strong presence there. He returned to China from the land route after crossing Hindu Kush with over 650 sanskrit texts, seven statues of the Buddha, and more than a hundred *sarira* relics.

Buddhism strengthened the ties between China and India. The Chinese emperor later sent another mission to Harsha, but Harsha was no more. A king from North Bihar named Arjuna opposed the mission. He captured the Chinese embassy. The leader of the embassy managed to escape and took refuge in Tibet, which was ruled by the son-in-law of Chinese emperor. The Tibetan king took revenge by attacking Arjuna and capturing him [75]. Like Ashoka, Harsha's last days were quite unfortunate. In 630 CE, he lost the battle against Chalukya king Pulakesi II, ending his dream of conquering the Deccan. He did add Bengal to his territory but only after Shashank died a natural death.

His vow of revenge against Shashank remained unfulfilled. In 647 CE, after Harsha died, his wife was imprisoned and both his sons killed by his own chief. North India again got divided into small empires.

6.7   The Clash of Civilizations

In 70 BCE the Jews had a religious crisis. Romans captured Palestine and destroyed the second temple. Many of the Jews fled to India, fearing prosecution by the Romans. In the midst of that crisis was born a charismatic faith healer in Nazareth. His name was Jesus Christ. Jesus and his followers revolted against the Roman rule. This resistance made the Romans angry, and they executed Jesus on political charges. Jesus was hailed as the Son of God who died for the sins of the people. Thus was born a new faith: Christianity [76]. The new religion appealed to the people of Rome, especially after the conversion of Roman king Constantine to Christianity in the fourth century. By the year 600, Christianity was a firmly established religion. At the same time, the Arabs became extremely successful in trading. The newfound wealth made them ludicrous. Discontented with his life in Mecca, a young man named Mohammad retreated to a cave in Mount Hira for meditation and reflection [77]. According to Islamic beliefs, it was here, at the age of 40 and in the month of Ramadan, where he received his first revelation from God. These revelations form the verses of the Koran, regarded by Muslims as the 'word of God'. It was the basis on which a new religion was born. To Mohammad *al-Lah* simply meant *the God* and was identical to the god worshiped by Jews and Christians. He did not believe that he was founding a new religion but saw himself bringing the old religion to his people. Islam means surrender, and a Muslim was one who submitted himself entirely to 'the God'. His only demand was that all human beings should behave with one another with justice, equity, and compassion [77].

Muhammad gained few followers early on, along with hostility from some Meccan tribes. To escape persecution, Muhammad sent some of his followers to Abyssinia before he and his remaining followers in Mecca migrated to Medina. This event, the Hijra, marks the beginning of the Islamic calendar, which is also known as the Hijri calendar. In Medina, Muhammad united the conflicting tribes. After eight years of fighting with the Meccan tribes, his followers, who by then had grown to 10,000, conquered Mecca. Before the prophet died in the year 632, he had already united the different tribes of Arab into a single Muslim religious polity.

Muhammad's death brought disagreement within the Muslim community. Yet the Islamic empire continued to expand. Soon Spain, much of Africa, and Central Asia were under Islamic rule. At the same time, the Tang Dynasty of China was creating the largest empire China has ever seen. Fergana and Samarkand became part of Chinese rule for the first time. The Tibetan Empire was also growing strong and posed a big threat to the Chinese. After Muhammad's death, Islam spread to Central Asia, defeating the Persian Sassanid Empire. The Arabs took over Bukhara and Samarkand, posing a direct challenge to the Chinese Empire. The Chinese allied with the Western Turks to resist the Islamic invasion. China also gave asylum to the son of the last Sassanid ruler of Persia. Buddhist Tibetan Empire saw an opportunity and allied with the Islamic

Arabs against the Turks and Tang Dynasty. The former alliance won, and the Chinese had to give away Fergana.

The rapid rise of Islam made the Christians insecure, just like the rising Christianity made the Jews insecure. Jerusalem, the sacred city of Christians, was now under the Islamic rule, and Spain had also been converted. This led to a series of religiously sanctioned military campaigns by the Christians against the Muslims. Fought between 1095 and 1291, the bloody wars are known as the Crusades. The Crusades originally had the goal of recapturing Jerusalem and their Holy Land from Muslim rule. This war, in the name of religion, became so deadly that even in the 21st century, the wounds are yet to heal. India became the collateral damage of this bloody battle. Muhammad bin Qasim, an Umayyad general, led the first Muslim troop to raid India in 710 E. The attack was a retaliation against the Sindhi king Raja Dahir who had helped the Persians. The fleeing Persian generals found shelter in India. There were also reports of loot and capture of an Arab ship carrying gifts from the king of Sri Lanka, by the Indian king. Qasim was sent with a strong army to attack Raja Dahir after failed negotiations. The attack was successful, and Dahir was defeated in the second attempt [78].

Islam survived the Crusades and continued to flourish. The insecurity from the Crusades turned Muslim rulers into further aggression. The success convinced them that they were the men of god. They started to destroy the old pagan faiths that thought otherwise. They raided the Persians, Hindus, and Buddhists living in Central Asia and India. Many Persians and Turks converted to the new faith. Some Persian Zoroastrians managed to escape to India to avoid persecution. Indian kings gave them shelter along the coasts in Gujarat and Mumbai, helping preserve the old religion. These Parsee communities have been, and still are, contributing a lot towards the growth of India. They left a strong influence in the industry sector with the likes of Tata, Godrej, and Wadia.

6.8   Paradise Rises

It was the age of empires. Brutal battles were common in the struggle for power. In such an era, two Indian kings united to push back the mighty Arabs. King Yashovarman created his own empire after defeating the kings of Magadha, Vanga, Thanesar, and Ayodhya and even controlled parts of Punjab and Haryana [79]. At the same time, a king from Kashmir was building upon his desire for a vast empire. King Lalitaditya Muktapida of Karakota Empire began his reign in the beginning of the eighth century [80]. We come to know about him mostly from Kashmiri writer Kalhana's book *Rajataranjini* and from some Arab and Chinese sources. The two ambitious rulers allied together to defeat the Arabs who had earlier invaded Sindh. Not unexpectedly, the alliance broke once the lost Indian territories were reclaimed. Yashovarman wanted to be the senior partner of the alliance much to the dislike of young Lalitaditya. Disagreements led to a battle that was finally won by the king of Kashmir. It was a decisive victory that made Lalitaditya the most powerful king of north India and the most powerful king of Kashmir ever. His glorious journey, however, had just begun. Lalitaditya assassinated the king of Vanga (Bengal) after inviting him to Kashmir. Seeking vengeance, a group of men from Vanga traveled to Kashmir. In a suicidal mission, they attacked Karakota Empire. They murdered a dignitary, pundered the temples in Parihaspur and Malta Keshaw, and set an old temple on fire. By the time the king could react, they escaped with their plunder and loot. Lalitaditya was unharmed, but the group achieved a lot of fame. Kalhana wrote, "Even the creator cannot achieve what the Gaurs [people of Bengal] did on that occasion and to this day the world is filled with the fame of the Gaur heros." [36]

Invasions from the west intensified after the Indians pushed back the Arabs. Lalitaditya took it upon himself to secure the borders. He defeated the dwellers of Upper Oxus (Tokharians) and the powerful Turks and became the last Indian king to control Central Asia. The day of his victory against the Turks was celebrated annually in Kashmir. Chanakya's teachings had not yet been forgotten, and Lalitaditya refrained from forcing his culture and faith upon the people he conquered. We come to know from Chinese writings that the king of Kashmir shared a healthy relationship with the Turks despite his victory. Lalitaditya made a wise Turk named Cankuna his minister [81]. He sent his embassies to the court of Chinese king Hiuen-tsung. With the Chinese alliance, he defeated the Tibetan king and the Dard tribes who threatened his borders [82]. Amid the wars, he did find time for constructing temples and palaces. The sun temple that he built at Martanda still survives. He also built three important cities and named them Parihasapura, Lalitpura, and Lokapunya [81].

Stories about the mysterious land north of Kashmir are as old as India itself. It was a place where there was no pain, no fear, and no disease—just peace and happiness. Here lived the legendary women of Strirajya. Women ruled this kingdom, and men could only stay temporarily. The women here used to practice polyandry, something still common in many parts of Ladakh. The land finds mention in *Ramayana* and *Mahabharata*. The legend spread through the Greek and Chinese writings as well. According to the legends, no one was able to conquer these powerful women until Lalitaditya's attention turned towards them. The queen of Strirajya fell in love with Lalitaditya. Taking advantage of the weakness, he attacked Strirajya. Legend has it that when the soldiers of Lalitaditya were attacking, the women of Strirajya distracted them by exposing their breasts [83]. The tactic worked for a short while but did not save this ancient kingdom.

At the peak of his power, Lalitaditya's influence extended from Bengal to Iran and as far north as Turkestan. The whole of India that lay north of the Vindhyans and Tibet was part of his empire. It covered an area that was larger than even the Gupta Empire. However, his thirst for conquest had not yet been quenched. The ambition that made him rise would also be the cause of his downfall. He died during one of his ambitious expeditions to the north of Kashmir in the dangerous terrains of the Himalayas. Some writings claim that he died while returning from his mission in an Arbamuck mountain called Deva Sui due to excessive snowfall. Others say that he committed suicide after being in a precarious situation in a war. While there are still some who hope that he retired with his army to the land of immortals, north of Kashmir [82]. The Karakota Empire survived till 982 CE but was ruled by kings much weaker than Lalitaditya. The paradise on earth went back to becoming a passive spectator of history.

6.9   Fight for Pride

Long before the humans walked the earth, at a time when the dinosaurs roamed, something happened deep within the earth that shaped the geopolitics of our country much later. The catastrophic Deccan eruption that happened 65 Mya probably killed the dinosaurs—at least some. What it also did was tilt the Indian plate towards the east. The rivers were forced to change their path and flow from the Western Ghats towards the east coast. While the sources of the rivers were up in the hills of Deccan, they created their fertile plains down in the plateaus of Andhra Pradesh and Tamil Naidu. This became the reason for persistent conflicts between the kings of these two regions over control of the rivers [24]. Two such empires that were locked in a battle for what seemed like eternity were Chalukyas of Deccan and Pallavas of Andhra. The battle that lasted for centuries saw the balance tilt from one side to the other.

Evil was gaining power in the world of mortals, and humanity was in desperate need of a hero. As the legend goes, Indra, the god of rain and thunderstorm, was quick to realize this. He went to Brahma, the creator, for help. Brahma was immersed in his regular prayers. On the request of Indra, he agreed to create a warrior in order to save the earth. The great creator took sacred water (Chalukya jala) in his palm and looked at it. From the water was born a great warrior who created the Chalukya Dynasty. That's what the court poets of Chalukya Dynasty would like us to believe. The true origin of the Chalukya Dynasty is debatable. Most scholars believe that they originated from Gujarat. The 11th-century Nilagunda inscription mentions that the Chalukyas were from Ayodhya [84]. Pulakesi I broke away from the Kadambas and created Chalukyas Dynasty with their base at Badami (mentioned as Badamoi by Greek writer Ptolemy of second century). The fort was created between two hills that formed a U-shaped valley of Badami, which was ideal for defense. There is a myth about how the two hills came into being. There were two brothers, named Vatapi and Ilvala, who treacherously killed people for food. Vatapi was a shape shifter who could become a goat. Ilvala would invite guests and serve them goat (Vatapi) meal. Once the guest ate Vatapi, Ilvala would call Vatapi to come out. Vatapi would emerge from the stomach of the guest, killing the person in the process. The brothers would then feed on the meat of their dead guest. They once tried the trick on Sage Agastya. The sage already knew about the brothers. After eating the meal, Agastya rubbed his stomach and said, "Vatapi be digested", and Vatapi was digested. When Ilvala called his brother, he did not come out. According to the legends, Vatapi and Ilvala are the two hills of Badami.

A reservoir was constructed in the valley at the center of the U-shaped hill. Pulakesi I expanded his empire to the western coast of Karnataka, gaining access to the marine trade [24]. However, it was under Pulakesi II (610 CE–642 CE), the great grandson of Pulakesi I, that the Chalukya Empire reached its peak. Pulakesi II defeated the army of Harsha in the Battle of Narmada and became Parameswara, the king of kings. Pulakeshi II made his brother, Vishnuvardhana, the governor of eastern territory which later became Eastern Chalukyas. It was not Harsha, however, but the Pallavas who were the real threat to the Chalukyas.

Constant war and instability had affected the psychology of Indians. The cult of devotion had spread its influence. In order to be respected by the people, every kingdom created its own myth of divine origin. Once upon a time, somewhere in southern India, a prince met and fell in love with a beautiful and enchanting princess. But their love could not last forever because the princess was a Naga (serpent) from the netherworld. The prince could not stay there forever. He had to leave while his wife was pregnant. While leaving, the prince told his beloved that if she sets their child adrift with a young twig (Pallava) tied to his body, he would recognize the child. He will give a part of his empire to his kid. A son was born to the Naga princess, and she did as asked. When the prince recognized his son, he gave him a part of his empire [24]. This new empire came to be known as the Pallava Dynasty. Like Chalukyas, the true origin of the Pallavas is also controversial. Some authors think that they were from north India while others propose a local Andhra origin. Though there is some evidence of early Pallava Dynasty dating back to third century, they became a politically significant power only in the mid-sixth century. It started under the leadership of King Simhavishnu. His son Mahendravarman I (590–630) extended the empire to the mainland of Tamil and even Sri Lanka. The exotic rock-cut temples of Mamallapuram were built during his reign.

Two growing powers, two ambitious kings, and a fight between them was inevitable. Pulakesi II attacked Mahendravarman I in 620 CE in the Battle of Pallalur. Though Mahendravarman I was defeated, he managed to escape and save his capital. Pallavas lost not only their northern territories but also their pride. Mahendravarman I tried many times to take revenge but in vain. The king died a decade later, carrying the shame of defeat with him. His son Narasimhavarman I took over the throne. He not only completed the temples his father started to build but also got the revenge that his father desperately sought. He attacked Pulakesi II in the battle of Vatapi fought in the year 642. Pulakesi II was killed in the decisive battle, and Pallavas gained control of Vatapi, avenging the loss of Pallalur. Narasimhavarman I looted the Ganesh idol and burnt the city of Pulakesi. It was the Chalukyan pride that was burning.

Vikramaditya I, who united the broken Chalukya Empire and managed to push back the Pallavas, followed Pulakesi II. He regained Vatapi and became the king of Chalukyas. He continued the battle with Narasimhavarman I's son Mahendravarman II and grandson Paramesvaravarman I. Vikramaditya I attacked Paramesvaravarman I in an attempt to capture the Pallava territory but was defeated. He fled back to the safety of his kingdom. The continued attack of Chalukyas enraged the Pallava king. Pallavas counterattacked and conquered most of the Chalukya Empire. They left only after the Chalukya Empire agreed to pay a yearly tribute. The Chalukyan humiliation continued. The victory made the Pallava Empire the most powerful empire in the south and was followed by a period of peace and growth. Pallava king Narasimhavarman II built the Shore Temple between 700 CE and 728 CE. His son Paramesvaravarman II succeeded him. Five years later, Vikramaditya II became the king of Chalukyas. After decades of silence, the peace was about to be broken.

Vikramaditya II was anxious to redeem the lost pride of the Chalukyas. He attacked Paramesvaravarman II and defeated him. Paramesvaravarman II tried to avenge his loss but was defeated again and killed. Paramesvaravarman II had no heir, leading to the end of Simhavishnu bloodline. Kingless Pallava Empire desperately needed an heir to stop the kingdom from disintegrating. Few key leaders and scholars of Pallava Empire gathered together to decide the fate of their kingdom. They had only one choice before them. Few chosen men took a gallant and adventurous voyage across Bay of Bengal in search of their new king. The great Simhavishnu had a brother named Bhimavarman. His sixth descendant, Kadavesa Hari Varma, was the king of Cambodia. The king had four sons who were the only legitimate heir of the Pallava Dynasty. The king rejected the proposal of making his son the king of Pallava Dynasty. After long negotiations the youngest son Nandivarman II agreed to the offer of becoming the king at a tender age of 14.

In 735 CE Vikramaditya II attacked the fragile Pallavas once again. The young king was not allowed to fight and was taken to safety. For the first time, the city of Pallavas came under the control of Chalukyas. His revenge was complete, and the Chalukyan humiliation was erased. It was here that the king did something unexpected. He ensured that the residents and the beautiful temples were not harmed. The loots from the war were returned. He donated a lot of money to rebuild the Pallava temples and returned back to Badami. An act of kindness brought peace to the land once more. It was Vikramaditya II who built the magnificent Pattadakal temple of Karnataka, now a World Heritage Site. He was succeeded by Kirtivarman II in the year 746. It was during this time that Dantidurga, a feudatory of the Chalukyas, became independent and established the Rashtrakuta Empire. Dantidurga allied with Pallava king Nandivarman II and defeated Kirtivarman II, marking the end of Chalukyas of Badami in 753 CE. While Nandivarman II's tender age seemed like his weakness, it actually became his strength. He outlived the Chalukyas, and the Pallava Dynasty continued to flourish till the last king Aparajitavarman was killed in 897 CE in a battle with the Chola king Aditya I. The conflicts between the Pallavas and Chalukyas led to exchange of architectural and sculptural styles between the two regions that are evident in the magnificient temples of south India.

6.10   Kanauj Triangle

The regional identity of India started to develop from the eighth century. Tamil became dominant in Tamil Naidu; the first crude form of Bengali language was developed in Bengal while Kannada became common in Karnataka. India was divided into three powerhouses: Rashtrakutas of Deccan, the Palas of Bengal, and the Pratiharas of Gujarat. The three dynasties fought it out for the prized city of Kanauj. It was the most important city of India since the fall of Patna. Rashtrakuta formed from the Chalukyas in the year 753. At their peak power, their territories included Maharashtra, Karnataka, and parts of Andhra Pradesh. Arts and literature flourished under their rule. They constructed the beautiful Kailasanatha Temple of Ellora and Jain Narayana temple at Pattadakal. Rashtrakuta Dynasty shared good trading relations with the Arabs. Many Arab traders settled along the west coast. Some of them also played active roles in the administration of Rashtrakuta Dynasty. Interestingly, the Jews, Christians, and the Zoroastrians were all present in the west coast of India. While they were fighting in the west, in India, all these communities managed to stay peacefully without any fight.

While the Arab authors wrote about Rashtrakuta Dynasty as one of the most powerful dynasties of the world, Gurjara Pratiharas were their greatest foe. The Arabs even considered them as an enemy of Islamic faith. Pratiharas are the first known Rajput Dynasty and probably originated from the White Huns or Gujars. They considered themselves as Agnivansha (Fire Dynasty) as opposed to Suryavansha (Solar Dynasty) or Chandravansha (Lunar Dynasty). There is an interesting story associated with the origins of Pratihara Dynasty. Parashuram, the incarnation of Vishnu, destroyed all the Kshatriyas (warriors). Without the Kshatriyas, there was no one to protect the people. Hence, sage Vasishta performed a yagna to save the world. From the fire of the yagna was created four Rajput clans: Pratiharas, Chauhans, Solankis, and Paramaras. Pratiharas were the first and the most powerful who ruled much of north India. Their capital was at Avanti. The myth was probably a symbolic representation of weakening of the Indian dynasties (Suryavansha and Chandravansha), and the growing influence of the Huns and Gurjars (the new Agnivansha). Pratihars defeated the Arabs in many battles. The Arabs lost all power in Sind and had to pay tributes to the Pratiharas. They gave up all attempts to concur any parts of India since then.

The third powerful dynasty of the era was in Bengal. After Shashank's rule, Bengal went into chaos. It was the Pala Empire that brought peace once again in the fertile lands of Bengal and started their golden era. The people of Bengal, through a democratic election in 750 CE, chose Gopala as the first Pala king. It was the first democratic election in India since the Mahajanapadas. People were fed up with the chaos and decided to make things right by choosing a king, something not unprecedented in Indian history. Khalimpur copper inscription says, "To put an end to the state of affairs similar to what happens among fishes, the people made the glorious Gopala, the crest jewel of the heads of kings, take the hand of Lakshmi, the goddess of fortune." [36]

There's an interesting story behind the election of Gopala. Bengal was without a king for a long time. People did elect many kings before Gopala, but a demoness killed all of them on the night of the election. When Gopala was elected, Goddess Chandi gave him a club. Gopala used the club to kill the demoness. That was how, according to the folklores, the Gopalas started the Pala Empire. The capital of Palas was Gaur. Palas were patrons of Buddhism. Universities like Vikramshila and Nalanda flourished under the Palas. Mahayana Buddhism spread to Tibet, Nepal, Bhutan, Myanmar, and the Malay Archipelago under their rule. Dharmapala constructed Somapura Mahavira, the biggest Buddhist Vihara in Indian subcontinent. One inscription says that Dharmapala offered prayers in Kedar (Himalayas) and Gokarna (a beach in Karnataka), indicating his dominance over North India. During its peak, under the rule of Dharmapala and Devapala, the Pala Empire extended from Assam to Kandahar and Punjab to Deccan. Their influence extended up to Indonesia and Malaysia. It was the golden era of Bengal. Literature also flourished during their rule. The famous poem *Ramacharitam* was written by Nandi during the Pala rule. Though Buddhist, their rule was secular, and many of the ministers in the king's court were Hindus.

The three powerful dynasties, Rashtrakuta, Gurjara Pratihara and Pala, were locked in a constant fight for Kanauj (figure 8). The powerful Pala king Dharmapala defeated the Pratihara king Indraraja and captured Kanauj. Pratihara king Vatsaraja took revenge by recapturing Kanauj only to be defeated by the Rashtrakuta king Dhruva. Dharmapala retrieved Kanauj from the Rashtrakutas, but the Pratihara king Nagabhata II once again conquered Kanauj. The continuous battles weakened all the three powerful empires, making India prone to invasion from the Turks. Amoghavarsha was the most powerful king of Rashtrakuta Dynasty. He ruled for 64 years. Amoghavarsha is often compared to Ashoka for his peaceful rule and less aggression with neighbouring kingdoms. Arab traveller Suleiman describes him as one of the four great monarchs of his time. Krishna II took over the throne after Amoghavarsha. After Krishna II, the empire started to decline. Rashtrakutas were the first to fall in 982 CE, and their kingdom was taken over by western Chalukyas. Pratihara Dynasty lasted till 1036, after which their feudatories broke away and claimed independence. The weaker Chauhans, Solankis, and Paramaras gained control of North India. The Pala Dynasty weakened under the oppressive rule of Mahipala II. There was a rebellion by lower-caste fishermen led by Divya. They ruled for half a century before the Palas reconqured the throne only to be defeated by the Sena Dynasty. Sena Dynasty was from Karnataka who migrated to Bengal and replaced the Pala Dynasty in 1174. Vijayasen was the first ruler of Sena Dynasty. His son, Ballalsen, consolidated the kingdom. He was an orthodox Hindu ruler under whose rule Brahminism strengthened in Bengal and Buddhism went on a decline. Exchanges with outside world were stopped, and traveling overseas was banned. It was the beginning of the fall of Bengal.

6.11 The Southern Brilliance

By the end of the first millennium of Common Era, the focus of Indian history had shifted south. Various dynasties rose to power and faded away in quick succession. Western Chalukyas, who claimed to be descendants of Badami Chalukyas, were feudatories to Rashtrakuta Empire. They replaced the Rashtrakuta Dynasty and became a dominant power of Deccan. By the end of 12th century, the Chalukyas were on the decline. Their feudatories like Hoysalas, Kakatiyas, and Yadavas of Devgiri took over from them. Hoysalas were hill tribes of Karnataka who saw opportunity in the weakening of Chalukya Dynasty and came down to control the plains. Kakatiyas ruled Andhra Pradesh. The most prominent ruler of the dynasty was a lady named Rudrama Devi. A woman ruler was a rarity in the history of the world of that era. She ruled from 1259 to 1289, succeeding her father when she was just 14 years old. She died like a true warrior, fighting in a battle. Yadavas of Devgiri, claimed to be originally from Mathura, took control of Deccan. There was one man, however, who would take control of the whole of southern India. He would grow his empire to become not just a king, but the king of kings. His name was Raja Raja Chola.

Cholas became a force to be reckoned with under the able leadership of Raja Raja Chola I. The Cheras and Pandyas were old adversaries of the Cholas. Raja Raja found himself surrounded by enemies after the Cheras and Pandyas allied with the Sri Lankan king. The Sri Lankan kings also shared good relationship with the Arab traders. Cholas wanted to control the marine trade that was now dominated by Arabs [24]. Alarmed by the strong alliance, Raja Raja attacked his opponents. He conquered Kerala, Karnataka,

Vengi (Andhra Pradesh), and Kalinga (Orissa). Raja Raja Chola I invaded Sri Lanka in 993 CE. He conquered the northern portion of the island and destroyed their capital city Anuradhapura. It was a brutal invasion where temples were destroyed, and treasures looted. The echoes of the war between the Tamil Cholas and Singhalese kingdom is still heard a thousand years later.

Raja Raja Chola I's son Rajendra Chola continued the domination, bringing the whole island of Sri Lanka under his rule in the year 1017. Cholas had been fighting with the Western Chalukyas for over a century. It was Rajendra who managed to subjugate them. He then went north and attacked Mahapala I of Bengal. Rajendra himself led the campaign. After defeating the northern empires, he marched up to River Ganges and brought the holy water back to his own country, along with a bronze idol of dancing Shiva. He also received elephants, women, and treasures from the Pala king Mahapala I. In 1025, Rajendra led a massive naval campaign to attack Srivijaya (figure 9). It was an instance of India's rare overseas aggression. The Cholas now had strong control over the marine trade, which made their economy flourish. Rajendra fought most of his wars with his son Rajadhiraja at his side. Rajadhiraja was a powerful warrior and a co-ruler from a young age. He died in a battle with the Chalukyas.

Chola's domination started to decline in the twelfth century. The Pandyas attacked them from the south and the Hoysalas from the north. Pandya Dynasty was one of the oldest empires of South India, along with Cheras and Cholas, originating before 500 BCE. They also continued for the longest, up till the 16th century. Sadayavarman Sundara Pandyan I, who ruled from 1251 to 1268, took the empire to its zenith. Under his rule, the Pandyas replaced the Cholas and the Hoysalas to become the dominant power of South India.

6.12   The Man with a Mission

Sankara, a higher-caste Brahmin, was in the holy city of Varanasi. As he was walking towards River Ganges, he found his path being blocked by an untouchable. The untouchable, a person belonging to the lowest strata of Indian society, had four white dogs with him. Sankara, fearing that he might touch him, ordered the untouchable to go away. The untouchable replied, "Why should I go away, and from what? Is it the physical body, or the self [atma]? If it is the body, then all bodies are made of same stuff, why should one body get away from the other? If it is the self, then the self is non-dual. It is here and everywhere, from what then it should go away? . . . Is there a difference between the sunlight reflected from the holy Ganges and from the pools in the streets where the untouchables live?." [85] The great priest had no answer and was humbled by the untouchable. The incident changed his view about life. Sankara spent the rest of his life trying to promote the Upanishadic philosophy of nondualism, or Advaita, around India.

Sankara, or Sankaracharya as he is commonly known, was born in the little known Ernakulam district of Kerala around eighth or ninth century. He belonged to an affluent and deeply religious family. He was a bright student and is said to have completed his formal education by the time he was just eight years old. He was inclined to become a sannyasi (sage), much to the dislike of his mother. At the age of 8, he traveled north in search of a mentor. In his journey, he met many learned men, but none of them could satisfy him. He realized that the original teachings of Upanishads had been forgotten. Religions had become corrupt and ritualistic. Instead of looking for the right mentor, he started to spread his idea of Advaita himself. His speeches and magnetic personality attracted many followers.

Sankaracharya started his tour of victory where he challenged the leaders of different philosophies who did not believe in nondualism. Purva-Mimamsa, or the ritualistic orthodox Vedic philosophy, was the most dominant religious practice at that time. He challenged the most adherent follower of Purva-Mimamsa, Mandana Mishra, on a debate duel. The deal was that the loser would convert and accept the philosophy of the winner. The debate between Mandana and Sankaracharya continued for months, judged by none other than Mandana's learned wife, Ubhaya Bharati.

While both Mandana and Sankaracharya accepted the authority of Vedas, Mandana believed that Brahmana was an abstract concept that cannot be revealed in words. It has no subject-object distinguishing feature. Vedas or Upanishads cannot be a proof of something so vague. The rituals and performance of actions (*karma*) mentioned in Vedas are real verbal testimony. As one performs his *karma*, as mentioned in Vedas, he gets merit. After his death, he gets a period of afterlife based on the merits. The people will lots of merits go to heaven for longer duration. They then come back to earth in a life based on his merits. He collects more merits based on his karma. Over many cycles of birth and death, the man attends *moksha* (salvation). Sankara argued that the Vedas describes two paths to get liberation: one through rituals and karma and the other through knowledge or Jnana. According to him, "Action cannot destroy ignorance, for it is not in conflict with or opposed to ignorance. Knowledge verily destroys ignorance as light destroys deep darkness." Karma was just the first step that prepared one for the experience of nonduality. Once experienced, the person is liberated from the cycles of birth and death. Such a person attends Moksha.

Towards the end of the long debate Mandana was loosing his ground. It was then that Ubhaya Bharati challenged Sankaracharya. She said that after marriage wife becomes half of the man. By defeating Mandana, he just defeated half of him. Ubhaya said, "You cannot claim complete success over my husband until I, his better half, have been defeated by you. Though you are an embodiment of divinity, I have a desire to debate with you." She was also an expert in the Vedas, and the debate lasted for 17 days. She realized that Sankaracharya was a celibate and started to target his weakness. She fired questions on Kama Sutra, the art of making love. That was an essential part of life, and those who do not have knowledge about love and sex do not possess all the knowledge of the universe. Sankaracharya was fairly given a month to learn this new art. According to the mythology, he went into the body of a dead king and received all the learnings from the queens who were happy to see their dead king return. Sankaracharya then came back and defeated her. After that, both Mandana and Ubhaya accepted him as their guru (teacher). Debates were important part of Indian society. It was logic, rather than sword, that was used as a weapon of debates. Logic was also the mantra of conversation. Losers were humble enough to accept the defeat and change their faith. Some of the debates, fights rather, that happen in modern social media are an assault to that spirit of debate.

Sankaracharya won all the debates he had with different spiritual leaders, and his number of followers soared. He converted many Buddhists, Jains, Saisaites, Vaishnavas, Saktas, Sauras, Ganapatyas, and Kaumaras into Advaita philosophy. Like the Buddhists, he established *mathas*, the temples of learning. He made four mathas at four corners of India: Dwarka in the west, Puri in the east, Sringeri in the south, and Badrinath in the north. Sankaracharya was not telling anything new. He was reiterating the philosophies of Upanishad in a new way so that it was easier for the mass to understand. His efforts united the different sects of Hinduism and made modern Hinduism the dominant religion of India. Buddhism, or whatever was left of it in India, rapidly declined after Sankaracharya's travels. Many myths and miracles were later added to Sankaracharya's life by his followers as has happened with many other religious leaders. He is considered by many to be the incarnation of Lord Shiva. Some people believe that Sankaracharya popularized vegetarianism among the Hindus, something that was earlier practiced by Buddhists and Jains.

Adi Sankaracharya too had his fair share of critics, Ramanuja being the most critical. While Sankaracharya's philosophy focused on jnana or knowledge, Ramanuja focused on the intellectual rationale for devotional practice within Hinduism. Ramanuja, born in Tamil Naidu around 1017, proposed qualified nondualism (Vishishadvaita). According to George Cronk:

> Ramanuja agrees that the sense of separate selfhood created by ego consciousness does not express true selfhood; the true Self is not the ego-created separate self [jiva], but the Atman.

> However, there is not just one Atman; there are many individual and personal Atman selves, each of which exists as a real part of and in fundamental union with Brahman. In Ramanuja's world-view, Brahman is the single, supreme, and all-encompassing reality; but within the essential nature of Brahman there exist real distinctions and differences between real material entities and between real individual selves. [86]

Thus, to him, god and people were real and not nonexistent. There was a difference between the two, and god was superior. He emphasized the importance of submission to god. One of the greatest contributions of Ramanuja was to open the door of the temples to the people of lower caste. His philosophy of *bhakti* (devotion), contrary to Sankaracharya's *jnana* (knowledge), was more appealing to the mass. Under his influence, Vaishnavism became the dominant branch of Hinduism. Though both Sankaracharya and Ramanuja shared different philosophies, both of them made major contributions in shaping the present form of Hinduism.

6.13   The Rise of the Nagas

Hindu religion, it is said, forbids people to cross the ocean that they call *kalapani,* or black waters. Beyond *kalapani* lay the realm of demons. Once you go there, you lose your identity and your religion. By losing your religion, one becomes an outcaste. It was probably a desperate effort from the Brahmins to stop the adventurous Indian traders who were making their own destiny. The traders were taking risks, growing rich and powerful, and challenging the authority of the priests. The efforts of the Brahmins went futile. Indian traders grew from strength to strength.

India's most valued trading partner was China. Since the time when Buddhism spread to China from India, Indians shared healthy relations with them. The marine route from India to China was undoubtedly the most important trading route of the ancient world. The legacy of this ancient route was left behind in Southeast Asia. Indian epics like *Ramayana* found a new home in this faraway land. Holy Indian cities were recreated, like Ayodhya at Ayutthaya. Grand Hindu and Buddhist temples, like those of Angkor Wat in Cambodia, speak of this ancient legacy. The marine trade route had to pass through the narrow Isthmus of Kra, connecting Malay Peninsula with the main land of Asia. This isthmus became the focal point through which Southeast Asia became 'Indianized'.

The people of Funan (now parts of Cambodia and Vietnam) controlled the Isthmus of Kra. Legend has it that a Naga (probably tribes having serpent as totem) princess of Funan, named Soma, attacked an Indian ship. However, an Indian named Kaundinya defeated her. He spared her life only when she agreed to marry him. They both got settled in Funan, and Kaundinya became its king. The couple had seven sons, and the king divided the vast land among each one of them. The Nagas mentioned in the story were probably clans having serpent as their totem. Huge serpents are sculpted at the gates of the temples of Angkor Wat. The story gives some clue about the interactions of Indians and the people of Funan. Firstly, the Indian sailors were common in this region. Secondly, people of Funan began as pirates who attacked the merchant ships. However, they were not strong enough to defeat the merchants. These Indian merchants put in some effort to stabilize the political scenario of the area for safe passage of their ships. This was the beginning of a long constructive effort that led to the consolidation and formation of the Kingdom of Funan. The story of the Naga princess is very similar to the myth of the beginning of Pallava Dynasty. One cannot help wonder how the origins of the dynasties of Funan and Pallava are linked. It is no wonder that son of the king of Cambodia was the only legitimate heir of the Pallava Dynasty after death of Paramesvaravarman II. Indians were well settled in Cambodia, a trend started by the Indian merchants. They helped spread Indian language and religion in the area.

The ports of Funan began as halting points for the ships to and from China. The local chieftains took active part in the trading activities. Sometimes they acted as middlemen by transferring the Chinese goods to Indians and Europeans and vice versa. Slowly, they started to introduce their own indigenous products in the market. Southeast Asian products like camphor, sandalwood, and spices were sold to the traders, boosting the economy of the land. The spices became so famous that Southeast Asia became the spice capital of the world.

By the end of fifth century, the Funan Kingdom was on a decline. The trade route had shifted from Isthmus of Kra to Indonesia. Indonesia had the best spices, and the traders now directly contacted them rather than Funan. There was a desperate attempt by Funan kings to change from a trade dependent economy to one that was agrarian. Many irrigational canals were built but could not stop the downfall. It was quite similar to the decline of ISVC. By the mid of sixth century, the Funan Kingdom was dead. The political instability pushed the people farther inland, and they settled around the great lake of Tonle Sap. It was here that the Khymer Empire began to take its root.

The cult of worshiping phallus, a symbol of fertility, was already prevalent in ancient Cambodia. Mountains were considered holy, a place where the ancestral spirit rested. The Cambodians easily accepted Lord Shiva, one who also resides in the mountain and symbolized by a phallus, as their own god. Soon other gods like Brahma and Vishnu were also assimilated into the Cambodian culture. The promotion of Indic religion was driven by local politics. Control of temples gave power over submissive local elites and thus the people under the elites. Jayavarman I (657 CE–681 CE) began to unite different Khymer clans by gaining authority over the local temples. This laid to the foundation of devrajya (divine king) cult in Cambodia.

Khymer Empire officially began in 802 CE under the leadership of Jayavarman II. He declared himself a *Chakravartin*, or king of the world, after claiming independence from Srivijaya Empire. His reign began with a consecration ritual in the holy mountain of Mahendraparvata, now known as Phnom Kulen. Mahendraparvata symbolized Mount Meru, the center of the universe. On the summit of the mountain was the abode of Indra, the king of Devas. With the ritual, Jayavarman II became the guardian of law and order, protector of religion, and defender of the land. The mountain is made of sandstone, which would later be quarried to make the temples in Angkor. On this mountain, we can still see beautiful sculptures of Brahma, Vishnu, Lakshmi, and thousands of Shiva Lingas.

The kings of Cambodia were considered as divine after their death. Though the royal temple was dedicated to the living monarch, it also became the mausoleum of the dead king, letting the new king draw on powers of his dead ancestors. This strengthened the position of the king whose authority could not be challenged by any outsider. Jayavarman II's successor, Indravarman, constructed a stone temple to shelter the royal Shivalinga named Indresvara linga. Inside it, resided Jayavarman II. This cult was continued by the successors, though the specific deity changed over time. Suryavarman II, who built Angkor Wat, was fond of Vishnu while Jayavarman VII became a Buddhist and constructed the Bayon temple complex of Angkor Thom.

The growing Khymer Empire came in conflict with Tambralinga kingdom. Khymer king Suryavarman I (1002–1050) requested help from Rajendra Chola of Chola Empire. On hearing the news of the powerful alliance, Tambralinga Kingdom asked help from Srivijaya Kingdom. By this time, Srivijaya has become the most powerful empire of Southeast Asia. They wanted to control the trade route between Indians and Chinese. Srivijaya taxed the people who used their ports heavily. Borobudur, the biggest Buddhist temple, is an evidence of Srivijaya's prosperity. The Indian Ocean ship panel of Borobudur Temple, dated to 800 CE, is an example of the maritime prowess of Srivijaya Kingdom. Around the mid of ninth century, many sailors from Srivijaya (Indonesia) started to populate Madagascar, taking with them the Indian language of Sanskrit. Srivijaya maintained friendly relationship with Cholas and the Palas of Bengal. However, their relation with the Cholas soured by the 11th century. Rajendra Chola led an aggressive naval expedition against Srivijaya Empire on request of the Khymer king. Srivijaya was not prepared for such an onslaught. They never expected the Cholas to sail far away from home with a huge army. Srivijaya and Tambralinga were routed. The defeat led to Srivijaya's decline and ended the monopoly they had over trading. Once the suzerainty of Cholas was recognized, the successful naval army returned. The golden era of Khymer Empire began after the defeat of Srivijaya as active trading resumed in Cambodia for the first time since the Funan.

Suryavarman I was the first strong ruler of the dynasty and he began to expand the empire. It was under Suryavarman II (reigned 1113–1150) that the empire reached its peak. While earlier rulers worshipped Shiva, Vishnu became popular under him. He built the grand temple of Angkor Wat in Dravidian style to represent Mount Meru. Champa Kingdom conquered Angkor in a battle fought in Tonle Sap Lake after the death of Suryavarman II. After 22 long years of battle, Champa was finally defeated, and Angkor was reconquered by Jayavarman VII. He renovated Angkor Wat and also built the Bayon in his new capital Angkor Thom. In this temple, we find the beautifully sculpted faces of boddhisattva Avalokiteshvara, often confused with Buddha. Many scholars think that the faces were of Jayavarman himself. He also built plenty of other temples, including Ta Prohm, Banteay Kdei, and Neak Pean. Ta Prohm is commonly known as *Tomb Raider* temple or Angelina Jolie Temple after the famous movie that was shot there. Khymer Kingdom began to shrink after the death of Jayavarman VII. The new Sukhothai Dynasty formed in Thailand pushed the Khymers back. Kublai Khan, the Mongol king, attacked Angkor, weakening it further. The dying kingdom finally perished when trading received a deadly blow due to Black Death that occurred in China in the 1330s. Angkor was lost from the pages of history as forests took over. A new empire, Ayutthaya, replaced Angkor to become the superpower of Southeast Asia.

6.14   Changing Times

India's cultural influence spread far and wide. Greeks were first to be acquainted, then Mongolia and China, followed by Southeast Asia, and finally the Arabs. It started from Afghanistan and ended in Southeast Asia as Far East as Philippines. India started its slow but steady decline post the Gupta era. There were few powerful kings who tried to rebuild the country, but none could sustain their glory for long. The chaos was more prominent in the north where several smaller empires fought among one another, trying to replace the powerful older dynasties. The same trend then followed in the Deccan. Soon after the decline of Cholas, even the south reached the same fate.

It was a time when the local languages and cultures of India took definite shape. For the first time under Rashtrakutas, we saw a fight between the south and north of India. The seeds of the conflict between Tamils and Singhalese were also planted. Deccan and Tamil started their share of hostility with the fights between Badami Chalukyas and Pallavas and then Western Chalukyas and Cholas. The fragmentation of India was reflected in the architectures. Architecture started to flourish in the south from sixth century. Chalukya Dynasty started the experiments in Aihole, Badami, and Pattadakal in Karnataka. There you can see the evolution of different styles of temples with time. The later temples have better sculptures. The sculptures are filled with the stories from *Ramayana*, *Mahabharata* and *Panchatantra*, along with daily life of local people. One can see the social status of people from the dress they wore. The rich wore more jewellery compared to the poor. One can also find sculptures of happy couple and angry fighting couples. Based on the style of temple architecture, India could clearly be separated into three regions: Aryavarta or North India that was situated north of Narmada, having Nagara architectural style; the Deccan in Western Ghats, with their Vesara style of architecture; and South India or Tamilahm having their own Dravida-style architecture. Not just language and architecture, even the dance forms became different in different regions. Bharatanatyam became the dominant style of dance in Tamil Naidu, Kathakali, and Mohiniyattam of Kerela, Kuchipudi of Andhra Pradesh, Kathak of Uttar Pradesh (with later Islamic influence), Odissi of Odisha, Manipuri of Manipur and Sattriya of Assam. These differences give an apparent image of India as never being a single entity.

Indian philosophy changed from Upanishads to the devotional Puranas. *Purana* means *old*. These ancient texts dealt with various topics, including history, science, and myths. There are eighteen major Puranas and nineteen minor ones. Most of them have been composed between third and tenth century. While Rig Veda questioned the origin of universe, the Puranas attempted to answer. According to Puranic cosmology, the universe evolves in continuous cycles of creation and destruction. Brahma is the God of creation, Vishnu of sustenance, and Shiva of destruction. Each cycle continues for 311.04 trillion years, which is equivalent to one life of Brahma. Current universe is said to be the fifty-first year of Brahma. One day of Brahma constitutes two *Kalpa* (one day and one night). Each *Kalpa* is 4.32 billion years, which is roughly equivalent to the modern estimate of the age of the earth. One *Kalpa* is equal to 14 *Manvantars*, and one *Manvantar* is equal to 71 *Chaturyugis*. One *Chaturyug* is equal to 4.32 million years. Each *Chaturyugis* is divided into four *Yugs* (eras): *Satya Yug* (Golden Age), *Treta Yug*, *Dwapara Yug*, and *Kali Yug* (Dark Age). We are now in *Kali Yug*. In one *Kalpa* the universe expands for first 7 *Manvantar*, stops for six *Chaturyugis*, and contracts till the 14th *Manvantar*. In first *Manvantar*, the sky forms, the air in the second, ocean in the third, fire in the fourth, and earth in the fifth. Vegetation starts in the sixth and animal in the seventh. Then the process reverses with animals to disappear first, followed by vegetation, and then the five elements. The destruction of the universe is called *pralaya*, which is followed by a new cycle of universe. The world, according to Puranas, was divided into seven regions separated by seven oceans. In the center was *Jambudvipa*, where India was situated. Star, moon, and the nine planets surrounded the world.

Along with Puranas, a new revolution of Bhakti movement started to become popular. It brought god to the common man of all castes. It undermined the importance of priests acting as a middleman between people and god. Tamil poet saints like Alvars and Nayanars made Bhakti cult popular. Other prominent poet saints of the time were Appar of Tamil Naidu, Basavanna of Karnataka, Jnaneshvar, and Tukaram of Maharashtra. The revolution that tried to shed the dominance of the higher caste gave the lower caste confidence to challenge their authority. Thousands of years of Vedic social order was broken, which angered the Brahmins. This probably made the orthodox Brahmins strict and rigid, enhancing the boundaries of the caste system. Studies done by researchers from the National Institute of Biomedical Genomics show that the Indians, who used to interbreed freely, suddenly stopped mixing seventy generations ago [87]. Considering 22.5 years as the span for one generation, the rigid caste system would have formed in the Gupta Era. In Bengal and Maharasthra, however, the rigidity was less prominent.

The society was less rigid about public discussion of sex. The debate between Sankaracharya and Ubhaya was interesting. Ubhaya was a learned scholar and was appointed as judge in the debate. She also spoke freely about sex in public, especially on a spiritual debate. Though celibacy helped in attaining liberation, knowledge of sex was important and not a sin. Sankaracharya had to learn the art of making love before claiming victory. Open debates about sex in public were also not considered a taboo. The story also points towards equality of women, especially among the well-to-do families. Knowledgeable women were respected in the society. However, women were married at a very young age. A 7-year-old girl was called *gauri* and was considered the best for marriage. A 10-year-old girl was called *nagnika*, 12-year-old as *kanyaka*, and all girls older than 12 years were called *rajasvala*. Rajasvala were considered the worst for marriage. Marriage could happen in eight different ways. In Brahma marriage, the best type of marriage, the bride was given to a noble family where the groom had knowledge in Vedas. In Daiva marriage, priest married the bride to a groom. Asra marriage was one in which the bride was given away to a sage after performing Vedic ritual and in exchange of cows. In Prajapatya marriage, the bride's father searches for a groom. Love marriage was called Gandharva marriage. In Ashura marriage, the bride's parents give their daughter to a groom after receiving money from him. If the bride was abducted and married with her consent, then it was Raksasa marriage while if it was forceful and without consent, then it was called Paishaca marriage. The last two were considered the lowest form of marriage.

There is a mis-conception among many that Indian's are traditionally vegetarians. That myth is busted when one visits the coasts of India, with probable excption of Gujarat and Tamil Naidu. Fish is a very popular food in the coastal belts. Drinking wine and eating meat was not uncommon even in the past. *Manasolassa*, an ancient text from second century, mentions blood sausage, goat's brain, barbecued rat, etc as common foods of that era. Kababs and tandoori were already present since ISVC. Drinking was also not a taboo. Lively pubs were common in cities since Mayurian era, especially Patna. Even today, half of Indian population eats non-vegetarian dishes.

Amid the decline in economy and political unrest, mathematics and astronomy continued to flourish. Scholars like Bhaskara I (600–680), Shridhara (650–850), Mahavira (ninth century), Aryabhata II (920-1000), Pavuluri Mallana, Hemachandra (1087–1172), and Bhaskara II (1114–1185) took Indian mathematics and astronomy to its peak. The period between 400 CE and 1200 CE is known as the classical period of Indian mathematics. The major contributions were in decimal number system, concept of zero as a number, negative numbers, arithmetic, algebra, and trigonometry. It inspired the Chinese and Arabs and helped develop the Arabian mathematics, which later went on to influence Europe and trigger its renaissance. The orthodoxy, however, slowly diluted scientific progress as India lost its political stability. Al Biruni observed, "Indian astronomical and mathematical literatures can be compared to a mixture of pearl shells and sour dates, or of costly crystals and common pebbles. Both kinds of things are equal in their eyes, since they cannot rise themselves to the methods of strictly scientific deduction." The cultural, spiritual, scientific, and economic decline of India happened alongside with its political decline. Various groups that have joined at different times in the long journey of survivors were now going to take the rough road.

Rise of Middle East (1200 to 1500 CE)

*Brahman became Prophet Muhammad, Vishnu became
Paigambar [prophet], Shiva became Adam, Ganesh became
Gazi, Kartik became Qazi, Goddess Chandi became Eve
and Padmavati became Prophet's daughter Fatima.*

—Sunya Puran

7.1   Raiders from the West

Abu al-Abbas al-Saffah, a descendant of Prophet
Mohammad's uncle, started the rule of Abbasid
Caliphate of Arab in 750 CE. He killed all the members of
Umayyad Dynasty he could lay hands on [77]. In a smart
move, the capital was shifted from Damascus to Baghdad in
the year 762. It brought the Abbasids close to the non-Arab
Turks, who supported them against the Umayyads. Under
Abbasid Caliphate, Islam reached its golden age. In 793 CE,
Sibawayh formalized Arabic language. Greek classics were

translated into Arabic, along with literatures from India and China. The Arabs learnt of Chinese inventions like the compass, paper, printing, and gunpowder and later passed them on to Europe. Arab mathematician Al-Khwarizmi wrote a book on Hindu numerals in the ninth century that led to the development of Arabic numerals. While progress in science slowed down in India, the Arabs took over and contributed to the growth of geometry, algebra, geography, astronomy, optics, chemistry, and medicine [88]. Arts, along with science and literature, flourished. The earliest versions of *One Thousand and One Nights*, more popular as *Arabian Nights*, can be dated to this period. Many of the stories of *Arabian Nights* were borrowed from famous tales from neighboring countries. Scientists and scholars enjoyed a great deal of intellectual and personal freedom unlike in Europe or Central Asia at that time. The culture and civilization of the Arabs flourished in a liberal and pro-scientific environment.

With the spread of Arabs there was a large-scale conversion of Persians and Turks into Islam. Many of them were taken as slaves. In 833 CE, Abbasid king Sultan al-Mutasim created a regiment of Turkish slaves [87]. That move would ultimately prove to be fatal for India. The Turk slaves were trained to become great soldiers. Many of them started to hold important positions in the army. Abu Mansur Sabuktigin was one such Turkish slave guard who went on to create the Ghaznavid Empire in Ghazna (Ghazni) province of Afghanistan. Sabuktigin seized Khurasan and Bukhara [87]. He was an orthodox Sunni and is said to have harshly suppressed any attempt of innovations in the Islamic creed. His son Mahmud succeeded him in the year 998. By 11th century, the golden era of the Arabs had started to decline and the Turks took over. Mahmud did give importance to scholars. He took all renowned scholars from areas he captured to his kingdom. Al-Biruni was one such scholar who was specifically sent to India to know about Indians. The Turks were ruthless; and their warfare stratagem consisted of rapid advance, retreat, and lightning-fast raids riding on their powerful horses [88].

Mahmud of Ghazni would soon have his eyes on the riches of India, an India that was fragile and divided. The Hindu Kabul Shahi Dynasty ruled Kabulistan (in modern Afghanistan) and Gandhara (in modern Pakistan). The Pratihara Dynasty, though successful in keeping the Arabs out of India, had declined and was replaced by number of smaller Rajput states. Gahadavalas took over Kanauj, Solankis ruled Gujarat, Paramaras ruled Malwa, and Chauhans ruled Ajmer. In Bengal, the weaker Sena Dynasty replaced the Pala Empire. Hoysalas, Kakatiyas, and Yadavas of Devgiri replaced the Chalukyas of Deccan. The internal fights resulted in building of numerous forts in India. The Jats built the Ranthambore fort; the Yadavas built the Devgiri fort in what is now known as Daulatabad. Surya Sen built the Gwalior fort, and Gond kings in Jabalpur built Madan Mohan fort. Quilla Rai Pethora was built by Chauhans in Delhi and the Jaisalmer fort by the Bhati Rajput ruler Rao Jaisal. Along with the forts, temple building also reached its zenith. Numerous Jain temples were constructed in Delhi, the relics of which can be seen in the Qutub Minar complex. Raja Bhoja built the incomplete Bhojeshwar Temple near Bhopal (figure 10). Temples with exotic sculptures like the Khajuraho temple, Modhera Sun Temple and the Konarak temple of Puri all belonged to this era.

Indian temples were rich, and Mahmud was attracted by the wealth. His first attack was on Anandapala, the ruler of Kabul Shahi Dynasty. Shahi Dynasty had fought the Turks successfully for many years. They were Hindu and Buddhist rulers who were probably linked to the Ashvakas of fourth century who put up a brave fight against Alexander's army. They also helped Chandragupta establish Mayurian Empire. The continuous fights, however, have made them weak. After a brave fight, Anandapala lost against Mahmud in the Battle of Chach in 1010. Within a decade, the Shahi Dynasty lost all its territories to the Turks. The successors fled to Kashmir where they were given shelter by the Kashmiri kings. Victories made Mahmud confident, and to take revenge for helping the Kabul Shahis, he attacked Kashmir. He was thoroughly defeated twice, and never again did he try to attack Kashmir. Mahmud went on to attack Somnath Temple instead.

In the winters of 1025, Mahmud made a surprise attack in Gujarat. Bhimdev I, the Solanki ruler, was unprepared and he had to run away to Kanthkot fort in Kutch. Mahmud plundered Somnath Temple for two days until Bhimdev managed to gather an army and attack Mahmud but was completely routed. Fifty thousand people are said to have died trying to protect the temple. The sacred floating Shiv Linga was broken into pieces, and all the riches had been looted. After realizing the strength of the enemy Bhimdev allied with the famed Raja Bhoja of Paramara Dynasty of Madhya Pradesh.

Raja Bhoja was not just a king but also a philosopher and an author who wrote eighty-four books. His writings covered a wide range of subjects from philosophy, poetry, medicine, veterinary science, phonetics, and yoga to even archery. There is a common saying in Hindi: 'Kanha Raja Bhoja, kanha Gangu Teli'. According to local folklore, the great king Bhoja had some problems while building his fort.

A priest suggested double sacrifice, a mother and her son, to overcome the obstracle. Oil-presser Gangu Teli's wife and newborn son accepted the offer. After the sacrifice, a temple was built in the name of Gangu Teli's wife. The quotation means that the poor and inconsequential people like Gangu will always make sacrifices for the powerful kings. It is generally used to compare two things having different status. The saying still survives, showing the popularity of Raja Bhoja and people's willingness to sacrifice their life for him. Raja Bhoja led the battle against Mahmud, along with Bhimdev and other Indian kings. Mahmud was no match for the huge army and had to run back to the comfort of this capital at Ghazni. Mahmud lost many men in the process. The Indian kings regained their lost territories. Bhoja and Bhimdev then went on to rebuild the Somnath Temple.

Mahmud's nephew, Salar Masud, attacked Somnath again with an army of more than 100,000 men and 50,000 cavalry. This time, the Indian kings were prepared. The main battle was fought at Bahraich. Seventeen Indian rulers allied together, with Raja Sukhdeo as their leader. Indian kings sent a warning message to Masud so that he would retreat from the Indian territory. After Masud's refusal, 120,000 soldiers attacked Masud's men. It was a fierce battle fought for hours. Masud's men were finally surrounded, and the Indians this time did not show any mercy to the Turks. Masud, along with most of his army, was slaughtered. The battles were against the raiders and not any religion. Muslim traders were still welcomed in the country. Colonies of many Muslim traders sprang up in various parts of India. Sufi preachers came to India and preached the gospel of love, faith, and dedication to the Muslim settlers [88]. The Hazrat Ghazi Saiyyad Salar Masud tomb of Uttar Pradesh is the grave of Masud, and both Hindus and Muslims still visit it to pay respect. In no other country will an invader get such respect. Therein lies the bewildering charm, the contradictory philosophies, and the confounding mystery that is India.

7.2 Ghori's Glory

Ghurids were vassals of the Ghaznavids until a Ghaznavid emperor treacherously poisoned a king of the former dynasty. It started the rivalry between the two groups. Shahabuddin Muhammad Ghori, the young Ghurid king, conquered the Ghaznavids in 1173. Ghori was an ambitious man; and he did what the Persians, Alexander's men, Arabs, or even Mahmud of Ghazni could not. He successfully raided deep into the heart of Indian territories. Ghori captured Punjab and, like Ghazni, tried to attack the Chalukyan Empire in Gujarat. It was considered that no man could defeat him. However, the challenge that he faced in Gujarat was not coming from a man. King Bala Mularaja was too young to rule. His mother Naikidevi, the regent queen, was controlling the kingdom. All knew the strength of the mighty king Ghori. But Naikidevi was not going to give her land to him without a fight. After Ghori attacked, a fierce battle took place between the two armies. It was near the village of Kayadara where Naikidevi inflicted a major defeat on Ghori and his men in 1178. Ghori's pride was shattered, and he never again tried to conquer Gujarat. He looked towards more vulnarable Punjab instead.

Prithviraj Chauhan was the most ambitious king of north India at the time. Before Hem Chandra Vikramaditya (popularly known as Hemu) of 16th century, Prithviraj was the last independent Hindu king of Delhi. Unfortunately, that is what made him more famous than his deeds. He came to power around 1177 at the age of 11. It was only when he was 16 that he started to control the administration. His policy was to expand his kingdom. Prithviraj's first target was the Chalukyan Empire in Gujarat. After being comprehensively defeated by the powerful Chalukyas, he looked towards east. Here he came face to face with Paramardi, the Chandel king of Mahoba. The battle between Chauhans and Chandels was made immortal by poet Jagnik Rao's famous ballad *Alha-Khand*. It is still recited by locals at many places in India. The hero in the ballad was not the victorious Prithviraj, but the generals of the Chandel king named Alha and Udal. They were brothers and great warriors. According to the poem, Alha impressed goddess Sharda by cutting his head and gifting it to her. In return, he received the boon of immortality from goddess. He also got a divine sword from his uncle that kept him undefeated. In the battle for Mahoba, Udal was fighting Prithviraj and injured him so badly that Prithviraj could not move. Just when Udal was about to kill him one of Prithviraj's general came to his rescue and killed Udal instead. Enraged, Alha rushed to kill paralyzed Prithviraj but was stopped by his guru. An injured man without arms should not be killed. Alha then left the battlefield and went to Himalayas in search of peace. He became the immortal hero of the ballad.

After gaining victory in Ganges Valley, Prithviraj turned towards Punjab. Prithviraj and Ghori were now directly pitted against each other. The outcome of the encounter would be decided in Tarain. The first battle of Tarain was fought in 1191. Ghori's horses were no match for Prithviraj's giant elephants. Ghori's men were thoroughly routed, and Ghori himself just managed to survive, saved by a Khilji horseman. Prithviraj then went on to capture Bhatinda. The easy victory made Prithviraj complacent. Instead of pushing for victory and capturing the weakened Ghurid Dynasty, he left them alone. This gave Ghori a chance to regroup his men. Ghori attacked again the next year. This time he was well prepared. Prithviraj had numbers on his side but lacked in strategy. His men were defeated, and Prithviraj himself was taken as a prisoner. This decisive victory marked the beginning of Islamic rule in India [88].

As per the version of Chand Bardai, the court poet of Prithviraj, Ghori was captured in the first battle. Only after he pleaded mercy and promised never to return to India that Prithviraj freed him. Ghori broke his promise and attacked again the next year with a bigger army. The Rajput army was taken by surprise when Ghori attacked in the dusk, a time when Rajputs do not fight. The confusion led to the defeat of the Rajputs, and Prithviraj was imprisoned and taken to Ghazni. There he was blinded after he dared to look straight into the eyes of Ghori. Days later, there was an archery contest, and Prithviraj wanted to take part in it. Courtiers laughed and gave Prithviraj an arrow to test the skills of a blind shooter. Chand Bardai was himself there to help Prithviraj aim. He was supposed to aim at a target just by hearing its sound after a man strikes it with a hammer. Prithviraj's perfect aim at his fist shot surprised Ghori. The moment Ghori said *shabash* (*well done*), Prithviraj shot the second arrow, aiming in the direction from where the sound came. It went straight through Ghori's throat. Gori died on the spot. Before the guards could kill Prithviraj, he and Chand Bardai killed each other. Prithviraj is buried in Afghanistan. Many Afghans are said to still stab on the grave of Prithviraj to vent their anger.

Ghori probably killed Prithviraj soon after the battle. He made his slave Qutb-ud-din Aibak, also a Turk, the first sultan of Delhi in 1206. Ghori died much later and was most likely assassinated by the Hindu Jat Khokhars. The Slave Dynasty of Aibak marked the beginning of Islamic rule in India. The Hindu kings of northern India, especially the Rajputs, failed to hold on to their land not because they lacked courage but because they were technologically inferior to the invaders. Though they were heavy on numbers, they lacked discipline and their battle plan was predictable, making India vulnerable.

7.3   The Tower of Victory

Ghori's victory had opened up the floodgates. Turks went on to conquer Bihar, Madhya Pradesh and Gujarat under leadership of Qutub-ud-din Aibak. The Chalukyas soon recaptured Gujarat, but the rest remained under Turk control. The raids led to the destruction of many villages, along with the Buddhist universities of Nalanda and Vikramasila. The monastries (*vihara*) of Bihar were raided and the monks were mistaken as 'shaven soldiers' [36]. The invaders called the whole country '*Bihar*' after the looted *viharas*. Bengal was the next big prize. The flourishing foreign trade has made the region very rich under the Sena Dynasty. Turks, under their general Bakhtiyar Khilji, attacked Sena king Lakshman Sen in Nabadwip. After his victory, Bakhtiyar was appointed as the governor of Bengal. Lakshman Sen fled to the south of Bengal where he continued to rule his small empire. It was Bakhtiyar who attacked and burnt down the Nalanda University. India lost a huge amount of its literature as one of the oldest and largest libraries of the world was burnt to ashes.

In 1206 Bakhtiyar attacked Assam in the lust of expanding his empire further. The shrewd Assam rulers allowed the Turks to enter deep inside their territory while quietly waiting for the right moment. Bakhtiyar's army was exhausted traveling on the difficult mountain terrain and wanted to retreat. Once the enemy was weak, tired, and frustrated, the Assamese attacked. Bakhtiyar's men were ambushed. While Bakhtiyar did manage to return back, he fell ill. His own men assassinated him in 1206. Qutub-ud-din Aibak also died soon after accidentally falling from his horse while playing polo. Before his death, he started to build Qutub Minar, a symbol of victory of Turks over India, but could not finish it (figure 11). It was finally completed by his successor Iltutmish.

Qutub Minar is a massive tower amidst the ruins of Iltutmish's empire. It was built at the center of Rai Pithora, the fortified city of Prithviraj Chauhan. King Angpal II of Tomar Dynasty originally built Rai Pithora in the 11th century. Angpal named it Lal Kot. It was later captured by Chauhans. Lal Kot is often called the first city of Delhi. The old city was destroyed. The Turks were now building a new city over the ruins of the old. The new cities were changing India's landscape once more. Eastern and western architectures fused together to gift to the world magnificent buildings like the Taj Mahal. In Qutub Minar we see arches in Indian architecture for the first time. The Turks learned it from the Arabs, who, in turn, learned it from the Romans. Another interesting structure still present in the complex is the iron pillar, the one built by Chandra Gupta II of Gupta Empire. It was originally placed on top of a hill but later moved here by a king named Angpal. Legend has it that the pillar was attached to the hood of the serpent king Vasuki. As long as the pillar was rooted in the ground, the empire of Angpal was supposed to remain firm. Angpal had no faith in old myths and asked the pillar to be uprooted. He brought it to Lal Kot as his prized possession. Soon after, his empire became unstable. According to the story named *Kili Dhilli Katha* (*Tale of the Loose Nail*), Delhi takes its name from *Dhili Kili* [89]. *Kili* was the iron pillar, and *Dilli* means that it was loose and unstable.

Turkish rule was also unstable like the iron pillar. Bengal along with parts of Madhya Pradesh and Rajasthan claimed independence. It was Iltutmish who went on to reconquer all of them. He, like his predecessors, tried to attack the Chalukyas of Gujarat but failed. His beloved daughter, Raziyya al-Din, succeeded Iltutmish in 1236. She was trained to handle armies and administer kingdoms. She refused the title of *Sultana*, which meant *wife or mistress of a sultan*, and used *Sultan* instead. Unlike Naikidevi, Raziyya was a ruler and not a regent. She wore men's clothing and removed the veil from her face. She practiced hunting like the kings and led her army to war. Despite early revolts against a woman ruler, she proved herself to be an able *Sultan*, and with time, people accepted her rule. She was kind towards non-Turk Muslims and tolerant towards people of other faith. Under her reign, many libraries, schools, and research institutes were established. Her liberal attitude led to a rebellion by the nobles in her kingdom. The governor of Bhatinda, Malik Altunia, attacked and imprisoned her. She was freed only after she agreed to marry him [88]. Raziyya never got back her throne as she died fighting the Jats in 1240.

Raziyya's death led to instability in Delhi until Ghiyas ud din Balban took the throne. Unlike Raziyya, Balban only entertained the highborn Muslims. Even the converted Indian Muslims were excluded from positions of power and authority. The Turkish rule continued to be fragile. The Hindu kings kept revolting, the roads were filled with dacoits, and there were frequent attacks on Balban's kingdom. In order to bring stability, Balban hunted down the rebels. Forests were burnt down, and the people of the rebellious villages in the forest were enslaved [89]. At the same time, threats from Mongols kept increasing in the western border. Balban was shocked when the Mongols killed his eldest son. Soon after that, he died. Balban's 17-year-old grandson, Muiz ud din Qaiqabad, succeeded him. Four years later, he was murdered by a Khilji chief, ending the rule of the First Sultanate.

7.4   Sikander-i-Sani

Balban's bias towards highborn Muslims has bred enemies. After his death, Delhi became unstable once more until the Khiljis took control. Jalaluddin Khilji took the throne in 1290 marking the beginning of the Second Sultanate. Khiljis were related to Turks but belonged from an Afghan village named Qalat-e Khilji. This made them Turko-Afghans and not pure Turks. Balban did not consider them as highborn Muslims. Ironically, few centuries ago, the Arabs considered themselves 'pure' Muslims and non-Arabs, including the Turks, were lowborn. The policy of favoritism neither worked for the Arabs nor for the Turks. The arrival of Khiljis broke the Turkish monopoly in high offices. Jalaluddin was a liberal ruler. He was quick to realize that a Hindu-dominated country cannot be sustainably ruled by trying to convert it forcefully into a truly Islamic state. Jalaluddin had a strong army that defeated the Mongols when they tried to capture Delhi in 1292. Defeated, the Mongols called for truce. Many Mongols settled in Delhi after the peace truce.

Jalaluddin's rule was short, and six years after his coronation, he was treacherously murdered by his cousin and son-in-law Allauddin Khilji [88]. Allauddin faced revolts from the nobles and even his own family members. But he curbed the rebels with brute force, confiscating their property and even killing them if needed. Inspired by Sikander (Alexander the Great), he called himself Al Sikander al Saquee (the Second Alexander). He became the most powerful ruler of the sultanate after conquering Gujarat, Ranthambore, Mewar, and Devgiri. He was the first Muslim ruler to successfully raid South India.

Gujarat resisted the Turks for a long time; finally, it was Alauddin Khilji's men who were able to conquer it in 1299. Khilji was desperate to have control over the trade route that was flourishing in Gujarat. Somnath Temple, which was rebuilt a century earlier, was demolished again. Even the Muslim settlers of Gujarat, who came for trading, were not spared. One soldier managed to run away on the order of the king of Gujarat. The king requested him to survive the day and take revenge later. Khilji's next battle was for Ranthambore.

After Prithviraj's death, the Chauhans moved to Ranthambore fort and had proved to be a nuisance for the sultanate. Jallauddin tried to attack Ranthambore fort, but was repulsed. It was Muhammad Shah who killed Jallauddin on the orders of Alauddin. Muhammad Shah, however, fell in love with one of the begums of Alauddin and conspired against the king. When the king came to know about the conspiracy, Muhammad ran away. He took shelter in the fort of Chauhan king Hamir Dev. Enraged, Alauddin attacked Ranthambore fort in 1301. The fort was too strong even for Alauddin's huge army, and Alauddin called for a truce. He asked Hamir to hand over Muhammad Shah and in return his army would go back to Delhi. Hamir was not a man who would turn back on his promise and was confident of protecting his fort. The battle resumed after Hamir's refusal to accept the terms of Khilji. Unfortunately, one of Hamir's officers named Bhoj Dev started to leak secret information about the fort's food and water supply. Alauddin used the critical information to stop the essential supplies to the fort. All he had to do now was wait. Hamir and his starving soldiers had no option but to open the gates and fight till death. Their women committed Jauhar, and Muhammad killed himself. Alauddin owed his victory to Bhoj Dev's treachery. Instead of rewarding Bhoj Dev, Alauddin ordered to behead him for betraying his own king.

Couple of years later, Alauddin turned towards Mewar. Legend has it that the beauty of the queen of Mewar, named Rani Padmini, attracted Alauddin. Alauddin wanted to attack Chittor fort, but it was heavily guarded. Alauddin then sent a message to Rawal Ratan Singh, king of Mewar, that he just wanted to catch a glimpse of the queen. Thinking about the safety of his people, Ratan Singh agreed to show his queen's reflection on the mirror. When Alauddin was allowed to enter the fort, he and his special men secretly surveyed it. While returning, Alauddin treacherously kidnapped Ratan Singh and demanded the queen in return of the king. The queen agreed. Next day, one hundred and fifty palanquins left Chittor fort for

Alauddin' s camp. Much to the surprise of Khilji's men, it wasn't the queen who sat inside the big palanquin but disguised armed soldiers of Chittor. They attacked the camp and freed Ratan Singh, bringing him back to the safety of the fort. This angered Alauddin, and he attacked Chittor once more. Even though Alauddin could not break through the fort, he ensured that the fort slowly ran out of resource, like he did in Ranthambore. Realizing that they were trapped, Ratan Singh ordered all his men to open the fort gates and engage on a direct combat with Alauddin's men. The soldiers fought bravely against the huge army of the sultanate till the last man was dead. Rani Padmini, along with the rest of the women, committed suicide (Jauhar). Victorious Alauddin entered Chittor. All he found was ashes of Rani Padmini [90].

After conquering Warangal, Alauddin became the prized possessor of the famous Koh-i-Noor diamond. He defeated the kings of Hoysalas, Kakatiyas, and Pandyan Empire in the south. Alauddin had four decisive victories against the Mongols at Jalandhar, Kili, Amroha, and Ravi [91]. Most of his resource was spent in maintaining a strong army in the western boundary to keep the Mongols at bay. The Mongol threat made Alauddin fortify his new capital at Siri, often called the third city of Delhi after Lal Kot and Mehruli. It is said that the heads of 8,000 Mongols, whom he defeated in the battle, still lie buried inside the foundation and walls of the buildings of Siri [89]. He built a magnificent reservoir called Hauz Khas inside Siri for the growing population of his new city. He also built a mosque and a madrasa inside the Qutub Minar complex. Alauddin started the construction of Alai Minar, planned to be twice as high as Qutub Minar. It was left incomplete because of his untimely death in 1316.

7.5   The Mad King

Allauddin did not die a natural death but was murdered by a man named Khusro Khan. Khan was originally a Hindu soldier from Gujarat. He was the one who managed to escape alive from the battle in which Allauddin had massacred his people. Khan did not run away to save his life but was ordered by his king to survive the lost battle and prepare for revenge. Killing Allauddin became the motto of his life. Khan was captured, enslaved, and converted to Islam. He suffered all the atrocities against him quietly, and managed to get admitted in Allauddin's army. He was a great warrior and easily rose up the ranks to become a military leader. Khan managed to gain Allauddin's confidence. He stayed close to his unsuspecting target and waited for the right opportunity. At the opportune moment, he managed to get Allauddin and his son murdered, ending the Khilji Dynasty. Khusro Khan became the new king of Delhi albeit just for four months. Khusro Khan wanted to remove all laws that were biased against the non-Muslims. He was against taxes based on religions. He also took strong measures to prevent sex slavery that were very common during that time. It is said that Khusra Khan even insulted the Muslim nobles in his court. His policies angered the nobles. They conspired with Ghazi Malik to get rid of him. Malik was loyal to Allauddin and was sent by Allauddin to fight the Mongols. He was a very successful military leader who conquered Multan, Uch, and Sindh. When Malik attacked Delhi, the nobles secretly opened the doors to him. Khusro Khan was killed in the battle. Khan did manage to take the revenge he promised his king, but his revenge was short-lived. Ghazi Malik, a.k.a. Ghiyas ud-Din Tughluq, laid the foundation of the Tughluq Dynasty in 1321.

Fearing attack from the Mughals, Ghiyas ud-Din started building a fortified city. Tughluqabad, the fourth city of Delhi, was created as the new capital. He could not savour it for long, though. A popular Sufi saint named Hazrat Muhammad Nizamuddin Auliya was building a tank for people at the same time. The king needed men to build his city. King's guards ordered the saint to let his men work for the king instead. Auliya refused and said that the new city is doomed to become the abode of jackals. The tank was more important for the people. This angered the king, but he was in Bengal. Ghiyas ud-Din decided to deal with the saint once he was back. Fearing for the life of the saint, his followers requested him to run away from Delhi before the king returns. The saint replied, "Delhi dur hai [Delhi is yet far away]." Ghiyas ud-Din died accidentally when he was returning. A structure he hastily built to celebrate his victory over Bengal collapsed on him. To some, Ghiyas ud-Din's death was a curse of the saint; to others, it was a conspiracy by his own son Muhammad bin Tughluq.

Muhammad came to throne in 1325. His kingdom extended from Punjab to Bengal and from Delhi to Madurai. One of his governors in the south rebelled against him and declared himself sultan. But he soon realized that it was not possible to control South India from Delhi. He moved his capital to Deogir, renamed it as Daulatabad. Tughluqabad indeed was doomed, and it became the abode of jackals as Nizamuddin predicted. The Devgiri fort of the Yadavas was enlarged to create Daulatabad Fort. Roads were built, connecting Delhi to Deogir. This new city was also far away from the threat of Mughals. Many of his men were ordered to shift to the new capital. However, the distance of 1,500 kilometres proved to be fatal for the many who died while traveling the long and treacherous path. It was a mistake. Though it was easier to control south from Deogir, Muhammad was fast losing his control over north. Muhammad learned a wrong lesson from his mistake. He decided to shift his entire capital again, this time back to Delhi. This mad experiment was a big failure, and he ended up with many disgruntled men. The madness, however, managed to diffuse Turkish art and culture to south and increased the cultural interaction between the northern and southern regions of India.

Muhammad used to torture his enemies in horrible ways. Ibn Battuta wrote it down when he was there in his office. Though he was afraid of Muhammad's eccentricity, he came to Delhi in hopes of a high paying job. People were executed every day. They were skinned, cut into half, or beheaded. Treacherous leaders were captured and thrown to elephants. Sharp blades were placed on the tusks. The elephants would throw the prisoners in the air, cut them into pieces, and thrash them with their legs as drums and music were played all along. Ibn noticed that 'the sultan was far too free in shedding blood'; and he would do that without caring if the person was a noble, poor, or a scholar. At least everyone was equal in the eyes of the king. One Sufi saint was tortured and every beard plucked out hair by hair just because he refused to get involved in the king's politics. The saint only wanted to live a simple religious life. He was banished from Delhi. Later, he refused to come back to Delhi when Muhammad ordered. The saint was then captured, tortured, and beheaded. Ibn was a friend of the saint. He also married the daughter of an official in Muhammad's court who plotted a rebellion and was later executed. There was enough reason to suspect Ibn, and he was imprisoned. Ibn thought he would be executed too but was freed. To his surprise, he was sent as an ambassador to the Mongol court of China. He liked his new job because of his passion for traveling, which to him leaves you speechless and turns you into a storyteller.

Muhammad, for the first time, introduced the concept of 'token currency' in India. The Mughals in other parts of Asia already successfully implemented it. This experiment too was a failure as people soon managed to forge the currency leading to coins being greatly devalued in the market. He had to recall the token currencies. That was not his last mistake. He divided Delhi's fertile lands into separate developmental blocks, each headed by an official. The officials received money to give loan to the cultivators to grow superior crops. Inexperience and dishonesty led to the failure of this policy as well. Muhammad bin Tughluq thus became the mad king of failed reforms. It was not because his policies were wrong but because they were much ahead of his time. The failed policies led to a great famine in 1335 that lasted for seven years. His empire collapsed, but his name was never forgotten. He died on his way to Sindh to curb a rebellion.

Firoz Shah Tughlaq took over the throne of Delhi after the death of his cousin in 1351. His policies favored stability rather than expansion. He kept the nobles happy and did not try to regain the lost territories. He made a new capital and called it Firozabad, relics of which can be found in Firoz Shah Kotla. This was the fifth city of Delhi. He brought a large sandstone pillar from Ambala to Delhi that locals said belonged to Bhim. He could not dechipher the inscription written on it. The inscription was deciphered centuries after Firoz died. The pillar actually belonged to Ashoka and bore his inscription. Firoz also constructed five large canals, of which the Western Yamuna canal still exists. Ten years after his death, in 1398, Timur invaded and devastated the city once more. After 16 years of chaos, the Sayyid Dynasty took control of Delhi, claiming to be the decedents of Prophet Muhammad. They ruled as vassals to Timurs as evident from the coins. The last king of Sayyid Dynasty, Ala-ud-Din Alam Shah, gifted his throne of Delhi to his governor, Bahlul Khan Lodi, in 1451.

The rule of the Lodi Dynasty was not a strong one, and they controlled only parts of north India. His son Sikander Lodi succeeded Bahlul Khan. He was a non-tolerant king who was particularly harsh towards Hindus. His main enemy was the king of Gwalior, Maharaja Mansingh. Sikander made Agra, being closer to Gwalior, the second capital. He attacked Gwalior fort five times and failed every single time. Sikander died in 1517, with his throne passing on to his son Ibrahim Lodi. His grave still resides in Lodi Gardens, Delhi. Ibrahim was the last ruler of the sultanate who was defeated by the Mughal king Babur in the battle of Panipat in 1526.

7.6   Two Brothers

A rabbit chased a dog away—a miracle, an inspiration that help built one of the most powerful Hindu empires of medieval India. With the mighty Tungabhadra River in the north and the impassable hills in the south, Hampi was the perfect spot. Even today, it is a perfect place for the tourist. As we walked from one ruin to the other, we could feel the magnificence of the once-splendid empire that was built by two brothers after they lost not only their territories but also their religion. Having over 500,000 inhabitants, Vijayanagar Empire was the second largest city of the world in the 16th century, thrice the size of Paris. Vijayanagar means the *city of victory*. It is also known as Vidyanagara after sage Vidyaranya, one who masterminded the rise of Vijayanagar Empire. The ruins of over 500 monuments of this once-lost city are spread over 26 square kilometres of area in and around Hampi (figure 12).

Hampi is a place filled with mythological events. The place takes its name from the original name of Tungabhadra River, Pampa. Pampa, Brahma's daughter, was a devotee of Shiva. Impressed with her devotion, Shiva asked her for a wish. All she wanted was to marry him, and Shiva could not refuse. During their marriage, gods showered golds, from which was formed Hemakuta Hills. Hemakuta literally means a *heap of god*. Vijayanagara Empire was built on the south of the Tungabhadra River, while on its north lay the ancient land of Kishkinda—the abode of monkey gods. Anjaneya Hill in Kishkinda is the birthplace of Hanuman. The first thing that is going to catch your eye in Kishkinda is it's breathtaking landscape. The large boulders scattered around, similar but grander than Alabama, is going to make you wonder what happened here. Legend has it that the boulders made their way here because of the war between Bali and Sugreeva, fighting for the throne of Monkey Kingdom. During the fight, they threw boulders at each other that got piled up all around. The boring truth, however, is that the unusual landscape formed by millions of years of (spheroidal) erosion of the granites, solidified acidic magma, that formed billions of years ago below the surface of Hampi.

The brothers, Harihara Raya I and Bukka Raya I, were commanders in the army of Hoysala Empire. They were defeated and taken as prisoners by Muhammad Tughlaq. Both of them converted to Islam and joined Muhammad's army. When Muhammad went back to North India, there were many rebellions in the south. The brothers were sent south to restore order. Instead, they gave up Islam and created an independent kingdom. Sage Vidyaranya helped the brothers convert back to Hinduism and guided them to become efficient rulers. According to local legend, the great saint asked the brothers to choose a spot where they would establish their kingdom. While travelling together, the brothers saw a small courageous rabbit chasing away a dog that definitely looked more powerful than the rabbit. The brothers decided to build their empire in that place. They were the small rabbit with a dream of chasing away the powerful invaders. The empire soon grew big and powerful and came to be known as the Vijayanagara Empire.

Harihara was crowned in 1336 and was later succeeded by his brother Bukka I in 1356. His son Kumara Kampana established Hindu rule far south of India defeating the Sultan of Madurai. Under Krishna Deva Raya, who reigned from 1509 to 1529, Vijayanagara Empire became the most powerful empire in the subcontinent that lasted for two centuries. He was often known as the destroyers of Turks. Krishna Deva extended his kingdom to Andhra Pradesh, Odisha, and even parts of Bengal. It was under him that most of the temples and palaces were built. One can understand from the temples that his rule was a secular one. There were many Muslim officers in his army. Art and literature flourished under Krishna Deva Raya. He had eight great court poets called *astadiggagas* (after the mythological eight, or *asta*; elephants, or *gagas*, which hold the earth from eight directions, or *dig*). The famous and witty Tenali Rama was one of the court poets. The key enemy of Vijayanagar was the Bahmani Kingdom founded by Afghan adventurer Alauddin Hasan after revolts against

Muhammad Tughlaq. Many wars were fought between Vijayanagar and Bahmani for the control of fertile Krishna Godavari basin, not something new in the history of this area. Bahmani Kingdom collapsed after they were badly defeated by Krishna Deva Raya.

After demise of Krishna Deva, the Vijayanagara Empire started to decline. The sultans had been on the back foot for many years. Now they finally decided to unite against Vijayanagara Empire. The first battle was fought in 1564 where the sultans suffered a heavy defeat. The sultans of the surrounding regions regrouped and attacked a year later with a much bigger army. In this famous battle of Talikota, millions are said to have participated in the war. Vijayanagara again had the upper hand until two Muslim officers in Vijayanagara army turned against them. The confusion in the Vijayanagara camp had finally led to their defeat. The king Rama Raya was captured and beheaded, and his brother fled with royal treasure. Thus came to end the last powerful Hindu Empire of South India. The capital city of Vijayanagar Empire was plundered and looted. With time, the City of Victory was lost in history.

7.7   Parrot of India

Saifuddin was a Turkish officer who fled from Samarkand, during the Mongol raids, to Balkh. Iltutmish invited him to Delhi. He got married to the daughter of King Balban's war minister. They had four children, one of whom went on to become a famous Sufi musician, poet, and scholar. His name was Amir Khusrow. Khusrow was a disciple of Hazrat Muhammad Nizamuddin Auliya, the famous sufi saint of Chishti order who believed that one can reach God through renunciation of the world and service to humanity. Once Auliya wanted to put his disciples to test. Accompanied by his disciples he went to a bothel. The students waited downstairs. The prostitute was pleased to see the great saint. She asked what service she can provide. Auliya told her to tell her maid to bring water in a liquor bottle so that his students could see. The disciples were shocked that their teacher went to a prostitute and drank alcohol. Ashamed, they slowly started to leave. By the time Auliya came down, only one of his disciple was left. It was Amir Khusrow. When asked why he did not leave, Khusrow replied, "O Master! I might have left, but where could I have gone except towards your lotus feet?" Auliya was glad to find a true follower and said with a smile, "Your wait is now over. You are accomplished."

Khusrow is often called the father of *qawwali*. He also introduced the famous *gazal* style of song in India. It was Khusrow who invented the popular musical instrument *tabla*. He also composed many famous poems, including the famous 'Layla and Majnun'. Amir Khusrow did not believe in the rigidity of religion. He said, "I am a pagan and a worshipper of love. The creed [or Muslims] I do not need; every vein of mine become taunt like a wire. The [Brahmin's] girdle I do not need." Because of his melodious poems and music, he was called the parrot of India. The Sufi version of Islam was liberal and compatible with the Bhakti movement of the Hindus. It became very popular in India. Khusrow died in 1325, six months after the death of Hazrat Nizamuddin Auliya, but not before revolutionizing Indian music.

There was another person who was bringing revolution in Hinduism. Bishwanbhar was born in a Brahmin family of Odissa. He, along with his family, migrated to Sylhet and, from there, to Nabadwip in Bengal. In 1510, Bishwanbhar left his home and wife to become a saint. He took the name of Shri Krishna Chaitanya. He opposed caste system and ritualistic practices. Some orthodix Brahmins and qazis opposed him and complained to the sultan of Bengal. Sultan Hussain Shah was a secular king, and he realized after enquiry that Chaitanya was a man of god. The king warned, "Let him engage himself happily with others in kirtan or stay in seclusion if his mind so desires. If anybody troubles him, whether qazi or kotwal, he will pay with his life." [36] Chaitanya believed Krishna as the only god, and complete devotion to him through love and chanting was the path to liberation. He sang, "Chant the Name of the Lord and his glory unceasingly. That the mirror of the heart may be wiped clean." He spent most of his later life in Jagannath, Puri. Under him, the Vaishnava tradition of Bhakti Cult was revived.

7.8   The Sultanate Rule

The sultanate rule of over 300 years was a strange one. It was a period of change socially, culturally, and architecturally. Hinduism became more rigid after the invasions. Al-Biruni wrote, "The repugnance of the Hindus against foreigners increased more and more when the Muslims began to make inroads into the country." He agreed that Mahmud of Ghazni 'utterly ruined the prosperity of the country' and created a hatred of Muslims amongst the locals. Indians have already seen the fate of Buddhists and Zoroastrians after the rise of Islamic kingdoms beyond their western border. The invasions and brutal assault on their culture by the invaders have made them intolerant even towards secular Muslims like Al-Biruni. While acknowledging the excellent philosophers, mathematicians, and astronomers of India, Al-Biruni also noticed that the Hindus believed that there was no country, king, religion, or science better than theirs. They withhold their knowledge from foreigners and also people of other caste. Such orthodoxy resulted from the invasions. Al-Biruni adds, "Their ancestors were not as narrow-minded as the present generation is."

Purdah, the practice of covering women's face with a veil in presence of strangers to prevent vulgar gaze, became a normal practice. Purdah was common among women of Iran and Greece, later adopted by Arabs and Turks, and finally transferred to India [88]. Like most things, India assimilated that too. The caste system was already very dominant. People of different castes did not intermix. The caste system of Hindus slowly started to penetrate into the Muslim society as well, adding to their ethnic divisions of Turks, Iranians, Afghans, and Indian Muslims.

The rulers of Delhi Sultanate, though not all, had often been intolerant towards those of other faith. Sharia became the law of states ruled by Muslim rulers. Sharia meant the 'right path' in Arabic. It was the law in all Muslim-ruled kingdoms. According to Sharia law, Jizya tax was imposed on the non-Muslims. The money was taken as a promise of protection. Those who could not pay the tax were either killed or enslaved. The tax was meant to promote conversion. However, since the tax brought a lot of revenue, some kings prohibited conversion. Building of new monastries, churches, or temples were prohibited as per the Sharia Law. The second-class status made Hindus feel unwelcome in their own land. The Muslims, though they enjoyed the power in the areas they ruled, were outnumbered and surrounded by a culture largely alien and hostile to them. The turmoil gave life to the Bhakti movement. According to it, the only path towards salvation was complete devotion to god. Salvation was the solution to the troubles, of which there were plenty. The movement started in south India and soon spread north. This extreme devotional form of Hinduism, still very common among the Indians, can be credited to the saints like Sankardeva, Vallabhacharya, Chaitanya Mahaprabhu, and Kabir. The Bhakti movement, along with the Sufi movement, helped in diffusing the tensions between the two communities.

Islam spread rapidly in areas, like Bengal and Kashmir, where the Islamic oppression was less and Islam was flexible enough to mould itself to local customs. In places, like Delhi, where there was a strong hold of Islamic rulers and Islam was rigid, it did not find many followers. In Bengal the Muslims learnt Sanskrit and composed literature in Bengali with Hindu theme. Early invaders of Bengal did break temples and created mosques (like Adina mosque) from the broken pieces of the temples. But kings like Hussain Shah of Gaur (Bengal) were liberal and created an environment where Hindu saints like Chaitanya Mahaprabhu could flourish. He was loved by his people and often called as the reincarnation of Krishna. Under the rule of liberal Muslim rulers, Satyanarayana of Hindus became Satyapir of Muslims. As per the story of *Shunya Puran, Dharma* becomes the savior of Muslims and "Brahman became prophet, Vishnu became Paigambar (a prophet), Shiva became Adam, Ganesh became Gazi, Kartik became Qazi, Goddess Chandi became Eve and Padmavati became Prophet's daughter Fatima." [36]

There were four major groups of Muslims in India. The first group was those who emigrated from Iran, Turkey, and Arab. The second group of people was those who were forcefully converted. The third group consisted of those who converted willfully for jobs and better opportunities and to evict the *Jizya* tax. The final group was those who liked the new religion. They were either lower-caste Hindus who were oppressed by the upper-caste Brahmins or the Buddhists who, like in Islam, did not believe in caste system and idol worship. Many of these Buddhists converted to Hinduism during the rule of Sena Dynasty. Now they wanted to convert back to a religion that was closer to Buddhism. India was going to change once more as new group of people joined the journey of survivors.

The Era of Mongols (1500 to 1700 CE)

[India during Akbar's rule] was a vast, mighty and
magnificent empire, brilliantly organized and culturally
unified, which dominated a massive swathe of earth.

—Alex von Tunzelmann, *Indian Summer*

8.1   The Wrath of Genghis

An interesting study done in 2011 by Julia Pongratz revealed how Genghis (Chingis is probably close to original; Genghis is the name we are more accustomed to) Khan helped cool the earth [92]. Genghis Khan has been one of the most brutal invaders the world has ever known. He attacked and destroyed numerous villages and is said to have killed over 40 million people. Vast lands that were under cultivation became vacant, helping forests take over. The study claims that the reforestation event had helped absorb 700 million tons of carbon from the atmosphere.

That had cooled down the earth considerably. Apart from killing, he also took the beautiful women from different regions he conquered. No wonder, one in every 200 men alive today is related to the great Khan. Genghis Khan, however, was more than just a brutal killer. He was a true leader, one who united the different tribes of Mongols and created one of the largest empires that covered around 22 per cent of the earth's surface.

Mongols comprised of many different hunting and gathering tribes, in constant war against one another. Had it not been for Genghis Khan, the name of the tribes would have been lost in the pages of history. Surviving from the jaws of death, he united the tribes into the most powerful army of its time. He was born in the middle of 12th century as Temujin to Yesügei, leader of the Borjigin clan. It is said that he was born with a clot of blood in his hand, ominous signs for his future. The Tartars, an enemy clan, killed his father when he was just 9 years old. Borjigin clan refused to accept Yesügei's young sons as their leader. A new leader was chosen. Temujin's family was abandoned and left to die of cold and starvation. Despite the odds, Temujin's family managed to survive in the wild. [93]

During the exile Temujin killed his eldest brother in a fight over the spoils of their hunting game, making him the leader of his family. He was later captured by one of the enemy Mongol clans. Temujin managed to escape from the clutches of his enemy. The great escape made him famous. In Mongolia fame was exactly what was needed to gain followers. He married Borte of the Onggirat tribe, as already arranged by his father. The marriage and the resulting alliance gave him political power. Borte was captured by the Merkit clan of Monguls and raped before Temujin could rescue her. Though Temujin took many wives later, Borte remained his only empress.

Temujin's strength and success in raids had already earned him recognition amongst the Mongols. He slowly, but steadily, grew in power by allying with other tribes. Father killed, family betrayed by their own clan, and wife raped, Temujin knew that the only way to peace was blood. There was a desperate need to unite all the different Mongol clans into one group, and that's exactly what Temujin sought. He fiercely attacked and conquered the tribes who did not ally with him, and then made their people his own. By 1206, he managed to unite Merkits, Naimans, Mongols, Keraits, Tatars, Uyghurs, and many other smaller tribes. Temujin thus became Genghis Khan, one who brought peace to plains of Mongol. Peace, however, would soon become a luxury for the rest of the world.

The first country to feel the heat of Genghis was China. Western Xia Dynasty shared its border with the Mongol Empire and was a threat. After repeated attacks, Genghis finally managed to break through in 1209 and conquer them. His next target was the big fish: Jin Dynasty. Mongols had long been vassals to them. Now it was time to turn the tables. By 1215, Genghis managed to sack Beijing. Soon the Kara-Khitan Khanate of Western Liao fell too, extending Genghis's empire up to Lake Balkhash, which bordered the Khwarezmid Empire. Muhammad Ghori was assassinated after establishing the first sultanate in India. After his death, Khwarezmid Empire replaced the Ghurid Dynasty. They controlled the important trade routes, and Genghis wanted them to be his trading partner. He had no intention to expand his kingdom any further; all he wanted was a diplomatic relationship that could create wealth for him and his people. Genghis sent a 500-man caravan to

Khwarezmid king, Shah to establish a tie. As Shah claimed them to be spies, the caravan was attacked by Khwarezmid army. Considering it a mistake, Genghis Khan sent a second group of administrators, including a Muslim, to meet the governor of Khwarezmid Empire. It seemed that the Shah had no interest in the diplomatic tie. He shaved all three men and beheaded the Muslim ambassador. This foolish act would unleash the fury of Genghis, and the world would not be the same again.

Genghis Khan gathered all his men and personally led the campaign, one of the largest invasion campaigns under him. It would also be one of the deadliest. The great Khan declared, "I am the punishment of God. . . . If you had not committed great sins, God would not have sent a punishment like me upon you." Khwarezmid Empire fell, and Shah fled. Many from their army ran away and joined the Delhi Sultanate. There was a large-scale massacre of civilians. The entire city, along with the villages, was destroyed. While returning, Genghis divided his men into two groups. He returned through Afghanistan while the other group came back through Caucasus and Russia. Both armies destroyed every civilization they found on their path. The only loss Genghis's men suffered in the entire campaign was against Volga Bulgaria. After the victories, Genghis Khan became the most powerful person of his time. Genghis Khan died four years later in the August of 1227. The exact cause of his death is unknown, just like the location of his graveyard. As per the traditions of Mongols, his burial place was kept a secret.

Genghis Khan was not just a soldier but also a visionary. He was tolerant towards all religion, something that was rare in other parts of the world at that time. His battles were more political than religious. He also attempted to create a civil state where every man and woman shared equal status. Differences were based on merit and not birth. It was just the beginning, and the Mongol Empire would continue to grow under his successors.

8.2   Timur the Lame

Genghis's successors continued the expansion of his empire. Korea was conquered in 1235, followed by Russia, Poland, Hungary, and southern China. The Mongol Empire spread from Central Europe to Sea of Japan and became the largest adjoining land empire in history. After centuries of violence, Eurasia finally saw a period of peace under the unified Mongol rule. Trading flourished due to the stability along the Mongol controlled Silk Route. The connection between the western and eastern empires became efficient. The Mongols established Yam, the first postal system connecting east with west. This was the beginning of globalization.

The expansion of Mongols had dramatic effect on the Islamic world. They ruined most of the Muslim cities, leaving behind just carcasses. The wrath of Genghis almost destroyed Islamic states. It was only the Baibars who could stop the Mongols when they defeated the latter in 1260. Apart from the empire of Great Khan in China, the Mongols built four separate empires in Asia. The Mongol clans were not biased by religion, and they preferred to build their empire on the local traditions. In China, they became like the Chinese, and the four other empires got converted in Islam as per their local tradition. The liberal attitude of Mongols led to the flourish of Sufi saints like Rumi who believed in the validity of all religions. However, the deadly

Mongol attacks left many Muslims insecure, and they became conservative. Muslim madrassas became strict, Koran became the only truth, and non-Muslims were barred from visiting holy cities. Much was lost in the attack, and many Islamic texts were burnt. The conservative groups tried hard to protect whatever was left. [77]

The Mongol empire started to decline in the 14th century with the rise of conflict between the different groups. What also aided the fall of the giant was one of the most devastating pandemics in human history: the Black Death. The cause of Black Death (1348–1358) is still a mystery but is said to have its origin in China. The flourish of Silk Route for trading under the Mongols also helped in transferring the infected rats from China to Europe. This triggered the pandemic that wiped out more the 50 million people. Black Death changed the course of European history. The rapid growth of population in Europe was straining the resources, leading to malnutrition. The dramatic reduction of population after Black Death meant that a huge amount of resource was left behind for the smaller number of survivors via inheritance or loot. The lack of labor led to the end of feudal system, and the increase in wealth of individuals led to better lifestyle. The struggle also made Europeans question god and religion at a time when Islamic world was becoming more conservative. Black Death changed the course of not only European history but also that of the Mongols. It accelerated their decline, and instability returned in Central Asia until one man started to unite the Mongols once again.

Timur was born a Muslim to the Turko-Mongol Barlas Tribe in 1336. An invading group of Mongols captured him and his family and took them to Samarkand. He and his small band grew up raiding travellers. During one such raid, he was shot by two arrows. One chopped off two of his fingers, and the other made him lame. Despite the odds, he gained prominence as a military leader due to his intellectual tactics. He could not call himself a Khan, the supreme title of the Mongols, as he was not a direct descendant of Genghis. Instead, he married a direct descendant of Genghis Khan to make himself qualify as their heir. Similarly, he could not claim to be a caliph, the supreme title of the Islamic world, as he was not a direct descendant of Muhammad. However, he acted as a protector of Islam, one ordained by god for the prosperity of Islamic World. Timur was an opportunist, and he converted his disadvantages to his advantage and managed to unite both the Islamic world and the world of the Mongols. His military success added to his cause, and by 1387, he conquered the whole of Persia. His deadly campaigns had wiped out about 5 per cent of world population of that time. He was feared throughout Europe, Africa, and Asia. Timur's next target was India.

Delhi Sultanate had been fairly successful in keeping the Mongols at bay. Khilji built the whole city of Siri over the corpses of thousands of Mongols. However, the Delhi Sultanate was now weak and vulnerable while the Mongols had been rejuvenated. Timur's attack on India was brutal even by his own standards. He justified his attacks on India as a religious war against a country that followed un-Islamic faith. He captured and massacred the cities in Pakistan on his way to Delhi. Delhi was one of the richest cities of the time. There he faced the army of Mahmud Shah Tughluq and his fierce elephants. Timur's army was afraid of the giants that were well armored and had poison in their tusks. Timur, being the cunning tactician that he was, had just the right idea to counter the elephants:

his camels. He loaded the camels with wood and then set them ablaze. The camels ran towards the elephants. The elephants panicked and turned back towards the defense of Tughluq. The chaos helped Timur put an end to the Delhi Sultanate. Delhi was captured, people massacred, and the city was left in ruins once more. Timur went back with all his loots leaving behind the Sayyids as his vassals. He kept expanding his empire until he died at an old age of 68 years while trying to attack the Ming Dynasty of China. He made the desperate attack during harsh winters. An aged Timur could not survive the extreme cold weather.

In 1941 a Soviet anthropologist brought out Timur's body from his tomb in Samarkand. The body confirmed Timur's wounds. Timur was tall and well built. A warning written in his tomb read, "When I rise from the dead, the world shall tremble." There was, however, an even more dangerous message inside the casket. It read, "Whomsoever opens my tomb shall unleash an invader more terrible than I." Quite ironically, just a couple of days later, Hitler invaded the Soviet Union [94].

8.3   Babur's Brawls

In Samarkand, Timur's descendants were fighting over what was left of the once great empire. Meanwhile, three other forces were gaining strength in Asia. The Turko-Mongol Uzbeks who converted to Islam, the Safavid Dynasty of Iran who claimed to be descendants of the prophet, and the Ottoman Empire of Turkey. The Ottomans were once defeated badly by Timur, but they were regaining their strength and would soon turn into one of the most powerful empires that lasted from the 15th century to the

World War I. The stage was set for another conflict between the rising empires, and for the Mongols to come to India.

Babur was a descendant of Genghis Khan through his mother and of Timur through his father, the king of Fergana. With a legacy like that, it is hardly a surprise that his ambitions matched those of his forefathers. Babur wanted to be the king of Samarkand and sit on the throne of his powerful ancestors. His father's sudden demise gave him the crown at the very young age of 13 years. It also made him the target of those who lusted for that crown. He wished that he could run away to the mountains and was not shy of confessing it years later when he wrote *Baburnama*, the first true autobiography by a Muslim king.

Babur was a brutal conqueror whose life had been filled with battles. He massacred many villages while conquering Delhi. He is said to have destroyed a temple in Ayodhya and erect a mosque over it. The mosque was in turn demolished in the winter of 1992 by Hindu fanatics, triggering communal clashes throughout India. Inscriptions in the mosque show that it was erected not by Babur but by one of his generals. It is also possible that the general repaired an old mosque and dedicated it to his king. The old mosque might have been built over a temple, but then who knows the truth? Truth takes a backseat when politics, religion, and history get comingled. Truth, however, was something Babur was not afraid of as he openly confessed his life in his autobiography. He wrote about his persistent wish for coming to India; he spoke of his dislike of this alien land once he came here; he wrote of his affection for a young market boy; he spoke of the wars, of women's chambers where he went for advice, and of his fondness for wines and melons. The king wrote, "My own soul is my most faithful friend. My own heart, my truest confidant." By nature, he was more Mongol than a Turk.

Babur came very close to his dream of being the king of Samarkand more than once. He was able to conquer Samarkand in 1497. However, he had to return to Farghana to stop the mutiny caused by his treacherous brother. As Babur took his army and attacked Farghana, he lost control of Samarkand to the rival prince. He ended up losing both kingdoms. Four years later, he attacked Samarkand again and won. This time the Uzbek leader Muhammad Shaybani Khan dethroned him. Shaybani Khan ran over the rest of the Timur's Empire, forcing Babur to move to Kabul, which the latter conquered in 1504. Babur wondered where these Uzbeks came from. He wondered how he lost his ancestors' land to these barbarians.

Shaybani Khan captured Babur's sister and forcefully married her. Babur allied with Safavid king Shah Ismail to defeat Shaybani. Shah Ismail, was a Shiite and enemies of Sunni Uzbeks. He killed Shaybani Khan in a famous battle near Merv and made Babur the King of Samarkand for the third time. Shah made a golden cup fashioned from Shaybani's skull, and the stuffed skin of his head was presented to the Ottoman Turks as a warning. Babur was reunited with his sister. As fate would have it, Babur lost Samarkand once more to the Uzbeks after the latter allied with the Ottomans. The Ottoman rulers killed Shah Ismail, leaving Babur with no hope of reconquering Samarkand. Babur's only option was to look towards India for wealth and protection. In the beginning, he only wanted to capture Punjab, the land once ruled by his ancestor Timur. But that brought him in direct confrontation with the Lodi Dynasty. This led to the first Battle of Panipat in 1526. Though Babur's army was outnumbered, they had the power of gunpowder that they have received from the Ottoman Empire. Ibrahim Lodi was not prepared for this new weapon of destruction, and he died in the battle. Babur became the first Mughal ('Mughal' is used to represent the Indian Empire rather than 'Mongol') king of Delhi.

The Battle of Panipat laid the foundation of the great Mughal Empire in India. However, Babur's rule was still far from being established as he faced new challenges. Rana Sanga was an ambitious Rajput king of Mewar. He conquered Malwa, Ranthambore, and won many battles against Ibrahim Lodi. Rana captured much of Rajasthan and was pushing towards Agra. Initially, he allied with Babur to defeat Lodi, hoping that Babur will leave India just like Timur. However, Babur's intentions of staying back meant that the battle between Rana and Babur was now inevitable. Rana's reputation made Babur's soldiers weary. To inspire them, Babur declared jihad. Babur, a person who was addicted to wine and opium, became a staunch Muslim overnight by breaking his bottles of wine. Religion was the excuse he uses to inspire his followers. He banned the consumption of wine within his empire and abolished customs tax for Muslims.

The fateful battle between Rana and Babur eventually took place in Khanwa on 1527. Rana made fierce attacks on Babur's right wing, almost breaching it when Babur's artillery forced them back. The critical moment came when the Tomar Rajput king Raja Shiladitya betrayed Rana and switched sides. The confusion divided the Rajput armies and eventually led to the defeat of Rana. Rana managed to escape but was poisoned by his own men, securing Babur's throne in India. After a long gap in history, Afghanistan was once again ruled from Delhi. It gave India back the added security from invasions and thus political stability.

Babur died at the age of 47 due to a serious illness. It is said that when his favorite son Humayun had fallen ill, he prayed for his son's health in exchange for his own life. His prayers were answered. Humayun recovered, but Babur became bedridden. He died soon, and his body was buried in Kabul, as per his wish.

8.4   Humayun's Tussles

His father shaped an empire; his son took it to its zenith, but he almost lost it to an Afghan general. Humayun, it is said, was a bit eccentric. He believed that there were hidden messages written in the stars and even wore dresses of specific color on specific days to get lucky. He was addicted to opium like his father, which could be a reason for his eccentricity. Humayun was also a decent and polite man, which earned him the title of Insān-i-Kamil (Perfect Man) among the Mughals. His father's sudden death meant that the new Moghul kingdom was now divided between the two brothers as per Mongol customs. Humayun ruled northern India while his half-brother Kamran Mirza ruled Kabul and Lahore. Humayun's main rivals were Bahadur Shah of Gujarat and Sher Shah of Bengal.

Bahadur Shah was fighting his own battles with not just the Mughals on land but also the Portuguese coming through the sea. The Portuguese were creating the first global empire. As a continuation of the Crusades, they fought and conquered southern Spain from the Moors. The success was a beginning of a new era of European colonialism. They were looking to control the trade routes, especially the spice trade of Asia. It started with exploration and exploitation of the African coasts. Vasco da Gama finally made his way to India in 1498. Helped by Indian traders he landed in Calicut, Kerala. Taking advantage of local rivalry, the Portuguese established their base in India and built Fort Kochi. In 1509 they won a decisive battle in Diu and established a firm base there. A year later, Goa was taken, helping the Portuguese dominate the marine trade in Indian Ocean. Portuguese dominion of India was established in Goa with help of king Krishna Deva Raya of Vijayanagara Empire. Krishna Deva allied with Portuguese against the Sultans who were in turn supported by the Ottoman Empire. The echoes of the fight between the Christian Europe and Muslim Middle East were heard on Indian soil.

Bahadur Shah ascended the throne in 1526. He conquered Malwa, Chittor, and Ajmer, making him a threat Humayun could not ignore. Humayun attacked Shah and conquered Malwa and Gujarat. Bahadur Shah fled from the battlefield and made peace with the Portuguese after conceding Daman, Diu, Mumbai, and Vasai to them. Bahadur's empire shrank as fast as it grew. He was killed by the Portuguese in 1537 that led to the siege of Diu a year later. It was a battle fought between the Ottoman Empire and the Portuguese on India soil which the latter won. Diu would never again be part of India until 1961 when the Indian Army launched a massive air, land, and naval attack on the Portuguese and won a vital victory.

While Humayun was busy in Gujarat, Sher Shah consolidated his rule in Bengal and Bihar. Other Afghan groups joined him. With the western part of his empire secured, Humayun could now look eastward. Humayun attacked and captured Chunar after a hard fought battle that lasted for six months. Sher Shah, meanwhile, moved east and captured Gaur. Humayun followed him to Bengal.

Sher Shah slipped away once again, this time to south Bihar. While Humayun was busy in Bengal, his brother was looking towards the throne of Agra. Humayun had to hastily leave for Agra in order to save his throne before getting rid of Sher Shah. Though Humayun managed to save his throne in Delhi, it would prove to be a costly mistake.

In 1539 Humayun and Sher Shah finally met in the battle of Chausa on the bank of Ganges. Sher Shah chose the battlefield strategically in a swampy area to neutralize the heavy Moghul artilleries. Literally knee deep in mud, Humayun sought a diplomatic solution through Muhammad Aziz. Humayun agreed to let Sher Shah rule Bengal and Bihar but only as provinces granted by him. As per the agreement, Humayun's army was supposed to charge at the Sher Shah, and the latter was supposed to act as if they were running away. The agreement worked as per plan, and the Moghul army relaxed after their assumed victory. Sher Shah, however, had other plans. He returned and attacked that very night, surprising Babur's army. The Moghuls were slaughtered. Humayun just managed to escape alive and reach Agra. Had he died, it would have been the end of Moghul rule in India.

Tables were turned, and it was Sher Shah who was now chasing Humayun. He attacked Humayun at Kanauj. Moghul army was no match for the Afghans. Agra was lost and Humayun fled to Lahore. Sher Shah was still not satisfied. He followed Humayun until the latter had no choice but to retreat farther west into his brother's territory. Humayun's brother had no interest in welcoming him, leaving the king without a kingdom. Humayun wandered across the tough terrains at a time when his wife was pregnant. Soon after Humayun's wife gave birth to a son, Humayun's brother captured the baby. The young kid grew up in his uncle's house while his parents took shelter in the court of an Iranian king.

Sher Shah was the new king of northern India ruling from Bengal to Indus. He was an able administrator who reestablished law and order in northern India. Sher Shah renovated and extended the Grand Trunk road, improving the communication across India. His new policies helped trade and commerce flourish. The strict, and sometimes harsh, laws imposed by Sher Shah meant that there were hardly any theft, robbery, or murder across the trade routes. He introduced the three metal currencies made of gold known as mohur, silver known as rupiah, and copper as dam. One mohur was 169 grams, and one rupiah was 178 grams. Rupiah is still used as a currency in India, along with Pakistan, Nepal, Sri Lanka, Indonesia, Mauritius, Maldives, and Seychelles. He also built many forts including the Rohtas Fort in Pakistan, Old Fort of Delhi, and Rohtasgarh Fort in Bihar. Some of his policies were continued by Akbar, which helped the later in consolidating the Moghul Empire. Sher Shah's rule was however cut short by his accidental death. He died from an accidental gunpowder explosion in his own camp while trying to siege Kalinjar fort in 1545. His son Ismail Shah Suri succeeded him. Ismail died nine years later, ending the Sur Dynasty.

8.5 Guru's Message

When Babar and Humayun were busy creating a vast empire, there was another man whose sole aim was to heal the earth. His name was Guru Nanak, and he was born in an era when chaos prevailed in the subcontinent. Different powers, both internal and external, were trying to get a piece of whatever was left of this wealthy land. Babur imprisoned Guru Nanak when the later sacked Multan. The guards soon realized that Nanak was no ordinary man but a true saint. The news spread to Babur, who personally came and visited the Guru. Babur took blessings from Nanak and granted him liberty.

Nanak was born in 1469 in western Punjab, now in Pakistan. He received education from both Hindu priests and Muslim maulvis. One day, at the age of 30, he vanished while taking a bath in a river. After searching for days, his family gave up hope and thought that he was dead. On the fourth day, he appeared, much to the surprise of his family including his wife and sons. However, their happiness did not last long. Nanak was now a changed man and has already taken the first steps towards his long journey in quest of spiritual harmony. Nanak realized that Hindu and Muslims are one and the same; they are not two different entities. Only fools fight in the name of religion. Religion was meant for peace and harmony, not war and destruction. It was a powerful message that he wanted to spread around the world:

> Owing to ignorance of the rope the rope appears to be a snake; owing to ignorance of the self the transient state arises of the individualized, limited, phenomenal aspect of the self. (Guru Nanak)

Guru Nanak left his family and went around the world, spreading the message of peace. Nanak got ample support in his spiritual quest from his sister Bibi Nanaki. He undertook four major journeys in four directions between

1500 and 1524. Bhai Bala and Bhai Mardana accompanied him in his journey. His first journey was to Bengal and Assam, and then he went up to Sri Lanka in the south. His third travel took him as far north as Kashmir, Laddak, and Tibet. His final journey was westwards to Baghdad, Mecca, Medina, and Arabian Peninsula. In one such journey, a small village invited them. The villagers were very nice to Nanak and his companions. They listened to his sermons and honoured the guests. While leaving, Nanak cursed them by saying, "Be uprooted and dispersed!" They then came across another village. The villagers were unfriendly and hostile. While leaving that village, Nanak blessed them, "Stay safe, stay here, and prosper!" Bhai Mardana and Bhai Bala were surprised by the unfair behaviour of their guru. They asked him why he cursed the good villagers and blessed the rude ones. To that, Nanak said, "If the good villagers were uprooted, then they would spread around the world, teaching their good behaviour. The rude ones should stay where they are. Similarly, if the good ones stayed in a small village forever, it would be unfair to the world. If the rude ones spread, they will cause havoc wherever they would go. Now tell me if I was unfair."

Guru Nanak's teachings have three main pillars:

Vand Chakko: Sharing with others whatever you have

Kirat Karo: Earn your living in an honest way

Naam Japo: Sing hymns for the god

According to his teachings, all gods are one and the same. *Vahiguru*, or god, is omnipresent, *nirankar* (shapeless), *akaal* (timeless), and *alekh* (once who cannot be perceived).

Nanak revolted against the Hindu caste system and against the Brahmins who exploited the lower castes. He also went against the Muslim kings who killed people in the name of religion. Nanak said, "Even Kings and emperors with heaps of wealth and vast dominion cannot compare with an ant filled with the love of God." While his main aim was to unite Hindus and Muslims, he angered the powerful people of both communities. Not everyone was open to the new message their closed minds failed to grasp. Nanak died at an age of 70 years in the year 1539 and was succeeded by Guru Angad.

The poems that he wrote were in Punjabi, which inhibited the religion to spread outside Punjab. The message, however, was loud and clear.

Religion lieth not in visiting tombs

Nor in visiting places where they burn the dead

Nor in sitting entranced in contemplation

Nor in wandering in countryside or foreign lands

Nor in bathing at places of pilgrimage.

If thou must the path of true religion see,

Amongst the world's impurities, be of impurities free. (Guru Nanak) [83]

After reading this section, my friend Maddy said, "In the mad frenzy of conquests and bloodlust, Guru Nanak comes as sweet summer rain upon the parched Earth." I agree.

8.6 The Return of the King

A son was born to Humayun and Hamida Banu Begam on 14 October 1542. The baby, named Jalal ud-din, was born inside the Rajput fortress of Umarkot. Only a year later, Humayun had to flee to Iran with his wife after his brother attacked. Humayun's brother Askari kidnapped their son. Jalal ud-din was kept in his uncle's palace as his father prepared to get him back. In Iran, Humayun developed good relations with the Persians. With help from the Persians, Humayun gathered a strong army. In 1545 Humayun started to move with his army towards Qandahar. Askari, on getting the news, sent Jalal ud-din to Kabul in the custody of Humayun's other brother, Kamran. Jalal ud-din grew up in Kabul under the guidance of his foster mother Maham Anga. He learned to hunt and fight but received no formal education. His illiteracy, however, did not hinder his hunger for knowledge.

Kamran once bought a painted drum meant for his son, Ibrahim Mirza, on the occasion of Shab-i-Barat. Jalal ud-din developed a liking for it. Ibrahim was older and stronger. Kamran got a perfect opportunity to humiliate Jalal ud-din and, through him, his much-loathed brother Humayun. Kamran called for a wrestling match between Ibrahim and Jalal ud-din. Winner gets the drum. Jalal ud-din was just 3 years old, and much to the surprise of all, he defeated Ibrahim [95]. It was an ominous sign for

Kamran. But for Humayun, it was the beginning of good times. Humayun conquered Qandahar and Askari was sent to Hajj. He then marched into Kabul and was reunited with his son just 17 days since that wrestling match. Humayun, despite persuasion by his people to kill him, had Kamran blinded and sent to Mecca. The king got back his throne. Humayun's greatest rival Sher Shah was also dead, and Delhi was fragile again.

His most able and trusted military commander, Bairam Khan, helped Humayun in his quest for Delhi. Humayun honored him as Khan Khanan, or king of kings. After two hard-fought battles, Humayun reconquered Delhi in 1555 [88]. While Babur's rule in India was short, Humayun's was even shorter. Humayun died on January 1556 when his son was away, fighting the Afghans in Punjab. He was on the roof of his library, trying to see the rise of Venus, when he heard the call for evening prayer. As he hurried down the stairs, his leg got entangled in his trouser, and he toppled over. Not a fancy way for a king to die. His death was kept a secret till Jalal ud-din returned. On 14 February 1556, Jalal ud-din was crowned king at the tender age of 13 years. Since he was young, it was Bairam Khan who ruled on his behalf till Jalal ud-din became the Akbar we all know.

A 10-year-old Akbar painted a body with all its part scattered. When asked what he drew, he replied Hemu. Hemu's reputation was known throughout the subcontinent. He was the most serious threat to the Mughal ambition. Hemu, a.k.a. Hem Chandra Vikramaditya, started as a cereal supplier to Sher Shah's army. He became the superintendent of market under Islam Shah. Then he rapidly rose to the position of prime minister under Adil Shah. Hemu was never defeated in the twenty-two battles he fought against the Afghan rebels and the Moghuls from

Punjab to Bengal. This included the famous battle of Delhi against Akbar's army. Most of his battles were fought from Gwalior Fort. His success made him popular among both the Hindus and the Muslim Afghans. They united under Hemu against the Moghuls, who were foreigners to this land. Again, the wars that were fought were not communal but political. Hemu became the king of north India in 1556. He was the first Hindu king of North India in the last 350 years.

Hemu's reputation disheartened Akbar's army. There was a strong opinion among the nobles to go back to Kabul, where they had a firmer grip. Turning back then would have made the Moghuls a minor distraction in the pages of Indian history like Alexander. That changed when Bairam Khan decided to stay back and fight. This led to the second battle of Panipat, fought on the November of 1556. Young Akbar did not participate in the battle. He was kept away in safe distance guarded by special forces. Hemu held the upper hand in the battle until an arrow hit him in the eye and he fainted. The incident unsettled Hemu's army. The Moghuls finally had their victory. Hemu was beheaded, and his head was sent to Kabul for display. Bairam Khan ordered a mass execution of the enemy. Towers were built with the heads of the rivals as a lesson for the others. It was this bloody battle that truly laid the foundation of Moghul rule in India.

Native Indians, especially those living in northern India, had a troubled life for the last few centuries. Many had adopted the strategy of running away and hiding in the forests during the wars. It also helped them escape forceful conversion. People had no faith in their king, and after having to survive on limited resources, they lost faith in each other. In the beginning, the Moghuls, not surprisingly, were seen with cynicism. The new Moghul rule under Akbar gave India stability. The chaos that prevailed in north India subsided.

8.7 Akbar the Great

"My Khan Baba [Bairam Khan]. Though there may arise quarrel between father and son, yet neither can be indifferent to each other. Since you are our Khan Baba, the same relationship applies between us. Inspite of this grief and hurt and improper and unworthy acts [from you], we hold you in our affection and favor and I love you . . . you may prepare to proceed to pilgrimage to the holy places (hajj) as requested by you in your petition," wrote Akbar in 1560. [95] It was Bairam Khan who was responsible for the firm establishment of Moghul rule in India. Although Akbar was the king, it was Bairam Khan who ruled. He was the mentor of Akbar, a fatherlike figure. The king, however, was growing up. There were differences between Akbar and Bairam Khan, and it must have gone out of proportions. Bairam Khan was a Shia and was disliked by the Sunni-dominated nobles in Akbar's court. His opponents humiliated him to the point when he was forced to rebel, much to the dislike of Akbar [88]. His foster mother Maham Anaga, who did not like Bairam, might well have influenced Akbar. Bairam Khan left for Mecca, and it was Akbar who now held the supreme authority. On his way, Bairam Khan was killed by an Afghan. Akbar married his wife and brought up his son as his own.

Akbar's rule (1556–1605) was contemporaneous with Queen Elizabeth I (1558–1603) of England but richer and more powerful. Many Europeans visited his court, including those sent by Elizabeth. The writers have left behind a good description of the great king. Akbar was of medium height, broad shouldered, and well built. He had shaved his beard but wore a mustache. Contrary to his religious custom, he kept long hair and wore turban, much like the Indians. He had a wheatish complexion with black Asian eyes. There was a mole on the left side of his nose, which many believed brought him luck. He was predominating with his nobles who dared not look into his eyes while being very friendly with a common man. As a king he was accessible to everyone irrespective of religion or status. [88] Akbar was kind to his subjects but was ruthless with offenders, no matter how close they were to him. He killed his foster brother Adam Khan for murdering Atka and his maternal uncle Muazzam for murdering his own wife. Justice took priority over relationships.

Akbar was a very successful leader. He moved his capital from Delhi to Agra. Akbar went on to capture Malwa and Gondwana. With North India under control, Akbar eyed Rajputana. Chittor was the heart of Rajput power and key to the control of Rajputana. Akbar attacked Chittor in 1567. Rana Uday Singh, the king of Mewar, retired to the hills leaving behind two powerful soldiers, Jaimal and Patta, to protect the fort. Uday Singh founded Udaipur near the hills. Jaimal and Patta defended the fort with all their might. It took Akbar six months to conquer the fort. The women in the fort committed suicide. The Rajput warriors, true to their character, opened the gates of the fort and fought till the last man. Over 30,000 people died defending the fort, which included the peasants. It was the first and the last time Akbar took part in such a massacre. In respect of their courage, Akbar built idols of Jaimal and Patta riding elephants outside the chief gate of Agra Fort. The heroic of Jaimal and Patta reminds one of the battle Udal and Alha fought with Prithviraj. After Chittor, Ranthambore fell too. Soon other Rajput kings, except Mewar, accepted submission. Control of Rajputana brought security to Akbar's throne. His next mission was to control the riches of Bengal and Gujarat, the hotspots of marine trade.

Akbar conquered Gujarat quite easily, in memory of which he built the Buland Darwaza (figure 13). But the moment he left Gujarat, there was an uprising. Akbar reached Ahmedabad from Agra in just 11 days, a journey that generally took 6 weeks, to stop the rebellion. Gujarat was regained in 1573, and a tower was built with the heads of the rebel leaders. Bengal was his next mission. In 1576, Akbar conquered Bengal, ending the Afghan rule in India. Meanwhile, Rana Uday Singh's son, Maharana Pratap, became the king of Udaipur. He was eager to reconquer Chittor. This led to the Battle of Haldighati on June 1576. Maharana Pratap's men were outnumbered. Maharana Pratap ran away into the Aravallis, from where he kept on attacking the Moghuls using guerilla tactics. He was able to gain back much of his lost territories, but Chittor continued to elude him. His innovative guerilla tactics became famous and later helped the Marathas rise against the Mughals.

With most of northern India under control, Akbar focused on consolidating his empire. He built on the strong framework made by Sher Shah and organized his army and tax system. Akbar's rule was a liberal one. He gave equal importance to all religion. Akbar stopped forceful conversion to Islam. He abolished Jizya taxes and removed the ban on construction of new temples. Unlike his predecessors who were loyal to the caliphate, Akbar did not recognize external authority over his rule. He also let the Hindus who were forcefully converted to Islam regain their religion. He celebrated Diwali throughout his empire. He aided the building of the holy Sikh shrine Harmandir Sahib (popularly known as Golden Temple) of Amritsar. *Ibadat Khana* (House of Worship) was held by Akbar where spiritual leaders of different faith gathered to have debates. This reminds us of another great king Ashoka, who also held such debates. Akbar's liberal attitude attracted enemies. Orthodox Islamic scholars like Ahmad Sirhindi opposed Akbar and his attempt to secularize the Islamic rule in India. He called for reforms to go back to orthodoxy. His thoughts affected later rulers, like Aurangzeb.

Akbar divided his empire into twelve subas: Bengal, Bihar, Allahabad, Awadh, Agra, Delhi, Lahore, Multan, Kabul, Ajmer, Malwa, and Gujarat. [88] Orderly government was established in each of the regions. To increase the stability for his vast kingdom, Akbar entered into matrimonial alliance with the Rajputs and even let his Hindu wives keep their religion. Akbar managed to keep diplomatic relation, if not friendly, with both the Ottoman Empire and the Portuguese. Trade and commerce flourished under Akbar. He became one of the richest kings of his time, if not the richest.

Seeing the conflicts among different religions at the debates in his *Ibadat Khana*, Akbar wanted to create another religion, one that would unite all. He called it *din-e-ilahi*. He was not a follower of tradition. According to him, "if following tradition was commendable, the prophets would have merely followed their predecessors". *Din-e-ilahi* had the intention of merging the best of all religions. It prohibited lust, pride, and slander while promoting compassion and prudence. Priestly hierarchy, animal sacrifice, scriptures were made redundant. He opposed child marriage and said, "The marriage of a young child is displeasing to God for the object which is intended is still remote, and there is immediate possibility of injury. In a religion which forbids the remarriage of the widow, the hardship is much greater." He was also against sati and thought that 'it is a strange commentary on the magnanimity of men that they should seek their deliverance by means of their wives' [95]. Akbar was also against circumcision of children. He wrote, "it is very strange for men to insist on the necessity of the ceremony of circumcision for children who are otherwise excused from the burden of all obligations". [95] Akbar knew that the religious divide was one of the biggest weaknesses of his empire. Unfortunately, his concept of *din-e-ilahi* died with him. India was not ready for it. He only had few converts, which included the famous Birbal, Abu al-Fazal who wrote *Akbarnama*, and Akbar's finance minister Raja Todarmal. The lack of converts also shows that Akbar did not force his new religion to his subjects.

Todarmal brought revolutionary changes in the tax system that was applied throughout Akbar's empire, except Bengal, Bihar, and Gujarat. Todarmal standardized all forms of measurements. Lands and settlements were surveyed, and lots of data, including crop yield and prices, were collected for the first time in India and probably the world. He introduced a new revenue system called *zabt* and a new taxation method called *dahshala*. The highly organized and efficient system brought transparency and economic growth during Akbar's rule. The other convert, Raja Birbal, was a Brahmin Kshatriya born as Mahesh Das, known for his wits and has been glorified in folk tales. He was a poet and singer and later became military advisor and took part in military missions. He died in one such mission against the Afghans. He was Akbar's favorite among the nine gems in his court, which also included the famous Indian classical singer Tansen. Tansen was born as a Hindu named Ramtanu. He converted to Islam and became Mohammad Ata Khan. Tansen gave Indian music a new dimension. The important positions held by Indians of different faiths in Akbar's court is proof of his liberal attitude and the key to his success.

8.8   In the Name of Love

Salim saw her for the first time in Lahore. Her beauty enchanted him. She was dancing to the tunes of the *mujra* ordered by the king, as if she was a free soul. Free, however, she wasn't. She was a slave girl, the most beautiful slave in King Akbar's court. Her name was Anarkali. It was love at first sight for both. Thus began the tragic love story between Salim and Anarkali. When Akbar came to know of the affair between his son and heir Salim with a slave girl, he was enraged. Anarkali was attested immediately. She managed to escape with the help of Salim's friend. This led to a war between the king and his son, in which the latter was humbled. Anarkali secretly went to Akbar and begged to him for Salim's life. She asked him to let her spent one night with Salim as her last wish. That night Salim was happy in the arms of Anarkali. Little did he know that it would be the last night with his beloved. Anarkali drugged Salim, and as Salim slept, she quietly slipped away and surrendered to Akbar. She was imprisoned in a closed chamber, where she probably died.

This legendary story has no historical basis, just like the famous love story between Akbar and Rajput princess

Jodha Bai. What was true, however, was the conflict between Akbar and Salim. Salim, popular as Jahangir, was the eldest surviving son of Akbar and Mariam-uz-Zamani, commonly mistaken as Jodha Bai. Mariam was the first and chief Rajput wife of Akbar, and also the longest-serving Hindu empress. Jahangir was addicted to alcohol, opium, and women. His addictions made Akbar doubt his leadership qualities. Akbar wanted Khusrau Mirza, Jahangir's eldest son, to be his heir. This made Jahangir rebel against his father. His fictional love story was probably written to justify this upheaval. Such rebellion between father and son was not common for Moghuls, and it set a bad precedence. Jahangir became the king after Akbar's death at an age of 36 years. Akbar died in 1605 of acute dysentery. His body was buried in a mausoleum in Sikandra, Agra. Khusrau Mirza rebelled against his father. Khusrau, however, was defeated, imprisoned, and blinded. Sikh Guru Arjan Dev was also made captive and tortured for helping Khusrau, apart from the reason that he was responsible for converting many Muslims to Sikhism. Arjan Dev was the fifth Sikh guru who completed the construction of Golden Temple and also compiled the Adi Granth. The guru died in custody starting the hostile relation between the Moghuls and the Sikhs.

Jahangir was a tolerant ruler, with the exception of his aggression towards Sikhs. Once there was a dispute between Portuguese missionaries and Islamic scholars. To solve their problem Jahangir lit a fire and asked the fighting scholars to jump in it to prove the strength of their faith. None of them did, and the problem was solved. He ruled for 22 years, during which he was busy creating stability in the huge empire Akbar fashioned. He also ruled from Agra and ignored Delhi, which became the city of rats. Jahangir's ambition of conquering the Deccan was left unfulfilled because of the heroics of Malik Ambar. Malik was an Abyssinian, born in Ethiopia, sold as a slave in Baghdad, and brought to Deccan by a merchant. He worked for the Deccan sultans and defeated the Moghuls with the aid of his Maratha followers. It was during this time that many Marathi leaders like Shahaji Bhosale, father of Shivaji, gained prominence. Along with the failure in Deccan, Jahangir also lost Qandhar to the Persians, hurting his pride. Jahangir's health started to degrade. Insurgence broke out among his sons for the throne. Shah Jahan rebelled against Jahangir, continuing the example set by Jahangir himself, but he soon made peace. Jahangir succumbed to illness in 1627. This brought the Moghul empress, Nur Jahan, into fame.

Nur Jahan, a Persian born as Mehr-un-Nissa in Afghanistan, was married to general Sher Afghan. The governor of Bengal murdered Sher Afghan. Nur was brought to Jahangir's harem as a personal assistant to one of Akbar's wife. Jahangir saw her beauty and fell in love, this time for real. Jahangir married her in 1611 as his twelfth wife. She was his last legal wife and the most favored one. She was a strong woman who went on hunting expeditions with Jahangir. She had considerable influence in the decisions made by her husband as king, especially after Jahangir got addicted to opium. She had her own textile business and even owned ships that took people to Mecca. She was proclaimed the Barshah Begam and coins were minted in her name. It was the first and only such instance of a coin bearing the name of a woman in Moghul era. Jahangir's death led to the struggle for throne among his sons. Nur Jahan feared that Shah Jahan would become the new king and she would lose her power. She favored the weaker

Shahryay whom she could influence. But her ambitions were shattered when Shah Jahan defeated Shahryay. Nur Jahan retired with her daughter to Agra. There she oversaw the building of Tomb of I'timad-ud-Daulah in memory of her father. It is considered as the draft for Taj Mahal. Her influence is immense in the architectural renaissance in India during Shah Jahan's regime. After she died, she was buried in Lahore inside a tomb that she had made herself. The following words are inscribed in her tomb, describing her final sentiments:

> On the grave of this poor stranger, let there be neither lamp nor rose. Let neither butterfly's wing burn nor nightingale sing.

Shah Jahan was crowned as the fifth Moghul king in 1628. Shah Jahan means king of the World, which he became by executing his chief rivals the moment he came to power. A couple of years earlier, Malik Ambar died, ending the Deccan resistance. This helped Shah Jahan, and later his son, conquer Deccan and invade southern India. It was Shah Jahan who shifted the capital back to Delhi as the streets of Agra were too narrow for his royal processions. The tension between the Sikhs and the Moghuls grew during Shah Jahan's regime. The Sikhs had to take up arms to survive and were ably led by Guru Har Govind. The Sikhs went on the offense, bought horses, and learned martial arts. Shah Jahan's troops were defeated by Sikhs in Amritsar despite the advantage of numbers. His victory demonstrated the strength of Sikh unity and inspired them. Shah Jahan did manage to take Guru Har Govind into custody but had to release him owing to his popularity among the people.

While he was not successful against the Sikhs, he did manage to taste victory against the Portuguese.

The Portuguese pirates were very active in the coast of Bengal. The Portuguese armada fleet carried them to India. The Bengal word for a bad person *haramzada* is said to be derieved from *armada*. One of the famous Bengal coastal tribes who joined the Portuguese pirates was the Mog or Magh tribe. They were Buddhists from Arakan who settled down in Tripura and Chittagong. There is a famous term in Bengali called *Mog-er-mulluk* (Kingdom of Mogs), which means *anarchy*. Mog tribes did not surrender to Mughals and kept attacking them. They had their own rules. Portuguese had an alliance with Mog king Thiri, who believed he was a future Buddha. When the nuisance became too much, Shah Jahan threw the Portuguese out of the Hooghly port and Bandel in Bengal, spoiling the latter's imperial ambition.

It was, however, not for wars but architecture that Shah Jahan became famous. Indian architecture reached a new zenith during his reign. Jama Masjid, Red Fort, and Agra Fort were among his numerous marvels. But the most famous of them all is the wonder called Taj Mahal. Taj Mahal was built in memory of Shah Jahan's wife, Mumtaz Mahal. Mumtaz was the most favored wife of Shah Jahan. The thirteen children she bore is a testimony of that. In fact, she died of complication while giving birth to the fourteenth child at the age of 40 years. She was buried in Zainabad, but later, her body was transferred to Taj Mahal after its construction. Artisans were brought from all over the empire, including Central Asia and Iran. The translucent white marble came from Makrana, Rajastan. The cost of building the wonder was four crore (40 million) at a time when gold was just 15INR per *tola* (11.66g). The view of Taj Mahal is so fascinating that after visiting it American novelist Bayard Taylor said:

> Did you ever build a castle in the air? Here is one, brought down to earth and fixed for the wonder of ages.

8.9 Bargi Comes our Way!

> Khoka ghumalo, para juralo . . . Bargi elo deshe.

> Bulbuli-te dhan kheyeche . . . khajna debo kishe?

Thus goes the Bengali folk song. A rough translation of that would be:

> The child sleeps; village is silent . . . Bargi comes our way.

> The birds have eaten the crops . . . Tax, how shall we pay?

The song depicts how the villagers of Bengal were traumatized by the name of Bargi. Bargi, a group of Maratha soldiers, raided the villages of Bengal ruled by the Muslim kings. If their demands were not met, they would massacre the villages. Even kids were not spared the sword. Their inhuman terror was at its peak in the mid-18th century when this song was composed. Bargis, however, were famous not for their vandalism but for their bravery. They were the key reason for the downfall of the mighty Mughals.

Bargis, or Marathas, started as peasants in the villages of Deccan. They were recruited by the Deccan sultanates as loose auxiliaries or bargirs [88] and hence the name. Most of the Maratha leaders were powerful *zamindars* (landlords), not independent rulers like the Rajputs. This was a reason why many Brahmins did not accept them as Kshatriyas in the beginning. The Marathas were independent soldiers who were recruited by the rulers. Their loyalty depended on the side that recruited them. Many Marathas even served the Mughals. They became important after they won many key battles with Mallik Ambar.

It was Shahaji Raje Bhonsle who first carved out an independent empire for himself. He rose to prominence in the Battle of Bhatvadi fought near Ahmednagar in 1624. He allied with the Nizam. With just 20,000 soldiers, he marched against the huge army of Shah Jahan who had 2 lakh soldiers. The Mughals required a lot of food and water supply to last the battle. They camped with all their resources near the bank of Mehkari River. While the Mughals were sleeping, Shahaji and his men broke the dam located upstream from the Mughal camp. The river got flooded leading to chaos in the Mughal camp. Shahaji won the battle and captured many prominent Moghul soldiers. Shahaji became a hero, but his son would become a legend.

Shivaji, Shahaji's son, was born in the hill-fort of Shivneri near Pune in 1630. By the age of 18, he won many forts in Pune, thus expanding his father's empire. His battle tactics were guerilla warfare rather than direct combat. Shivaji took control of Sinhagad Fort in 1647 (figure 14). In 1657 he conquered Javali from another Maratha leader. Then he killed Afzal Khan and routed his army in the Battle of Pratapgarh two years later. Shivaji was still not satisfied and went on to capture Panhala fort, South Konkan and

Kolhapur districts. The victories made Shivaji a living legend. Support started pouring in as many Maratha and Afghan leaders joined him. Shivaji, while praising Aurangzeb's predecessors, warned the Mughal king not to discriminate based on religion, else his empire would be reduced to ashes 'in the fire of their anger'. However, Sivaji's fight was political and not communal. His rule was liberal, and he allied with many Muslim leaders.

Towards the end of his regime, Shah Jahan became ill. Anticipating his death, his sons were engaged in a bloody battle for succession. One of his sons, Shah Shuja, was the governor of Bengal. When Shah's concubine was ill and complained of stomach pain, a British doctor named Mr Boughton cured her after all local doctors failed. In return, Mr Boughton was granted duty exemption only for personal trade. The exemption was, however, misused by the British to open a profitable trade in Bengal. The British, somewhat treacherously, opened a factory in Hooghly in the name of the company [96]. Shah Shuja, meanwhile, declared independence after his father became ill. Shah Jahan tried to stop the struggle for his throne and declared his son Dara as his successor, which only aggravated the matter. Dara was an able leader and a secular person. It was Dara who translated many ancient Indian texts, like the Upanishads, into Persian. Shah Shuja fought with Dara for Agra but was defeated. Aurangzeb, in turn, defeated Dara in 1659, and Shah Jahan was made captive in the women's quarter of Agra Fort. He was not ill treated by Aurangzeb but was robbed of all his powers. Aurangzeb went on to defeat Shah Shuja in 1660. The later managed to flee to Manipur with his family. Aurangzeb executed Dara and his other brother Murad to become the undisputed king. Later, he did try to make amends with his family by letting his children marry the children of his dead brothers.

Aurangzeb ruled for 50 long years and expanded his kingdom by continued warfare. At its peak, the Mughal Empire under him covered a huge area from Kashmir in the north to Tamil Naidu in the south and from Afghanistan in the west to Bangladesh in the east. There was one place, however, that even he failed to conquer. Aurangzeb sent a massive army to concur Guwahati. Lachit Borphukan, the commander of Ahom Kingdom, knew that they were no match for the Mughals on open ground. He had to choose the battlefield carefully. Guwahati, a hilly terrain, was the ideal spot. Several battles were fought for over four months without much progress for any side. Lachit's tactic was to frustrate the Mughals without much fighting, and it worked. The final battle took place in Saraighat when the mighty Mughals attacked from the river. Many of Lachit's men were afraid and ran away, but the brave Lachit went ahead with his troop. They silently built bridges across the Brahmaputra River, made of boats placed side by side. The Mughals went forward with full force, pushing for victory after they saw just few Ahom ships holding guard. The few Ahom ships standing on the way of the mighty Mughal army were just bait. Lachit had other plans. His main force quietly went behind the Mughals and made a swift attack from the rear, surprising their enemy. The Mughals had no option but to retreat. They suffered heavy casualties. Despite all odds stacked against him, Lachit and his men won the battle. It was not just a loss but also a disaster for Aurangzeb's men.

Despite the odd defeat, the Mughal Empire flourished. Aurangzeb probably died as the richest man on earth. But the Mughal Empire came crumbling down after his demise. One reason for that has been his policy of religious intolerance, something that started during Shah Jahan's regime. Construction of new temples was banned, though repairing of old ones were still permitted. Aurangzeb himself demolished many temples for various reasons. Some, like the Somnath Temple, were destroyed to teach the rebellious Hindu kings a lesson. The others, like the Viswanath temple, were destroyed because of the banned practice by many Hindus and Muslims to come to these temples and learn from the Brahmins. Most of the vandalism took place later in his rule when he became suspicious of the Hindu rulers. Aurangzeb undid the liberalization brought by his great-grandfather. He reintroduced Jizya tax on the non-Muslims. This further angered the Hindu rulers. However, poor people who were unable to work or were unemployed were exempted from the tax. The amount of tax was also fixed based on people's ability.

The Marathas, Rajputs, and Jats kept on plotting against the king. Even the ones who accepted him as overlords betrayed him at times, making him insecure. By 1680, when this throne was secure, he stopped demolishing temples. He also executed the ninth Sikh Guru Tegh Bahadur in 1675, renewing the conflict with the Sikhs. This led to Sikh movement commanded by Guru Tegh Bahadur's son and the tenth guru, Guru Govindh Singh. He turned the movement into a military brotherhood, Khalsa. He bestowed the title of *Singh* or *lion* to the first five disciples. Women were made part of the Khalsa with the title of *Kaur*, or *princess*. He introduced the five Ks—*Kesh* (uncut hair), *Kanga* (wooden comb), *Kara* (iron bracelet), *Kirpan* (sword), and *Kacchera* (undergarment)—that needed to be carried by Sikhs all the time. Though the Govindh Singh was not able to stand the might of Mughal for long or establish an independent Sikh state, he was able to unite the Sikhs and give them an identity [88]. By the end of Aurangzeb's reign, the rebellions from Rajputs of Marwar and Mewar, Jats, Afghans, and Sikhs were straining the Mughals. However, none of them were as dangerous as the rise of the Marathas under Shivaji. Shivaji now posed the biggest threat to the ambitions of Aurangzeb and the survival of the Mughals in India.

8.10   The Beginning of the End

Capturing Deccan had remained a dream for Mughals since Akbar's time. It was Aurangzeb, the last great Mughal Empire, under whose rule the final frontier was conquered. Deccan, however, proved to be Mughal's Achilles' heel. The key powers in Deccan, after the fall of Ahmednagar to the Mughals, were Sultans of Bijapur and Golconda and the Marathas. Until 1657, the Marathas under Shivaji were busy expanding their control over Konkan. They were in no mood to upset the mighty Mughals. Shivaji even helped Aurangzeb capture the strategic location of Bijapur. Success made Shivaji overconfident and he started to raid the Mughal territories of Ahmednagar and Junnar. Aurangzeb responded by attacking the Marathas. Shivaji was forced into the Treaty of August 1657 in which Shivaji lost most of the territories he occupied. That same year Shah Jahan fell ill, and Aurangzeb became busy in the war of succession. This gave Shivaji the perfect opportunity to get back some of his lost territories.

Shivaji's main fight was with the Siddis. Siddis were descendants of Bantu people of Africa brought to India as slaves by the Arab and Portuguese merchants. They are mostly Muslims and still live in various places in the west coast of India and in Pakistan. The Portuguese, who were also alarmed by the rise of Shivaji, helped Siddis. The main concern for the Portuguese was that Shivaji had started building war vessels with trained navy, something the land-based Mughals ignored. That would pose a direct threat to the Portuguese dominance over the Arabian Sea. Meanwhile, on the persuasion of Aurangzeb, Adil Shah of Bijapur ordered Afzal Khan to attack Shivaji. Shivaji was not able to defend all his territories from Afzal. He called for a truce and asked Afzal to meet him in Pratapgad. The meeting did not go well, and there was a fight between the two in which Shivaji killed Afzal Khan. The Persian writers blame Shivaji of treachery while the Marathas blame Afzal Khan of striking the first blow. Shivaji's men then routed Afzal's army. The victory changed the combination of allies. Portugal realized Shivaji's power and was contemplating an alliance while Adil Shah was fed up with the constant presence of Mughal army in his territory and tried to build better relations with Shivaji instead.

Maratha victories were an insult to the Mughals. Aurangzeb did not want to take any more chances. He went to his best man to finish the job. Rajput king of Amber, and senior general of the Mughals, Raja Jai Singh I was given the task of dealing with the nuisance of Shivaji. The first thing Raja Jai Singh did was to isolate the Marathas from their possible allies, including the Portuguese and Adil Shah. Jai Singh then went on to capture Purandar fort in 1665 and forced Shivaji to yield. Shivaji was made to sign the Treaty of Purandar, in which he had to surrender twenty-three forts. Shivaji was left with just twelve small forts and had to pay a compensation of 400,000 rupees. As per the treaty,

Shivaji's son Sambhaji was made a Mughal sardar and was to serve in the Mughal army.

The year after, Shivaji was called to Aurangzeb's court with the promise of being given royal favors. He was persuaded by Jai Singh and was assured of protection. Shivaji came to the king's court but felt insulted and went out of the court protesting. According to the Marathas, the Mughals insulted Shivaji by treating him like a man of low status. According to Mughal authors, Shivaji was rude to his king and misbehaved. The Rajput account mentions that people respected Shivaji, before he came to Aurangzeb's court, for his bravery. But after the audacity he showed in the king's court, people started praising his courage even more. Shivaji's behavior angered Aurangzeb, and he was persuaded by the nobles to imprison and probably kill Shivaji. Shivaji came to know of Aurangzeb's intentions and managed to escape with his son, disguised as saints. Jai Singh might have helped him in the escape. After a lot of struggle and lucky escapes, Shivaji made it to Rajgad. Letting Shivaji escape was the biggest mistake the Mughals made. Aurangzeb remembered the mistake on his deathbed 50 years later.

Thereafter, Shivaji managed to develop better relation with Mughals. Aurangzeb gave him the title of *Raja* (*king*) as desired by Shivaji. He still was Aurangzeb's vassal, and the entire Deccan remained under the control of the Mughals. Shivaji seized Bijapur with the permission of the Mughals. He then made a swift and successful attack on the Portuguese-controlled territory of Goa. The Portuguese strength had weakened, and they were no more a threat to Shivaji. Shivaji also managed to ally with Golconda and Bijapur, thus uniting the Deccan. The peace with the Mughals lasted only till 1670. Shivaji attacked and regained the forts he lost to the Mughals five years ago. With the Mughals busy fighting the Pathans, it was the right time for Shivaji's coronation, which took place on 6 June 1674. He started printing his own coins, thus declaring independence from the Mughals [97]. Shivaji's army was strengthened when he was joined with 30,000-armed Karnataki foot soldiers sent by the Berar chief. Shivaji died, as a free king, of fever and probable blood dysentery at the age of 52 years. His son Sambhaji succeeded him.

Aurangzeb ignored the Deccan until 1681 when the Marathas gave his rebel son Akbar shelter. Aurangzeb reached Deccan with his men in pursuit of his son. This time, Aurangzeb attacked with his best men, taking part in the battle himself. Bijapur and Golconda fell to Aurangzeb. In 1689, Sambhaji was captured, tortured and executed. His half-brother, Rajaram Bhonsle, succeeded Sambhaji. Aurangzeb attacked Rajaram, who managed to escape to Jinji in the east coast. From there, he kept on attacking the Mughals. Though he was getting old and tired, Aurangzeb never stopped fighting in order to gain what he thought was rightfully his. He wanted to end the Marathas once and for all. In his mad quest, Aurangzeb probably stretched himself too much. His treasury was drained, and his army became tired and weary. Mughals attacked Jinji in 1968 and captured it. Rajaram managed to escape again but died in Pune two years later. His infant son succeeded him. Rajaram's wife Tarabai acted as his regent and continued the Maratha onslaught against Mughals. Aurangzeb finally realized that he was running out of time and conquering the whole of Deccan was not feasible. He retired to Aurangabad where he fell ill. While ill, he is said to have told the following lines to his son, "I came alone and I go as a stranger. I do not know who I am, nor what I have been doing." Aurangzeb died in 1707 at the old age of 88 years. He was buried in a modest grave as per his strict Islamic faith. Before his death he wrote, "Now I go away with this stupendous caravan of sins." The Mughal Empire declined rapidly after his death, mostly due to incompetent rulers and internal revolts. Aurangzeb's aggression and centralization of power had created many enemies. The constant attacks by the Marathas weakened them. By the mid of 18th century, the Marathas defeated the Mughals and expanded their territory from Deccan to Bengal.

8.11   India under Mughals

The description of foreign writers about India through time depicts the changing condition of the Indians. Greek authors 2,100 years ago wrote about Indians who were clean and well dressed. They wore 'elaborately trimmed shoes of white leather having variegated and high soles'. They loved finery and ornaments. India was still economically stable and a safe haven when Faxian visited in the fourth century. However, just three centuries later, Indian roads were not very safe. Pirates had attacked Xuanzang several times while he was in India. It points towards an unstable Indian economy post the Gupta era. However, the Indian cities were still large and prosperous. They were supported by the surplus in the villages. The Indian bazaars (markets) were the center of social and cultural activity, along with economic transactions, as described by Ibn Buttuta in 14th century. The fertile soil and enough rain meant that the agriculture was still flourishing. While agriculture was the backbone, trading brought lots of foreign money. Center provided all facilities for traders. The Indian postal system was very efficient and helped the merchants communicate over long distances. There were two types of postal systems. The *uluq* was run by royal horses stationed every 6.5 kilometres, and *dawa* was like a relay race where the postman ran from one village to another having a distance of around 500 metres. Quite contrary to intuitions, *dawa* was faster than *uluq*.

Post 14th century, things started to worsen. The constant wars and invasions destabilized Indian economy, especially in northern India. A lot of Indians moved south where conditions were still stable while many ran away and took shelter in the forests. This affected agriculture as well as trading. Those who took shelter in the forest became robbers. Ibn Butta was once a victim of such robbery when he was on his mission to China. All he was left with was his trousers. He did, however, manage to find his team and complete his mission. When Babur came to India, he was surprised to see the poor condition of peasants and ordinary men. The poor hardly had clothes to wear, and most people were barefooted as compared to the trimmed leather shoes worn by their ancestors. Villagers had modest houses made of mud with scanty furniture, quite like modern Indian villages.

In the beginning of the 17th century, India's population was around 125 million. There was enough land for cultivation; however, the agricultural conditions were not very good. No new technology had been added in the past century to increase the productivity of crops unlike Europe at that time. Income inequality was very evident during the Mughal era. The lowest status in the villages was that of the untouchables or *kamin*. They were hired, and often exploited, by the peasants who had land and called themselves *khudkasth*. The *khudkasth* were, in turn, exploited by the *zamindars*. [88] The nobles and the *zamindars* were pretty rich. The salaries of nobles in Mughal courts were higher than anywhere else in the world. This attracted a lot of foreigners, like Ibn Battuta, who came to India and settled down as nobles. The *zamindars* collected land revenue from the *khudkasth* and gave it to the *rajas*. In return, they would receive a portion of the tax money, which could go up to 25 per cent [88]. Above the *zamindars* were the *rajas* who worked for the king. The rajas had some power within their territory and were even allowed to keep armed soldiers. The hierarchy was a result of decentralization of power. India was so vast that ruling it directly from the center was not possible. However, the *rajas* had to pay tax to the king. To pay the tax and maintain their luxurious lifestyles, they needed to exploit the people under them. This led to the decline of agriculture in villages, which indirectly affected the stability of the cities. Growth in both agriculture and trading was not keeping pace with the growing demand. The poor became poorer while the rich became richer.

The Mughal era was the time of architectural renaissance in India. The Mughals brought with them the knowledge of Persian architecture. It mixed with the Indian style of architecture to create masterpieces like the Taj Mahal. The Mughals were experts at turning the landscape into beautiful gardens. The Mughal gardens still exist at various places in India. They also brought with them the delicious cuisines, which include mughlai parantha, butter chicken, murg mussalam, malai kofta, reshmi kabab, boti kabab, mutton rogan josh, and rezala.

The medieval era was the time for various religious movements across India. The Bhakti cult gained prominence among the lower caste, challenging the authority of

Brahmins. It originated in Tamil Naidu but soon spread all across the country. It opened the path of salvation to everyone. Ramananda, Chaitanya Mahaprabhu, Surdas, Meera Bai, Kabir, Tulsidas, Tukaram, and Ramadas were among the many prominent leaders of Bhakti movement. While Bhakti movement, along with Sufism and Sikhism, tried to promote mutual tolerance and harmony between the Hindus and Muslims, there had been many incidents of Muslim kings destroying Hindu temples. It has remained a very sensitive and political issue in modern India.

The destruction of temples reduced during Akbar's rule but happened again in the later part of Aurangzeb's regime. The trend of temple destruction is not unique to Muslim rulers in India. Looting of royal idols from the temples of enemy king was common amongst Hindu rulers since times immemorial. A fifth-century Jain temple in Paharpur has been converted to Buddhist monastery by Pala kings in eighth century. Harsha destroyed many temples to teach greedy Brahmins a lesson. Similar fate befell the Buddhists temples in Kashmir after there were charges of corruption and superstition. The 'Gaur Heros' destroyed the state deity Vishnu belonging to King Lalitaditya as an act of revenge. Rashtrakuta king Indra III demolished Kalpapriya temple belonging to the Pratiharas in tenth century. In the early 13th century, the kings of Paramara Dynasty ruined numerous Jain temples in Gujarat. [98] Many Buddhist temples were demolished when Indian kings attacked Sri Lanka. Temple destruction got a religious angle when the Muslim Afghan and Turk raiders looted the Hindu temples in the name of religion. They were raiders and not rulers of India. The pattern of temple destruction by Indian rulers showed that destruction were driven more by political will than religion. The temples destroyed either belonged to an enemy king or to persons who committed treason or were disloyal to the king. Temples under the rule of the Muslim kings were protected and sometimes even repaired using royal treasury. During rule of liberal kings like Akbar, new temples were built as well.

The Delhi sultanate could not form a stable empire because of constant revolts. The Mughals too were busy with internal disturbances and neglected science and technology. The Mughals had been a land-based power, and they did not bother about developing a navy. Under the Mughals India lost her dominance over sea. The Mughals were still very rich. Their wealth and power made them oblivious to the rise of Europe. While Europe armed itself with powerful weapons, India became weak, divided, and vulnerable.

European Imperialism (1700 to 1857 CE)

A country not only divided between Mahommedan and Hindoo, but between tribe and tribe, between caste and caste; a society whose framework was based on a sort of equilibrium, resulting from a general repulsion and constitutional exclusiveness between all its members. Such a country and such a society, were they not the predestined prey of conquest?

—Karl Marx, *The Future Results of British Rule in India*

9.1   The Beginnings

After the eventful year of 1492, Europe would rapidly rise to become a world superpower. They would begin an era of exploration and discoveries. It would also be a brutal age of wars and bloodshed. Europe's rise would be as much through adventure and innovation as through slavery and exploitation. There would also be a bit of luck involved. Eastern Europe developed under the Greeks and Romans while Western Europe was yet to catch up. By the end of fourth century, the Roman Empire became weak, especially from the attack of Huns and internal revolts. The empire was divided into Eastern and Western Roman Empire. Various groups of Germanic people invaded the weak Western Rome while Eastern Rome survived as the Byzantine Empire. Frankish Empire was the most powerful of the Germans, which later became France and Germany. The Germans also took Port of Cale from the Romans, which became Portugal. The Germanic Anglo-Saxon tribe conquered the British Isles and created the Kingdom of England. By tenth century, most of the countries of Europe had taken shape.

Meanwhile, the Islamic world was experiencing their golden era. They conquered Iberian Peninsula in 711. It included Spain, Portugal, and southern France. The Muslims here were known as Moors. The Crusades followed, headed by the churches. Crusades drained a lot of money and were unsuccessful. Europe, however, managed to free itself from the Moors by 1492, a success that is fancifully called the Reconquista [99]. The era of Crusades was dark times for Europe. Black Death and Hundred Years' War added to people's woes. In 1453, Constantinople (the capital of Byzantine Empire) fell to the Ottoman attack. It marked the end of the great Roman Empire. Many scholars, mostly Greeks, fled to Italy and other countries in fear of persecution. They brought with them the ancient Greek texts that helped trigger the European Renaissance.

The events were changing the psychology of the people of Europe. Europeans were getting increasingly polarized between the orthodox people and those trying to break away from orthodoxy. There was revolution within the church against corruption. Effort was made to separate religion from politics. The Protestant Reformation took place between sixteenth and seventeenth century. It led to a series of wars, culminating into the Thirty Years' War fought among various nations of Europe. Jews and Muslims in Europe were forcefully converted or persecuted, and women suspected as witches were hunted down and burnt alive. In that very year (1492), Jews in Spain were forced to convert to Christianity. Many fled to Portugal and Ottoman Empire. Parallely, there was an intellectual awareness that affected arts, science, literature, religion, and almost everything else in Europe. This intellectual revolution, known as European Renaissance, started in Italy in the fourteenth century. It slowly spread to the rest of Europe by sixteenth century. The halos disappeared from the paintings that once depicted gods and angels. Paintings became more realistic as people started to feel that they were no more at the mercy of some higher power. Instead of resigning their fate to gods, they began to take risks. Risk brought huge profits to those who were successful, and it triggered the age of exploration and discovery [100].

Interestingly, India also played its part in Europe's rise. New inventions and the discoveries of the New World, the civilizations beyond known world, were possible because of the development of advanced mathematics and accurate measurements. [100] Scholars like Fibonacci of Pisa (1170–1250) learned about Indian mathematics from the Arabs, who, in turn, had learned it from India. Introduction of zero and decimal system revolutionized the way Europeans counted. [101] It led to rapid progress in astronomy and navigation and thus exploitation of the New World. Even Einstein agreed, "We owe it to Indians who taught us how to count, without which no worthwhile scientific discovery could have been made." In India, however, science was lost in chaos and superstition.

Europe was fascinated about India. To them, it was a land of fantasy and riches. Their idea of India was created by the writings of Western authors. The Greeks wrote about the rich and beautiful land of India that it was during the time of the Maurya Empire. Europeans believed that there was a glorious Christian kingdom beyond the Islamic lands. A legendary king by the name Prester John lived there. To them the Gates of Alexander and the Fountain of Youth were present in this mysterious land that bordered the 'earthly paradise'. The stories of the apostle Saint Thomas's preaching in India in the book *The Acts of Thomas* were taken as evidence. The fantasy was supplemented by the fictitious writings of Mandeville. He claimed to have traveled to India and seen the flourishing Kingdom of Prester John. What Mandeville also said, this time correctly, was that the earth was round and India could be found even by sailing west [56]. In that famous year of 1492, three years before young Babur became king of Farghana, Christopher Columbus set sail for his legendary journey towards west in search of the mysterious land of India and in search of spices. He took Mandeville's statement too literally.

9.2   Sugar, Slaves, and Guns

Europe's trade with Asia was hampered once Ottoman Empire took control of the Silk Route. They were in dire need of an alternate path. The Portuguese tried the sea route westward, but they only made it up to the Cape of Good Hope. Christopher Columbus wanted to try the eastern route. After a lot of persuasion, he managed to get funding from the Spanish Crown. He set sail on 1492 in search of India. He got his calculations wrong and underestimated the distance to India. When he found Cuba, he thought that it was Japan and mistook America for India. The natives of America became Indians, a name by which they are still called. Columbus, unknowingly, discovered a New World, and so did the natives. Interestingly, the new continent got its name not after Columbus but after Amerigo Vespucci, who visited the continent 15 years after Columbus. Waldseemuller and Ringmann named the continent after Amerigo as they were not aware of Columbus's achievement. Though Amerigo did not discover America, he was the first to realize that this piece of land was not a part of Asia. To be fair, Columbus did not truly discover America. The natives had been living there for thousands of years, and for them, it was the Europeans who came from a New World. Chinese boats, some historians claim, had landed in America before Columbus. Columbus was not even the first European to visit America. The Vikings had reached there long before him. However, the age of European colonization of the New World did begin with Columbus's voyage. Columbus did not find traders as he expected to find in India, and more importantly, there was no gold around. At first, the natives were friendly, and they shared most of what they had. But one thing they did not want to share was their woman. The Europeans forced themselves upon the weak natives. They took many as slaves. Columbus had to make the best use off this new place and justify the money spent by the Spanish Crown.

If any European country had the chance to find India through the sea route, it was the Portuguese. They were expert navigators and had the best maps. Every time they sailed, they built upon the previous voyages. Helped by few Gujarati traders, a man named Vasco da Gamma managed to reach India. He landed in Calicut, Kerala, on 20 May 1498. Gamma brought with him goods for trading that had high demand in Africa. In India those goods were already cheap and available aplenty and thus had no value. Gamma's first expedition to India was not a commercial success. Gamma, however, went back with some good news. Finding India put Portugal one step ahead of Spain. This was not a country of naked natives like Columbus found. This country was rich. India was the key to spice trade as spices were nearly thirty times cheaper here than in Europe. More importantly, he realized that Europeans were much stronger than the Indians in terms of better ships and better guns. [102]

Columbus found a way to make the new land profitable. He started planting sugarcane, a plant that grew well in tropical climates. Soon sugarcane spread to other colonies. Sugarcane originated in Southeast Asia and India. The Arabs had taken the plant and subsequently passed it on to Europe. There was huge profit to be made from sugar. However, there was shortage of manpower in the New World. The natives were not immune to the germs carried over by the Europeans. Their number decreased drastically as they died of diseases previously unknown to them. This is where the Portuguese came to rescue. Portuguese had already established colonies in Africa. They were making profit by trading gold, ivory, pepper etc. Africa also had a huge resource of slaves. Slaves, mostly from Africa, were the main labor force in the Arab sugar industry. The Europeans took a leaf out of Arabs' book. Slaves were sold by the African states to the Europeans in return of valuables, especially guns. There were conflicts and rivalry among the Africans, which led to the war. War increased the demands for European weapons. The prisoners of war were sold as slaves. African slaves were stronger than the natives of America and were immune to European germs. Europeans started importing a lot of slaves from Africa to America. The slaves acted as labors to help grow sugarcane. Sugar was sent from America to Europe. Europe sold the products and made profit. The profit was used to buy more slaves. This hugely profitable business was known as the infamous triangular trade. The first slaves arrived in America in 1505, a trend that continued for the next 300 years. [103] Fifteen to 25 million African slaves were transported to America between 1518 and 1860. That was half the number of slaves that began their journey from African coast. The other half died before they could reach the shore [104].

Triangular trade boosted European economy, creating the base for Industrial Revolution. It was not just the money and exploitation but also technological inventions that kept Europe a step ahead of the rest of the world. [102] The innovations started long before the renaissance. Invention of waterwheel between the third and first century BCE helped in better irrigation and also acted as a power source. This power would soon run the big industries of Europe. Invention of eyeglasses doubled the work life of skilled craftsmen. Lenses also helped Leeuwenhoek revolutionize the world of microorganism, germs, and thus medicine while scientists like Copernicus, Kepler, and Galileo peeped into the world beyond ours. Mechanical clocks made people more organized and helped in planning. Printing machines helped spread information quickly. Precise compasses and better maps made marine navigation so much easier. The most important invention of them all was the gunpowder. Though it originated in China, it was the Europeans who created powerful weapons out of it. Weapons made Europe invincible. There was no power in the world to match their artillery.

Though Spain and Portuguese had a head start in exploring new lands, they were soon left behind by other European nations. Spain grew rich from sugar industry and silver mining. Silver meant money, but import of too much silver reduced its demand. Silver prices dropped, affecting Spanish economy. Spain and Portugal also wasted a lot of their wealth in wars, like their failed attempt to conquer Britain. This further weakened their economy. They were very orthodox, and their strict religious beliefs made them close the doors to Industrial Revolution. It was the Dutch, and then the British, who took over to create their own global empires.

9.3   Empire on which the Sun Never Set

The Portuguese established their first trading center at Kollam, Kerala, in 1502. It marked the beginning of the colonial era in India, decades before the Mughals came. They built good relationship with Vijayanagara Empire and used the latter's grievance against the sultans to establish Portuguese dominion of India in Goa. Portuguese men married local Indian girls and left behind their culture, relicts of which can be found in Goa. They promoted Catholic Christianity in their dominions. Many churches were built by the Portuguese along the coast, Basilica of Bom Jesus in Goa being the most famous of them. Christianity, however, had already entered India long before Portuguese arrived. Saint Thomas converted many locals to Christianity in 70 CE. This version of Christianity was totally unknown to the Portuguese. When they met these Syrian Christians, they tried to Latinize them by force. Non-Christians were converted to Christianity or were tortured to death. Many locals fled and settled in the neighboring kingdoms.

The Portuguese strengthened their base in Goa, Daman, Salsette Island, Mumbai, Vasai, Diu, and Mangalore with their military might. Gradually, they started flexing their muscles. They built forts to protect their dominions. Control of all the important ports in west coast of India gave them monopoly over marine trade in Arabian Sea. The Portuguese also settled down in Hooghly (Bengal) during Akbar's reign. They established a port in Bandel and founded the Bandel Church. Their good relations with Mughals did not last long. Shah Jahan attacked and threw them out of Hooghly in 1632 after a few Portuguese pirates created nuisance. The Portuguese left their influence in Bengali vocabulary as Portuguese words like *chave* became *chabi* (*key*), *balde* became *balti* (*bucket*), and *pareka* became *perek* (*nail*). [105]

Dutch and British wanted to break into the triangular trade monopoly held by Spain and Portugal. They started by attacking their ships. This, along with the religious disturbances between Protestants supported by England and Netherlands (Dutch) and the Catholics of Spain and Portugal, led to the Anglo-Spanish wars that started in 1585. Spain wanted to invade England but was defeated. The battles provided British and Dutch with the experience of naval warfare. They went ahead to create their own colonies, with its main aim being piracy against the Spanish empire. Like the Spanish, Britain also started sugar plantation with the help of slaves brought by the Dutch. Britain established their first American colony in Jamestown, Virginia, on May 1607. [106] They soon took over most of what is now USA. The Dutch, on the other hand, took over many colonies from Spain and became the most powerful marine power in Europe. They became the main rival to British supremacy and friends became foes. There were series of wars between the Dutch and Britain. The Dutch had a minor setback in the first war between 1652 and 1654. But they soon reestablished their dominance in the following wars of 1665–75 and 1672–74. Portuguese and Spanish alliance also broke. Constant wars and religious orthodoxy slowly made Portugal weak. By 1661 Portugal was at war with Spain, and they needed the alliance of British, whose power was growing. Princess Catherine of Portugal got married to Charles II of England. The less-inhabited areas of southern Mumbai were given to England as dowry.

The Dutch went on to colonize Indonesia, the land where the spices originated. They took over from Portuguese to become the dominant marine trade power of Asia. British responded by establishing their base in India. India had the best cotton in the world, and the cotton trade proved to be more profitable than the spice trade. It was a masterstroke that would change British fortunes forever. Soon Indian cotton would dress up everyone in the streets of Europe, and Britain was the country that controlled it. Bengal was the key to trading in Asia. By 17th century, French made a colony in Chandannagar, Danes at Srirampur, and Dutch at Chinsurah. [56] British tried to establish EIC (from here on, EIC would mean British East India Company) in Hooghly but were forced to retreat when they had problems with the local Mughals.

USA declared independence from Britain after the American Revolutions of 1765–83. This shifted British focus from America towards Asia. Huge profits were made from the cotton industries, and it triggered a series of innovations that led to Industrial Revolution. One invention that happened out of necessity for something helped trigger another one in an entirely different field. There was also some social reorganization. Majority of Britain's population were farmers who had nothing much to do during the winter. The merchants used the farmer's free time to produce quality cotton cloth at cheap prices. New method of agriculture called enclosure was introduced in Britain where farmers acquired large plots of enclosed land that was more profitable. The smaller farmers lost their land and had to move to the cities. They got employment in the cotton industries. Coal mining also became common as it fueled the growing industries. The coalmines often got flooded. Steam engine was invented to pump the water out of these mines. The new innovation from a minefield created efficient and powerful machines like the steam locomotives that revolutionized transportation in Europe. The society rapidly changed from agrarian to industrial. Agrarian society depended on surplus of agriculture to flourish. Development was restricted by availability of land. Such societies do not have the resource to keep experimenting and innovating. [99] But the new industrial society depended on young minds finding new ideas and breaking the old dogma. There was enough resource for innovation and thus for technological advancement.

Wars and revolutions continued in Europe through 18th and 19th centuries. French Revolution (1789–99) took away power from the monarchies and churches and gave rise to democracy and nationalism. It was followed by the Napoleonic Wars (1803–1815) between France and the opponents led by Britain. The wars united Italy and Germany, an alliance that would continue till the world wars. Napoleon conquered most of Europe and weakened Spanish grip over its colonies. Latin American colonies declared freedom from Spain and Portugal. However, Napoleon's disastrous attempt of invading Russia and his final defeat at Waterloo ended France's dreams. British empire emerged as the dominant world power, only challenged to some extent by Russia. It became the largest empire the world had ever seen, extending from Canada in the west to New Zealand in the east. It was 'the empire on which the sun never set'.

9.4 Tale of Three Cities

British EIC was formed on the eve of 1600 by a group of adventurous merchants and aristocrats, with support from the Queen. The aim was to control the Asian spice trade. It is said that it all started for just five shillings. After the Dutch increased the price of pepper from three shillings to eight shillings, the British merchant joined hands and decided to form the new trading firm. Spice originated from Indonesia, but the Dutch were already controlling it. India, however, held the key to the spice trade. Indian cotton was in great demand in Indonesia, and it was the Indian cotton that was traded in return of spices. Moreover, the ships to Indonesia had to travel through Indian ports and were dependent on it for supply and repair. EIC had no ambition of ruling India. All they wanted was to establish trade and make profit from it. Sir Thomas Roe, who represented EIC, warned, "If you seek profit, seek it at sea, and in quiet trade – it is an error to afford garrisons and lead wars in India." [36] EIC followed the advice in the beginning. They started by establishing three key trading hubs.

Madras Day, the day Chennai was born, is celebrated every year on 22nd August. Back in 1639, an English gentleman named Francis Day bought a piece of land on the eastern coast of southern India from the local king of Vijayanagara emperor. The EIC employed Francis, and he was granted to build a factory and warehouse for trading. There was, however, constant threat from the Dutch and Portuguese competitors. To safeguard their interest, St George Fort was built in 1644, which still exists as the seat of the government of Tamil Naidu. Soon, St George Fort started to boom with activity as trading brought huge profits. Merchants and artisans started to arrive and settle in this new city that grew in size to become Madras [107]. In 1746, St George Fort was captured, and the French plundered the city. The British regained its control three years later.

Mumbai was an archipelago of seven islands namely Bombay Island, Parel, Mazagaon, Mahim, Colaba, Worli, and Little Colaba. It was given to Portuguese in 1534 by the Gujarat Sultanate in return of getting help in fighting the Mughals. Portuguese gifted it to Charles II of England. The king in turn leased it to the EIC. EIC ignored Mumbai and was active in Surat instead. It was a time when the Marathas, under Shivaji, were fighting against Mughals. Marathas attacked Goa and Mumbai and looted away treasures that funded their war. They also attacked Surat where the British already had a strong presence. The employees of the EIC, along with the traders, fought and managed to save their property from the invading Marathas. EIC showed its strength in protecting itself impressing the Mughals, the enemy of Marathas. It was an important event as it brought the British closer to the Mughals. [107] Mumbai, meanwhile, remained in the shadows. It was only after 1687, when the headquarters of EIC was moved from Surat to Mumbai, that it became a bustling town. The city became headquarters for Bombay Presidency. From 1782, the different islands were connected into single amalgamated mass. After the opening of Suez Canal in 1869, Mumbai transformed into the largest seaport in Arabian Sea.

British's Bengal experience was different from what they encountered in other places of India. Bengal was well served with rivers. It had cheap and good-quality cottons that were at demand in Southeast Asia with whom Bengal already had a well-established trade relation. Food was cheap, water was plenty, and hence cost of maintenance was low. It was a perfect place for trading. But unlike Mumbai, Chennai, or Surat, the strong Mughal government under Shah Jahan directly ruled Bengal. As discussed earlier, British misused the exemption granted to them by Shah Jahan's son Shah Shuja. The Mughals preferred the British to the Portuguese who were thrown out of Bengal few decades back. Profit brought a large number of private European traders in Bengal who competed against the company. The company did not want competition as it thrived on monopoly. The job of repairing this unwanted scenario was finally given to the most experienced company officer in Bengal: Job Charnock.

Charnock started his career in Bihar as a procurer of saltpeter, used to make gunpowder. He fell in love with a beautiful young Rajput girl. It is said that he rescued her from her husband's funeral pyre. Charnock called her Maria, and they had three children. He began to dress like Indians did and became fluent in Hindi. He moved to Bengal in 1669, and by 1685, he became the second in command of EIC in Bengal. The company came in conflict with the Mughals when the later imposed a customs tax of 3.5 per cent. Though against his wish, Charnock was forced by the company to attack the Mughals. The strong Mughal army routed the British. Charnock fled to Chennai after a little halt at Sutanuti, for which he had other plans. It was during this time that Charnock also lost his beloved wife. Maria was buried like a Christian, but every year on her death anniversary, Charnock sacrificed a cock over her grave as per her native custom. It was Aurangzeb who finally allowed Charnock to return to Bengal in 1690. After some perusal, Charnock managed to create Bengal Presidency, which was independent of Madras. The loss of his wife affected him, and in his last years, he became ill tempered and moody.

In 1695 an English pirate named Henry Every looted a Mughal ship heading towards Mecca. The Mughal ship was the largest ship operating in Indian Ocean at the time, and it was the richest loot by a pirate ever. This incident angered Aurangzeb, and his fury almost wiped out EIC from India. The company was saved only after an official apology from Britain. EIC purchased three villages—Kalikata, Sutanuti, and Gogindapur—for just 1,300 rupees from the *zamindars* belonging to Sabarna Roy Choudhury family. [107] Charnock already surveyed this place while running away from the Mughal. This was a good place from security point of view. The Ganges tributary (Hooghly River) ran on the west and the marshy salt lake to the east. To the north, there was a creek connecting Hooghly to the salt lake; and to the south, there was the tiger-infested dense forest of sundarban. With permission from the Mughals, Fort William was constructed there in 1712. Bengali merchants started to settle in the new town that grew up to become Kolkata. Rudyard Kipling wrote, "Thus from the mid-day halt of Charnock/ Grew up a city / As the fungus sprouts chaotic from its bed / So it spread." [36] Due to the Maratha raids, many villagers abandoned their house and fled to a safer Kolkata, and the population of the city soared. English dug a canal, called Maratha ditch, to prevent the Maratha raiders from entering the city.

EIC set up ports and trading hubs away from the old ones controlled by local rulers. Instead of Masulipatnam, it was Chennai, Mumbai instead of Surat, and now it was Kolkata rather than Hooghly. Moreover, all the new cities were fortified. So when the Mughals became weak and there was power struggle in India, the three cities were relatively safe. The power struggle affected trade, and by 18th century, EIC began its military expansion in India to protect their trade. After Aurangzeb's death, the Mughals were no more a power to reckon with. The struggle for India was now between the British, the French, the rising sultan of Mysore, and the Marathas.

9.5   India Divided

The crazy demand of spices in Europe was probably because it was essential in preservation of meat at a time when there were no refrigerators. It could also have been a status symbol as these expensive spices came from the exotic lands of the East. More than the spices, however, Europe of 18th century became crazy about the Indian cotton clothes. The clothes printed in India with block painting, hand painting, and embroidery became the new fashion statement of Europe. [107] The profit from trade attracted not just Dutch and English but also the French to India. The ripple of Anglo-French rivalry in Europe was being felt in the Indian subcontinent.

European sailors and merchants settled along the coasts of India. The harsh and risky life that they led required feminine comfort. Since the wealthy Indian women were out of reach, comfort was found in the less wealthy women who lived near the coast. Many of these Europeans married the Indian girls. European officers marrying Indian women of low origin hurt the 'white-man's pride'. To prevent the 'nuisance', ships filled with young European women were sent to India. The first ship brought unmarried Portuguese women from Lisbon to Goa in 1510. [108] British followed the Portuguese tactics, which backfired. Many of these women took a liking for the filthy rich Indian kings. Those who could not find a suitable partner returned back or became prostitutes. Both were not acceptable to European men. Though restricted by caste and religion, marriages between Indians and Europeans became very common. It was not easy for the European women to get accustomed to a foreign culture, and the family of the Indian kings did not immediately accept a foreigner. EIC also tried hard to discourage European women from marrying Indians. These women were not welcomed in social gatherings. With time, things only became worse as India became unstable and EIC became aggressive.

The Mughal Empire disintegrated after Aurangzeb's death in 1707. The local rulers started fighting to fill in the void. Decline of Mughal power adversely affected trade as roads became infested with thieves and pirates. Murshid Quli Khan, the Nawab of Bengal, declared himself independent from the Mughals. Murshid was born in a Brahmin family but was sold to a Persian nobleman. He lived his life in Persia before joining the Mughals in revenue department. Aurangzeb appointed him as the *dewan* of Bengal in 1700. After Aurangzeb's death, he became the de facto ruler of Bengal. His liberal rule led to peace and prosperity. It was the beginning of independent Nawabs of Bengal.

Young Siraj-ud-Daulah became the Nawab of Bengal in 1756. When he came to know about British ploy against him and fortification of Fort Williams, he attacked and seized Kolkata. Over five dozen captives were locked up in a cell meant for just six as a temporary arrangement. Unfortunately, they were kept there overnight due to miscommunication. Forty-three captives, including few British women, died inside the cell that has been named black hole. European media exaggerated the news and created a perfect opportunity to settle the matters. Robert Clive sailed from Chennai with his army to recapture Bengal. He first attacked and defeated the French who were supporting the Nawab in Chandernagar. The British then attacked Siraj in Plassey on the banks of Hooghly. Siraj lost the battle even before it began as few of his own men conspired against him. The betrayal made it an easy win for the British in what was supposed to be the most decisive battle in the history of the world. Siraj managed to run away but was caught and murdered.

The British put Siraj's uncle, Mir Jafar, on the throne. It did not take much time for Mir Jafar to realize that he had made a deal with the devil. Mir became friendly with the Dutch after the constant British interference in his political matters and their huge demand for money. Realizing the Dutch threat, British fought and defeated them in the battle of Chinsurah. After getting rid of the French and the Dutch and defeating the local rulers, EIC became the supreme power of East India. They now controlled a large area that included Bengal, Bihar, Odissa, Jharkhand, and Uttar Pradesh. The Mughals now came under the protection of the EIC. British strategy changed from 'quiet trade' to aggression as evident from one British document which stated, "We acquired our influence and our possessions by force, it is by force that we must maintain and preserve them and that no neighbouring subah, nawab or rajah will suffer to remain in tranquility except from fear, and a conviction that they cannot disturb us without danger to themselves, come what may." The consequence of the change of rule and lack of concern for the locals was the Bengal Famine. Over a third of the population of Bengal and Bihar were wiped out due to the famine. There was revolt against the British by the *Fakirs* and *Sannyasis* (ascetics) after British officers executed 150 of them without any reasons. These ascetics made pilgrimage to Bengal where they were paid handsome amount by the *zamindars*. After the EIC increased the taxes, it became difficult for the *zamindars* to pay both. EIC thought that the ascetics were looting their tax money and forcefully stopped them. The ascetics then fought back. It was difficult even for the organized British Army to stop the sporadic attacks, especially in hilly terrians and in the forests. The Fakir-Sanyasi Rebellion was the first protest against the British by ordinary men. It was the beginning of British imperialism in India, and it started with a bad taste.

After the fall of Mughals, Marathas rose to become the dominant power. They almost conquered Delhi, only to be interrupted by the invasion of Nadir Shah of Persia who plundered the city in 1739. Nadir went back with the Koh-i-noor diamond, the peacock throne, and lots of wealth. Maratha power continued to grow in northern India until 1761 when they were defeated in Panipat by the Afghan invader Ahmad Shah Durrani. They, however, were still a power to reckon with, especially in their home ground: the Deccan. Marathas defeated the British in the first Anglo-Maratha war (1775–1782), resulting in the Treaty of Salbai where Marathas regained all territories west of Yamuna River.

British were also threatened by the growing power of sultan of Mysore. Hyder Ali was the de facto ruler of Mysore. He was illiterate but intelligent and an able ruler. He realized the British threat, and like Shivaji earlier, he understood the importance of naval power. He tried to contact the Marathas and other powers of India but received little help. Hyder Ali went on his own to build his navy, with Maldives as its headquarters. He is also credited for inventing the deadly Mysorean Rockets. Despite suffering from cancer, he resisted the advance of British EIC. After his death, his son Tipu Sultan took over the throne. Tipu was an aggressive leader and was known for his bravery and the way he fought the British. His father lost to the Marathas and accepted their authority. Tipu wanted to break out of it, bringing him in direct confrontations with the Marathas. Tipu Sultan's army destroyed many temples and forcefully converted many Hindus and Christans to Islam during the wars. The worst affected were the Kodavas of southwest Karnataka. His aggression was cut short as he too lost to the Marathas and was forced to negotiate a deal with them. Tipu, however, was more worried about the British threat. He allied with Napoleon and the sultan of Constantinople. Napoleon almost conquered Egypt in order to join with Tipu Sultan and defeat the common enemy. Before they could meet, Napoleon was defeated in Waterloo, and Tipu Sultan fell in the fourth Anglo-Mysore war in 1799. Ironically, the same man named Arthur Wellesley defeated both.

While one enemy of British fell, another took its place. Maharaja Ranjit Singh founded the Sikh empire in Punjab the same year Tipu died. His successful campaign against the Afghans weakened the later and made the western border of India stable again. Ranjit Singh went on to capture Peshawar, Multan, Jammu and Kashmir, and parts of Himachal. The Sikh and British empires did not want to come in direct confrontation yet. Meanwhile, the British were looking to invade Nepal. The Gorkha war was fought between 1814 and 1816, in which the British gained one-third of Nepal's territories. British could never invade entire Nepal, and the Sugauli Treaty brought peace between them. Gorkhas later became important part of British Army. Once the Gorkha wars were over, British focused on eliminating their only challenge: the Marathas. Marathas by then were already weak, divided, and on the decline. They did not put much effort in keeping themselves updated with the new weapons. Britain managed to use the rivalry between the Indian kings to weaken them further. When the Marathas met the British in the third and the final Anglo-Maratha war (1817–1818), they were no match for the Europeans. The loss gave British control over most of the subcontinent apart from Punjab.

Russia's victory in Persia and Turkey brought them closer to India. In an attempt to stop the Russians, the British Army invaded Afghanistan. Sikhs allied with the British in the first Anglo-Afghan war (1839–1842). It was a disaster for the British Army. Not long after the battle, Ranjit Singh died weakening the Sikh empire. British found a perfect opportunity to gain control over the remaining part of India. The first Anglo-Sikh war was fought between 1845 and 1846. Sikhs lost most of their territories to British. Sikhs tried to regain the lost territories in the second

Anglo-Sikh war three years later. They lost again, and this time, Punjab surrendered to the British. The fighting spirit shown by the Sikhs impressed the British, and like the Gorkhas, Sikhs became an integral part of British Army in India. The whole subcontinent came under control of EIC. The British triumph was a result of lack of unity among the Indian rulers. The sultans of Mysore, the Marathas, the Rajputs, and the Sikhs never got united to fight the common enemy. The shortsightedness and greed for throne, along with ignorance of new technologies, led to their downfall. For most of the common people, apart from those affected by famines like in Bengal, the stability brought by the single rule came as a relief. Uniform system of government and education all over the country brought peace, for the time being.

9.6   Frail India and Drugged China

Chinese tea became very popular in Europe, just like the Indian cotton. With India as its base, EIC looked to extend its control over China. Silver from America, mined by Spain, was used by the British to buy Indian cotton and Chinese tea to sell in European markets. EIC made huge profits, and the money brought power. However, their aggressive policies and trade monopoly did not receive support in Britain. After several protests to remove trade monopoly of EIC, the Queen of England passed the Government of India Act of 1833. EIC was now to be governed by a Board of Control, which listened to the Queen. Their political and administrative control over India was renewed. Each presidency of EIC—which included Calcutta, Bombay, and Madras—maintained its own army. The total army consisted of 38,000 British, 340,000 Indians, and around 524 field guns. [109] Though the dominant force, Indian sepoys were never promoted to the highest level. The discrimination against the locals along with arrogant and racist behavior of some of the British officers created resentment among the sepoys.

To boost the local industry in Britain, Indian clothes and other products were banned in British market. It was the Indian industry that suffered resulting in a rapid rise in unemployment. From leaders in manufacturing and trading, India was reduced to just an exporter of raw materials. Closure of British market to Indian products affected EIC's profits further. Instead of European markets, the EIC now looked at Indian market. Cotton was bought cheaply from India, taken to Europe to manufacture different products, which was then sold back to India at high prices. While India's economy was declining, the cost of living increased. EIC was desperate to make as much money as possible from India and China after losing control over trade monopoly. Chinese tea was still popular in Europe, but there wasn't enough silver to buy them. EIC found the next best substitute: opium. Opium was grown in India, especially in Bihar, and illegally sold in China. With a lot of money coming from opium, it replaced traditional crops in India. Other commercial crops like jute, cotton, and indigo were also cultivated in abundance. Because of this shift in focus of agriculture, wheat and rice suffered. The money did not trickle down to the peasants. The peasants became poorer and had no money to invest in new technologies. This resulted in numerous famines in India between 1770 and 1857. [110]

Salt tax was an entirely new tax invented by the EIC and became a heavy burden on the common people. Locals were banned from manufacturing salt, increasing the price of salt by fifteen to thirty times. The high price meant that most Indians could not afford it, and the poor people started to eat ashes as alternative. The most significant problem, however, was the land taxes. EIC had increased the tax by five to ten times of what Mughals used to take. *Zamindars* were appointed by them and given full control over the land that they governed. In turn, the *zamindars* had to pay fixed, but huge, sums of money to the EIC. They were replaced if they failed to do so. Zamindars were under the kings who were under protection of British crown. The kings used to draw attractive salary (rupees~70,000,000 per annum) from the Crown. The British Raj purposefully spoilt the Indian kings. The young kings did not have much power or responsibility but all the luxury. They studied in British schools and enjoyed lavish lifestyle. British administration ensured that the kings were never a threat to them. The salary of the kings came from the tax taken from poor people. The new regulations encouraged *zamindars* to oppress the poor and become rich or perish. Police worked for the EIC and thus the *zamindars*. Their job was to help the *zamindars* in oppression, which would start the fragile relation between the Indian police and the common man that persists till date. As demand from the East India Company increased, the tenants (mostly farmers) felt the pressure. They often did not have money to pay the taxes. It gave small traders the opportunity to lend money to the poor and illiterate people and exploit them. The traders took to this immoral business as their real business suffered from competition with the British traders. The administrative system was also very bureaucratic.

To control the vast land of India and maintain effective trading, EIC needed to build infrastructure. It was 16 April

1853 when *Sultan*, *Sindh*, and *Sahib*, the three locomotives, dragged thirteen carriages from Bombay (now Mumbai) to Thane. It was the first-ever train journey in India. Taking the historical trip was a gentleman named Jaganath Shunkerseth. *Nana* Shunkerseth was an Indian businessman from Mumbai. Nana, along with Jamsetjee Jejeebhoy, became rich by partnering with British and trading cotton and opium. They were philanthropists, and a large portion of the money they earned was returned back to the poor. Not quite the philanthropist but a brilliant and sharp Indian industrialist of the era was a Bengali zamindar named Dwarkanath Tagore, grandfather of Nobel Prize winner Rabindranath Tagore. He was among the growing section of Western-educated Bengalis. His ruthless professionalism, innovative ideas, and entrepreneurship skills made him a legend. He bought the first coal mining company of India in Ranigaunj, which later became Bengal Coal Company. Dwarkanath was instrumental in creating the first political association of modern India called Zamandari Association [111]. From it was formed the Bengal British India Society, which would later inspire the Indian National Congress. Indian companies like M/s. Carr & Tagore Company of Dwarkanath Tagore were used as proxy by EIC after the Qing Government of China banned the British from opium trade. The continuous British effort to drug the Chinese despite opposition from the Chinese authorities resulted in the first opium war (1839–42). China lost, and the British forced them into an unequal treaty. Five ports—Canton, Shanghai, Amoy, Ningpo, and Foochow—were opened to foreign trade, which mostly meant opium. Foreigners were no more under the control of Chinese jurisdiction [112]. France and USA followed Britain, and China was helpless. Christian missionaries started to pour in. Forceful conversion to Christianity and people's resent against the fading Qing Empire led to the Taiping Rebellion. Around 20 million people died, and China was further weakened. Britain found an excuse to attack China once more, but the sudden Indian Revolt of 1857 postponed the second opium war.

William Edward Forster, a British statesman, gave a lecture in 1858 before Leeds Philosophical Institution on how the EIC tax India [113]. His book helps us understand why the revolt of 1857 took place. It was till date the most dramatic rebellion by any natives against the British rule, which at that time ruled majority of the world. If Forster's report is correct, for the year ending April 1856, the gross India revenue was £28,812,097 [114]. In today's value, that would be almost 300 billion Indian rupees. It came from six parts:

1 Customs, including duty on imported salt:	£ 1,934,906
2 Opium monopoly:	£ 4,871,227
3 Excise:	£ 1,183,073
4 Salt tax:	£ 2,435,389
5 Land tax:	£15,913,942
6 Miscellaneous:	£ 2,435,398

Add to that the money that they got by trading and looting. India was being sucked dry.

Major Ludlow wrote in mid of 19th century, "It [EIC] has failed in every one of the requisites of good government. It has to give security to person or property throughout by far the greater portion of India; sometimes by leaving the subject exposed to the open violence of brigands; always by placing him at the mercy of oppressive and fraudulent officials. Its judicial system is dilatory, costly, and inefficient. Its revenue system . . . seems devised in its different branches, so as to promote the largest possible amount of oppression, extortion, and immorality." [115] His quote summarizes the condition of India under EIC. Make no mistake about the fact that the condition of average Indian was already bad when Europeans arrived in India. It just went from bad to worse under the rule of the EIC. Everyone was affected, not just the poor.

Many Indian nationalists prefer to call the revolt as India's first war of independence. However, it wasn't the first war by Indian rulers against British nor were the people fighting for India. Different groups had different agendas, united by a common aim of uprooting a foreign rule that oppressed and exploited them. The British give it the name of Sepoy (army) Mutiny in an effort to hide their mismanagement that led to the war. According to the British story, Indians in the army thought that the new advanced cartridge was covered by fat of beef and pork. They had to open it using their teeth, and it was against their religion. The rumors angered the Indian sepoys and were seen as a conspiracy against their religion. The rebellion started when a sepoy of 34th Bengal Native Inventory, Mangal Pandey, attempted to shoot at a British lieutenant. He was arrested and executed, and his entire regiment was disbanded. No other incidents of revolt were reported from West Bengal after that.

The episode of Mangal Pandey, along with another curious development, alarmed the British officers. Rumors spread about mysterious rotis been distributed all across Central India. Rotis, homemade Indian breads, were passed from hand to hand and from villages to villages at a speed of 100 to 200 miles per night by people known as night runners. The first report of the Chapati Movement, as it was called, came in February 1857 [116]. One watchman would give a single chapati (Indian bread) to another watchman. He was supposed to make four such chapatis and distribute to four watchmen of nearby villages. The rotis sometimes carried messages like 'Sab lal ho jayega [Everything will turn red]'. The watchmen themselves did not know the reason for distributing the breads. They just followed the order. It is said that the movement originated in Indore, a land under the Marathas. It spread rapidly throughout North India. Few months later, the revolt of 1857 started, and the bloodshed indeed turned everything red. Does the revolt have anything to do with the Chapati Movement? Were the night runners spreading the news of usurp? We will never come to know as whatever reason there was for the spread of the rotis, it was meant to be a secret; and for once, the secret was well kept.

9.7   Death of a Poet

Naa kisi ki aankh kaa nuur huin, naa kisii ke dil kaa qaraar huin

Jo kisi ke kaam na aa saake, main woh ek musht-e-gubaar huun

(Neither the light of anyone's eyes, nor solace of the heart . . . I am.

A wasted fistful of mud, that's what . . . I am.)

Thus wrote the last king of the legendary Mughal Dynasty, Bahadur Shah Zafar. There was pain in his voice—and understandably so. He was a great man born in a wrong time. Zafar was a liberal ruler unlike Aurangzeb. Once a group of Muslims asked him to allow cow slaughter, something that is unholy for the Hindus. Zafar angrily replied that Islam does not depend on sacrifice of cows. Once an empire that ruled most of Hindustan, Pakistan, Afghanistan, and even parts of Iran has shrunk and now was restricted within the walls of Red Fort. Even that was soon taken away from Jafar. Three of his sons were murdered by the British in cold blood near the gateway, now known as Khooni Darwaza (Deadly/Murderous Door). Zafar was captured and imprisoned when he was already feeble and gloomy and into his 80s. He was not even given a pen and paper to continue his favourite hobby: writing poetry. So he wrote on the walls with a burnt stick before his death:

umr-e-daraz mang ke laye thhe char din, do aarzoo mein kat gaye do intezar mein

din zindagi ke khatm huye shaam ho gayi, phaila ke paon soyen-ge kunj-e-mazaar mein

kitna hai bad-naseeb zafar dafn ke liye, do gaz zamin bhi na mili ku-e-yar mein

(Days I asked and received four. Two passed in desire, and in waiting two more.

Life at its brink as dusk sets; with outstretched legs in grave, my body rests

For his burial, how unfortunate Zafar; Not even
two yards, his beloved land can offer.)

It all started on 10 May 1857 in Meerut when numerous
Indian sepoys were imprisoned because they refused to use
cartridges that were suspected to have cow and pig fat. As
noted by Sir John Malcolm, witness to the Sepoy Mutiny,
the Indian sepoys were loyal to the EIC until 1796 [117].
After 1796, the structure of the regiments changed as more
European officers joined the army and Indian sepoys got
stuck in the lower ranks. They were also forced to travel
overseas, something their religion prohibited. The angry
sepoys, treated as second-class citizens in their own land,
revolted. They killed some European officers in Meerut,
crossed the Yamuna River, burnt down the tollhouse,
marched into Delhi, and asked Zafar to lead them. The
poet king was in no mood for action in this old age, and he
stayed silent. Zafar took the throne when he was already
63 years old. He had no big ambition. He was happy in his
court, listening to the great poets like Ghalib and Zauq.
Revolt, however, spread throughout the city. Few British
officers were killed, and the unruly rebels did not spare
even their families. British officers panicked and open
fired at the sepoys, including those who were fighting for
the EIC. Things went out of control, and the next day, Zafar
reluctantly accepted alliance of the sepoys. The support
of a Mughal king gave the movement momentum, and
it spread rapidly across northern India. In Kanpur, the
fight was led by Nana Saheb and Tantia Tope, in Lucknow
by Begam Hazrat Mahal, in Bareilly by Khan Bahadur,
in Jagdishpur by Kunwar Singh, and in Jhansi by Rani
Lakshmibai [110]. Occasional rebellions also took place in
Bengal and Bombay Presidency while Chennai remained

silent. The Sikhs allied with the EIC as their hatred for the Mughals was much more than that towards the British. The deaths of their gurus in the hand of Mughal kings were not forgotten easily. The British Army brought in all support that they could get from Britain, Persia, and those on their way to China to fight the opium war. India was the crown of British empire. They could ill afford to lose it. What followed was a ruthless battle.

In Kanpur the rebels slaughtered hundreds of Europeans, including women and children. The British officers, in turn, burnt down villages after villages, killing rebels and civilians alike. As per the records, 100,000 Indian sepoys were killed. That statistics does not take into account the dead civilians and rebels who did not belong to the British Army. Amaresh Misra, in his controversial book, termed it as an 'untold holocaust' where the Britishers killed 10 million Indians in over ten years since 1857 [118]. Even though the British were slow to retaliate, Indians could not grab that opportunity. Lack of faith in one another, the resulting lack of coordination, and betrayals by own men led to the defeat of the Indians. The supply of artillery belonging to the rebels also exhausted. The British forces slowly regained all their lost territories. Delhi fell on September 1857 when Jafar was captured from Humayun's tomb. Rani of Jhansi, called by a British officer as the only man among the men, died fighting on 17 June 1857. The old Kunwar Singh managed to escape the British troops till his death on 9 May 1858. Tantia Tope was betrayed by Man Singh and was captured and executed on April 1859 [118]. Though the revolt failed, it managed to achieve an impossible task of uniting the Indians, to some extent at least. Years later, it would inspire Indians in their fight for independence from the British rule. The war also marked the end of two great powers of India: the Mughals and the EIC. The Queen of England took over from the EIC and established the British Raj. As for the Mughals, the dynasty ended with the death of Bahadur Shah Jafar. He once wrote a poem as if he knew his end was near:

Bar rahi hai hameshaa zakhm pe zakhm, dil kaa chaaraagaron khudaa haafiz

Aaj hai kuchh ziyaadaa betaabii, dil-e-betaab ko khudaa haafiz

Kyon hifaazat ham aur ki dhundhen, har nafas jab ki hai khudaa haafiz

Chaahe rukhsat ho raah-e-ishq mein, ai 'Zafar' jaane do khudaa haafiz

(Increasing forever pain on pain, Oh healers of heart . . . Goodbye!

Today I am unusually impatient, Oh restlessness . . . Goodbye!

Why search for protection from others, When every part of me said . . . Goodbye!

Even if ceases the road to love, Oh 'Zafar' let go . . . Goodbye!)

Fight for Independence (1857 to 1947)

Bombs and pistols do not make revolution. The sword of revolution is sharpened on the whetting-stone of ideas.

—Bhagat Singh

10.1 The Bong Connection

C hanges were taking place around the world in the last half of 19th century that would shape the course of our modern world. Far west, Edwin Drake's oil discovery in 1859 would help create one of the most powerful industries the world has ever seen. In Europe, Germany was formed after unification from Prussia. Young Germany started to compete for supremacy with the well-established European powers. The tension created by the unification of Germany resulted in the Franco-German War of 1870. The war triggered an arms race among the European nations, planting the seed for the World War I.

The dream of modernization and peace was broken by the increasing tension. Europeans soon realized the flipside of industrialization. Some people moved to the peaceful countryside, away from the hustle of the busy cities, in search of peace. Many European writers and painters portrayed a dark and gloomy future, where the big cities were destroyed and lay in ruins.

Farther east, the powerful Ottoman Empire was on the decline. The sultan tried to bring reforms but was too late. They had to take huge loans from Britain, giving the latter control over its finances. Same thing happened in Egypt. The Islamic states had seen the power of industrialization when Napoleon invaded, and they wanted that power too. It took centuries for Europe to break away from the orthodoxy of the church and acclimatize to modernity. Time was against the Islamic states for such a change overnight. The failed attempt at modernization, along with insecurity of a dying culture resulting from losing its control to the Christian European powers, led to the rise of fundamentalism.

In the East, Japan woke from its deep slumber of 200 years and finally opened up to the outside world. Japan's closure to the outside world and its reluctance to follow the West help it preserve not just Japanese culture but also Indian culture. Benoy K Behl, an art historian, has taken many pictures of Indian traditions preserved in Japan that have been lost in India. Japan absorbed Indian culture via China. Eighty per cent of Japanese gods are originally Indian gods. Japanese alphabet *kana* has its root in Sanskrit. Sixth-century Indian script Siddham is found in Japan and not India. When Japan did open up, to the surprise of everyone, it took no time for Japan to develop into an industrialized nation. Japan went on the aggressive path while its bigger brother China took a back step. The Qing Dynasty of China had weakened after the Opium Wars and the internal rebellions. The unrest resulted in the end of dynastic rule in China and the beginning of the republic. Back in India, power changed hands from the EIC to that of the Queen after the revolt of 1857, marking the beginning of the British Raj. There was also a renewed sense of patriotism being generated among the Indians, and it all began with the Bengal Renaissance.

Presence of the British had extreme effects on Bengal. While on one hand the ruthless policies led to famines that killed millions, on the other hand, it opened Bengal to the science and philosophies of the West. There was a new breed of English-educated Indians in Bengal who got access to the Western books. The renaissance and the revolts that happened in Europe inspired the young Indian minds. The European interest in Vedas and Upanishads reintroduced the ancient Indian texts to the Indian. Young India found a reason to be proud of their country's past. One must not forget that the ancient Vedic science was not entirely lost. Jantar Mantar was built in New Delhi, Jaipur, Ujjain, Mathura and Varanasi by Rajput king Sawai Jai Singh based on Vedic astronomy between 1724 to 1735 CE. The practice of rhinoplasty based on ancient Indian methods also continued at various places across India. The newfound pride and knowledge, however, resulted in the Bengal Renaissance. It paralleled the Italian Renaissance in a way that both were promodern revolutions against medieval orthodoxy inspired by the ancient texts.

The roots of Bengal Renaissance can be found in Raja Rammohan Roy's new theist society called Brahmo Sabha, created in 1828. K M Pannikar described him as the 'first modern man of modern India'. His pro-West sentiments were criticized by many, but Rammohan stood for what he thought was right. His main opponent was Radhakanta Deb, who opened Dharma Sabha to counteract Brahmo Sabha. Rammohan Roy vehemently opposed the cruel custom of *sati* and was a pioneer in its abolishment. He vowed to abolish the evil practice after being shocked by forceful burning of his sister-in-law after his brother's death. Because of his efforts, the British introduced Bengal Sati Regulation Act of 1829. The act made the practice of *sati* illegal in British-controlled India. He also fought for the property rights of women. Rammohan Roy was instrumental in introduction of modern education in Bengal. He established colleges that created educated middle-class Indians who would later lead the freedom movement. He, along with an English clockmaker David Hare, founded Hindu College in 1817, now known as Presidency College. From Hindu College sprang a new extreme culture of Young Bengal, led by an Anglo-Portuguese teacher named Henry Vivian Derozio. These young minds were intoxicated by free thoughts and liberation. They started mocking the orthodox ritualistic Hinduism in their monthly journal *Athenium*. In order to break away from traditional prejudices, they drank wine and ate beef. They fought for women's education, freedom of press, and many other sociopolitical issues. They denied the existence of god and opposed idolatry, priestcraft, and the evils of colonialism. In a way, they were like the Charvakas (atheists). The revolution was inspired by the French Revolution but lacked depth to go the distance.

Another legend of the Bengal Renaissance was a poor Brahmin boy named Ishwar Chandra Vidyasagar. Educated in a Sanskrit school, he learned English by himself. He read both Indian and English texts and learned the best of both worlds. He wrote numerous books on Sanskrit and Bengali for beginners in a lucid way. His book *Barno Porichoy* is still read by Bengali children. He helped open numerous schools for boys and girls in Bengal. He fought against child marriage and polygamy. But his main contribution was the promotion of widow remarriage in Bengal. Pioneering scientists like Jagadish Chandra Bose, Satyendra Nath Bose, Upendranath Brahmachari, and Meghnad Saha were born from the new education system. Jagadish Chandra Bose was the inventor of wireless telecommunications, and showing his true greatness, he refused to patent his invention. He was the first to realize that plants have life and believed that plants can 'feel pain and understand affection'. He was also the father of Indian science fiction. Satyendra Nath Bose is well known around the world for his contributions to quantum mechanics. The quantum particles 'bosons' are named after him. Not just science but literature also flourished during Bengal Renaissance. The Renaissance fashioned great authors like Ram Mohan Roy, Akshay Kumar Datta, Ishwar Chandra Vidyasagar, Michael Madhusudan Dutt, Sharat Chandra Chatterji, Bankim Chandra Chatterjee, Dina Bandhu Mitra, Kaji Najrul Islam, and Rabindranath Tagore. It was also the time of spiritual reawakening. Ramakrishna Paramahamsa's teachings brought new revolutions to the Bhakti movement. His ideologies inspired young minds like Swami Vivekananda. Vivekananda's famous speech in Parliament of the World's Religions in Chicago introduced vedanta and yoga to the world. Four years later, in 1897, Vivekananda founded Ramkrishna Mission for social justice. It still exists today. Another great personality who helped promote the Vedas was Aurobindo Ghosh. He studied in England for Indian Civil Service. Back in India, he became actively involved in freedom movement, which he left early, and became a spiritual leader.

The political maturity of Bengal gave it an advantage over other states of India. While the revolt of 1857 failed due to lack of coordination, the nonviolent Indgio Rebellion of Bengal happening at the same time was a huge success. It was a peasant movement of the poor indigo farmers against the influential British indigo planters who oppressed and exploited the former. The revolt saw both Hindus and Muslims coming together against the far more powerful Indigo planters. By the Act of 1833, the planters were granted free hand in the oppression of the peasants. The oppression was visible, and the officials did not interfere because of the huge profit that came from indigo farming. The protests from the poor farmers did not receive any attention till the educated Bengali middle class joined them. They gave the movement its tooth. Dinabandhu Mitra's controversial play *Neel Darpan* (*The Mirror of Indigo*) depicted the poor condition of the farmers. In short time, it became widely popular. Various articles were written to spread awareness. The peasants decided not to sow a single seed. The British government tried to suppress the movement ruthlessly and massacred many peasants. But the peasants did not fight back. They kept protesting nonviolently. Government's brutality only ended up making the revolution stronger. Indigo farming was ultimately stopped. Passive resistance found its first victory in India, a decade before Gandhi was born.

One of the most important events of Bengal Renaissance was the establishment of British Indian Association on 31 October 1851. It was formed after Landholders' Society merged with the Bengal British India Society. British Indian Association was an all-Indian organization that had political agendas. It helped create political awareness among Indians that spread throughout India. It would later help in the formation of Indian National Congress (INC). Its weakness was in the fact that the movement was restricted to a few educated elites. Majority of the poor Indians could not benefit from the movement. Moreover, most Indian Muslims kept themselves away from the Western education. Their reluctance to accept the new ideas pushed them away from not just educated middle class and the British but also Hindus in general. The Western scientific thoughts that led to the Bengal Renaissance were the greatest gift to India from the British. It helped India break away from the medieval religious taboos, it gave women equal rights, and more importantly, the renaissance generated nationalism among Indians that would ultimately lead to the fall of British Raj. Britishers themselves favored the Hindus in the beginning. But after the educated Hindus started to press for more reforms, the British changed tactics in the 1870s and started favouring the Muslims instead. This widened the gap between the two communities even in Bengal, where they used to live in peace and harmony. The preferential treatment slowly turned into the 'divide and rule' policy, which led to the partition of Bengal and ultimately that of India.

10.2   Act Accordingly

"God has appointed blood for her [Bhowanee] food, saying 'khoon tum khao', feed thou upon blood." This was the motto of the Indian tribe who killed in the name of Bhowanee, a goddess who would destroy all humanity if she were not fed blood. By feeding her, they claimed, they were saving the human race. These deadly people were not poor thieves stealing to live their daily lives. They were professionals for whom stealing itself was life. They befriended travellers. At the right opportunity, they would kill them and run away with all their possessions. A lot of time, they would spare the children, take them, and train them like one of their own. Known as Thugs, they were traveling tribes who passed their legacy to their kin. The more familiar English word *thug* is derived from this tribe. They are extinct now, thanks to the efforts of British civil servant William Sleeman.

William left no stones unturned as he executed and imprisoned the Thugs until there were no more Thugs left. To stop the menace of the Thugs, Criminal Tribes Act was passed in 1871. This listed tribes that were considered as criminal offenders. The adult males of the tribe had to report to the police every week, and the police had the right to arrest them without reason. Ironically, barring few, all the tribes were innocent. Many tribes, like the Banjaras, were carriers of merchandise from one part of the country to the other [11]. After British improved the connectivity in India through roads and railways, these tribes lost their earnings and were forced to take up criminal activities. Indian tribes were later exploited based on the Criminal Tribes Act, which was abolished only after independence. The tribal rebellions were one of the reasons for passing such an act, and Thugs were just the kind of excuse the British government needed to suppress them.

The tribal communities of India had traditionally been isolated, self-sufficient, having their own culture and rules. They also occupied lands that were rich in natural resources. The British invaded their freedom and made them angry. The Santhals of Bihar, Bengal, and Odissa revolted. Sidhu and Kanu were the heroes of the Santhal rebellion [119]. Not surprisingly, the British Army crushed the rebellion but not before their heroics inspired other natives. The Jaintias and the Garos of Meghalaya revolted against the British who were strategically constructing roads through their locality in the 1860s. House tax and income tax introduced by the British further aggravated the situation. The British government again crushed the rebellion with full force. One of their leaders, Kiang Nongbah, was executed in full public view. Instead of deterring, it encouraged further revolts. Munda tribes revolted against the British under the leadership of Birsa Munda. Birsa became a messiah among his followers, who claimed that he had divine powers. He protested as the lands of his ancestors were taken away, their way of life was forcefully changed, and the aborigines were reduced to being labors in the farms of rich men. Birsa was arrested on 3 March 1900, and he died in jail under mysterious circumstances [119]. Many of his men were sent to Kalapani or cellular jail in Andaman constructed after the revolt of 1857.

There was still no peace for the British. The American Civil War in the early 1860s led to increase in demand for cotton. However, after the end of Civil War in 1864, the demand died and cotton prices came crashing down. To increase the profit, British government raised the land revenue by 50 per cent at a time when the harvest was bad. Nothing was going right for the Indian peasants. They had to borrow money at high interest from the moneylenders who made their life miserable. The peasants revolted in the winter of 1874. It began in Kardah; but revolts soon spread to Deccan, Punjab, and Assam [110]. There were occasions when the moneylenders were attacked and the debt bonds and deeds were burnt down. The peasants of Deccan got support from Poona Sarvajanik Sangha led by Justice Renade. The government did manage to suppress the rebellion but not before passing the Deccan Agriculturists' Relief Act of 1879.

After the Queen took over from EIC, numerous acts were passed. Some helped in eradicating social evils while others were meant purely for exploitation. Prostitution existed in India for thousands of years as evident from the second century BCE play *Micchakatika*. Prostitutes were respected and accepted as part of the society. Even today, the idol of Durga is incomplete without the mud brought by the prostitutes. One needs to beg to receive the soil from the prostitute as a gift and blessing. Many of the acts were passed in a hurry before the British understood the complexity of Indian society. The Cantonment Act of 1864 gave the British government control over local prostitution. Twelve to fifteen native women were provided as prostitutes for each regiment. Prostitution spread rapidly under the British rule, but the status and respect they got in the society decreased. Unfortunately, for the soldiers, their fun did not last long as many of them became victims of venereal disease. The prostitutes were then forced to undergo regular examination. If they were infected, they were treated in special hospitals meant just for them, often forcefully. The infected male British officers, however, roamed free [120]. After massive protests from Indians and human rights activists from UK, the law was finally scrapped. Ironically, the same British government did not hesitate to make Devadasis illegal, probably because the Devadasis were not meant to entertain the British officers. Devadasi is an ancient Indian custom of girls dedicating their entire life to a god or a temple. They danced and sang in the temple unlike the rajadasis who performed in king's court for public entertainment. Devadasis were respected by everybody and enjoyed high status. They were second only to the temple priests. The status of the Devadasis deteriorated during the Middle Ages. During British Raj, all rituals related to Devadasis were made illegal. Slowly, Devadasis and prostitutes became synonymous, a form in which the custom still exists secretly in many parts of southern India.

The biggest victims of the new laws were the transgender and the transsexual communities of India. Indian mythology is full of transsexual and transgender people. Hijras, or the third gender, have been integral part of our culture. Our ancestors easily accepted gender diversity. In fact, erotic sculptures in temples depicted homosexual relationships. Such open culture was a shock for the British under influence of Victorian orthodoxy. They banned homosexual relations in 1861 under section 377 of the Indian Penal Code. Hijras were labeled as a 'criminal tribe' in 1871 and stigmatized. Gradually, the orthodox British culture became part of our own as we forgot the traditions of our once ironically progressive past. While the century-old section 377 was struck down in 2009 by Delhi High Court, it was recriminalized by the Supreme Court in December 2013. The sad irony is that United Kingdom had moved on and made gay sex legal. We, however, hold on to its wrong legacy.

Not all acts passed by the British government were detrimental. There were new laws that helped India getting rid of evil medieval customs like *sati*. Age of Consent Act of 1891 increased consensual sexual intercourse for all girls to 12 years age in an effort to abolish child marriage. Caste Disabilities Removal Act of 1850 abolished the laws that affected the rights of persons who got converted to a different religion or caste. The Bengal Rent Act of 1862 gave protection to tenants from the exploitation by the rent-owner. British rule also challenged India's caste system. All Indians, probably for the first time, were the same in front of the law. A higher-caste Brahmin and a lower-caste Surda would face similar punishment for similar criminal offence. People, irrespective of caste, were recruited in Indian Civil Service and Indian Army. Every regiment of the army, however, was still divided in terms of one's religion and caste. The fair system gave opportunity to Dalits, like Ambedkar, to flourish. The key motive of colonialism in any part of the world was profit, not charity. More than half of the government spending was on military, justice, police, and jails and very few on agriculture and development [121]. It is understandable why the British had passed some of the acts. What cannot be understood is why many of such old acts still exist. There is an immediate and pressing need of reform.

10.3   Nations by Themselves Are Made

Sons of Ind, why sit ye idle,/Wait ye for some Deva's aid?

Buckle to, be up and doing!/Nations by themselves are made!

Yours the land, lives, all, at stake, tho'/Not by you the cards are played;

Are ye dumb? Speak up and claim them!/By themselves are nations made!

What avail your wealth, your learning,/Empty
titles, sordid trade?

True self-rule were worth them all!/Nations by
themselves are made!

Whispered murmurs darkly creeping,/Hidden
worms beneath the glade,

Not by such shall wrong be righted!/Nations by
themselves are made!

Are ye Serfs or are ye Freemen,/Ye that grovel in
the shade?

In your own hands rest the issues!/By themselves
are nations made!

Sons of Ind, be up and doing,/Let your course by
none be stayed;

Lo! the Dawn is in the east;/By themselves are
nations made!

- A O Hume, *Old Man's Hope* [122]

This beautiful poem was not written by an Indian but
by A O Hume. There were many Englishmen, like Hume, who
sympathized with the Indians and protested against the
atrocities of the British Raj. Born in 1829, he came to India
to join the Indian Civil Service at the young age of 20 years.
Just after nine years, he faced, and survived, the revolt of
1857. Instead of the Indians, he blamed the incompetence

of EIC for the outbreak. Hume took the initiative to provide education for the Indians. He started free primary schools and arranged for scholarship for higher education. Hume criticized the land revenue policy that was the leading cause of poverty in India. Not surprisingly, his open criticism of the government was not taken well. He was forced to resign in 1882. Hume continued to stay in India. He had a unique hobby of collecting and preserving different bird specimens from India. He is rightly called the father of Indian ornithology. His most important contribution for India, however, was the foundation of INC. Hume wrote, "Every nation secures precisely as good a Government as it merits." If Indians are not ready to 'strike a blow' for the sake of their country, then they deserve to be in the mess they are.

Regional political parties had already taken shape in various parts of India, led by the educated Indians. Associations like the British Indian Association of Bengal, Bombay Association, Madras Native Association, Indian Association, Madras Mahajan Sabha, Bombay Presidency Association, and Poona Sarvajanik Sabha were working individually at regional level [110]. Educated Indians were slowly making sense of the legal and political structure of the British Raj. The Indian intellectuals had successfully fought the Indigo Revolution and the Deccan agricultural revolt. But most of their other protests were unsuccessful. The main reason was the lack of unity between the different associations. Hume realized it, and he believed that the educated Indians could come together and fight against the injustice of imperialism. With that aim in mind, he founded the INC in 1885, only to be disappointed by the inaptness of Indian leaders. Frustrated, Hume went back to UK a decade later. It would take INC some more time to mature and fulfill its objectives. One of the major problems INC had was that it only represented the elite English-educated Indians. It did not represent the entire strata of the Indian society. The foundation, however, was set to unite the Indians against a common enemy and develop a sense of national pride.

Another major development in India that would help in the rise of nationalism was the Indian press. India's adventure with the press began long back in January 1780 when an eccentric Irishman named James Augustus Hicky published the *Bengal Gazette*. It claimed to be 'a weekly political and commercial paper open to all parties but influenced by none'. His attack on the government and especially on Mrs Hastings led to his downfall. *Indian Gazette* was published on November 1780 to compete against *Bengal Gazette*, with probable support from none other than Mr Hastings [123]. Soon, other weekly journals started to appear in Madras (now Chennai) and Bombay (now Mumbai). Government, quick to realize the danger of free press from its experience in UK, tried to control the menace. Journalists, all Westerners till then, who had written against the government were deported from India. New regulations were passed in 1799 to completely control press, which made publishing any paper without government inspection punishable. Despite restrictions, the popularity of newspaper kept growing. The first regional newspaper published in India was in Bengali and was called *Samachar Darpan* [124]. Soon other regional languages followed. Nationalistic newspapers spread to all parts of the country, including remote villages. The government was criticized tactfully without trying to directly insult the establishment. Protests started to happen in favor of freedom of press, ably led by Bal Gangadhar Tilak. The struggle is far from over. Even today, India is ranked very low at 140th in World Press Freedom Index (2014) despite having an independent press that is not controlled by the government [125]. The contribution of the Indian press towards the identity of India was enormous. Fight for freedom of press went side by side with India's freedom struggle. Almost every freedom fighter wrote for one of the papers or the other. The press, along with the political bodies like INC, would help in the freedom movement that would spread like wildfire throughout the nation in the 20th century.

10.4   Rise of Extremism

At the turn of the century, three developments happened in India that threatened the Raj. First was the unity of Hindu and Muslim peasants against the oppression by a common enemy, second was the reach of Indian press and its influence on developing nationalistic sentiments, and third was the rise of a single native political party that was beginning to expose the fallacies of the British government. The government was projecting itself as the protector of India. According to them, they were maintaining law and order in India and investing foreign capital in helping her develop into an industrialized nation. Many Indian leaders bought the idea until some of them started to do a detailed economic analysis of British Raj. The person who led the research was none other than the Grand Old Man of India, Dadabhai Nairoji. He was the first Indian to become a British member of Parliament and was also one of the founding members of INC.

The findings from the economic analysis were revealing. Foreign capital was invested in India not for developing her as the British projected but to exploit her natural resources. India was made into an exporter of cheap raw materials and importer of expensive British-manufactured goods. The policy of free trade ruined traditional handicrafts, and the competition from the developed British industries hampered the growth of indigenous industries in India [110]. British projected Indian railways as a great contribution towards developing India. However, the economic studies showed that the Indian railways promoted exploitation of natural resources and spread of foreign goods rather than development of Indian economy. The railways made extraction of cotton and other raw materials from India, for the European manufacturers, very cheap. The railways that discriminated based on skin colour was not making ordinary Indian's life any better. The tax structure, especially land revenue, was a burden on the poor. It was the leading cause of increasing poverty in India. India's wealth was drained to Britain as salaries and pensions of British officials working in India [110]. A large portion of the wealth went in maintaining the army that helped Britain maintain its world dominance. Majority of Indian people were poor and illiterate. If the British government were really concerned about Indians, the percentage of illiteracy would not have been as high as 88 per cent when they left. Only a fifth of the children were receiving any form of primary education. That too happened only because the government required native clerks [121]. The nationalists brought this 'drain theory' out among the mass and helped people realize who the real enemy was.

While the moderates like Dadabhai, Gopal Krishna Gokhale, Pherozeshah Mehta, and most of the members of INC questioned the motives of the Raj, they were loyal to

British. They wanted reforms in favor of Indians and not independence. The moderates failed to attract the majority of the Muslim community. Syed Ahmad Khan founded the first Muslim political body, the All-India Muslim League (AIML), in 1905. AIML worked closely with INC in the beginning. INC's moderate methods were clearly not working, and few members started to lose their patience. One of the early opponents of the moderate approach was Bal Gangadhar Tilak, popularly known as Lokmanya Tilak. He was the first person to propose swaraj, or self-rule, as the final objective. He famously declared, "Swaraj is my birth-right and I shall have it." Tilak received support from strong personalities like Bipin Chandra Pal, Arobindo Ghosh, and Lala Lajpat Rai. This new form of extremism gained ground after partition of Bengal by Lord Curzon in 1905. The partition was made on communal ground, and Indians saw in it a plan to divide and rule India.

Protesters flooded the streets of Bengal, and *Vande Mataram* (praise to the mother) became the new slogan. The river near Hooghly Bridge was filled with people from the morning. They took bath in the holy river. Then the people of all communities tied rakhi on the wrists of each other to show unity. All foreign goods were boycotted. Despite the large gathering, there was no violence or rowdyism. Few Muslim leaders did support the partition as they saw an opportunity to get hold of a land where they were clear majority. The protests, however, were successful, and Bengal was finally reunited in 1911. But not before creating further divide between the Hindus and Muslims. Muslim political leaders became insecure of becoming a minority in Hindu-dominated India. This feeling came for the first time after the Revolt of 1857 and the end of Mughal Empire when they were stripped of most of their powers.

Majority of the Muslim population, skeptical of English education, denied themselves the opportunity of economic development. This increased the gap between the Hindus and Muslims. Nowhere was the gap more prominent than in Bengal.

In the late 19th century, the British shifted from 'pro-Hindu' to 'pro-Muslim' policy because of revolts from the Hindu political class. The British successfully fueled the growing anti-Hindu sentiment of the Muslims. British policies tempted the Muslims to become loyal as evident from the Morley-Minto reforms. Separate electorates were created for Muslims, and only Muslims could vote in those electorates. This enhanced the political barrier on religious grounds. Soon there were separate Muslim trade unions, student organizations, and merchants chamber [122]. Seeds for partition were thus planted. Similar division happened between the educated Hindus, dominated by upper castes, and the *Dalits*. INC can be blamed partly for not identifying the vested interest of British and not being able to encourage and provide confidence to majority of the Muslim and Dalit communities to join their party.

Post the partition of Bengal, the gulf between the moderates and extremists increased, which finally led to the split within INC in 1907. Both Dadabhai and Tilak realized the danger of a split but could do nothing to stop it. New form of violent extremism spread in Bengal. Secret organizations like Anushilan Samiti and Jugantar gained followers. It was the beginning of armed revolution against the Raj. Young Khudiram Bose and Prafulla Chaki bombed a carriage mistaking it for Magistrate D H Kingford's carriage. Instead, two British women were killed [110]. From Bengal, this violent patriotism spread to Punjab. The Punjabi NRIs started the Ghadar movement. The movement purposefully made the Punjabis feel ashamed of allying with the British during Revolt of 1857 and inspired them to fight back this time. Many Bengalis, like Rash Behari Bose, supported the movement while the moderates opposed this extreme form of revolt. The British government gave hope to the moderates and took them on their side while ruthlessly curbing the extremist group. Most of the extremist leaders, including Tilak and Arubindo, were arrested. Many leaders of the Gadhar Movement were executed.

British managed to weaken both the Hindu-Muslim unity and INC at the same time. The next objective for the British was to control the press. With that in mind, the Press Act was passed in 1910, imposing strict censorship on any publication, especially those directed against the government. Numerous presses were shut down and many more fined. Just when India looked to be coming fully under the control of the British government, World War I broke out.

10.5   The Forgotten Heroes

In the beginning of 20th century, Germany was leading the steel and chemical industry and grew considerably in coal. They now looked to challenge the British supremacy over sea. They started to build a railway track from Berlin, through the Austro-Hungarian Empire and Bulgaria, into Baghdad, belonging to the Ottoman Empire. If the track was completed, it would generate enormous wealth for the Germans, and the railway line would be inaccessible to Britain. It would also bring Germany within striking distance of British Egyptian interest and from there to Persian Gulf and finally into their prized possession: India.

It was crucial for the British to stop the German menace, and they needed an excuse [126]. Serbia parted from the weak Ottoman Empire with the motto of regaining the glorious past of the Slavs. When Hungary took over Bosnia, they faced resistance from the nationalistic Bosnian Slavs. The nationalists considered themselves to be ethnically closer to Serbia than Hungary. The nationalists assassinated Austria-Hungarian Archduke Franz Ferdinand and his wife in June 1914. The world got the excuse to explode.

Competition among the European nations led to a strange sort of military alliance among the different countries. According to the alliance agreement, a country had to join in the war if its ally was attacked. Germany had an agreement with Austria-Hungary while Japan with Britain, Britain with Belgium and France, France with Russia, and Russia with Serbia [127]. So when Austria-Hungary attacked Serbia after Ferdinand's death, Russia joined the war to save Serbia. Germany attacked Russia to save Austria-Hungary that brought France into the game. When Germany attacked its old rival France, Britain had to join the war. The Ottoman Empire joined the Central powers led by Germans while Japan and Italy took side with the Allies. America was dragged into the war when a German U-boat sunk a British ocean liner with 159 Americans onboard. Russia, however, withdrew after a quick treaty with Germany because of their internal conflicts.

The war had no relevance to India, but even then, she sent more than 1.1 million armies, whom the world forgot. Over 60,000 Indians died fighting someone else's war. Not just men, India also sent horses and other animals and over 100 million pounds to support the British [128]. Quite contrary to British feeling that Indians would take the opportunity to revolt, majority of Indians remained loyal to the Crown. Indians hoped that the British Raj would be kinder to them and grant them their demand for home rule once the war was over. Occasional rebellions did occur inspired by extremist groups like Jugantar in India the Ghadar movement of USA and the Indian Independence Committee of Germany. Bal Gangadhar Tilak's release from jail in 1914 boosted the nationalists. A British lady named Annie Basant helped him immensely. Both of them promoted the home rule and spread the message throughout India. INC welcomed Tilak and his men back. Personalities like Jawaharlal and Jinnah joined AIML. The movement reached its peak in 1917. The government was forced to bring in the Montagu Declaration. It was a policy to accommodate more Indians in every branch of administration 'with view to the progressive realization of responsible government in India' [129]. It was a bait from the British government to pacify the Indians, and it worked. The movement for home rule fizzed out by 1918.

Omissi's book [128] opens us to the life of the forgotten Indian soldiers of the Great War through the letters they wrote. The quotes that follow are taken from those letters. Indian soldiers mostly belonged to the poor and illiterate peasant class. They were happy that the British government provided them employment. They fought not just for money but also for pride. According to one soldier, "it was fitting for anyone who has eaten the salt of the great government to die [for the government]". [128] They were brave and had some success. A Sikh soldier wrote, "With a shout to our Guru we hurl ourselves forward. The enemy bullets scorch our heroes, while machine guns and cannons spread their shot upon us. We leap the wire entanglements and overwhelm the enemy, killing some and capturing the rest."[128]

Indian Army was weak due to lack of proper training. British never wanted them to become too powerful. They were poorly equipped and were in cold and unfamiliar conditions. They were often used as pawns and were given positions at the frontline [128]. After the experienced officers died, inexperienced and inept officers replaced them just because they could speak 'Indian'. Lack of skill and leadership meant that they suffered heavy casualties. It left a dark impact in their mind as the war progressed. They compared the deadly war to *Mahabharata* and Karbala. A wounded soldier once wrote to his relative in India from England: "Do not think that this is war. This is not war; it is the ending of the world." [128] The soldiers sometimes used code words in their letters send to their family to express discontent. Most of the codes were easy to decipher like the one that said, "Black pepper is finished. Now red pepper is being used, but, occasionally, the black pepper proves useful. Black pepper is very pungent and the red pepper is not so strong. This is a secret, but you are a wise man." [128] *Black pepper* meant Indians, and *red pepper* meant the Europeans. The morale of these Indian soldiers were expectedly going downhill. There were further affected by the harsh winter. Some soldiers even wounded themselves to avoid going into the battlefield. Various techniques to appear wounded or sick were described in the letters, like smoke from some plant that causes swelling. Most often, the tactics did not work as even wounded soldiers were sent back to the battlefield. One Indian soldier wrote, "I have been wounded twice, and now this is the third time that I am being sent to the trenches. . . . The butcher does not let the goat escape."[128]

The soldiers did receive good treatment in the hospitals. There were times when the Queen herself came to meet the wounded Indian soldiers. They seemed to be very impressed by the French, especially the French women. Their writings suggest that the French did not discriminate between 'brown' and 'white', unlike the British. It seemed like there were occasional sexual encounters between Indian jawans and the European women. It hurt the pride of European men who tried to prevent such nuisance. It was one of the reasons why all the letters were checked in detail. Indians praised the cleanliness, compassion, and literacy of the local Europeans and were disappointed by the poverty and backwardness back in India. At the same time, many were homesick and just wanted to return and eat homemade Indian food. Indian infantry were finally withdrawn from the frontline duties by the end of 1915 while the cavalry remained. They were then placed in the familiar and warmer climate of Mesopotamia to fight the Ottoman Turks. Indian soldiers played a pivotal role in capturing Baghdad and defeating the Ottoman Empire [128].

The war was fought between machines, and the machines were powered by oil. Men, munitions, and money had little value without oil; and that is where the Allies had a distinctive advantage [130]. With the big oil companies, including Standard Oil of New Jersey, Royal Dutch Shell, and Anglo-Persian Oil Company on their side, their ships and automobiles became more agile. New killer machines like tanks and warplanes came into existence, and the weapons became more powerful than ever before. Allies, with their newfound mobility and efficiency, came out victorious. Germany agreed to a ceasefire on Armistice Day, 11 November 1918. On 28 June 1919, the peace treaty named Treaty of Versailles was signed. It was a controversial and unfair treaty that laid impetus for another war in years to follow. The deadly battle claimed lives of over 9 million combatants and 7 million civilians [129]. The boundaries of countries were redefined. When one looks back at the 'great' war now, one wonders why. The war left not just wounded bodies but wounded souls. Once the war ended, the Indians were very happy to return to their country as changed men.

10.6   Was Gandhi a Hero?

India's freedom struggle took a new turn after the Great War. It was Mohandas Karamchand Gandhi who took the center stage in the final battle against the British Raj. Gandhi is widely regarded as a saint, a mahatma, who showed the whole world that battles can be won without violence. Einstein said, "Generations to come will scarce believe that such a one as this walked the earth in flesh and blood." Yet Gandhi had his fair share of critics. He has been labeled as a 'sexual weirdo' who slept with his young niece, and there have been protests against building his statue in London. He has been called a racist and has been accused of being in a homosexual relationship with a German bodybuilder. So before we go into our next phase of freedom struggle, it is very important that we understand Gandhi.

Selected writings by Gandhi in *My Experiments with Truth* [131] throw some light on his life. Gandhi was a little boy of 18 when he dared to go against his people who threatened to outcaste him. He crossed *kalapani* and sailed to England with a dream of a bright future in law in 1888. He got permission from his mother to go abroad only after he promised her three things: no meat, no alcohol, and, most importantly, no sex. His friends in England warned him that he would not survive the cold conditions without meat, but he was adamant. He was also inspired by the new vegetarian revolution in England. Not having wine also had its own advantage, especially when Gandhi was called to the bar at the end of his course. There were two bottles of wine for a group of four. Since there was scarcity of nondrinkers, he was in demand. Everyone wanted him so that the rest three in the group could finish two bottles. While he kept his first two promises easily, it was the third that seemed most difficult. There were times when he came very close to breaking the most important vow. First time in Portsmouth and second much later while sailing to South Africa. But each time, he managed to stop himself before crossing the limit, even though it meant dirty thoughts and sleepless nights.

Gandhi was ashamed of the fact that he was married at such a young age and even had a kid. His first child was born when he was just 15 but survived only few days. Like a coward, he hid the fact that he was married when he was in England. He finally confessed to an old lady who loved him like a son and was looking to engage him with a young British lady. Gandhi was also very, very shy. He trembled when he had to speak in public, and often, someone else had to read his speech on his behalf. It was in his second year when Gandhi read *Gita* for the first time. He started reading other religious books as well like *The Light of Asia* and was impressed by Hindu philosophy. He realized that superstition was not part of Hinduism. In later life, he fought hard to abolish all forms of superstition from Hindu religion. He also began to like English customs and dresses. Gandhi survived England and came back to India after three years, only to hear the news of his mother's demise.

It was kept a secret from him so that it did not affect his studies.

The Indian episode wasn't a happy one. His shyness prevented him from becoming a successful lawyer. His relation with his wife, Kasturba, was also not amicable. There were times when he made her life miserable. Later he realized his mistake and even had the guts to acknowledge it in his writings. He revealed that he learnt nonviolence from his wife who would later be an active participant in the freedom struggle. In 1893 he got an offer from Dada Abdulla & Company and went to South Africa, where the third phase of his life began.

Gandhi was surprised to see the poor condition of Indians in Africa. Indians were often insulted by the Englishmen who addressed them as *Coolie* or *Sami*, quite oblivious to the fact that *Sami*, which came from *Swami*, meant *master*. Gandhi was thus called the 'Coolie barrister'. Not all Englishmen were rude. There was one gentleman who fought with the guards and allowed Gandhi to travel with him in first-class train compartment, generally reserved for the 'whites'. He even ate dinner with many Europeans in Johnson's family hotel. It was in South Africa where he came to know about Islam and Christianity and also sharpened his knowledge of Hinduism. However, it was the racism he faced in South Africa that prepared him for the battle in India. He had to fight to keep his turban on while inside the court. He was once thrown off the first-class compartment despite having legal tickets because he was a 'brown'. In the same journey, Gandhi was beaten up after he refused to sit on the floor of a coach for which he had tickets. He was also denied to stay in many hotels because of his skin colour. There were places where Indians were not allowed to walk on the streets at night.

He was once pushed and kicked by a guard for walking on a footpath, barred for nonwhites, at night.

Gandhi was a well-educated barrister. If he was treated like this, he wondered what would be the condition of the poorer Indians. Once his work in South Africa was finished, he was preparing to leave for India. In his farewell party, he chanced upon an article in the newspaper. It was about a bill before the House of Legislature, which, if passed, would disallow the Indians their right to elect the members of Natal Legislative Assembly. That changed his plans, and he decided to stay back and fight for justice. He started to study the condition of Indians in South Africa in detail. He put in effort to make Indians aware about cleanliness and educate them. He promoted unity of Indians despite the differences in language, religion, and caste. While Gandhi was worried about his countrymen, he did not care much about the native Africans whose conditions were even worse. Gandhi firmly believed that the Indians, having a richer civilization, were superior to the natives and deserved better treatment. He founded Natal Indian Congress in 1894, which fought for the rights of Indians in South Africa. Gandhi came to India two years later to get support from Indian political leaders. His popularity attracted many enemies, mostly British. He was attacked by mobs when he returned to South Africa but somehow managed to escape. His wife too joined him in South Africa during this time.

Gandhi encouraged recruitment of Indians when the British were fighting Boer war in 1899 and again in 1906 against the Zulu kingdom. It is during this time that Gandhi met Pingali Venkayya, a geologist who would later design India's flag. During the wars, Gandhi came to realize the power of British Army. He knew it would be futile for the weak countries to fight the British with arms. Instead, he chose nonviolent resistance, or *satyagrahya*, as his new weapon. He had been put to jail for his nonviolent protests. It was in the jail where he had interactions with the native Africans. That helped him erase his prejudice against them. He met the rich German-born Jewish architect Hermann Kallenbach in 1904 and became very good friends. Kallenbach donated his farm to Gandhi, which became a shelter for the *Satyagrahis* (the nonviolent protesters). It was named Tolstoy Farm. Gandhi is said to have written to his friend the following lines: "How completely you have taken possession of my body. This is slavery with a vengeance." [132] The lines have widely been misinterpreted and taken as a proof that Gandhi was gay, even though none of Gandhi's letters to his German friend had sexual connotations.

Gandhi's new method of *satyagrahya* (nonviolent protest) became successful. Funds started to pour in from India, donated by Sir Ratan Tata, Nizam of Hyderabad, INC, and the AIML, along with many others [131]. Gandhi succeeded in uniting Indians of different class and religion. He finally returned to India in January 1915, beginning the fourth and final episode of his life. In India, he was involved in the much-controversial Brahmacharya experiments, especially with his young grandniece Manu. In this weird experiment, he slept with the naked ladies. His obsession with Brahmacharya developed from a childhood experience. When his father was sick, he spent a lot of time massaging his feet. One night his uncle took over from him, and he went straight to his room where his pregnant wife was. They had sex that night, after which he got the news that his father was dead. The child born later also did not survive. Gandhi blamed his lust for the tragedy. Now he wanted to end that lust by controlling it. His own men, including Sardar Vallabhbhai Patel and Nirmal Bose, disliked the Brahmacharya experiment and urged him to stop. But Gandhi was adamant and even frank about what he wanted. Gandhi's reply to his critics was "If I don't let Manu sleep with me, though I regard it as essential that she should, wouldn't that be a sign of weakness in me?" [133] Manu's diaries throw light on the kind of effect the experiments had on her. She was devoted to Gandhi and was not forced to stay in there. Manu wrote, "Bapu is a mother to me. He is initiating me to a higher human plane through the Brahmacharya experiments, part of his Mahayagna of character building. Any loose talk about the experiment is most condemnable." [134] The relation she shared with Gandhi was like 'Mirabai who lived only for her Shyamlo [Krishna].' Manu was standing beside Gandhi when the latter was shot. She was shocked. She wrote, "As the pyre was lit and Bapu's body was consigned to the flames, I wanted to sit there forever. It was all a bit difficult for me to accept; only a few days ago Bapu was with me, now I am completely lonely, completely helpless." Gandhi's methods might have been weird, but he was not a 'sexual weirdo' as many try to project out of political malice or colonial prejudice. He did not lust for sex. He wanted to end that lust forever.

Gandhi was not a saint. He was an ordinary man who was put through extraordinary situations. Facing injustice from a powerful force, he did not accept it like most men—he revolted. Sometimes he was right and at times wrong. He was orthodox, he was too religious, he was strict with his children, and he had flaws—like we all do. But what makes him different was that he stood for what he thought was right. He was a shy person who was afraid to speak in public but had the magnetic personality to attract millions of followers. Only because of Gandhi, the freedom movement reached the poor and illetarate mass instead of being a monopoly of few foreign-educated lawyers. He brought in a new method of satyagrahya that taught the world about nonviolent protest. It is for these reasons that he is, and will remain, one of the greatest heroes of the world. Gandhi once said, "See me please in the nakedness of my working, and in my limitation, you will then know me."

10.7 Rising Voices

The reluctance of the British government to give India self-rule after the war, along with the worsening of her economic condition, led to frustration among the youths. Young Indians took to the path of violence to get rid of the Raj. Few members of Indian Army were disgruntled with the British for treating them like slaves and secretly supplied arms to the extremist groups in India. The occasional incidents of violence by nationalists in Bengal, Punjab, and Maharashtra led to the enactment of Rowlatt's Act in March 1919. It gave the British government the authority to arrest and imprison any person suspected of terrorism without warrant or trial. The Indian political leaders, especially Gandhi who was now becoming active in Indian politics, criticized the act. On 6 April, Gandhi began his first *satyagrahya* on Indian soil against the 'black act'.

Five years earlier, a young tribesman named Jatra Oraon started a religious movement called Tana Bhagat. It was a nonviolent movement against not just the Zamindars, missionaries, and the British, but also their own tribal lifestyle. As the Indian tribes increasingly mixed with the outside world, they got influenced by other dominant religions. The Mizos got inclined to Christianity while Hinduism influenced the Tana Bhagats. They became ashamed of their rituals and customs like polygamy. The movement inspired the tribals to give up superstitions, alcohol, meat, and sometimes even agriculture. The Tana Bhagats let all their cattle go free and resigned in the forest for salvation [11]. They became followers of Gandhi and took active part in his *satyagrahya*. The modern Tana Bhagats still believe in Gandhi's philosophy of ahimsa and wear khadi clothes, dhoti, and Gandhi cap with a tricolour flag on it.

After Rowlatt's Act was passed, Dr Satyapal and Dr Saifuddin Kitchlew were arrested in suspicion of spreading terrorism. Huge crowds gathered in front of police station, demanding their release. Panicked, police fired at the mob, killing several protesters. The angry mob went rampant, attacking British officers and killing three in the process. A European teacher was also attacked, saved only by few Indians who hid her under a table. Gandhi had to call off *satyagrahya* due to these incidents of violence. Brigadier General Dyer, son of an Indian-born Anglo brewer, was transferred to Amritsar to handle the growing unrest. He banned gathering of large crowd in Punjab.

Like every year at the time of Baishakhi festival, on 13 April 1919, people gathered inside Jallianwala Bagh for a public meeting. Dyer thought that his instructions were being disobeyed. He ordered his fifty Gorkha riflemen to surround the garden and shoot at the gathering without any warning. Bullets were fired at innocent men for ten minutes, where almost a thousand (official British figure of 379) people died. While the brutal incident shocked the entire nation, many Britons, including Rudyard Kipling, supported Dyer. Dyer was, however, criticized in the House of Commons and was forced to retire the next year. Dyer's last few years were not happy, and he died eight years since the incident from cerebral hemorrhage after multiple strokes paralyzed him. He said in his deathbed: "So many people who knew the condition of Amritsar say I did right . . . but so many others say I did wrong. I only want to die and know from my Maker whether I did right or wrong." [135]

Rabindranath Tagore, the first non-European to win Nobel Prize for Literature, renounced his knighthood in protest. He said that it 'make(s) our shame glaring in the incongruous context of humiliation'. Tagore wrote after the massacre: "He who causes suffering becomes small when his victims have the power to rise above it by their heroism of fearlessness. This is the lesson which Gandhi has been trying to preach to his countrymen."[136] Gandhi, angry with the British, called for non-cooperation movement throughout India. He also supported the Khilafat movement in an effort to unite the Indian Muslims against the common enemy. The British often cited the tension between the Hindus and Muslims as a reason for not leaving India. Both communities had to unite if they wanted to claim independence.

The idea of Khilafat movement was rooted in the belief that caliphate was the ideal Islamic symbol that provided divine justice in this world. The God who speaks through his messengers rules the world. Men must listen to the messenger or the one who takes his place. After prophet's death, it was the caliph that took his place and was thus the supreme guide of men. When Ottoman Empire lost in the Great War and was divided, the caliphate was in danger. Most Muslim kings of India, apart from Akbar, had always been loyal to the caliphate. As discussed by Dr Khimjeen, in mind of Indian Muslims, the authority of universal caliph was accepted as a necessity. Some Indian Muslims were afraid that they would be left at the mercy of British and Hindus once their protector caliphate collapsed. The British only helped in promoting such ideas [137].

The insecurities of Muslims in India increased after few key incidences. The British government gave in to the demands of the Hindu-dominated Bengalis who protested against partition of Bengal on religious lines. The Muslim leaders who favored the partition thought that the government betrayed them. In another incident, British government decided to build a road that passed through a mosque and a temple. After protests, the government decided to bend the road instead of destroying the temple. However, the government went ahead with destroying part of the mosque that was not considered sacred. When the Muslims protested, the government ordered open fire. Many Muslims, including children, were killed in the firing. The increasing anti-British feelings of Indian Muslims culminated in the Khilafat movement. One of the pioneers of the movement was Muhammad Ali Jauhor, who was also part of the AIML. He was a nationalist who dreamt of 'united faiths of India'. He became the leader of Khilafat Committee. Ulama of the Deobandi and the Firangi Mahal were trying hard to promote survival of the caliphate and later became active in the Khilafat movement. Firangi Mahal, which once housed the European Indigo merchants, became a grand center of Islamic education. They promoted Hindu-Muslim unity and were very close to Gandhi. When Gandhi visited Lucknow, he stayed at the Firangi Mahal. All Muslim families abstained from cooking meat during his stay out of respect. Gandhi, and his supporters who were mostly Hindus, supported the Khilafat movement while the AIML, in turn, supported Gandhi's non-cooperation movement. Hindus and Muslims joined hands and chanted 'Hindu-Muslim Bhai Bhai'. It happened despite the sudden attack on India by Amanullah of Afghanistan during third Anglo-Afghan war in the summer of 1919 that brought back medieval fears in the mind of the Indian Hindus.

Non-cooperation movement was launched on 1 August 1920, a day that started with the death of Lokamanya Tilak. It was a day of mourning as thousands of people gathered and observed fasts. Gandhi and Ali brothers, later being important Khilafat leaders, went on a nationwide tour to promote their cause. Indian-manufactured goods were promoted. Gandhi appealed to boycott foreign clothes and urged villagers to make cloth using weaving and hand-spinning wheels. Foreign cloths were burnt all over India and *khadi* (Indian handwoven cloth) became the new fashion. Some students complained to Gandhi that *khadi* was costly. Wear less clothes was his answer. From that day, Gandhi renounced *dhoti* and *kurta*, wore just a *langot*, and became the 'half-naked fakir'. The demand of foreign clothes fell, and its value dropped from INR 120 crore in 1920 to just INR 57 crore the next year [134]. The movement was working, and the British were alarmed.

Just when the movement was at its peak, three things happened that would lead to its abrupt end. First, Mappila Muslims of Malabar became aggressive and attacked the police stations and then the Hindu landlords in 1921. Second was the Chauri Chaura incident, where angry mobs set a police station on fire, killing twenty-one officers. Gandhi immediately called off his non-cooperation movement. The decision surprised many Indians, and the Muslims felt betrayed. Gandhi justified that India was not ready for nonviolent protests yet as any act of violence will give British forces enough reason to curb the entire movement. The third incident was the abolishment of the caliphate by the Grand National Assembly in Turkey on 1924. The Khilafat movement in India lost all significance after that. All these incidents had remarkable repercussion in India. The Hindu-Muslim unity broke, and it was followed by numerous incidents of communal violence.

10.8　The Cult of Chakara

Gandhi saw in industrialization a hidden evil that tied men into a vicious web of the materialistic world. The promise of science, technology, and prosperity were illusions that threatened not just our nation but also the souls of our men. Running blindly after Westernization made our youth lose their identity. Wearing English clothes, learning in English-medium school, working in industries controlled by British masked as modern and liberal and which Indians were proud of were only created for the profit of our oppressor [138]. British advertised the so-called 'modern' attitude because it bred industries, like the Manchester clothes. These industries made a huge profit by selling costly products in India while the 'out of fashion' indigenous industries suffered. In this culture, both consumer and worker became a slave to the machines controlled by the big industries in Britain. It was a culture that promoted suspicion, hatred, racism, and exploitation [139]. Such industries only ended up making us poorer. Gandhi called for the renunciation of everything Western. He wanted complete non-cooperation with the government. Gandhi advocated following a simple lifestyle and using indigenous products. *Chakara*, or the spinning wheel, was the symbol of such simplicity. Gandhi started the chakara agitation, inviting all Indians to spin the wheel and make India self-sufficient. Rabindranath Tagore, one of Gandhi's greatest admirers who is credited for giving Gandhi the title *Mahatma* (some give the credit to an unknown journalist), criticized this extreme view.

Tagore started the reorganization of Indian villages long before Gandhi returned from Africa. He was educating the villagers and promoting agriculture, cotton, and village industries [140]. Tagore himself wanted to get rid of the British Raj and was an adherent follower of nonviolence. When he found that the young patriotic minds were leaning towards violence, and especially after Khudiram and his friends killed innocent European women, he distanced himself from the movement. Some called him a betrayer. But that did not change his mind as he was against 'blind nationalism' [141]. According to Tagore, those who uphold the ideals of nationalism are the most conservative in their social practice. It becomes more problematic in a country like India where there is a physical repulsion between different castes. To Tagore, renunciation of everything Western, including science and technology, was stupid. Saying everything Western is bad is as ridiculous as saying everything Western is good. While to Gandhi poverty was a virtue, for Tagore, it was a problem that we needed to get rid of. Chakara, to Tagore, was not a symbol of progress but of poverty and everything that was wrong with India. According to the poet, "Western science should merge with eastern spirituality to create a complete society that is without the self-created borders".

Nationality, to Tagore, was the root cause of our problems, not industries. Nationalism threatens humanity as it ultimately promotes exploitation of one country by another. Colonization is rooted in the idea of nationalism [141]. The two world wars were enough proof to support Tagore's thought. Hitler was a product of extreme nationalism. Non-cooperation movement was doing exactly that by creating hatred for everything Western. The poor were forced to buy khadi clothes that were more expensive. Students were told to boycott English-medium schools, thus hampering their education. Tagore was against the idea of youths blindly following a cult and losing their ability of reasoning. In the eyes of Tagore, 'what India most needed was constructive work coming from within herself' [141]. In poet's words, he wanted an India 'where the mind is without fear, head is held high, knowledge is free and world was not broken into fragments'.

Indian customs, like caste system, bind a person to a specific duty chosen by one's ancestor. It helps in gaining labor but kills the free mind by binding one to repeat the same job over and over for ages without question. Such mind always required a ruler or a saint to tell them what to do, and hence, such minds can never be free. Tagore saw the same ignorance in the blind followers of Gandhi who 'follow him like rats' without questioning. Gandhi himself became a cult. Sarojini Naidu once said that it cost a lot to keep Gandhi in poverty. The protection he required to continue with his simple way of life was a costly affair. It was symbolic and necessary, as the freedom struggle required the mass of India. The chakara was part of that cult that Tagore did not like. Tagore firmly said, "Lest I should be a party to the raising of the charkha to a higher place than is its due, thereby distracting attention from other more important factors in our task of all-round reconstruction." [142]

Gandhi replied to Tagore, assuring him that there was nothing to fear. Gandhi had a lot of respect for Tagore and often asked him for advice. He used to call Tagore *Gurudev*. Gandhi explained that he was not trying to build a China Wall between East and West. He was protesting against forceful cooperation rather than voluntary cooperation based on mutual trust and respect [143]. Gandhi disagreed with Rabindranath about the students' education. According to him, "training by itself adds not an inch to one's moral height and that character-building is independent of literary training. I [Gandhi] am firmly of opinion that the Government schools have unmanned us, rendered us helpless and Godless" [143]. Non-cooperation with the bad is as important as cooperation with the good. Gandhi went on to say, "I am certain that it does not require ages for Hindus to discard the error of untouchability, for Hindus and Mussulmans to shed enmity and accept friendship as an eternal factor of national life, for all to adopt the charkha as the only universal means of attaining India's economic salvation and finally for all to believe that India's freedom lies only through non-violence, and no other method." [143] Tagore was still not convinced, so when Gandhi said, "Everyone must spin. Let Tagore spin like the others. Let him burn his foreign clothes; that is his duty today. God will take care of the morrow" Tagore was quick to reply, "The charka does not require anyone to think; one simply turns the wheel of the antiquated invention endlessly, using the minimum of judgment and stamina." [141] Tagore wondered why a person with skill to do better things would waste his talent in spinning a chakara. Tagore did not want India to become isolated from the rest of the world. Instead, he believed in fluid borders of countries where every country learned from the other and grew together. Both Mahatma and Gurudev were right in their own way. Despite the differences, both continued to have immense respect towards each other.

After the withdrawal of non-cooperation movement, Gandhi was arrested. It was followed by disagreements within INC. When Gandhi was released on February 1924 due to poor health, it seemed like INC was going to split again. C R Das and Motilal Nehru wanted to end the boycott and enter legislative councils to expose the government. People like Vallabhbhai Patel, Rajendra Prasad, and C Radhagopalachary opposed it. Though Gandhi was against it, he made a pact with C R Das and Motilal to end the split. The latter group entered legislative councils as Swarajists. The freedom movement, however, seemed to have lost track. There were a few separate incidents, like the rebel of Koya tribes in Andhra led by Ramachandra Raju in 1922–24, revolt by Akalis in Punjab, Satyagrahis defending the honor of the national flag in Nagpur in 1923. But there was no sign of British retreat [110]. Dismayed by the turn of events, Gandhi wrote to Tagore, "I am furiously thinking day and night but I do not see light coming out of the surrounding darkness." [136]

10.9   Call for Swaraj

The UK elections were due in 1929. Indian Nationalists used the opportunity and pressured the British government to give them self-rule. Under pressure, the government formed the Indian Statutory Commission in February 1928. It was more popularly known as Simon Commission. The main purpose of the commission was to buy time and let the elections pass. According to Lord Birkenhead, "(Britain) must not run the slightest risk of the delay in selection. It is, of course, obvious that the mere anti-dating of the Commission, while it would probably give satisfaction in India, would deprive [British Government] of nothing valuable" [144]. The British ploy was obvious when no Indian members were chosen as part of the committee that would decide India's fate. This angered the Indians, leading to protests all through India. When Mr Simon came to India, he was greeted with black flags wherever he went. Police restored to lathi charge on several occasions to clear the protesting mob. In once such attack, Lala Lajpat Rai was seriously injured. He succumbed to injuries few months later.

After the protests, Lord Birkenhead challenged Indians to 'form a unanimous constitution and present it to [British government] and [they] will implement it' [145]. Indian leaders accepted the challenge. But there was one problem. The number of Hindu-Muslim riots had increased since Gandhi called off the non-cooperation movement. More than twenty-five riots have been reported between April and September of 1927. The riots mostly happened during religious celebrations. Hindus played loud music near mosques, and Muslims killed cows near temples [146]. The incidents created further divide between the two communities, just like the British hoped. The Hindus and the Muslims could not come to a common agreement. After the failed third meeting, Nehru Report was framed by a smaller group of people, chaired by Motilal Nehru [147]. The report asked for dominion status for India. Among the only two Muslim delegates, Syed Ali Imam could not attend due to sickness and Shoaib Qureshi refused to sign, arguing that the rights of minorities were ignored. Jinnah himself went ahead recommending fourteen points to protect the interest of the minorities [148]. His points did not get the support of the majority and were rejected. Jinnah was dejected, and the gap between INC and AIML grew further. The Indian Liberal Party and AIML opposed Nehru Report. Young Subhas Chandra Bose and Jawaharlal Nehru did not like the dominion status either. More importantly, the British government ignored it and refused to introduce any political reform.

The British apathy frustrated INC and they were finally ready to go on the aggressive path. In the Lahore session of INC, Gandhi was people's first choice for president, followed by Sardar Vallabhbhai Patel. Though Jawaharlal Nehru was not the most popular, he became the president on Gandhi's insistence. Surprisingly, Subhas and Srinivasa Iyenger were excluded from the Congress Working Committee. Tricolor Indian flag with the spinning wheel in middle was hoisted in Lahore. Independence pledge was read out, and 26 January was declared as the Independence Day, or Poorna Swaraj.

Gandhi called for the civil disobedience movement, which included nonpayment of taxes. He also launched salt satyagraha with Dandi March on 12 March 1930. Many, including Jawaharlal, ridiculed the idea of protesting against British salt monopoly instead of bigger issues. But Gandhi knew well that bigger political concerns do not connect to the masses. He was more concerned with issues of the poor in order to bring them into the movement of civil disobedience. It was a huge success that made the British government concerned. Thousands of Indians were put behind bars, including Gandhi, for making illegal salt. Ghaffar Khan, with over 50,000 followers, joined the movement to fill in for those put behind bars. After Ghaffar Khan's arrest, thousands of Indians gathered to protest.

The British police were ordered to open fire on the peaceful protesters. Over 250 people were killed, but the protesters stood firmly in front of the bullets without any violence.

After all key leaders were arrested, 76-year-old Abbas Tyabji and Gandhi's wife, Kasturba, followed Dandi March with the Dharasana March; and after their arrest, Sarojini Naidu took the lead. Women, for the first time, became actively involved in freedom struggle of India. American journalist Webb Miller published the atrocities of British rule against nonviolent protests and helped turn the world opinion against the British rule in India. *Time Magazine* declared Gandhi as The Man of the Year in 1930. Webb had immense respect for the naked fakir. He used to carry a cigarette case, and in one of his meetings with Gandhi, the latter promised to sign it only if he never smoked again. Webb Miller maintained his promise till he died. Even after the massive protests, the salt tax was not reduced. The movement, however, united the Indians and also managed to get the support of the world for India's cause. Gandhi was released from prison and was called to a round table conference, the first time for an Indian as an equal.

10.10   Sarfaroshi Ki Tamanna

Just for a handful of silver he left us / Just for a ribbon to stick in his coat—

Found the one gift of which fortune bereft us / Lost all the others she lets us devote;

. . .

We that had loved him so, followed him, honored him / Lived in his mild and magnificent eye,

Learned his great language, caught his clear accents / Made him our pattern to live and to die!

. . .

He alone breaks from the van and the freemen,

He alone sinks to the rear and the slaves!

We shall march prospering—not thro' his presence;

Songs may inspirit us—not from his lyre; [149]

Robert Browning's famous poem was printed on a pamphlet issued by Bhagat Singh and his men. On the cover of it was a poster of Lajpat Rai, a.k.a. Sher-e-Punjab. Bhagat Singh had so much respect for Lajpat Rai that nothing was said against him. It was a silent protest against a great man who was turning to communal politics towards the end stages of his life. Bhagat Singh was an atheist and firmly believed that the narrow old customs of religion should be criticized and discarded one by one [110]. He, like many young Indian of that time, was influenced by the revolution in Russia and the idea of Marxism that was popularized in Punjab by the Ghadar movement. Bhagat Singh belonged to a family of freedom fighters and was inclined to the non-cooperation movement. His heart was broken after Gandhi called off the movement when it was at its peak. Later, he joined the armed revolutionaries. He was not a terrorist but a man with a vision who wanted the dead souls of India to wake up. He was humane, fighting against inhumanity. Singh is known more as an angry young man who killed a British officer to avenge Lala Lajpat Rai's death. His logical thoughts and free mind are often undermined. Bhagat Singh was not the only one to take up arms. Armed revolution was gaining ground in India as the youngsters were losing patience and faith in the old political leaders due to their lack of action.

On 9 August 1925, the eight-down train slowly approached Kakori from Shahjahanpur. Ten well-trained armed men pulled the chain of the train. They took position to rob British money that the train was carrying. It was just 8,000 rupees that they managed to rob. But the purpose was not just the money but to shake the very foundation of British administration. The mission was a success, apart from a mishap where a passenger was accidentally shot. The gang ran away and spread to different locations. Police cracked down heavily, and all but one member of the gang were arrested. Ram Prasad Bismil, Ashfaqullah Khan, Rajendra Nath Lahiri, and Roshan Singh were sentenced to death. The one who kept deluding the British authorities was Chandra Shekhar Azad, the master of disguise. He had made a promise to himself that he would never surrender to the British.

Azad mentored Bhagat Singh and other members of Hindustan Social Republican Association (HSRA). On 17 December 1928, Azad, Singh, and Rajguru assassinated police officer Saunders, who was involved in beating up Lajpat Rai. HSRA soon published, "We are sorry to have killed a man. But this man was a part of a cruel, despicable and unjust system and killing him was a necessity." [150] Their next action was to bomb the Central Legislative Assembly to protest against the passing of Public Safety

Bill and Trade Disputes Bill. Singh and B K Dutt threw a bomb in the assembly. The bomb was weak and not meant to kill anybody. Both of them surrendered to the police as per plan. HSRA pamphlet declared, "It takes a loud voice to make the deaf hear. With these immortal words uttered on a similar occasion by Valliant, a French anarchist martyr, do we strongly justify this action of ours." [150] Rajguru and many others were soon arrested. Azad managed to fool the police once again. Singh, Rajguru, and Dutt went to the courtroom confidently every time they were summoned, singing patriotic songs like 'Sarfaroshi ki tamanna aab hamare dil mein hai' or 'Mera rang de basanti chola'. They undertook hunger strike in jail, protesting against the discrimination of Indian prisoners compared to the Europeans. The sound of their revolution echoed around every corner of India. The whole nation was angered when they heard that Dutt, Singh, and Rajguru were to be hanged. Meanwhile, Azad's luck ran out, and he had to shoot himself when he was surrounded by police and saw no chance of escaping. Azad kept his promise of never surrendering.

Meanwhile, in Bengal, the armed revolution had taken one step ahead. Instead of individual heroism or small groups, there was a new form of organized mass-scale armed revolution. Surya Sen, popularly known as Masterda, led one of the most active groups. Like his father, Masterda was also a teacher in a government college in Chittagong. He was a member of INC and participated actively in the non-cooperation movement. Like Bhagat Singh, he was disappointed that the movement was called off. He brought together a group of like-minded people who could work towards his master plan. The plan was to free Chittagong by capturing the two armories and blocking all connectivity including telephone, telegraph, and railways. Around sixty-five men took part in the plan that was executed on the night of 18 April 1930. They were divided into a number of teams, each with their specific agenda. Both armories were captured, telephone and telegraph lines were destroyed, and the train service was disrupted. Unfortunately, they could not find the ammunitions. All of them gathered outside the police armory and hoisted the Indian national flag. The flag was saluted with the proclamation of Provisional Revolutionary Government. The group then took shelter in a nearby hill where they fought the British Army bravely. Twelve of Masterda's men died while over eighty British troops were killed [110]. But their ammunition was limited, and Masterda ordered the group to disperse into the nearby villages. Most of Masterda's men were captured by police and punished. The villagers, mostly Muslims, helped the revolutionaries hide for three years until Netra Sen disclosed the hideout of Masterda. A revolutionary, however, killed Netra before the British could give him his reward. Masterda was arrested, tortured, his teeth hammered, nails plucked out, and limbs broken. Whatever was left of him was hanged on 12 January 1934. His last letter said, "Death is knocking at my door. My mind is flying away towards eternity. . . . At such a pleasant, at such a grave, at such a solemn moment, what shall I leave behind you? Only one thing that is my dream, a golden dream—the dream of Free India." [151] His letter inspired thousands of young minds. Recruitments for the armed revolution soared.

Meanwhile, the British government called Gandhi for a Round Table Conference (RTC) held in London. After weeks of heated discussion with Irwin, the British government agreed only on the following six points [152]:

1. Withdrawal of all ordinances and end of prosecutions
2. Release of all political prisoners, except those found guilty of violence
3. Permit peaceful picketing of liquor and foreign cloth shops
4. Restore the confiscated properties of the freedom fighters
5. Permit free collection or manufacture of salt by persons near the seacoast
6. Lift the ban over the INC

Realizing that he could not do anything more, Gandhi signed the Gandhi-Irwin Pact on 5 March 1931. It was the end of civil disobedience movement. The pact was less than satisfactory for the Indians, but they did not have much to bargain with. The nonviolent civil disobedience movement was putting strain on the Indians and was fast losing strength. But to the Indians who had high expectations, Gandhi failed them once more. Gandhi discussed about the release of Singh, Rajguru, and Dutt but in vain. By the time Gandhi returned to India Bhagat Singh and his friends had been executed. Within days from being the greatest hero, Gandhi turned into a villain. This time it was him, rather than a British, who was greeted with black flags by Indians.

10.11   Confrontations

Jinnah was one of the brightest political leaders of India. He studied in a madrassa in Karachi and was trained as a barrister in Lincoln's Inn. He was the youngest Indian to be called to the bar in England. Jinnah was working towards Hindu-Muslim unity and was part of the moderate faction of Congress. By the time Gandhi joined INC, the moderates had become weak and Jinnah was left alone. He joined AIML to bridge the growing gap between the League and Congress. Jinnah did not like Gandhi's over-religious approach to politics and the mass hysteria he created. To him, 'politics is a gentleman's game'. When his fourteen points to protect the minorities were rejected by INC, he parted ways with them. After his wife's death, Jinnah settled in London with his daughter Dina. His sister came to London to support him as Jinnah was getting old and was also suffering from lung disease. His relation with his daughter strained after she married a Christian. Jinnah came back to politics to represent the AIML in RTC. Disappointed as the INC rejected separate electorate for Muslims, he went back to London—to his favorite smoke and whiskey. That would have been the end of his political carieer. When he heard from his friend that Jawaharlal said 'Jinnah is finished', he returned to politics and to India with vengeance [153].

In the several RTCs, Jinnah proposed separate electorates for Muslims, just like Ambedkar for the untouchables. After the end of the RTCs, the government announced Communal Award in 1932, creating separate electorates for each minority religion and for the untouchables. Though INC did not like it, they did not disapprove either. Gandhi, however, was not happy with the separate electorate for untouchables. According to him, it would create further division within the Hindu community. Gandhi was fighting to remove the evil of untouchability from the society. He traveled across India, spreading the awareness. Gandhi was not against the caste system, and he did not approve intercaste marriage. He was only trying to abolish discrimination, exploitation, and inequality among the different castes. This is where Ambedkar differed. Ambedkar wanted to abolish the caste system because, according to him, as long as it existed, there would be discrimination. Until the caste system was abolished, he wanted separate electorates to protect the untouchables. That brought him in direct confrontation with Gandhi. Gandhi went on hunger strike till death in Yerwada Central Jail of Poona, protesting against the separate electorates for untouchables. Gandhi's fast created widespread unrest, and Ambedkar was compelled to agree with Gandhi's demands. It was agreed that there would be reserved seats for the 'depressed castes' instead. The agreement, known as Poona Pact, was signed on 24 September 1932. Tagore was there when Gandhi broke his fast, and he sang a Bengali song [136].

Tagore later changed his stance about the Poona Pact. He said, "Communal award advocated by the Pact . . . will inflict a serious injury upon the social and political life of Bengal." [136] Many Dalits still hate Gandhi for his fast. Gandhi was slowly going away from politics and was more involved with social reforms and removal of untouchability. To him, without that, India could never achieve true freedom. Gandhi described the earthquake of January 1934 as 'divine chastisement for the great sin we have committed against the Harijans [untouchables]'. Tagore was again prompt to protest, "Feel profoundly hurt when any words from his [Gandhi's] mouth may emphasize the elements of unreason." [136] He added, "It is all the more unfortunate because this kind of unscientific view of [natural] phenomenon in too readily accepted by a large section of our countrymen." [31]

Gandhi left Jawaharlal Nehru as his successor. Gandhi's relation with his sons was not amicable. It was in Jawaharlal that he found the son he always wanted, even though Jawaharlal's personality was quite contrasting to Gandhi's. Jawaharlal studied in Harrow and was sharp, smart, and liberal. Socialist movements influenced him, like Subhas Chandra Bose. It made Jawaharlal more radical than his moderate father. He worked with Subhas to develop good relations between INC and other free countries. Jawaharlal was not against Westernization, like Gandhi. He was not religious, and he never understood why Gandhi considered sex as sin. He once sent a letter to Gandhi expressing his difference of opinion.

Jawaharlal's wife, Kamala, however, was very much influenced by Gandhi. In her later life, she abstained from sex, much to the dislike of Jawaharlal. Kamala was not well and was suffering from tuberculosis. Kamala became close to Jawaharlal's friend Syed Mahmud. She once wrote to him that "I want you men to be put in purdah for some years, and then I should ask you what it is like." [153] It shows her strong feminist side. Her daughter Indira inherited the personality from her mother. Jawaharlal being busy and Kamala being sick, Indira was lonely. A Parsee named Firoze Gandhy fell in love with her. He kept proposing to her till she finally agreed at a time when they were in Paris. Jawaharlal was not happy about the affair, but he agreed after his daughter's firm perusal. Indira and Firoze married five years after the proposal. Firoze later changed the spelling of his surname from Gandhy to Gandhi, which would have enormous significance in Indira's political career.

For India, 1937 was important because it was the year when the government of India came into force. For the first time, 35 million people of India were allowed to vote. INC, led by Jawaharlal, won 716 out of 1,161 seats while AIML led by Jinnah suffered a heavy defeat. Elected representatives took office after an oath of loyalty to the king. INC ignored AIML and offered to cooperate with them only if the AIML was dissolved and merged with INC. AIML saw itself as the only representative of Muslim community and was offended by the behavior of INC. After the results of the election, AIML started their campaign for partition. The new country would be called Pakistan, meaning *the land of pure*. It also had the initials of Punjab, Afghan, Kashmir, and Sindh. To achieve this objective, Jinnah brought himself close to the British government.

The new Congress government tried to bring in reforms. They managed to give the untouchables access to temples, public offices, public waters, and other public places. Most freedom fighters were released from jail. However, they did not have enough power to do something more substantial. Meanwhile, INC was splitting again. As a leader of INC, Jawaharlal was becoming a bit autocratic. Many, like in the article 'The Rashtrapari' published in *Modern Review*, criticized him for the same. Jawaharlal understood it and corrected himself. He was the president of INC in 1936 and 1937. In 1938, when Jawaharlal was in Europe, Subhas became the new president of INC with support from Gandhi. Subhas, however, would soon part ways with Congress, Gandhi, and Jawaharlal.

10.12   The Misguided Patriot

It was the summer of 1934 when a young Austrian lady appeared for an interview to assist Subhas Chandra

Bose in writing a book. Her name was Emilie Schenkl, a Catholic and a daughter of a veterinarian. Subhas was a risk for the British government if he was roaming free in India. His deteriorating health, along with his mass support, made it difficult for them to keep him in jail. Unlike Jinnah or Jawaharlal's wife, Kamala, Subhas was not allowed to enter Britain where he already had a large number of followers. He was sent to Austria instead, where the British authorities watched him closely. Subhas was approached by the publishing company Wishart to write a book on India's freedom struggle. Subhas required help in writing the book. The Great Depression caused unemployment, and Emilie was eager for the job. With time, the two different personalities from two different cultures came closer. Subhas was attracted by her caring yet bold and straightforward nature. He called her *Baghini*, meaning *tigress* [154]. It was Subhas who first approached her, and she accepted. For Subhas, his first love has always been his country. Instead of a peaceful life in Austria with the one he loved, he chose the difficult path of going away from Emilie and continue fighting the elusive battle for India's freedom.

Subhas Chandra Bose was born in Cuttack towards the end of 19th century. He was a brilliant student. His father sent him to Presidency College in Kolkata not just to build his career but also to keep him away from his notorious friends. Subhas was once expelled from his college with the blame that he assaulted Professor Oaten. Oaten manhandled some students, and the students retaliated. Subhas was merely present at the site. He was blamed because he already had the reputation of being rebellious. From his childhood, Subhas was inclined towards psychology and spirituality. He confessed that, had he been born in a free country, he would have preferred psychology to politics. He once ran away with a friend in search of a true guru. He found none and came back disappointed. When he was 15 years old, he was introduced to Vivekananda's books. He was deeply influenced by Vivekananda's and Ramakrishna's teachings. It was Vivekananda who became his true guru and remained so throughout his life. Had Vivekananda been alive then, Subhas would probably have become his disciple. He became a politician instead.

Subhas went to Cambridge University, and as promised to his father, he joined ICS after coming fourth in Indian Civil Service Examination. The boring job did not interest him, and he resigned. Subhas had no intentions of working under an alien government. He was the first Indian at that time who dared to resign from ICS and set an example for others. Like many young Indians of his time, the Jallianwala Bagh massacre left a deep impression on him. Subhas came back to India and joined politics in 1921. The Oaten incident and his leaving ICS put him on the radar of the British officials. Subhas became active in the Indian freedom struggle and was quick to gain the popularity of people. He was arrested without evidence or trial and sent to Mandalay prison for alleged involvement in revolutionary movements. It was in this prison that he contracted Tuberculosis, which would make him sick for the rest of his life. After his release in 1927, he became general secretary of INC. Subhas became the Mayor of Kolkata in 1930. He, along with Jawaharlal, traveled around the world to build good relations with other nations.

Subhas and Tagore cut short Bankim Chandra's poem 'Vande Mataram' to the first two words so that Muslims were not offended. The song was originally dedicated to Goddesses Durga, which did not represent all religious communities. Also, it was taken from Bankim's *Anandamath*, which was anti-Muslim [155]. Subhas was arguably the most popular non-Muslim leader among the Muslims. He tried to talk with Jinnah against partition. Subhas wanted Jinnah to be the first prime minister of free India to remove the insecurity of the minorities. Jinnah ignored his plea. Subhas had a long discussion with Gandhi in February 1931 before the Irwin Pact and expressed his concern about the political prisoners that the pact excluded. After mobs protested against Gandhi for execution of Bhagat Singh, Sukhdev, and Rajguru, Gandhi labeled the protesters as 'Subhas Youths'.

In 1932 Subhas was sent to Europe to recover from his illness and to keep him away from Indian politics. During this time, Hitler's Nazi Party became the largest elected party in Germany and Hitler became the chancellor. On 27 February 1933, a young Dutch Council communist started a fire in Reichstag Buildingin Berlin. Adolf Hitler took the opportunity to influence the president and pass emergrncy decree. Hitler then obliterated the Communist Party of Germany and consolidated his power. Subhas spent a lot of time during his exile in Europe to understand the world politics. He tried to build good rapport with the countries that had troubled relationship with Britain, like Germany, Italy, and Ireland [156]. Subhas was definitely not a fan of Nazis just like Hitler was no fan of Indians. Hitler considered Indians as non-Aryans and hence inferior. When Subhas was asked if he really could ally himself with the Satan's representatives, he answered, "It is dreadful, but it must be done. It is our only way out. India must gain independence, cost what may . . . British imperialism [in India] can be just as intolerable as your Nazism here." [156] In Europe, Subhas developed a liking towards fascism. He later accepted that "we in India wanted our national freedom, and having won it, we wanted to move in the direction of Socialism. . . . When I was writing the book, Fascism had not started on its imperialist expedition, and it appeared to me merely an aggressive form of nationalism." [156] A dejected Subhas returned "to India with the conviction that the new nationalism of Germany is not only narrow and selfish but arrogant. . . . The new racial philosophy which had very weak scientific foundation stands for the glorification of the white races in general and the German race in particular." [156]

Vithalbhai Patel, elder brother of Sardar Vallavbhai Patel, met Subhas when he came to Europe for a complex surgery. They both became very close, and Subhas finally found an experienced Indian freedom fighter to talk to. Vithalbhai and Subhas were openly critical of Gandhi's fast in Yerwada Jail against separate constitution for untouchables. Vithalbhai's health deteriorated, and it was Subhas who cared for him. Vithalbhai died in Europe on October 1933. Even Gandhi appreciated Subhas's 'magnificence and devoted nursing . . . at much risk to his own health' [156]. Vallavbhai, however, was not very happy with Subhas. He was especially concerned about the money his elder brother left to Subhas in his will. He took the will to court, claiming that it was fake, and managed to make it null and void [156].

After the Government of India Act of 1935 was passed, Subhas decided to return to India despite the warnings from the British government. Subhas was arrested immediately after he set foot in India. Jawaharlal called for a nationwide protest against Subhas's arrest. Subhas was finally released a year later. After his release, Subhas became an active member of INC. He went to Europe in 1937 and secretly married his girlfriend Emilie on 26 December. In early 1938, Subhas still in Europe, Gandhi initiated the process of making Subhas the president of INC, much to the dislike of Vallabhbhai. Jawaharlal was already president for three terms, and apart from him, Subhas was the most popular INC leader. The next year, however, Gandhi was against Subhas as president because of the latter's view of complete independence and use of force if required. To Gandhi, Subhas was 'a patriot of patriots' but 'misguided'. In 1939 Subhas won the vote for presidency against Pattabhi Sitaramayya, Gandhi's nominated candidate. Subhas was supported by his friend U Muthuramalingam Thevar. A major chunk of the vote from South India went in favor of Subhas because of Thevar. Gandhi took it as a personal loss and wanted Subhas to resign. Subhas had to leave his post after all the members of the Congress Working Committee led by Vallabhbhai, excluding Jawaharlal and Sarat Chandra Bose, resigned in protest against Subhas. Tagore tried to persuade Gandhi not to make the mistake of ignoring the great leader, but Gandhi was adamant. Subhas went on to establish Forward Bloc, with its main hold in Bengal, and was joined by Thevar. Within the next couple of years, INC and Subhas went further apart. Jawaharlal wrote in 1940, "Subhas Bose is going to pieces and had definitely ranged himself against the Congress." [156] Gandhi still had faith in Subhas and told him that "for the time being you are my lost sleep. Someday I shall find you returning to the fold, if I am right and my love is pure" [156].

Meanwhile, World War II had started, and Subhas was trying to establish links with Russia. The viceroy Lord Linlithgow declared that India was participating in the war against Germany without consulting the Indian leaders. Subhas saw in the war an opportunity to get India independence. He openly urged people not to support Britain in the war. In his final battle, he would require the Hindus and Muslims to unite. He called for the removal of Holwell Monument made in memory of Britons who allegedly died in a closed jail under Siraj-ud-daula [155]. Subhas glorified the Muslim ruler and even celebrated his birthday. After Subhas was arrested on July 1940, he went on a hunger strike against his arrest. He continued for a week till he was sent home in an ambulance with the plan of rearresting him once he recovered. Tight security was put outside and spies inside the house. All visitors were monitored and all letters checked. Subhas went on religious seclusion for a period of time with a plan to escape. With help from his nephew Sisir, Subhas, disguised as a Muslim named Muhammad Ziauddin, left the house. Apart from few members, none, including Subhas's mother, knew about the plan. Misinformation was spread to confuse the British spies. At the opportune moment, on a moonlit night, he sneaked out of the house, got into his Wanderer BLA 7169, and Sishir drove him away from the main gate. British intelligence was fooled and left embarrassed. While Kolkata was sleeping, Subhas was embarked on a long journey to awake the entire nation. In the last letter before Subhas left, Gandhi wrote to him, "You are irrepressible whether ill or well. Do get well before going in for fireworks." [155]

10.13   World War II: Do or Die

Experiments with democracy failed around the world. The peace treaty after World War I left a bitter legacy. There was the rise of nationalists and dictators fueled by the Great Depression that started in 1929. Russia became a communist country from where communism spread to China. The fascist party of Mussolini was in power in Italy, Franco's dictatorship took over Spain, and Hitler came to power in Germany. Hitler declared rearmament, and Germans believed that Hitler was the one who could overturn the unfair Versailles Treaty signed after their defeat in the World War I. Munich Agreement of 1938 led to annexation of German-speaking parts of Czechoslovakia into Hitler's domain. Surprising the world, Hitler signed a pact of nonaggression with Russia. Britain and France went on to sign an alliance with Poland. After Germany and Russia invaded Poland on 1 September 1939, Britain and France declared war on Germany. Poland was defeated within two weeks and was divided between Germany and Russia. Germany went on to invade Norway, Netherlands, Luxembourg, Belgium, and France while Italy went on to invade France and Egypt. World War II had begun. The new developments were closely watched by Subhas as he planned his great escape.

After Subhas fled from Kolkata, he went to Russia via Afghanistan. Meanwhile, Russia and Germany's pact fell apart, and Hitler decided to invade Russia. Subhas was not received well in Russia as they did not want to upset the British empire. Instead, they gave him a safe passage to Germany. In Germany, Subhas created the Free India Legion, or Azad Hind Fauj, as part of Nazi German army. The army was made of Indian students in Germany and the Indian prisoners of war. Subhas also started Azad Hind Radio through which he requested all Indians in India and abroad to stand together to uproot the British Raj [157]. Subhas's enchanting oratory skills fired up the nationalists in India.

Gandhi took no side in the war as to him it was a war between two imperialist powers. Subhas supported the Axis because to him an enemy's enemy was a friend. Jawaharlal, however, was against the Axis powers and declared that "Hitler and Japan must go to hell. I shall fight them to the end, and this is my policy. I shall also fight Mr Subhas Bose and his party along with Japan if he comes to India" [153]. Jawaharlal, however, wanted complete independence before offering full support to Britain, which the latter was in no mood to give. Despite opposition from Indian political leaders, over 2.5 million Indians fought for the British in World War II, the largest volunteer army in history. In protest, all INC ministers resigned on 10 November 1939. Jinnah was happy that the Congress regime finally ended. He requested all Muslims to celebrate it as the 'day of deliverance' and thanksgiving. Jinnah's appeal upset many in INC including Abul Kalam Azad, who stated, "It is difficult to imagine any group of Muslims, howsoever at loggerheads with the Indian National Congress, would tolerate to be presented to the world in such colors." [158] Jinnah found support from B R Ambedkar who was present with Jinnah during the celebrations. To Ambedkar, INC had oppressed the Dalits much more than they had oppressed the Muslims.

During such fragile times, India needed inspiration from outside. Subhas spoke from Berlin, "Every Indian has to answer immediately: 'Do I want Britain and America to win this war?' If Britain has recognized full independence of India there would have been some justification for desiring her to win, but the British have stubbornly refused to grant us our liberty. Perhaps they feel if India is lost, their Empire will virtually cease to exist. The Indian people have refused to accept the empty promise of Dominion Status after the war and are convinced that and Anglo-American victory will mean a continued enslavement of India and several other nations." [157] Subhas inspired not just the Indian civilians but also the Indian Army under British to revolt. When Japan attacked Christmas Island, Indian soldiers revolted against the British officers and handed over the Island to them. Encouraged by the German success, Japan attacked Pearl Harbor in December 1941, bringing USA directly into the war. USA was already helping China with aids and arms. Pearl Harbor was an USA military base created to keep Japan in check. Japan attacked without consulting Germany. In fact, both were fighting the war separately, the only similarity between them being that they were fighting a common enemy. Hitler thought of Asians as a poorer race while Japan did not approve of German aggression against Russia. British troops suffered humiliating defeats against Japan in Burma, Malaya, and Singapore. Japan's success made Britain wary, and they feared of Japan taking over India.

After Britain's failure to guarantee India complete independence, Gandhi launched Quit India Movement in August 1942. He gave the ultimatum: 'Do or die'. It was a moral dilemma for many Indians who hated the Nazis for killing the innocent Jews and the Romani people. The Romani people were a group of Indian-origin migrants who left India over 1,000 years ago. At the same time, the Indians could not support the arrogant British, especially after the bitter experience of World War I. The British government was quick to suppress the movement, especially because Japan had already invaded Burma and were closing in on India. Over 100,000 Indians were imprisoned, including Gandhi and all top leaders of Congress. The movement would have been left leaderless but for Subhas who continued to inspire the Indians from abroad through radio.

Subhas was disappointed by Hitler's madness of invading Russia and his reluctance to help India in its freedom struggle. To Hitler, if the British were out of India, Russia would take control of it, which he did not want [155]. Subhas wrote, "The march of German troops towards east will be regarded as the approach, not of a friend but of an enemy." So far, Subhas had kept himself away from Japan because of its unfair attacks on China, but he was encouraged after Japan's success. He now wanted to be in Southeast Asia, closer to home. In Europe, Subhas stayed a few months with his wife, Emilie. They had a daughter on 29 November 1942. Two months later, Subhas handed Emilie a letter for his brother, thanking him and asking him to take care of his wife and child. He knew it was the last time he would see her. He left Germany in a cramped U-180, changed over midway to Japanese submarine I-29, and reached Japan.

Rash Behari Bose, still remembered for the Indian curry he introduced in Japan, had created the foundation for Indian revolution there. Masterminded by the Japanese, with help from Mohan Singh and Rash Behari Bose, Indian National Army was formed. It soon lost its way only to be revived by Subhas when he reached there. The force had no barrier of religion, caste, or sex. Possibly the first time in the world, outside Russia, a women's regiment was formed. It was aptly named the Rani of Jhansi Regiment. Provisional government and Indian National Army were established in Andaman and Nicobar, but for all practical purposes, it was under Japanese control. Subhas then shifted his base to Burma.

On 9 February 1943, old but still strong, Gandhi went for a 21-day fast in jail. The British Raj was unmoved, and Linlithdow wrote, "Gandhi should be allowed to fast to death." [153] All preparations were made for his funeral, and an ambulance was left on standby. Roosevelt tried to get Gandhi released but failed. Gandhi was temporarily released to meet his ailing wife. She died on Gandhi's lap. Gandhi did not allow doctors to give her Western medicine. Instead, Gandhi and his followers were singing devotional songs. Long back, Gandhi said that it was difficult for someone to be his wife and only Kasturba could manage it. How could he allow Western medicine to save the life of his wife? How could he betray the image that he created of himself? How else could the millions of Indians follow him? When Gandhi went back to prison, few people saw him cry, probably for the first time. Gandhi contracted malaria in jail, and his health deteriorated. He was finally released on 6 May 1944. One month later, Subhas broadcasted to Gandhi, whom he addressed as the 'father of nation', that "India's last war of Independence has begun. . . . In this holy war of India's liberation, we ask for your blessing and good wishes." [110]

10.14 The Final Frontier

By the end of 1946, the sterling debts that the British owed to India was over an astounding 1,700 crores [159]. These were the cumulative value of all the goods and services taken away from India during World War II for British soldiers as well as civilians while many Indians died of hunger. The export of rice and wheat from India, along with the capture of the dominant rice exporter Burma by Japan, led to its lack of supply in India. Conditions worsened after the severe cyclone that spoilt the harvest of 1942. The agricultural wages also declined at the same time. Rice became so costly that the poor could afford it no more. Parents killed their children, dogs fed on the dead, young girls became prostitutes and their fathers' pimps. There were corpses lying all around with no one to cremate them. There was no statistics available for the government to work on. Census of population was reliably unreliable. Estimates of the number of people who died in the famine range from 1.5 to 4 million. Compare that to the 6 million Jews massacred by the Nazis in 12 years. No wonder many call the Bengal Famine of 1942–43 as India's forgotten holocaust, a mass murder that could have been avoided. About 1.5 million INR profit was made from buying and selling rice during the famine. Considering the conservative estimate of 1.5 million deaths, every death was balanced by roughly 1,000 INR of excess profit. The government was in denial, and they kept maintaining their propaganda of 'no shortage'. When the Indian viceroy Wavell and secretary Leo Amery repeatedly asked Churchill for help, he wondered instead why Gandhi was still alive. Indians, Churchill thought, were 'beastly people with beastly religion', who 'bred like rabbits' [160]. Churchill refused to release the available stocks with an excuse that the Britons might require it when the war was over [153]. Subhas's offer of sending rice from Myanmar was ignored, and ships carrying wheat from Australia bypassed India [161].

Bengal Famine was one of the greatest disasters the world had yet seen, and it was followed by one of the deadliest battles ever fought—a war that would be among the top four turning points of World War II. On one side was the army of Subhas fighting with Japan, and on the other side, it was the Indian Army fighting for British empire. Japan launched Operation U-Go, with the aim of capturing Imphal and Kohima with about a 100,000 men [162]. This was the final battle Subhas and his army were looking forward to. Provisional Indian Government was set up on October 1943 and war was declared against Britain and America. The Japanese force and Indian National Army first attacked the coastal belt of Arakan and then moved towards Imphal and Kohima. The British and Indian forces had the advantage of numbers apart from better infrastructure to mobilize troops. The Indian Army was also better trained to fight in the wet jungles of northeast India. Moreover, they had air supply unlike the Japanese. Despite that, the Japanese made a good start, and the British forces withdrew from Imphal. Indian National Army marched ahead singing 'Kadam kadam barhaye ja [Move ahead step by step]' and shouting 'Chalo Delhi [Let's go Delhi]'. Cornel Mallik of Indian National Army hoisted the Indian National Army flag for the first time in India at Moirang on 14 April [163]. Indian National Army flag had the tricolor of Congress with the tiger of Tipu Sultan in the center instead of the Chakara. 'Jana gana mana' was chosen by Subhas as the national anthem and 'Jai Hind' as the national greetings.

Kolkata, being the closest big city to China and Burma, was the main center of military operations. Howrah Bridge was the key connection to Kolkata, and Japan wanted to destroy it. Suspecting an attack, the whole city of Kolkata was blacked out. No lights were lit on the roads, and all windows were painted black. The Japanese attacked only at night because of Kolkata's good air defense system. The first bombings happened on 20 December 1942 and continued for the next couple of years. Heavy bombings happened in Khidderpore dockyard, along with many other places in Kolkata, but Howrah Bridge remained safe.

The Japanese army defeated the forces in Sangshak but not before the defenders put up a brave fight to delay Japanese progress enough for British forces to reorganize. That year the monsoon came early, spoiling Japan's plan. The Japanese, who took the gamble of traveling with light arms and ammunitions and were dependent on rapid victory, now found themselves depleted of their ammunition supply. Indian National Army and Japanese army were defeated in Kohima, and by the time they arrived near Imphal, they were exhausted. They were in no position to advance and finally decided to retreat on 18 July. It was a retreat worse than that of Napoleon. Many soldiers died due to starvation and disease. Their bodies lay scattered around the forest with no one to bury them. The Japanese had 55,000 casualties in the war, their worst loss ever, while the British-Indian Army had casualty of just 17,500 men. Fighting in the jungle during monsoons is one of the toughest. The European soldiers were depressed and homesick just like Indian soldiers were during the World War I in the harsh winters of Europe. Malaria and diarrhea made matters worse. The Indian Army was more comfortable at home and fought bravely. The victory was one of their greatest military achievements till date. The army then advanced to capture Burma. Subhas publicly announced the Imphal failure on 21 August 1944 through radio. One reason for the failure was betrayal of a few people from Indian National Army who gave away secret information to the British. Success of Indian National Army was heavily dependent on the internal rebellion in India during the war. British forces, due to the leak of information, easily countered the threat. Most of the revolutionaries within India were identified and put behind the bars, if not killed.

By the end of 1944, America and Britain had broken Japan's dominance in Asia, Italy was already defeated, while the aggression of Russia has pushed Germany on the back foot. By February 1945, Russia closed in on Hitler. Mussolini was killed on 28 April. The next day Hitler quietly married the women he loved, and then within 40 hours, the newlywed couple committed suicide. By the time Russia invaded Berlin, Hitler's body had been burnt as per his last wish. Germany signed total and unconditional surrender on 7 May. Japan was now 'threatened by world's four most powerful nations and history's most awe-inspiring weapon' (*Statesman Late City Edition*, Calcutta, 10 August 1945). Japan continued their fight until America dropped two atom bombs over Hiroshima and Nagasaki. Russia also declared war against them, forcing Japan to surrender on 15 August 1944. The war was finally over. Britain had won the war but lost the empire. Their men were tired, and their economy destabilized.

Out of 15,000 Indian National Army soldiers, 750 died in battle, 1,500 of disease, 2,000 escaped to Bangkok, 3,000 surrendered, and 7,000 were captured by the British. British Army was ready to capture Indian National Army in Singapore but were in a dilemma about how to deal with Subhas. If he was sentenced to death, India would be free that very moment. If he was kept alive, the huge mass following would have made it difficult to keep him in jail. Subhas wanted to stay with his men in Singapore during surrender, but his cabinet advised him against it [164]. Before he left, Subhas said, "Roads to Delhi are many, and Delhi still remains our goal. The sacrifice of your immortal comrades and yourselves will certainly achieve fulfillness." [156] On 17 August, Subhas flew away from Bangkok with some of his comrades to Saigon and from there to Tourane. He was finalizing how Indian National Army should surrender along with the Japanese and was planning to go to Russia. Next day he flew to Taipei, and from Taipei, he took the ill-fated and overloaded Japanese bomber.

Emelie was watching television in her house in Vienna when the new was splashed in the TV that Subhas died in a plane crash. She quietly went upstairs and knelt beside the bed where her little daughter Anita was sleeping and wept [156]. India was shocked. Even Gandhi did not believe Subhas had died. There had been similar news of his death years before, but it had turned out to be a hoax. The entire nation hoped against hope that it was a hoax this time as well. The British were confused by the news. They doubted that they had got rid of their biggest enemy so easily. Subhas's body was not recovered, and accounts of eyewitness about the plane crash contradicted. Some secret files (No. 870/11/p/16/92/Pol) released by the government in 2016 gives a hint that he was alive after the crash. Subhas probably even broadcasted three messages between December 1945 and February 1946. The authenticity of the broadcasts has not been proved yet. There are enough reasons to doubt that he died in the plane crash, and the mystery of his death is not solved yet. The money and gold that he collected for his army, and was with him during the flight, also went missing. The Indian government has been unwilling to release the documents related to his death, citing the reason of national interest as it might lead to chaos, safely keeping them away as top secret. The whole of India sympathized with the alleged death of their most popular leader. The British could no more trust the Indian Army as Indian National Army became their national heroes. An Indian National Army soldier once said, "We fought for India, but India was something vague. Netaji (Subhas) was the symbol for which we fought." [164] There in lay the victory for Subhas. He managed to create unity despite the vagueness in the concept of India, putting the final nail in the coffin of the Raj.

10.15   Rainbow of Hope

By the end of the war, USA and Russia emerged as the new world leaders. The biggest loser was Britain. They took huge loans not just from USA but also owed £450 million to Egypt, £250 million to Ireland, £200 million each to Australia and New Zealand, and, the highest of all, £1,250 million to India [153]. The Labor Party of UK withdrew support from the coalition government, and in the re-elections, they won handsomely under Clement Attlee. Attlee was in a hurry to settle the inevitable Indian freedom. Ban on INC was lifted, its leaders freed, and elections called. INC won by a huge margin while AIML swept the Muslim constituencies. The religious polarization was clear from the results, something that was absent during the last election. Vallabhbhai Patel was supposed to be the president of INC but stepped down in favor of Jawaharlal at the request of Gandhi.

The British, in their arrogance and stupidity, gave death sentence to Indian National Army officers despite violent opposition. The three officers sentenced were Shah Nawaz Khan, Gurubaksh Singh Dhillon, and Prem Sahgal, all belonging to different communities. For the last time, INC and AIML stood together in protest. INC believed that they represent no religious group. AIML represented only the Muslim community. In contrast, Subhas's Indian National Army represented all communities. That was the reason why the pain of Indian National Army officers united the whole of India. The 'misguided' Indian National Army soldiers became national heroes. Indian Army under British Raj revolted, and mutiny broke out in the Indian Royal Navy on February 1946. A revolt that started in Bombay spread from Karachi to Kolkata. Posters threatening '20 British dogs' for sentence of every Indian National Army officer made the British insecure [110]. It was the loyalty of Indian Army that helped the British control the Raj. Without their help, the British had no power. According to Jawaharlal, "never before in Indian history had such unified sentiments and feelings been manifested by various divergent sections of Indian population as it had been done with regard to the question of the Azad Hind Fauj" [110]. Subhas's aim was finally achieved, and British were now convinced that they have to leave India for good.

Cabinet Mission was called in March 1946 by Attlee to finalize a graceful exit from India. The purpose was to discuss the method of framing the constitution with the elected representatives and set up a constitution body and an executive council. Different plans were proposed, but none got the agreement of both INC and AIML. Jinnah called on the Muslims for Direct Action Day on 16 August 1946 in demand of creating Pakistan. He warned that he will have 'either a divided India or a destroyed India', and he got both [153]. AIML planned large-scale meetings in Bengal to promote the idea of Pakistan. They requested for declaration of public holiday to avoid violence. Bengal Congress and Hindu Mahasabha opposed the holiday and urged for the shops to remain open. Muslims tried to close the shops forcefully while Hindus attacked the Muslim processions. It was a feedback mechanism as the violence escalated to a disaster as people raped and killed any opponent in their path. Violence spread from Bengal to Bihar, Assam, Punjab, and North-West Frontier Province. Thousands of innocents died irrespective of their religion because of the stubbornness of Indian political leaders. The British finally realized the Frankenstein created by their divide-and-rule policy. The difficult responsibility of final British exit fell on the reluctant shoulders of 'accident prone' 'master of disaster' Lord Mountbatten [153].

Mountbatten found himself in a country where civil war was inevitable. All Britain wanted was to leave India before it started. India was divided into so many groups, not just in terms of language, religion, and caste but, more importantly, politics. Russia was already sponsoring the Communist parties bringing India into the radar of USA. Jinnah wanted a separate nation for Muslims of India as they felt insecure in India dominated by Hindus and Congress. Ambedkar favored partition, acknowledging the huge differences between two communities. He wanted a separate constituency for untouchables who were victimized by the upper castes. The far-right Hindu groups like Hindu Mahasabha were against INC's pro-Muslim attitude and at the same time opposed partition. The Sikhs wanted partition of Punjab instead of getting clubbed with a dominant Muslim province. INC opposed partition of India and rightly tried hard to represent all communities and all castes in a not so right way. Though everybody wanted freedom, there was no common consensus to earn it. Mountbatten wrote to Attlee: "The scene here is one of unrelieved gloom. . . . The Cabinet is fiercely divided on communal lines; each party has its own solution and does not at present show any sign of being prepared to consider another . . . unless I act quickly I may well find the real beginnings of a civil war on my hands." [153] It was Mountbatten's wife, Edwina, rather than him who found it easier to deal with the Indian leaders. She was comfortable with Gandhi, Ambedkar, and even Jinnah. However, it was Jawaharlal with whom she grew the closest. Even a decade later, they would remember the first time they met. Some would call it platonic love. Her contributions should not be undermined in the events that followed.

Mountbatten went to London to finalize the quick exit. A new plan was drafted and proposed to the Indian leaders. Independence date was fixed to 15 August 1947, a good ten months before the deadline. Mountbatten chose the date as it was the 'second anniversary of VJ [victory over Japan] day, nothing more significant than that' [153]. It was decided that India was to be partitioned. Reluctantly, Jawaharlal and Jinnah agreed with the plan. Only Gandhi was still against it. He said, "I find myself all alone, even the Sardar and Jawaharlal think my reading of the situation is wrong and peace is sure to return if partitioning was agreed upon . . . the future of independence gained at this price is going to be dark." [153] The immediate future was one of the darkest indeed.

In July 1947, the Indian Independence Bill was introduced into House of Commons in London. Conservative Party led by Churchill protested against independence and wanted dominion status for India. Churchill was ignored, and the plan went ahead. North-West Frontier Province voted to be part of Pakistan while Punjab and Bengal voted for partition. Kashmir remained a tricky issue. It was a Muslim dominated land ruled by a Hindu king who wanted an independent nation. For India, it was a necessity that it retained the natural defense of Himalayas; else, it would be an easy target for Afghanistan, Russia, and China. Many other states like Travancore, Bhopal, Jodhpur, Junagadh, Hyderabad, and Nagas of Assam wanted to be separate. The dirty job of demarcating the boundary of India and Pakistan was given to a man who had never been to India before. Sir Cyril Radcilffe had just 40 days to complete a task that should ideally take four years. Once he hurriedly drew the borders, he was told to keep the map safe and secret until independence (figure 15). Without borders, the people of Punjab were confused whose independence they should celebrate: India or Pakistan. The bloodbath was soon to follow. Seeing the deadly aftermath of his creation, Radcilffe would later reject his salary.

On 14 August, one day before India, Pakistan celebrated independence. Jinnah and Mountbatten boldly rode an open car through the crowded streets of Karachi despite an assassination attempt threatening them. In a speech three days earlier, Jinnah had declared that Pakistan would be a secular country where 'in course of time all these angularities of the majority and minority communities, the Hindu Community and the Muslim Community . . . will vanish . . . if you ask me, this has been the biggest hindrance in the way of India to attain freedom and independence, and but for this we would have been free people long long ago' [153]. The midnight of 14 August, India's first prime minister Jawaharlal gave his famous speech inside the chamber of constituent assembly, "At the stroke of the midnight hour, when the world sleeps, India will awake to life and freedom. A moment comes, which comes but rarely in history, when we step out from the old to the new, when an age ends, and when the soul of a nation, long suppressed, finds utterance."

One-fifth of human race (400 million people) got freedom on 15 August 1947. Gandhi was not there to celebrate freedom. He was in Kolkata, trying to stop the riots. It was not the freedom he fought for. Nor was this freedom due to him. When Atelee was asked about the reason for leaving India, he cited various reasons, "The most important were the activities of Netaji Subhas Chandra Bose which weakened the very foundation of the attachment of the Indian land and naval forces to the British Government." When asked on the contribution of Gandhi, 'Attlee's lips widened in a smile of disdain and he uttered, slowly, putting emphasis on each single letter "mi-ni-mal"' [165]. One must not, however, forget Gandhi's contribution of bringing the mass into the freedom movement. There was a joyful atmosphere in Delhi as the whole city lit up in orange, white, and green. The huge crowd that gathered not just cheered for the Indian leaders but also shouted 'Mountbatten Zindabad' and 'Lord Sahib Zindabad' [166]. A photographer present in the event later said emotionally, "At last, after 200-years, Britain has conquered India." [153] The Indian flag was hoisted up on 16 August. Amid the huge cheer and salute, a rainbow broke in the sky at the perfect moment as if to welcome the new beginning.

10.16   The Bloodbath

It was August, and monsoon was yet to arrive. The hot Indian summer of 1947 was also a lot drier than usual. The weather probably reflected the dark evil that engulfed the mind of Indians. A large group of Muslim women were stripped not just of their clothes but their soul and paraded naked in Amritsar as violent mobs of Sikhs raped and murdered them. Few women managed to survive the ordeal, only because of some brave Sikh men who hid them inside the Golden Temple [153]. Sikhs were avenging the March massacre where the Muslims in Pakistan raped and murdered the Sikhs. Here it was the Sikhs, in other places it was the Muslims or the Hindus, but the victims of this brutal form of revenge and counter-revenge were inevitably women. The few who survived had their hands and breasts cut off, genitals mutilated, or the name of their rapist tattooed on their body. If they survived to cross the border in one piece, there were pimps waiting to gift them one of the oldest professions in a man's world: prostitution. It was the lucky ones who died because a life worse than hell awaited the ones who survived. A very conservative estimate by the government of India suggests that 83,000 women were violated during partition [167]. The irony of life is that the ones who least want the wars are the ones who suffer from it the most. Rape is as old as war itself, and it has been used systematically as a weapon of war in every corner of the world since time immemorial. What happened during the partition of Punjab was not unique as it was not just a riot but also a war. Imperialism, the new and more powerful enemy, had shifted our focus from our old foes. Now that the giant was slayed, the old wounds surfaced once more. Muslim extremist groups, Sikh Akali Dal, Hindu Mahasabha, and the likes fueled the violence.

Over 12 million people were displaced from their homes and had to migrate across the border with death chasing them at every step. It was the largest mass migration in human history. Around a million died in the process. The riots that began in Bengal took the most brutal form in Punjab. These were the two states partitioned by Radcilffe line. In Punjab the Sikhs, Hindus, and Muslims were evenly spread unlike in Bengal where the Hindus were dominant in the west and Muslims in the east. That made it that much harder to cut Punjab into two half. Bengal, which had already experienced partition, got its boundary declared couple of days before Punjab on 15 August. This aggravated the violence in Punjab. More importantly, Bengal had Gandhi. It was in Bengal that Gandhi became a saint because it was in Bengal where he performed a miracle.

When India leaders were celebrating Independence Day, Gandhi was taking a difficult journey through the riot-stricken areas to calm people down. He first went to Bihar; and from there, he traveled to Bengal, which had been the heart of communal violence for a year since Jinnah declared Direct Action Day. Gandhi's plan was to be with the Hindus of East Bengal during the partition. His plans changed when the terrified Muslim leaders in Kolkata invited him to stay with them. They assured him that if there was no riot in Kolkata, there would be no riot in the rest of Bengal. If the Hindus of Kolkata did not harm the Muslims, the Muslim-dominated regions of East Bengal would not harm the Hindus. With that assurance, Gandhi went to Kolkata and stayed in a Muslim house. Angry Hindu mob shouted at Gandhi, telling him to go back. They blamed him for supporting the Muslims and were asking for the blood of Shaheed Suhrawardy, the Muslim leader and ex-chief minister of Bengal. Gandhi brought Suhrawardy forward with a hand placed firmly over his shoulders. The crowd asked Shaheed if he took the responsibility for the killings of Hindus last year. Surprising everyone, Suhrawardy accepted the blame and said that he was ashamed of it. By accepting his mistake, he won over the crowd. Soon there were Hindus and Muslims hoisting the Indian flag together amid the huge cheer from the crowd [168]. On 15 August, Kolkata became the city of joy. The fairy tale did not last long as within a week violence returned. The old man, who had already distanced himself from politics and considered by many as a spent force, decided to go on a fast until people stopped killing one another. The city calmed down once more. Leaders from all faith came to him and put down their weapons and pledged not to fight. One could hear the resounding cries of '*Hindu Muslim Ek ho*', '*Jai Hind*', '*Inquilab Zindabad*' in the streets of Kolkata. Lorries, buses, and taxis filled with Hindus and Muslims drove around the street, shouting the slogans of brotherhood. Bengal survived because of the old man's miracle, but Punjab was not that lucky.

Seventy-year-old Gandhi started his journey towards Punjab. Meanwhile, riots spread to Delhi, breaking Gandhi's journey in between. The emotionally charged Sikhs and Hindus migrating from Pakistan attacked the Muslims in Delhi. Fearing for their lives, the Muslims ran away to fortified places like Jama Masjid and Old Fort. A frustrated Jawaharlal warned people through radio, "We are dealing with a situation analogous to war, and we are going to deal with it on a war basis in every sense of the word." [153]

Gandhi visited the hospitals to meet all victims. He requested Hindus, Muslims, and Sikhs to stop the violence so that he could continue his journey towards Punjab. When violence did not stop, he resorted to another fast, trying to emulate the success in Bengal. Hindu, Muslim, and Sikh leaders came together and pledged to stop the violence. Gandhi broke his fast. Delhi, however, did not calm down like Kolkata. Two days later, there was an unsuccessful attempt to assassinate Gandhi. Gandhi ignored the attack and kept meeting the people in Delhi. On 30 January, ten days since the attack, Gandhi walked towards the prayer meeting ground. The frail old man was supported himself on the shoulders of his two granddaughters. A 36-year-old Maratha-Hindu named Nathuram Godse fired four shots at Gandhi from two yards for what he thought was a pro-Muslim fast. One bullet pierced Gandhi's stomach, and he collapsed immediately. Gandhi was rushed to Birla House for treatment. At 5.45pm, the news of Gandhi's death was announced. After seeing Gandhi's dead body, Sardar Patel said, "On his face was written the usual spirit of forgiveness. There was no expression of anger or annoyance anywhere. It was the expression of his usual kindness and forgiveness."

The members of the congregation immediately seized Godse. He surrendered without resistance. He went to court with his head held high without any sign of remorse. He proudly gave his last speech, "If devotion to one's country amounts to a sin, I admit I have committed that sin. If it is meritorious, I humbly claim the merit thereof. I fully and confidently believe that if there be any other court of justice beyond the one founded by the mortals, my act will not be taken as unjust. If after the death there be no such place to reach or to go, there is nothing to be said. I have resorted to the action I did purely for the benefit of the humanity. I do say that my shots were fired at the person whose policy and action had brought rack and ruin and destruction to lakhs of Hindus." [169] He was the first person to be hanged in Independent India.

Godse, like many other extreme right-wing Hindus, hated the Muslims not just for invading and ruling India but also for being pro-British during the fight for independence. Vinayak Damodar Savarkar led the *Hindutva* sentiment in India. Savarkar fought for India's independence and was imprisoned in Andaman Jail. In jail, he got the permission to open a library where he taught his fellow prisoners.

He was released after signing a plea for clemency with a promise of not taking any further part in India's freedom struggle. The Khilafat movement, where some section of Muslim community showed more loyalty to Muslims outside India than the Indians, strengthened his belief of *Hindu Rashtra*. To him, *Hindu Rashtra* was not a place for people of a particular religion but a place where 'people who live as children of a common motherland, adoring a common holy land'. Sikhs, Jains and Buddhists were part of his bigger Hindu culture. His idea did not receive the support of the majority. But it did gain some followers. The irony is that Jinnah and Savarkar, the leaders of right-wing Hindu and Muslim groups, were both atheists.

Godse was wrong in understanding Gandhi. Gandhi wanted the Hindus and Sikhs to put down arms so that the Muslims in Pakistan also did the same. As long as there was violence in India, he could do nothing to stop violence in Pakistan. Most Indian Muslims were not disloyal to our nation as Godse thought. It was the political parties that created the divide for their own political gain. Jamiat Ulema-e-Hind opposed partition and promoted nationalistic feelings among Indian Muslims. People like Maulana Kalam Azad, Ghaffar Khan, and the Muslim soldiers of Indian National Army were Indians first. There were Muslims who stayed back after partition and wanted to be part of India rather than Pakistan. They happily raised the Indian flag together with the Hindus after independence. In a Hindu temple of Banaras, it was a Muslim who unfurled the Indian flag; two Hindu and Muslim boy-girl pairs unfurled the national flag in Shillong [170]. There was hope for India even in such trying times of despair.

The riots might have been stopped had Mountbatten not rushed with independence. Riots as well as partition would not have taken place if the British gave India independence after the World War I as promised. The riots could have been stopped had Jinnah not been so desperate for Pakistan. The riots could have been stopped had INC been more considerate to AIML. It was Gandhi, and the million who died during partition, who paid the price of the mistakes.

The *Statesman* editorial wrote on 1 February 1948, "Numb with sudden tragedy, the people of India mourns their dead leader whom they lately hailed as Father of the Nation. They seem conscious as yet mainly of their loss and the love they bore him. Hearts overflow. But on many lips are questions. What does this calamity portend? He who in many past crises has been there to interpret, to counsel, to lead, is gone." Gandhi's death was a shock for the whole nation, especially for Jawaharlal and Patel. Gandhi's death united the two men who mattered the most for India, especially at a time when India was most vulnerable. Putting all grievances aside, both men came together to build a nation. The world gave India no chance to survive. India was the least likely nation for democracy to subsist. Everybody predicted doom. The new journey of the survivors was written in blood, and doomsday seemed to be near for India but for Jawaharlal and Patel.

Modern India (1947 to 2015)

The liberation of spirit that has come to India [since 1947] could not come as release alone. In India, with its layer below layer of distress and cruelty, it had to come as disturbance. It had to come as rage and revolt. India was now a country of million little mutinies

—V S Naipaul, *India: A Million Mutinies Now*

11.1 Pieces of Puzzle

B ritish rule created infrastructures, and revived India's science and literature. They tried to get rid of evil customs like sati, caste-system, and child marriage. However, there rule had pushed India's ecomony back by many decades. According to a report, there were thirty-one serious famines during the British rule compared to just seventeen 'reported' famines in the 2,000 years before their rule. The famines, which happened due to the British policies, killed up to 29 million Indians [153]. Poverty increased as the Raj drained India's wealth. When they left, 88 per cent of Indians were illiterate, and only a fifth of the children were receiving any form of primary education. India's indigenous industries were destroyed. There were reports of hands and thumbs of hundreds of weavers of Bengal being cut to stop the weaving industry. India, along with some other British colonies, was forced to remain in silver standard, introduced by Sher Shah in 16th century. Countries like Germany, USA, and France moved to gold along with Britain. With a lot of silver being discovered by Spain, the value of silver decreased compared to gold. India, who was mostly trading with gold-standard countries, suffered. The value of rupee fell along with silver, affecting India's economy. India finally adopted gold standard in 1898.

The divide-and-rule policy shattered the fragile communal harmony in India. The lie of Aryan-Dravidian division was repeated so many times that it became a fact. The strong central control took away power from people. This led to a lack of mutual respect and ownership for one's own country. The dowry extortions increased when the traditional property rights of women were taken away [170]. In the last century of the British rule, Victorian conservatism became part of the Indian culture. Homosexuality was criminalized, and sex became a sin.

The medieval thoughts and customs were also deeply rooted in the minds of most Indians. Educated people like Radhakanta Deb opposed the abolishment of custom of sati, Lokmanya Tilak was against abolishment of child marriage, and even Gandhi did not allow doctors to administer medicine to his wife before she died and sang devotional songs instead. When the leaders of our society found it difficult to get out of the rigid mind-set, think about the millions of poor and illiterate. India was in dire straits when she gained her independence. The partition only made matters worse. While the British railways and education system gave India a head start, the bureaucracy dragged her back. The Indians learned two things from the British and mastered it – cricket and bureaucracy. The future of the country looked bleak.

Jinnah's dream of Pakistan was granted, but the Pakistan he got was not the Pakistan he wanted. East Pakistan without Kolkata was dominantly agricultural and poor. West Pakistan fared only a bit better. Not satisfied with what he got, he now wanted India to suffer the same fate. India's borders were not yet defined. The princely states wanted to remain independent, and the kings were in no mood to lose control over their people. Jinnah encouraged these states to part from India. But there was one man who was standing between Jinnah and his wish: the iron man of India. Sardar Vallabbhai Patel was born in a village of Gujarat in 1875. His birthday, on 31 October, is celebrated every year as Rashtriya Ekta Diwas. As first home minister and deputy prime minister of Independent India, he was instrumental in setting relief for the refugees in Delhi and Punjab. It was he who convinced Congress to accept the partition of India to fast-track independence. Now his task was to unite the rest of India.

Patel, along with Mountbatten and V P Menon, spoke with all the princes and tried to convince them to join India. Most of the 562 princely states, including Bikaner and Jawhar, joined India. Junagadh, Bhopal, Hyderabad, Travancore, and Kashmir wanted to remain separate. Hyderabad, a Hindu-dominated kingdom ruled by a Muslim king, was rich and was already communicating with Portugal to buy Goa and get access to the sea while also keeping in touch with Britain to make their case for independence. The situation in Kashmir was just the opposite. It was a Muslim-dominated state ruled by an unpopular Hindu king. Most people expected Kashmir to join Pakistan. The king, however, wanted to be independent. Bhopal was the second largest Muslim-ruled state in India after Hyderabad. It was in the middle of the subcontinent, surrounded by states that were already part of India. People revolted against the Nawab when he wanted to be separate. Patel's job became easy, and Bhopal became part of India in 1949. Similarly, when the Nawab of Junagadh decided to be part of Pakistan despite Mountbatten's warning, there was revolt. The animal-loving Nawab who had over 300 dogs and is responsible for saving the Asiatic lions from becoming extinct, could not save his own kingdom. After Pakistan accepted Junagadh's accession, the suzerainty of Junagadh—Mangrol and Babariawad—protested and decided to be part of India. Amid the protests, the Nawab, his family, along with all his dogs, and Prime Minister Shah Nawaz Bhutto fled to Pakistan. The Bhutto family, belonging to a Rajput clan from Sindh, would become dominant leaders in Pakistan Peoples Party. After Nawab fled, Patel sent the Indian Army to take over Junagarh, and a plebiscite was held. Just 91 people voted for Pakistan while 190,779 voted for India [153]. Junagarh also became part of India.

In Travancore, the Prime Minister C P Ramaswami Iyer wanted to build an independent nation that modeled itself after USA. The region had one of the highest literacy rates and had recently discovered thorium-rich placer deposits, increasing its strategic importance. They were ready to barter the find with USA to stay independent. The state

Communist party revolted against Iyer, but Travancore Army crushed the revolt. However, after narrowly escaping an assassination attempt by a communist comrade, Iyer resigned. With Patel mounting pressure, the king of Travancore agreed to merge with India.

After Travancore joined India, the position of the Nizam of Hyderabad was weakened. He was still adamant to stay independent. Unfortunately, for the Nizam, like Bhopal, Hyderabad was also surrounded by Indian territory from all sides and had no sea connection. Meanwhile, the internal trouble from the peasant class intensified. The communist party led the Telangana Rebellion against the ruling class. The Nizam fought back with his army, called the Razakars, led by Muslim politician Kasim Razvi. The Communist Party used guerrilla techniques to take over more than 1,000 villages from the landlords [170]. The agricultural land was divided among the landless peasants. However, the Razakars crushed the communists ruthlessly and were responsible for the death and rape of thousands of peasants. INC was banned in Hyderabad, and even the Muslims who wanted to join India were victimized. The Nizam was preparing for a war with India. He received arms from both Pakistan and Portugal. There was a large-scale recruitment in the Razakar army. This made Patel furious, and he sent the Indian Army to take care of the situation. It was a massive operation named Polo, which started on September 1948. The Indian Army was too strong, and Razakar army was defeated within a few days. The retaliation by the Indian Army was equally, if not more, ruthless. According to the official estimates, 27,000 to 40,000 people died in the war. Pakistan protested in vain as another princely state was merged with India. For Patel and India, there was only one final battle left: Kashmir.

Jinnah was frantic for Kashmir as it was key for Pakistan's economy. Jawaharlal was also desperate for Kashmir not only because it was his homeland but also because it was a symbol of his secular India. King Hari Singh, being a Hindu, was not comfortable to be part of Pakistan. He was also unwilling to join India as he was against Congress, a party that was close to his enemy Sheikh Abdullah. Abdullah was head of Kashmir Muslim Conference. Kashmir means *desiccated land*, and myth has it that it was once a lake that was drained by the great sage Kashyap to create land for Brahmins to settle. It has one of the oldest continuous human settlements in the world. In the 15th century, it came under the influence of Islamic rule but managed to maintain its own identity. Kashmiri Sufism was born out of that grand fusion. After the British won Kashmir in the First Anglo-Sikh War, they sold it to the Hindu king of Jammu. Jammu had more Hindus, Ladakh was dominated by Buddhists, while the valley had a Muslim majority. The communities remained in harmony for centuries until partition. It was one Muslim-dominated region of India where the Muslim League had little influence. Hari Singh was not very popular among his Muslim subjects, and it is rumored that he was on a mission of ethnic cleansing of Muslims in Poonch and Southern Jammu [153]. Sheikh Abdullah, grandfather of Omar Abdullah, was fighting against the king. He wanted a democratically elected government without any communal affiliation and renamed his party as National Conference. Hindus and Sikhs with grievances against the Maharaj also became part of the party. It was a strange situation. The Hindu king did not wanted to be part of India while the most popular Muslim leader did not want to join Pakistan. Abdullah criticized Muslim League for their communal agenda and partitioning of India. Muslim League and their idea of Pakistan did not inspire the Muslims of Kashmir.

Meanwhile, the Pathan tribes of North-West Frontier Provience, mostly Afridis and Mahsuds, entered Kashmir to take revenge of the Muslims killed in Punjab. They killed, raped, and looted at whim. It was a massacre in which even the local Muslims, being indistinguishable from the Hindus, were not spared. The invaders were heading towards Srinagar. Hari Singh feared for his life and asked Indian government for help. Officially, India could not help until Kashmir accepted to join with India. Desperate, Hari Singh signed an instrument of accession, and Patel sent Indian troops to fight the tribes. Jawaharlal suspected that Jinnah helped the tribes to get into Kashmir while Jinnah blamed Jawaharlal of using power to seize Kashmir. Indian Army flew to Srinagar on 27 October 1947, securing the city. Jinnah, alarmed by the presence of Indian troops, ordered Pakistani Army to defend Kashmir. There was some resistance among the British members of Pakistan troop who were not willing to fight the British members of Indian Army. Nevertheless, the Pakistan Army did join the war that stopped only due to the harsh winters of 1948. Azad Kashmiri army, mostly militants, took control of northern and western part of Kashmir while Indian Army took control of the rest. Jawaharlal, under pressure from Mountbatten, took the matter to UN Security Council without cabinet permission. It further complicated matters. Abdullah was against interference of UN as he was convinced that the Indian Army could take over entire Kashmir from Pakistan. Jawaharlal later repented, taking the issue to UN, as Britain and America were favoring Pakistan for its strategic location after the cold war intensified [170]. Ceasefire was called with a promise of plebiscite to decide the ultimate fate of Kashmir. The plebiscite never took place as Pakistan was not ready to withdraw Azad Kashmiri army before the plebiscite, and India was not ready to have a plebiscite in the presence of Azad Kashmiri army.

Jinnah died on 11 September 1948. There were rumors that he repented the creation of Pakistan just before his death. Mountbatten had resigned and was replaced by C Rajagopalachari. Gandhi was already dead. Patel was now in full charge, and within two days after Jinnah's death, Hyderabad fell to the Indian Army. In 1950, when the constitution of India came into force, Kashmir too became part of India with special provisions. Pakistan-occupied Kashmir went under Pakistani administration. Kashmir dispute remain unsettled as the tension between the two nuclear capable countries continue to threaten the subcontinent. Some might think that Gandhi's 'nonviolent' India was a bit aggressive in their policy of creating united India. But even Mountbatten agreed a divided India would never have survived, especially with the new world powers trying to fill in the gap left by the old one. Breaking down the entire infrastructure and all the manpower in a complex society would have led to more border tensions. Patel and his men saved India by uniting it like no one had ever done, not even Ashoka or Akbar.

11.2   Idea of India

The making of the constitution of India was one of the toughest jobs in the world. It has been criticized for being copied, but copying the right thing that suits a country as complex as India is no mean feat. No country has a copyright over their constitution; thus, anyone is free to take inspiration. It was a constitution that helped bind a country like India, making it the largest democracy—a democracy that no one expected to last a year. Yes, it was written in complex language; and it was not based on the philosophy of Gandhi. But it represented the idea of India, an idea that was not just about the different religions, separate castes, multiple languages, or diverse cultures but also about the different ideologies. This difficult task fell on the members of the constituent assembly, chosen by the elected members of provincial assemblies. The key members of the assembly that formed in 1946 were Dr B R Ambedkar, Sanjay Phakey, Jawaharlal Nehru, C Rajagopalachari, Sardar Vallabhbhai Patel, Kanaiyalal Munshi, Purushottam Mavalankar, Sandipkumar Patel, Maulana Abul Kalam Azad, Shyama Prasad Mukherjee, Nalini Ranjan Ghosh, and Balwantrai Mehta with Rajendra Prasad as the president. B R Ambedkar himself became part of the constituency with Jinnah's help. Jinnah, a close friend of Ambedkar, asked Jogindranath Mandal to resign to create a vacancy for Ambedkar who had been defeated in the elections of Bombay Presidency. He was thus elected from East Bengal [171].

After independence, a drafting committee was formed to frame the constitution, with B R Ambedkar as the chairman. The draft of the constitution was, however, already in place. Sir Benegal Narsing Rau, not a member of the committee, was the key man who prepared the first draft. He traveled around the world to get ideas and was an experienced man who had already drafted the constitution of Burma. After almost three years of hard work, the world's longest constitution was adopted by the Constituent Assembly and came into force on 26 January 1950. With that, India became an independent republic from being under the dominion of British Commonwealth. The date 26 January is thus celebrated as the Republic Day, a day chosen in the memory of the declaration of *Purna Swaraj* (complete freedom). Ambedkar gave a moving speech, summing up the work of the drafting committee, and more importantly gave three warnings. First was to abandon not just the methods of extremism but also the Gandhian methods of protests that were good against imperialism but had no place in a democratic society. His second warning was against the hero-worshipping nature of Indians as it 'is a sure road to degradation and to eventual dictatorship' [170]. The third warning was against being satisfied with just political democracy. His warnings are true even to this day. Ambedkar was also against article 370 that gave Kashmir a special status. But Patel got it passed through Jawaharlal after special request from Sheikh Abdullah.

The constitution was adopted from various countries. It provided for parliamentary democracy like Britain, having a federal structure like Canada. The distribution of power between center and state was also taken from Canada. There were some members of the constituent assembly who wanted decentralization of power, but most of them voted for strong center, especially after the increase in communal violence during partition. The separation of power among the different arms of the government and also the establishment of the Supreme Court, highest constitutional court with the power of constitutional review, was adopted from America. Directive Principles of State Policy, the guidelines to the central and state governments of India while framing laws and policies, were inspired from the constitution of Ireland. From Germany, was adopted the policy of emergency. President is the head of state of the Republic of India, and part of council of the Parliament of the Union along with Lok Sabha and Rajya Sabha. Lok Sabha, or the Lower House, consisted of elected members from 543 constituencies. Rajya Sabha, or the Higher House, consists of a maximum of 250 members, 12 of whom are elected by the president for their contributions to science, art, literature, and social services, rest being elected by the state and territorial legislatures. In practice, most of the executive authority of the president is executed by Council of Ministers, headed by the prime minister of India. According to article 74 of the constitution, 'there shall be a Council of Ministers with the Prime Minister at the head to aid and advise the president who shall, in the exercise of his functions, act in accordance with such advice'.

The preamble of Indian constitution sums up the idea of India:

> WE, THE PEOPLE OF INDIA, having solemnly resolved to constitute India into a SOVEREIGN SOCIALIST SECULAR DEMOCRATIC REPUBLIC and to secure to all its citizens:

> JUSTICE, social, economic and political;

> LIBERTY of thought, expression, belief, faith and worship;

> EQUALITY of status and of opportunity;

> and to promote among them all

FRATERNITY assuring the dignity of the individual and the unity and integrity of the Nation;

IN OUR CONSTITUENT ASSEMBLY this twenty-sixth day of November, 1949, do HEREBY ADOPT, ENACT AND GIVE TO OURSELVES THIS CONSTITUTION.

It is one of the rare constitutions where the word 'citizen' comes right at the beginning in the preamble. People of India being divided in terms of religion, language and caste, that one word 'citizen' helped bind all of them together. That is what saved India from disintegrating. The words 'socialist', 'secular' and 'integrity' were added later by Indira Gandhi.

Two versions of the constitution were made, one in English and other in Hindi. Three hundred and eight members of the assembly had to sign both. There was a lot of debate about the language in which it should be written. English reminded of imperialism and shame, but there was no other language, including Hindi, that everyone could agree upon. There were eleven pages of signature, with Jawaharlal being the first and Feroze Gandhi being the last to sign. Most people signed in English, with the exception being Abul Kalam Azad who signed in Urdu and Purushottam Das Tandon in Devanagari [170]. The artists of Shantiniketan decorated the handwritten constitution. Leading artists, like Nandalal Bose, painted in each page an art depicting the history of India. But the man who took the pain to write down the entire constitution by hand in flowing italic was Prem Behari Narain Raizada, a person we know little of. Jawaharlal asked him to write the constitution, and he accepted. His signature in the pages of the constitution was the only fee he claimed [172].

11.3   A Shaky Start

Jawaharlal, born in a rich family and educated abroad, was a secular person. He appreciated his share of food, wine, and art [175]. He was shocked to see few Indians rejoicing Gandhi's death. The divisions among Indians in terms of religion, caste, clan, and communities distressed him. Jawaharlal was against reservations and quotas but could do nothing to stop it. Patel was a patriot like Jawaharlal and was a devoted follower of Gandhi. It was on Gandhi's request that he stepped down and allowed Jawaharlal to be the prime minister of India. However, that's where the similarity ended. Patel's tough personality was quite contrasting to that of the emotional Jawaharlal. Patel was a nonalcoholic, nonsmoker vegetarian who worked hard and had little time for personal entertainment [170].

Jawaharlal was sympathetic towards the Left and very tough on the Hindu extremist group while Patel was against the communists, friendly with RSS, and very harsh towards Pakistan. Even though India's democracy had more similarity with America than the Marxism of the Soviets, Jawaharlal preferred the latter for economic and military aid. He saw in the Americans similar imperialistic traits as the British. Moreover, just an ocean controlled by the American navy separated India from America. Soviets, on the other hand, had neither an onland route nor a navy to control India directly. Even though India was officially neutral, USA took the India-Soviet relation as a threat and thus aided Pakistan. Russia's involvement in

Afghanistan made Pakistan strategically more important to USA. Even China saw the Indo-Soviet relationship as a threat as their relationship with Soviets deteriorated. Chinese involvement made control of Kashmir, which connected China to Pakistan, even more critical. The irony was that a Maoist China, along with democratic America, helped the military dictatorship of Pakistan to counter the relationship between democratic India and Marxist Soviets [176].

Jawaharlal's leftish policies, like the Licence Raj and Inspection Raj, created too many hurdles for the industry. It tied down India's growth. The labour-friendly policies made it difficult for companies to recruit staff because once hired, it was almost impossible to fire them. While India's population grew rapidly, the growth rate was very low. It was often derogatorily called the 'Hindu growth rate', which was just 1.3 per cent per capita income between 1950s and 1980s. Even Pakistan grew at 5 per cent, a rate significantly higher than India. Early economists blamed Hindu's contentedness with life and leaving everything to fate as responsible for such low growth. Later they realized that the government policies were the main culprit.

The first election of the Indian Republic took place in 1951–52. It was the largest and the most difficult election the world had ever seen until then. Over hundred million Indians cast their vote, hoping for a better future [170]. Jawaharlal won by a comfortable margin. Millions of illiterate Indians showed their maturity by participation in peaceful elections while, on the other side of the border, Pakistan's condition worsened. Unrest increased in East Pakistan over Urdu being enforced on the dominant Bengali Muslims. Police tried to oppress the protesters, killing a student in the process. A new constitution was framed in 1956 that made Pakistan an Islamic republic and gave Bengali an official status. The recognition came a bit too late. East Pakistan was now fighting to form a separate country.

India too was not spared of the language problem. After several protests, the state borders were redrawn based on linguistic lines. Andhra State was merged with Hyderabad to form Andhra Pradesh. Saurashtra-, Kutch-, and Marathi-speaking districts of Madhya Pradesh and Hyderabad merged with Bombay State. The new state, named Kerala, was formed. Mysore grew, incorporating nearby Kannad-speaking districts. It was later renamed as Karnataka. A lot of reorganization would take place since. Bombay Presidency would be divided into Maharashtra and Gujarat; Haryana would separate from Punjab; similar divisions would happen in Madhya Pradesh, Uttar Pradesh, Bihar, and Andhra Pradesh. India had to be divided in order to keep her united.

Jawaharlal's charisma helped Congress get majority in the second Lok Sabha elections, but the popularity of the party was decreasing. Dravidian movement started in South India as a protest against Brahminism and Aryan-speaking North Indians. The Dravida Munnetra Kazhagam (DMK) party wanted a separate country, Dravida Nadu, for South Indians. They rejected everything Aryan. Dravidian languages, culture, and literatures were promoted. Tamil theaters and movies helped in the propaganda of separate Dravidian culture. The old mythology that advanced civilization of Tamils lived in a separate continent called *Kumari Kandam* that later sunk beneath the ocean was promoted for political gains. The theory cited scientific evidence from some geological reports that spoke of a lost continent called Lemuria, interpreted from findings of similar fossils in India and Africa. The theory of the lost continent has long been rejected for all practical purpose but was alive for all political purposes in India. Slowly, the call for a separate nation faded, and the political parties focused more on reducing the North Indian dominance in Indian politics instead. DMK also led the anti-Hindi agitations against Hindi becoming the national language of India. The regional propaganda helped DMK replace Congress as the major party in Tamil Naidu.

Trouble also came from the tribal communities who had their own culture and never felt part of the bigger India. The biggest agitation came from Nagaland. Nagas were a group of separate tribes that claimed a shared origin. Legend has it that their ancestors lived together in harmony in a place called Mahkel. As the population grew, they split and spread to new lands but promised to reunite someday. The British conquered Naga territories, and the missionaries converted most of them in to Christianity. Christianity united the separate tribes who were fighting among one another, and their legacy came true. Many Nagas became well educated in English. Angami Zapu Phizo, the militant leader of NNC, claimed a separate nation for Nagas [177]. The Indian Army had to be brought in to maintain peace, and Nagaland became part of India in 1963.

To curb the unrests within India, the government passed the Armed Forces (Special Powers) Act (AFSPA) in 1958. It gave the Indian Army special powers in places classified as 'disturbed areas'. It was modeled on a British ordinance created to curb Quit India Movement, and no wonder it was controversial. The army had the power to arrest and even kill civilians in order to maintain law and order. They were provided legal immunity for their actions. Human rights activists who had been complaining of oppression, discrimination, and even rape by Indian Army condemned the act. The icon of such protests is Irom Chanu Sharmila. She began her fast on 2 November 2000 after the Indian Army mistakenly shot ten innocent civilians dead in Malom, Manipur. She was attested for charges of 'attempt to suicide' and was force-fed. She still continues her protest, making it the longest hunger strike in the world. While India managed to suppress the internal problems to some extent, threat from outside continued to loom across the borders.

India's relation with China deteriorated post-independence after the border disputes in Ladakh and Anurachal Pradesh. China rejected the McMahon line drawn by the British and laid claim on territories that India considered its own. Things got worse from 1959 after the Tibetan uprising as India gave asylum to the 14th Dalai Lama. This resulted in frequent clashes between the Indian and the Chinese army. Meanwhile, the Lok Sabha election was due in February 1962. At an apt time, just before the elections, the Indian government decided to free Goa. Goa was one of the first European colonies in India and also the last. Unlike the French, the Portuguese were adamant to keep their colony, and all diplomatic efforts from India failed. Inspired by British India's freedom struggle, the local Goans started resisting the foreign rule. Tristao de Braganza Cunha first led the fight for independence. Portuguese authorities ruthlessly suppressed all resistance. Nonviolent protests did not work, and armed groups like Azad Gomantak Dal was formed. They made strategic attacks on Portuguese authorities. Independent India did support the armed revolts to weaken the Portuguese government. On 24 November 1961, the Portuguese army fired at an Indian passenger boat, killing one person, escalating the tensions.

India attacked Goa on December 1961. The operation was code-named Vijay. Indian Army enclosed Goa from all sides, attacking from land, sea, and air. The small Portuguese army was no match for the Indians. It was a small-scale war, short and swift, in which twenty-two Indians and thirty Portuguese were killed. The long rule of 451 years ended in just 36 hours, and the Portuguese were defeated. Daman and Diu were also liberated soon. A dejected Portuguese government promised Portuguese citizenship to all Goans. They also offered a reward of US$10,000 for capturing Brigadier Sagat Singh, the commander of the first Indian troop that entered Panaji. There were protests and mass demonstration in Lisbon where people shouted 'death to Nehru' and 'Goa is ours'. India's action was backed by China and Russia but not by NATO countries, which included USA, France, and Britain. India did receive support from African nations. Ghana radio criticized the Western countries for their hypocrisy of speaking about 'Berlin as the symbol of democracy and liberty, while failing to speak up for the liberation of Goa from Portuguese colonial tyranny'. Pakistan criticized India's move as 'naked militarism'. The war did work for INC, and in the general elections couple of months later, Jawaharlal won comfortably for the fourth time.

Up in the north, the Indians and Chinese kept sending their armies to fill the uninhabited areas that they claimed as their own. Small skirmishes continued. But Jawaharlal was convinced that China would never attack India crossing the high mountains, especially after Chinese support for Operation Vijay. China surprised him by a full-scale attack on both eastern and western frontiers at the same time. It was a planned aggression, and India was caught unprepared. The Chinese had five times more troops than the Indians [170]. The Chinese army that had already been fighting in Tibet were used to high altitudes. Moreover, they had the advantage of occupying the flat plateau of Tibet where they had accessibility to all their supplies. The outdated war machineries of India were no match for the advanced arms used by China. The result was a humiliating defeat, and Aksai Chin came under control of China. On 22 November, China announced unilateral ceasefire after increasing international pressure and the approaching harsh winters. Around 1,383 Indian soldiers were killed in the war, 3,986 taken prisoner, while 1,696 are still missing. India finally realized the need of a strong army. In the next two years, the Indian Army doubled its manpower. Jawaharlal even took help from USA president John F Kennedy to upgrade the army equipment. A large amount of GDP was spent in strengthening the Indian Army that is now the third largest army in the world.

Jawaharlal's health started to decline after the war. He passed away on 27 May 1964. The *Statesman Kolkata* editorial wrote the next day, 'There was not another man—and no exception need be made—whose death could have saddened so many hearts in so many lands as Jawaharlal Nehru's. India was, quite simply, stunned, as never since the assassination of Mahatma Gandhi in January 1948.... To few has it been given to be in forefront of a movement of national liberation for over 30-years and, then, to lead the country's Government for nearly seventeen. Both were periods of great change.' Sad faces and tears could be seen even in the streets of Pakistan. The whole world was in grief as 'an epoch had ended'. India went into mourning for 12 days. The question everybody had in mind, a question that Nehru himself hated, was 'After Nehru, who?' Some even said, 'After Nehru, what?'

Shri Gulzari Lal Nanda replaced Jawaharlal temporarily. Lal Bahadur Shastri was then chosen as his successor. After India's loss to China, Pakistan strengthened its ties with the latter. Pakistan voted in China's favor for a seat in UN and in return settled their border disputes. With India defeated and Jawaharlal dead, Pakistan found the right opportunity to attack India, inspired by their new friend. This resulted in the second Indo-Pak war of 1965. Shastri's slogan *'Jai Jawan Jai Kisan'* (Hail the soldier, hail the farmer) became famous during the war. The war ended with Tashkent Declaration of 10 January 1966 after involvement of USA and Russia. As per the declaration, India and Pakistan agreed 'not to have recourse to force and to settle their disputes through peaceful means'. The ceasefire did not go down well with the citizens of India and Pakistan. This led to the downfall of Pakistan president Ayub Khan, while Indian prime minister Shastri mysteriously died in Tashkent after signing the ceasefire treaty. Indian government claims that he died of heart attack while Shastri's family believes that he was poisoned. First inquiry into his death was inconclusive, and the reports of the same are missing. Despite no postmortem being done, there were blue spots and cut marks in his abdomen. This added fuel to the fire of controversies. Like Subhas's death, this also remains an unsolved mystery for Indians. Nanda was sworn in as prime minister for the second time. India, however, survived the wars once more.

11.4   India is Indira and Indira is India

The death of two prime ministers within a couple of years shattered India and Congress. Indira Gandhi, daughter of Jawaharlal, was named the successor of Sastri in 1966. As the only woman prime minister India ever had, she also went on to become one of the most successful, and controversial, political leaders of India. Congress won the general elections in 1967, despite being their worst performance till date, and Indira started her first full term. Those were difficult times, and all the prophecies of doom for India had started to look real. People were frustrated with the corruption in Congress and its inability to improve the conditions of the poor and lower castes. As Congress lost its vote bank, the regional parties began to rise at its expense. DMK swept seats in Tamil Naidu, and the communists won in Kerala. Congress even lost their stronghold in Bengal against an alliance between the Bangla Congress and Communist Party of India (CPI). Swatantra and Janata parties became popular in Orissa while in Maharashtra the Shiv Sena was born. Up north, the Mizo National Front, having roots in Indian government's ignorance towards famines in Assam, created a major uprising in the state. Meanwhile, trouble with China continued. The Chinese army infiltrated Sikkim and came up to Nathula in what is known as the Chola Incident. India had learned from her past mistake, and this time, they were not giving up without a fight. In the battle, India lost just 88 soldiers while China lost over 300. The Chinese army was pushed back, and Sikkim became part of India. There was, however, a bigger threat that India was about to face.

On 23 March 2010, 81-year-old Kanu Sanyal committed suicide inside his residence. This once-energetic rebel was frustrated at the state of CPI and Maoists of India who, he thought, had lost their path. Kanu, along with Charu Majumdar, was the leader of the Naxalbari Movement of 1967. Back then in Naxalbari, the farmers were angry with their landlords who took all their crops as tax, leaving barely anything for them to eat. Despite independence, the practice of exploitation of farmers continued. Inspired by the ideologies of Mao Zedong, which spread through the writings of Charu Majumdar, the farmers decided to fight back. Police was called to stop the protests, and the farmers were arrested. One policeman was killed in the encounter as the farmers shot arrows at them. The police retaliated by firing on the crowd, killing eleven people. The police and landlords went after the rebels, forcing them to take up arms supplied by China. What followed was a brutal killing of the landlords. According to Charu Majumdar, it was 'liberation' of lands from the oppressors. The lands were forcefully snatched from the rich landlords and given to the poor tillers. The government left no stone unturned to crush the movement. Taking advantage of the president's rule in Bengal, Indira Gandhi mobilized the army in 1971. Most of the Naxal leaders, including Charu Majumdar, were arrested, killed, or went missing. Charu Majumdar died in prison in 1972. The Naxal movement, however, was only the beginning. It soon spread from Bengal to Bihar and Andhra Pradesh. The era of landlords was over, but the corruption in the government and exploitation by big companies had bred many disgruntled and poor Indians. They have kept the Naxalites, or Maoists as they call themselves, alive. Over the years, Maoists have grown in strength and now are a threat to India and its democracy.

Meanwhile, the cold war was becoming more intense. American president Nixon, was not very happy with India's nonalignment. He addressed Indian prime minister as 'old witch' and the Indians as 'slippery treacherous people' [178]. The support of China and America encouraged Pakistan to be aggressive with India once more. Pakistan made airstrikes on eleven Indian airbases on 3 December 1971. The operation was code-named Changez Khan in order to tempt India. As expected, India was tempted. It now became a full-fledged war. Both USA and China warned India against a war on Pakistan. USA dismissed the Indian Army as poor pilots who 'can't even get off the ground' [170]. They even requested China to use military force to intimidate India [178]. China, however, had an experience of the upgraded Indian Army in the Chola Incident and wisely refused. Moreover, the winter made sure that they stayed on the other side of the Himalayas. USA was busy in Vietnam and could not afford to mobilize their army to India. When they did mobilize their army, Russia got involved and USA promptly withdrew.

Pakistan made a gross error in judgment as they chose a wrong time to get into war with India. While Pakistan started their attack from the west, India looked towards east. The locals of East Pakistan gave away the key positions of Pakistan Army to the Indians. It was an easy victory for India and a humiliating defeat for Pakistan. Fearing that once the Indian Army was free from the east they would attack west Pakistan, they used their diplomatic ties to stop the war. Pakistan's general Niazi agreed for unconditional surrender on 16 December. But before the surrender, the Pakistan Army systematically raped and murdered around 3 million Bangladeshis. It was an unwritten holocaust, and many Bangladeshis fled to India as refugees. As per the Shimla Agreement of 1972, Pakistan recognized Bangladesh as an independent nation. Sheikh Mujibur Rahman came to power in Bangladesh. In Pakistan, President General Yahya Khan handed over the political power to Zulfikar Ali Bhutto of the Pakistan Peoples Party. The defeat did not go down well with the Pakistani population, and many Pakistani Hindus were murdered as retaliation.

The victory made Indira Gandhi the most popular personality in India. Even the opposition leader Atal Bihari Vajpayee hailed her as Goddess Durga. It seemed like Indira was able to put India back on track. She brought in some key policies. Green Revolution doubled the agricultural yield and made India self-sufficient in food. Operation Flood, started in the 70s, was a huge success. It made India a milk-sufficient nation. Other countries would successfully adopt India's model. India also tested its first nuclear weapon in 1974, strengthening its military arm. On 15th August 1972, India celebrated her silver jubilee of independence with pride. Just when everything looked perfect for Indira Gandhi, things would take an ugly turn.

It all started in 1972 when drought and poor kharif crop increased the food price in Gujarat. Young students were the first to protest against the rising food prices. The movement became known as Nav Nirman. Protesters turned against the corrupt Congress government of Gujarat, and the protests soon became violent. Many people, including students, were killed in police firing, and the government of Gujarat was finally forced to resign on February 1974. Students of Bihar, inspired by Gujarat, joined in the protest. Movement in Bihar got a boost when a well-known freedom fighter Jayaprakash Narayan, aka JP, agreed to lead the movement. Students were asked to boycott classes and leave their studies for a year and raise awareness against the increasing unemployment, rising food price, and corruption [170]. There were over 500 casualties as government hit back with force. Seventy of those casualties were fatal [179].

Just when JP and his supporters were becoming desperate, railway minister L N Mishra was assassinated and the chief justice was attacked [179]. Both were close to Indira. Increasing violence due to JP movement was blamed for the assassination, giving the government an excuse to stop the movement by force. JP was undeterred as he continued his protests with more vigor. The protests were no more restricted to Bihar. People's grievance against Indira increased after she allegedly used her influence to provide license for manufacturing cheap cars in India to her son, Sanjay. Sanjay, who had no experience in the business, started Maruti Udyog. Later it collaborated with the Japanese company Suzuki and launched the famous Maruti 800. Meanwhile, more trouble awaited Indira. She was charged with electoral malpractice, use of government machinery and officials for promoting her party before election, and excessive electoral expenditure. The opponents demanded her resignation. Sighting the excuse of lawlessness, President Fakhruddin Ali Ahmed was asked by Indira to declare emergency. On 25 June 1975, one of the darkest days in Indian history, the president gave in to Indira's demand. That night, power supply to all Delhi newspapers were switched off; opposition leaders including JP, Morarji Desai, A B Vajpayee, and L K Advani were arrested; and all civil liberties were suspended [170]. Those arrested still had the authority to challenge their detention in court. But Chief justice A N Ray, who was unfairly appointed by Indira herself ahead of two more senior judges, turned down all their appeals.

Indira started to tweak the Indian constitution in her favor. Indian judiciary, the reason for all her troubles, was the first to feel her heat. In July, a constitutional amendment was passed that barred judicial review of proclamations of emergency, whether made to meet external, internal, or financial threats. In August, another amendment was passed that placed the election of the president, the Vice president, the prime minister, and the Speaker of the Lok Sabha beyond the scrutiny of the Indian courts. The most controversial was the 42nd amendment passed on January 1977. It reduced the power of Supreme Court and High Court and laid down fundamental duties of Indian citizens to the nation. She added *secular* and *socialist* in the preamble to the constitution. There was a reason why Ambedkar avoided those two words. The whole constitution was framed in a way that it made the term *secular* redundant. *Socialist* was introduced to legalize the ever-increasing control of the central government. Ambedkar was against the term *socialist* as it went against the very idea of democracy. According to him, there might be some other form of social system that one may develop in the future that is better than a socialist system, and the constitution has no right to stop the people of India from choosing that better system [180].

It has been alleged that it was Indira's son Sanjay who was unofficially ruling India during emergency. Sanjay ordered cleaning of slums around Jama Masjid to beautify it and also woo Muslim votes. Police firing killed 150 people after the slum dwellers protested as their homes were being destroyed. Sanjay then went on with his aggressive population control plan. It was supposed to be voluntary but was enforced with brutality on millions of Indians, many of whom were unmarried or opponents. Indian media lost all its freedom, and even movies were censored. The famous movie *Sholay* too did not escape the scissors.

In the climax of the movie, ex-policeman Thakur, whose hands were cut and family killed by Gabbar, takes revenge by killing the dacoit leader. That would have been the end of the movie had it not been for emergency. The censor board denied an ex-police officer from killing a man, even though he was a criminal. So the ending of the movie was changed, and just when Thakur was about to kill Gabbar, the police stopped him. Ordinary people did not have the right to give the final justice. This is significant because the root of the emergency lay in the protests of ordinary people who were taking law in their own hands to get justice.

Few days into the emergency, Bombay edition of the *Times of India* published, "D'Ocracy DEM, beloved husband of T Ruth, loving father of L. I. Bertie, brother of Faith, Hope and Justice, expired on June 26." Sikh Akai Dal and RSS kept protesting against the emergency despite all measures by government to shut them up. Thousands were arrested and tortured while many died in custody. Finally in 1977, after 21 months, Indira called for fresh elections and released all political prisoners. Indira had overestimated her popularity, and Congress suffered their first humiliating defeat. Both Indira and Sanjay lost their seats. Democracy won again in India, and Morarji Desai became the first non-Congress prime minister of the country. Charges were framed against the Congress government for the atrocities committed during emergency. Many Congress leaders including Indira and Sanjay were arrested. But they were soon released as none of the charges could be proved.

11.5   Dance of Democracy

Moraji Desai lived to be 99 years old. The secret of his health, he claimed, was drinking his own urine. Urine therapy is an ancient therapy in many parts of the world, including India. It had its share of followers, which include Madonna and Sarah Miles. Moraji Desai, one who had served Congress for most part of his life, was now the first non-Congress prime minister of India. He was leading the Janata Party, formed when the opposition leaders united to stop the menace of Indira and Sanjay. One of the achievements of our fifth prime minister was to improve diplomatic relationship with China and Pakistan. In his tenure, some of the amendments made during the emergency were reverted. However, nothing much could be achieved as there was no unity within the different members in the government. The fragile unity of Janata Party collapsed in 1979. The incompetence of Janata Party, coupled with the sympathy for Indira Gandhi after she was arrested, meant Congress was back in the reckoning. Indira also entered into an agreement with Shahi Imam of Jama Masjid to secure the Muslim votes. The previous time the imam was upset with Sanjay's population control programme and had asked people to vote against Congress. The consequence was disastrous. This time, Indira made amends. The result was a landslide victory for Congress in the Lok Sabha elections of 1980. Indira's third term did not start well. Her favorite son, Sanjay, died in an air crash. With no one to trust, Indira forced her reluctant son, Rajiv, to join politics.

The '80s were a decade when television (TV) became a household name in India. The government promoted TV even in remote villages. It was a ploy to control the population by keeping people glued to the idiot box. Guess what? It worked. The first colored TV was introduced in India in 1982. The epic TV series of *Ramayan* started in 1987 followed by *Mahabharat* and *Bharat Ek Khoj* in 1988. The popularity of Rama and Krishna suddenly surpassed all the divisions among different Hindu communities. Hindus soon began to identify themselves with one common god. It has been argued that the popularity of *Ramayana* and *Mahabharata*, along with the preferential treatment Congress gave to the minority community for vote bank politics, gave Bharatiya Janata party (BJP) (formed after the disintegration of Janata Party) the opportunity to rise [181].

Two great tragedies struck India in that decade. The first one happened in Assam. There was a huge immigration of Bangladeshis in Assam, and the immigration was politically controlled as the immigrants were given right to vote. All Assam Students Union (AASU) demanded postponement of the state elections of 1983 till all foreigners were identified and their names deleted from electoral roles. Elections went ahead despite warnings, resulting in a deadly ethnic clash in Nellie. As per unofficial figures, over 5,000 people died, mostly Bangladeshi Muslims. The government of India then went on to pass one of the most unconstitutional acts, the Illegal Migrants (Determination by Tribunals) Act of 1984. The act made it easier for Bangladeshis in Assam to prove that they were Indians. Even the Supreme Court has condemned the act in 2005.

This was followed by the second tragedy on the other side of the country in Amritsar. Jarnail Singh Bhindranwale and his armed followers took shelter inside fortified Golden Temple. They demanded passing of Anandpur Resolution that was framed by Shiromani Akali Dal. The resolution demanded various favors for the Sikh community, which included larger share of water for irrigation and return of Chandigarh to Punjab. Thousands of people joined in the protest. Indira ignored the demand and instead spread misinformation. She said that the Akali Dal wanted a separate Khalistan. Calling herself a savior of India, she ordered the army to attack Shiromani and his gang of armed militants. The date for the assault was cunningly chosen as the holy day when Guru Arjan Dev, the founder of Golden Temple, died. It was a full-scale war where the Indian Army used tanks, artillery, helicopters, armored vehicles, and even chemical weapons on their own countrymen. Bhindranwale was killed, and the temple was taken over by the army. The Sikh library was burnt down and the holy Golden Temple massacred. As per the official figures, around 500 civilians died that day. The actual figures could be ten times more. As a revenge for the massacre, two Sikh bodyguards of Indira Gandhi shot her on 31 October 1984. Thirty bullets pierced her, and India's only female prime minister died in the hospital. Congress declared Rajiv as the successor after his mother's death.

What followed the murder was a massacre of the Sikhs. Angry mobs attacked Sikhs and indiscriminately killed them. Over 2,000 Sikhs died in Delhi alone. It has been alleged that Congress politicians held rallies and distributed money, weapons, and liquor to inspire the attackers. Delhi Police watched silently as people were butchered. While Indira's death was avenged, the thousands who were brutally murdered by the mob and politicians have not yet received full justice. Rajiv Gandhi shamelessly declared on national TV, "When a big tree falls, the earth shakes."

11.6   The Earth Shakes

It was a cold December morning, but that morning was different. Cough, suffocation, and irritation in the eyes were what the residents of Bhopal woke up to on that fateful morning of 3 December 1984. People panicked and ran out of their houses, trying to get away from the deadly white smoke that was fast engulfing them. Many died on the streets. Some managed to get to the nearby hospitals, which filled up rapidly. The hospitals of Bhopal were not equipped for a major disaster like this, and casualties were huge. Around 500,000 people were affected, and over 10,000 died from the poisonous gas that was accidentally released from the Union Carbide's Bhopal plant [182]. More than being an accident, it was the callousness and ignorance of the American firm Union Carbide Corporation (UCC) that was the architect of the worst industrial disaster the world has ever seen. The plant was poorly designed, much less safe than their older plant in Virginia. The people were not properly trained, 70 per cent being untrained. There were already many minor accidental leakages that were ignored [183]. Warnings were given to the company, and requests were made to the government to shift the plant away from the city. But all requests fell on deaf ears, and a tragedy was inevitable. Legal actions followed the disaster. UCC bargained their way out and paid just US$470 million. A case was framed against UCC CEO Warren Anderson. He was arrested but was soon released on bail. He escaped to USA and did not appear for any court hearings since then. While no case could be proved against him, eight Indian employees were found guilty and convicted. Anderson died without trial on September 2014. Weeks after the catastrophe, Lok Sabha elections were held.

Rajiv Gandhi worked as a professional pilot in Indian Airlines. He had no interest in politics. He fell in love with an Italian waitress named Albina Maino, now known as Sonia Gandhi. They married and had two kids, a son and a daughter. His life took a sudden turn in early 80s when two consecutive tragedies struck his family. The untimely death of his brother and mother landed the pilot into dirty Indian politics. Riding on people's sympathy, Rajiv Gandhi won the 1984 Lok Sabha elections emphatically. Congress received a record 49 per cent vote from all over India. Rajiv put in efforts to improve science and technology. The software and IT industry started to grow rapidly. India's relation with USA started to improve, and there was marked increase in foreign aids. During his tenure, free education from 6th to 12th grade was introduced. MTNL was created, helping spread public telephones all across India. Attempts were made to liberalize the economy by encouraging exports and reducing import duties, but the Licence Raj continued. Rajiv also introduced 30 per cent reservation for women in government bodies. He promoted nuclear disarmament around the globe and supported the anti-apartheid movement in South Africa. Being a man from the world outside politics, young Rajiv was seen as a clean leader. But politics was in his blood, and soon the inexperienced outsider began to think like a politician.

Shah Bano, a mother of five, in her early 60s suddenly found herself in the middle of a raging controversy. Her husband, Ahmed Khan, took a younger wife and within few years kicked Shah Bano and her children outside the house. As per the Indian law, Ahmed had to pay a pity sum of 179.20 INR every month to Bano for maintenance. After three months, Ahmed denied any payment to Bano as per Islamic laws. Ahmed's petition to Supreme Court against the payment of the maintenance was overruled. This led to a series of protests by orthodox Islamic groups. Bano was pressured and made an outcast in the society. Under pressure, she refused to accept the money from Ahmed. The fanatic Muslim extremists won the battle. Seeing this as an opportunity of securing Muslim votes, Rajiv Gandhi passed the Muslim Women Protection of Rights on Divorce Act of 1986. As per the act, husband had to pay divorced wife maintenance for only 90 days as per Islamic law. Supreme Court was once again humiliated by the politicians for doing what was right. Arif Mohammad Khan, who was in favor of Supreme Court's decision, resigned from Congress. Quite contrary to what the name suggests, the act snatched away the rights of Muslim women, leaving them unprotected. With Muslims pleased, Rajiv now turned to the Hindus. Under his influence, the district judge of Ayodhya ordered opening of locks to permit worship at a small Hindu shrine within Babri Masjid on 1 February 1986. It was a dangerous move. Rajiv unknowingly sowed the seed of the violence of 1992 [170].

Meanwhile, trouble started in Sri Lanka. After independence, the Sri Lankan government became pro-Singhalese, ignoring the minority Tamil community. Seven hundred thousand Tamils did not receive citizenship, and most of them returned to India. Sinhala was made the only official language, and many Tamils lost their job since they could not speak Sinhala fluently. Criteria were made in a way that admission to colleges became difficult for the Tamils. Buddhism was made the primary religion. Anti-Tamil riots left many Tamils dead or homeless. The tensions led to the formation of Liberation Tigers of Tamil Eelam (LTTE) in 1976. They were fighting for a separate homeland named Eelam to be created in the northern part of the country where Tamils were a majority. After the

Jaffna Library, containing many important books related to the Tamils of immense historical value, was burnt down by organized mob of Sinhalese, there was full-fledged civil war. LTTE, led by Prabhakaran, launched a deadly attack on the Sri Lankan Army in 1983. The brutal attacks of LTTE was retaliated with even more brutal force by the Sri Lankan army. Indian Army initially helped the Tamil civilians by dropping food and medicine. India's presence pressured the Sri Lankan government to provide few concessions to the demands of the Tamils. Rajiv Gandhi then made a blunder by sending the Indian Peace Keeping Force (IPKF) to Sri Lanka, with an aim of ending the civil war. Many Sri Lankans disliked the presence of Indian Army in their land. Absence of accurate maps and intelligence information meant that the IPKF suffered heavy casualties. The failure of IPKF led to the deterioration of relations between India and Sri Lanka. Rajiv Gandhi lost the Lok Sabha elections of 1987, and the newly elected prime minister, V P Singh, called IPKF back.

For Congress, their worries had just began. Chitra Subramaniam, a journalist in her advance stage of pregnancy [184], took the challenge to unveil one of the worst political scandals that happened in India. The first hint came in 16 April 1987 when the Swedish Radio claimed that Bofors, a Swedish arms manufacturer, has bribed top Indian politicians and defense officials to secure US$1.3 billion arms deal. N Ram, the editor of newspaper the *Hindu*, assigned Chitra the project to expose the scam. Chitra, with help from Swedish police chief Sten Lindstrom, got hold of hundreds of key documents that brought out the depth of corruption in Indian politics. Bofors was blacklisted in India, but nothing could be proved against Rajiv Gandhi. Many powerful politicians under him were named. CBI director Dr A P Mukherjee later revealed that Rajiv came to know that some politicians were taking commission for the arms deal. Rajiv wanted the commissions to be collected to reduce the dependency of the party on rich business and industrial houses [185]. The corruption charges tarnished the global image of India, which was once known for truth, spirituality, and nonviolence.

11.7 Going Bankrupt

V P Singh was the finance minister from 1984 to 1987. During his tenure, he took bold and aggressive steps to reduced gold smuggling and tax evasion. His raiding of high-profile personalities like the Ambanis (businessman) and Bachchans (film stars) did not go down well with Congress. He was soon transferred to the post of defense minister. As defense minister, he probably started to get a hint of the Bofor's deal and was sacked again. Singh left Congress and founded a new party called Jan Morcha, which later merged with other parties and became Janata Dal. Janata Dal allied with some regional parties and formed the National Front, which became the key opponent of Congress in 1989 Lok Sabha elections. V P Singh became the prime minister of India after United Front formed the government, with outside support from right-winged BJP and left-winged Communist Party. It was the first coalition government of India. Just like the earlier non-Congress government, this one too did not last long.

Mandal Commission, headed by B P Mandal, was set up by Moraji Desai in 1978 to identify the socially, economically, and educationally backward classes of India. As per the report, around 50 per cent of Indians belonged to OBC.

This half of Indian population was poorly represented in jobs. However, they were becoming important vote banks and strength of many anti-Congress regional parties like DMK, Lok Dal, and Socialist Parties [170]. To attract their votes, Singh gave reservation of 27 per cent of all vacancies in government jobs for other backward classes (OBC). This was in addition to the 22.5 per cent already present for the schedule castes (SC) and schedule tribes (ST). There were huge protests all over India against reservations based on castes as it went against the constitution. Many students committed suicide to protest against the reservations, but nothing changed.

Meanwhile, BJP president L K Advani decided to go on a *pad-yatra* (journey by foot) to unite the Hindus on the issue of Rama and his birthplace Ayodha. Babri Masjid, which the BJP and the kar sevaks claim to be a destroyed Rama Temple, was portrayed as a symbol of past slavery that needed to be erased. Pramod Mahajan suggested Advani that a yatra on a car would be much quicker. So instead of walking like Gandhi, Advani decided to travel in an air-conditioned Toyota van, decorated like a rath. So began the famous rath yatra (chariot journey) of 1990 from Somnath, Gujarat. The yatra left behind a trail of communal violence in various places of North India. Some people began to call the rath yatra as rakt yatra (blood journey). Laloo Prasad Yadav arrested Advani in Bihar for building up communal tension. Mulayam Yadav in Uttar Pradesh arrested more people. Security forces, brought in to maintain order, shot at the violent mob. Lots of people were injured, and many kar sevaks were killed. The dead kar sevaks were used as a tool to promote further communal violence. After the arrests, BJP stopped supporting the national front, and V P Singh had to resign. Chandra Shekhar took the opportunity to form the new government with outside support from Congress. While the communal tensions never quite calmed down, there was a fresh trouble for India.

Since 1985, India started having problems in balance of payments. It became a serious issue in the beginning of 90s. Indian government was close to default on loan payments, and it only had a foreign exchange to pay for three weeks of import. The Chandra Shekhar government secured a loan of 2.2 billion from International Monetary Fund (IMF) after agreeing to open up India's economy in the next budget. However, Rajiv withdrew support leading to fresh elections. Meanwhile, economic conditions worsened, and the caretaker government, led by Chandra Shekhar, had to sell 20 tons of gold in exchange of a loan of US$240 million.

While campaigning for the elections on 21 May 1991 in Sriperumbudur, near Chennai, Rajiv Gandhi was assassinated by a girl named Dhanu. Rajiv went ahead with the campaigning despite intelligence warnings. In one such campaign, Dhanu first greeted Rajiv with a garland and then bent down as if to touch his feet. It was then that she detonated the RDX explosives hidden under her dress. It was the first suicide bomb attack in India in which sixteen people died. Dhanu and her partners belonged to LTTE. It was a revenge against Rajiv for sending IPKF to Sri Lanka. There were occasional incidents of violence after Rajiv's death. An angry mob attacked the car of President Mr Venkataraman when he arrived to express his condolence. Red alert was declared in Bengal. But the Lok Sabha elections went ahead despite the tragedy. No party came out as clear winners. Congress was called to form the minority government as it got the maximum number of seats. P V Narasimha Rao became India's first prime minister from South India. The Rath Yatra successfully increased BJP's vote share from 11.36 per cent in 1989 to 20.11 per cent in 1991, and they became the dominant opposition party.

P V Narasimha Rao was a knowledgeable lawyer turned politician who could speak in seventeen languages. He made significant contributions to India's development as a prime minister. His own party often undermines his role. He took bold steps to bring in complete reforms at a time when Indian economy was in crisis. He renamed Congress Party from Congress (Indira) to Indian National Congress, giving hints to those who mattered that the party belonged to the people and not one family. It was Rao who broke Congress traditions and gave a nonparty member the important post of finance minister. It was necessary to give the post to someone who had international credibility, one who already favored an open economy, and, more importantly, one who can negotiate a loan from IMF.

Rao first looked towards I G Patel, who declined the offer. It was Manmohan Singh who got the post instead. Despite opposition within his own party, Rao gave Manmohan, a seasoned professional economist, complete freedom [186]. While taking loan from IMF, India agreed that the License Raj has to go and the state-controlled economy had to end. With that in mind, Manmohan became the architect who liberalized India's economy. Manmohan wrote a thesis way back in the '60s, suggesting the need for a more open-trade regime. Now he had the power to implement it. Rupee was devalued, quotas were removed from imports, the tariffs were reduced, FDI became easier, public sectors were privatized, exports were encouraged, domestic market was freed, and the service sector was given a boost [170]. Manmohan concluded his budget speech, saying, "No power on earth can stop an idea whose time has come. I suggest to this August House that the emergence of India as a major economic power in the world happens to be one such idea. Let the whole world hear it loud and clear. India is now wide-awake. We shall prevail. We shall overcome." [187]

Two separate episodes rocked India in the '80s that challenged her claim of a secular nation. After the success of Advani's rath yatra, BJP went ahead with their agenda of creating Rama temple in Ayodha. They came to power in Uttar Pradesh, and the BJP chief minister, Kalyan Singh, himself provided food and shelter to the thousands of volunteers (kar sevaks). They were coming to Ayodha to reclaim what they thought was the birthplace of Rama. It was 6 December 1992 when over 100,000 kar sevaks moved towards Babri Masjid. Few thousands of police were not enough to stop the mob, and they fled from the spot. The Hindu fanatics went in and crawled over the mosque with axes and hammers, bringing down the century-old structure within hours. Advani himself did not expect the turn of events and later expressed his regrets publicly. But the damage had already been done. What happened in Ayodha triggered a series of riots around India, from Gujarat, Delhi, Madhya Pradesh, Uttar Pradesh, and Karnataka to Assam, with Mumbai being the worst affected. On 7 December, near Muhammad Ali Road of Mumbai, Muslims raided Hindu shops, broke down temples, and attacked the police as an act of vengeance. In north Mumbai, members of BJP and Shiv Sena attacked Muslim homes and shops. Soon violence spread throughout the city. Before the army could bring the city under control, 800 people had already died, of which two-thirds were Muslims. The riots were followed by a series of bomb blasts in Mumbai, starting 12

March 1993. The attacks were made by the dreaded don Dawood Ibrahim as a revenge for the death of Muslims. This led to a division in Dawood's D-Company. His right hand, Chotta Rajan, split away after taking most of the Hindu gangsters with him.

The second episode was taking shape up north in the valley of Kashmir, once known as the paradise on earth. The separatist movement by Kashmir Liberation Front was now replaced by the shouts of Jihad by Hizb-ul-Mujahideen. Kashmiri Pandits constituted around 15 per cent of the population in the valley before independence. They were now the targets of the Muslim terrorist organizations. On 19 January 1990, mosques of Kashmir declared that the Pandits are kafirs and the males had to leave the valley, convert to Islam, or get killed. It has been alleged that the women were told to be left behind, to be used as sex slaves by the militants. What followed was a massacre of the Pandits and sexual violence against their women. Thousands of Hindus fled away from the valley, and the population of the Pandits in Kashmir was reduced to just 3 per cent. Many peaceful Muslims of the valley fled along with the Kashmiti pandits. Many of them settled down in the peaceful land of Goa. The Muslim terror organizations of Kashmir got support from Pakistan and ISI. After the end of cold war, all the extremists who were fighting against Russia in Afghanistan found a new ambition: liberation of Kashmir and disintegration of India. The terrorists blended easily with the locals, and their main target was the Indian Army. Hardly a week passed without an attack on the army. The army, in turn, retaliated with brute force, and sometimes the innocent civilians became the victims.

Rao's tenure had many positives. Along with the rise of communalism, numerous terrorist hijacks and kidnappings occurred during Rao's tenure, and he handled them pretty well without giving in to the terrorists' demands easily. Rao has also been praised for his proactiveness in proper planning and quickly sending relief after the deadly Latur earthquake of 1993. He holds the Guinness Book of World Records for winning an election by a record 500,000 vote margin. Rao was the first Indian prime minister to give a cabinet position to an opposition. He even sent A B Vajpayee, a member of BJP, to represent India in UN meeting. However, Rao's government has been charged with bribing members of the Jharkhand Mukti Morcha to vote for him during a confidence motion. He was alleged of forging documents to taint the image of V P Singh. He was later acquitted of both charges, but his image received a major blow. In 1996 Lok Sabha elections, Congress lost, and Rao was forced to step down as president of INC. INC vote share dropped to just 28.8 per cent while BJP's share remained at 20.29 per cent. Despite a lower vote share, BJP emerged as the single largest party and was called to form government by the president.

11.8   Dawn of New Era

Between 1996 and 1998, India had four prime ministers. Amid the two terms of A B Vajpayee, Deve Gowda and I K Gujral also took oath. Midterm elections were held in 1998, and the frustrated public gave the mandate to BJP. After coming to power, Vajpayee ordered nuclear tests in Pokran. Five nuclear tests were conducted between 11 May and 13 May 1998. The operation was code-named Operation Shakti. Vajpayee proudly declared India's nuclear capability to the world. The tests were a reaction to Pakistan's testing of medium-range ballistic missile Ghauri. The missile was provocatively named after Ghauri, the man who defeated Indian kings and established Islamic rule in India. Pakistan replied with six nuclear tests of their own on 28 May. Both India and Pakistan now joined the league of nuclear powers alongside USA, Russia, China, France, and UK. Just when the world thought nuclear threat was over after the end of cold war, a new threat loomed over the subcontinent.

The nuclear tests gained immense popularity within the country, even though the world heavily criticized India and Pakistan for starting a nuclear arms race in Asia. Aids to India were cut, and economic sanctions were imposed by countries, most of whom already possessed nuclear weapons. To release the pressure, India and Pakistan signed the Lahore Declaration on 21 February 1999. The objective was to promote peace between the two nations and prevent misuse of nuclear arsenals. However, the fear of nuclear war came true when Pakistan Army, disguised as Kashmiri militants, infiltrated eight to ten kilometers into the Indian territory [188]. They were able to block the vital Srinagar-Kargil-Leh Highway. It was the beginning of the first and the only direct warfare between nuclear-armed countries. Since India had the policy of no-first-use of nuclear weapon, Pakistan believed that their 'nuclear shield' would prevent Indians from going into a full-scale war. They underestimated the Indian Army.

The war was fought on high altitudes and difficult terrains. Pakistan Army had the advantage as they had occupied the higher ground while Indian Army had to take the difficult path of climbing up. Indians retaliated aggressively but strategically in order to avoid nuclear conflict. Indian Air Force flew over the occupied hills and bombed the infiltrators. They were not very effective due to the high altitude and bad weather. They acted as cover for the ground army that fought their way up the hills. Far away in Arabian Sea, the Indian Navy began aggressive patrolling. It affected Pakistan's oil supply and trade. Caught on the back foot by India's aggression, Pakistan's foreign secretary warned, "We will not hesitate to use any weapon in out arsenal to defend our territorial integrity." [188]

The most difficult and the most vital battle of Kargil War was for Tiger Hill. If Indian Army were not able to capture it, all other gains would have been nullified. Indian Army chose the most difficult and unexpected path to surprise the opponent. The path they chose was a vertical peak, and the climb was to take place in the dead of the night. By the time the Pakistan Army realized that there was an attack, it was a bit late. The Indian Army suffered heavy casualties as they were in the line of firing of the Pakistani soldiers. While the opponents could hide behind the rocks, the climbing Indian soldiers enjoyed no such advantage. Despite the odds heavily stacked against them, the Indian Army marched on. It took two months for the Indian Army to take back around 75 per cent of the intruded area. For Pakistan, it was a costly battle to maintain. Indian Intelligence got hold of a telephonic conversation between Pakistani general Pervez Musharraf and Lieutenant General Mohammad Aziz Khan that exposed the role of Pakistani Army. After Pakistan was exposed, international community demanded immediate withdrawal of Pakistani forces. USA also pressured Pakistan by blocking loans. Pakistan had to withdraw all their forces. The war finally ended on 26 July with Indian victory.

The war had positive results for India. Indians saw their army fight for the first time on TV. The Indian

Army became heroes, and the bodies of soldiers were welcomed with pride. Many unknown people, like Captain Anuj Nayyar, Captain Vikram Batra, and Lieutenant Manoj Pandey, became national heroes. The war glued the fragmented nation. India got a boost in terms of international diplomatic relations, and the national stock markets rose by 30 per cent over positive sentiments. Pakistan economy, on the other hand, was affected badly after the war as they faced isolation from the rest of the world. The withdrawal of forces from Kargil did not go down well with the Pakistan Army. Within a couple of months, there was a coup in which Nawaz was removed and was replaced by General Musharaf, the mastermind of Kargil War. Musharaf planned and executed the battle without informing the prime minister. Sharif realized, though very late, that he 'blundered in making [Pervez Musharraf] Army Chief' [188].

The battle also exposed India's weaknesses. The intelligence agencies completely failed to anticipate the massive infiltration plan of Pakistan Army. There was lack of cooperation between civilians and army [188] that led to the failure. Overexcited and uncontrolled Indian media also gave away some key strategies of the army to the opponents. The pieces of equipment that the army had were outdated. While the political parties were busy getting mileage out of the victory by posing with the wounded army or distributing gifts to them in front of camera, the real issues were hardly discussed. NDA, however, became popular after the war.

Fresh elections were held in 1999 after AIADMK withdrew support and NDA alliance collapsed. Vajpayee came back strongly and became the prime minister for the third time. Vajpayee continued his aggressive economic reforms despite ailing health. Highway Development Project and Pradhan Mantri Gram Sadak Yojana were launched by Vajpayee to improve the roadways of India. Within five years, Vajpayee government made half of the total length of roads made in the last thirty years. India's GDP grew more than 6 per cent. India's international image improved along with its economy. No more was India a third-world country but a developing nation. BJP did well in state elections of Rajasthan, Madhya Pradesh, and Chhattisgarh and was all set to return to power in 2004 Lok Sabha elections. But the India Shining campaign failed, and Indian public proved to be unpredictable.

Two things changed the equation. The economic growth did not trickle down to the farmers fast enough. The second factor was the Gujarat Riot. On 27 February 2002, the same date when the Reichstag fire brought Hitler to power, another tragedy happened. Several Hindu pilgrims were returning from a ceremony at the demolished Babri Masjid in Ayodha on the Sabarmati Express. Under controversial circumstances, four coaches caught fire, resulting in the death of 59 people. What caused the fire was uncertain, but local Gujarati media blamed Muslim terrorists. This triggered violence in Gujarat against the Muslim community. The violence soon went out of control, and state government headed by Chief Minister Narendra Modi was accused of inaction and negligence. Around 790 Muslims and 254 Hindus died in what was the worst communal violence in India since the anti-Sikh riots. Just like the anti-Sikh riots, the victims of Gujarat did not get justice. Communal tensions increased all over India. Eight Hindus were killed by Muslim mobs over a trivial issue of drinking water from a public tap in Marad on May 2003.

Angry farmers and rising communal tension eclipsed Shining India, and BJP was defeated in 2004.

United Progressive Alliance (UPA) led by INC came to power despite a fall in their vote share from 28.3 per cent in 1999 to 26.53 per cent in 2004. INC now had a problem that they would not mind having. It was the problem of a successor. Rahul Gandhi was too young, and Sonia was advised by senior INC members against becoming the prime minister. It was a fragile coalition, and every ally had to be kept happy by choosing the right candidate. At the same time, a strong prime minister like Rao was a threat to the Gandhi family. The ideal candidate was Dr Manmohan Singh, a humble person who was not from a political background but widely respected among the politicians. Manmohan became the first Sikh prime minister of India. It was Sonia who controlled the party while Rahul was groomed being for the future.

Manmohan Singh, along with his finance minister Chidambaram, continued the aggressive economic reforms, helping India's GDP grow up to 9 per cent. Manmohan was dubbed by Left as pro-business and neo-liberal. It was a big problem for UPA-1. The support of Left was crucial for survival while economic growth was crucial for the country. It was Sonia Gandhi who came as a saving grace. She was portrayed by INC as a socialist who opposed Manmohan. Left thus had enough reason to support INC and UPA while criticizing Manmohan for his economic policies [188]. Manmohan was instrumental in signing the critical civil nuclear cooperation agreement with USA despite disagreement with Left and members of his own party. It was a historic deal that carried forward the efforts made by Vajpayee government.

Manmohan's government brought three important acts in 2005. First one was the Right to Information (RTI) Act aimed at giving citizens more right to information, thus increasing the transparency and accountability of the government. The second was the Protection of Women from Domestic Violence Act that would give women protection against domestic violence that is prevalent in our society. The third was the Mahatma Gandhi National Rural Employment Guarantee Act' that promised security of livelihood in rural areas by providing at least 100 days per year of wage employment to every household whose able adult members would volunteer to do unskilled manual work. Manmohan also helped in breaking the ice on Kashmir issue. He improved diplomatic relations with Pakistan. President Musharraf was invited to India to watch the India-Pakistan cricket match. It was because of his initiative that First J&K Round Table Conference was held in 2006 that gave a platform to all leaders to freely express their opinion on the sensitive issue. The improvement of relations between the two countries was a threat to the extremist groups, and they intensified terror attacks.

On 29 October 2005, three bombs exploded in the crowded streets of Delhi, killing 62 people a couple of days before Diwali. Seven blasts rocked Mumbai Railways on 11 July 2006. Over 200 people died while over 700 were injured. Indian Mujahideen took responsibility for the attacks. Within a couple of years, Lashkar-e-Taiba with support from Pakistan's ISI carried out the deadliest attack on Indian soil. The terrorists entered India from Pakistan via Arabian Sea. Fully armed men attacked twelve places in Mumbai on 26 November. They fired indiscriminately at public and exploded timer bombs at various places. The places under attack included Chhatrapati Shivaji

Terminus, Leopold Café, Nariman House, Taj Mahal Hotel, and Oberoi Trident. The terrorists were guided on phone from Pakistan and given live updates about the movement of the police force with help from the detailed live telecast shown by the overenthusiastic media. Mumbai was not prepared for an attack of this scale, and the horror lasted for four days. About 164 people lost their lives, including the famous ATS chief Hemant Karkare. All ten terrorists were eventually shot down by the Indian Security Forces, barring Ajmal Kasab. He was arrested alive only after the brave subinspector Tukaram Omble died holding on to Kasab's AK-47 even as he was fired upon [188]. Kasab was later hanged in Yerwada Jail, not before he admitted to the crime and of Pakistan's involvement. The attacks were meant to trigger communal violence but failed in their objective. However, they did manage to slow down the peace talks with Pakistan.

The attacks came during the great global recession of 2008 after the Lehman Brother crisis. Indian government acted fast by boosting investor confidence, and the recession was avoided [188]. Despite the increase in terrorism and the global recession, UPA-1 was flourishing under Manmohan. It was the farmers who brought INC back to power; thus, before the next elections, it was the farmers who needed to be pleased. Huge debts were the main cause of increasing farmer suicides, and the government decided to completely relieve the loans given to small and marginal farmers. It would cost the government 720 billion rupees to save 40 million farmers [189]. It was not something unprecedented. It happened before in 1979. But this time, it was a move that brought UPA back to power in the 2009 Lok Sabha elections. Manmohan became the only prime minister of India after Jawaharlal to return to power for two consecutive terms.

11.9   Hoping Against Hope

UPA-2 was the undoing of Manmohan. His aggressive policies and favors to the farmers strained the government finance. Success depended on sustainable strong growth of Indian economy. However, though India managed to escape the recession of 2008, the economy did slow down. It was also the time for Congress to build the image of Rahul Gandhi. He was portrayed as an angry young man, a rebel who wanted to change the rotten old system. Rahul even did not shy away from insulting the prime minister publicly. Rahul's image was built at the cost of Manmohan's. Manmohan quietly went inside his cocoon and let Sonia and Rahul take over. His reputation took a hefty blow as media, and internet made a mockery of the man who had once changed India's fate by liberating her economy. Manmohan was criticized for his silence. His replied, "It has been my general practice not to respond to motivated criticism directed personally at me. My general attitude has been 'Hazaaron Jawabon Se Acchi Hai Meri Khamoshi, Na Jaane Kitne Sawaalon Ki Aabru Rakhe [My silence is better than a thousand questions; don't know how many answers it holds]'."

When UPA-1 came to power in 2004, they did so with help from the Left. Within four months, the Communist Party of India (Maoist) was formed after merging of some radical leftish groups. While Maoism was losing its grip in Mao's own China, in India, it was deepening its roots. With India's rising economy the industries and infrastructures were growing and fast encroaching into the tribal forests. While the farmers were taken care of by the government, the tribes were neglected. This laid a perfect foundation for the Maoists to thrive. The Maoists had already helped

Mamata Banerjee in Bengal by supporting her in Nandigram and Singur in the anti-land acquisition controversy with Tata. Five years later in 2009, when UPA was re-elected without the help of the Left, CPI (M) was declared as a terrorist organization. Manmohan called them the biggest threat to India. However, it was too late, and the Maoists had grown in strength. Chhattisgarh government tried to use the tribals who were angry with the Maoists to counter the Maoist threat by giving them arms. They knew the jungles well enough to counter the Maoists but were not as organized. Salwa Judum, as the tribals army was called, was a failure and was banned by Supreme Court in 2011. In 2009, COBRA, specialized unit of CRPF meant for the Maoists, and the state police killed thirty Maoist rebels in Dantewada. It was the only time before the retaliation happened.

In the early hours of 6 April 2010, the CRPF men committed a big tactical blunder as they chose a wrong place to camp for the night after returning from an operation in Dantewada. Over 300 Maoists slowly, but carefully, crawled into the CRPF camp and slaughtered the sleeping men. Some jawans managed to radio for help. The rescue vehicle took a well-known road towards the camp on which the Maoists already planted landmines. The rescue party was also annihilated. Seventy-six policemen died that night, and all their arms and ammunitions were looted. It was the deadliest attack by the Maoists in India and was a ruthless success. State and center took several measures to counter the Maoist threat after the Dantewada Massacre. The Maoists have been unsettled since their leaders Kishanji and Azad were killed. But the threat continues to loom in the dark tribal jungles of India. Unless the government helps the tribals get out of poverty, the Maoist terror would be difficult to neutralize.

The threat from Maoists is something that never affected the middle-class Indians. Now there was a new threat that brought them out of their comfort zone and onto the streets of India. On the night of 16 December 2012, a 16-year-old psychotherapist and her friend were returning home after watching a movie. It was 9.30pm when they boarded a bus from Munirka. There were five men already present in the bus, apart from the driver. After some time, the bus doors were locked, and it went off route. When the couple suspected something was wrong, the five men beat up the friend of psychotherapist and then took turns to rape her. They then inserted a blunt rod inside her vagina, causing severe damage to her genitals, uterus, and intestines. Both the victims were then thrown out of the bus. The brutality of the attack shocked the entire nation. The girl, named by media as Nirbhaya—the fearless—succumbed to injuries. The entire nation came out in protest. Police caught all the six culprits. The most violent of the six was a juvenile, and ironically, he got the least punishment by virtue of his age. Of the other five adults, one committed suicide while the rest were given death sentence. Delhi High Court upheld the verdict of death penalty on 13 March 2014. Supreme Court stayed the execution, and Nirbhaya is yet to get her justice. More brutal cases had happened in India in the past. Women have been raped and burnt alive. The tribal and Dalit girls have been repeatedly violated. But it was the Nirbhaya tragedy that struck a chord with the middle-class Indians. The widespread mass protests forced the government to amend some of the outdated laws, and the Criminal Law (Amendment) Act of 2013 was passed.

The mass protests were not the first of its kind in the recent past. There were protests in 2011 against the corruptions that affected the Indian government. A series of unprecedented scams—which included the coal scam, 2G Spectrum scam, CWG scam, Adarsh scam, and Satyam scam—have left Indian citizens disappointed. India's growing international image suffered a setback. The anticorruption movement of 2011, as it was called, gained momentum when Anna Hazare came to Jantar Mantar and began his hunger strike to force the government to pass a strong anticorruption law. The fast ended after government accepted his demands of passing the Jan Lokpal Bill. When Lok Sabha finally passed the bill on December 2011, it turned out to be a weaker version. Even that did not get passed in the winter session of Rajya Sabha, leading to further protests. The protests did not bear the fruit that was expected. Few members from Anna's team, headed by Arvind Kejriwal, moved away from the movement and joined politics with an oath to clean the system from within. Thus was formed the Aam Admi Party (AAP), not surprisingly having the symbol of a jharu (broom).

The rising corruption, a silent prime minister, and lack of a leader was hurting the prospects of UPA in the upcoming Lok Sabha elections. Projection of Rahul as the prime minister candidate did not help their cause either. As a last-ditch effort, Congress played their final trump cards in a hope to turn the middle class and the poor in their favor. Lokpal Bill was passed in 2013 to attract the middle class while for the poor Food Security Bill was brought in. INC played their card a bit too late. It was not just BJP who was a threat to INC. There was now a new kid in town: AAP. Kejriwal, former IRS officer educated from IIT, was the face of changing Indian politics. AAP surprised everyone by winning twenty-eight of seventy seats in 2013 Delhi Assembly elections. They formed the minority government with support from Congress. AAP reduced the electric bills and provided 20 kiloliters of free water per month to those houses having meters. This increased the popularity of AAP. However, they resigned after a failed attempt to introduce Jan Lokpal Bill in Delhi Assembly. Inspired by their success in Delhi, AAP contested in the Lok Sabha elections. As a new party, they stretched themselves too far and too thin, resulting in a dreadful performance. AAP came back strongly to win the Delhi Assembly during re-elections by winning sixty-seven out of seventy seats.

The 16th Lok Sabha elections held from 7 April to 12 May 2014 was the longest election in the country's history and the largest election ever held in the world. The two main candidates fighting for the post of prime minister of India were Rahul Gandhi (for INC) and Narendra Modi (for BJP). Modi belonged to a humble family and was inspired by RSS at an early age. He joined BJP and quickly rose through the ranks. Modi replaced Gujarat chief minister Keshubhai Patel when the latter could not properly handle the Bhuj earthquake of 2001. Modi grabbed the opportunity with both hands and won four consecutive state elections. Modi's success in Gujarat gave him an extra edge in the Lok Sabha. BJP's key agenda in 2014 were to fight corruption, speedy governance, boost economy, security for women, and clean River Ganges. BJP spent a lot of money on their *acche din* (good days) campaign, and it worked. The Modi wave was larger than people expected. BJP won the Lok Sabha elections with clear majority for the first time. After thirty long years, the era of coalition was finally over. Modi became the 15th prime minister of India. People hoped against hope for a change towards a better future. Since then, Modi has tried to improve foreign relationship with various countries. He launched the Make in India campaign and put in efforts to ease doing business with India. With only few seats in Rajya Sabha, BJP's challenge would be to get key bills, like GST, passed. The opponent will leave no stones unturned to prevent it. The new government has already been rocked by controversies like the Lalitgate and Vapyam scams. There had been protests against the perceived notion of rising intolerance. Whether it is true or not, only time will tell. As the world economy is slowing down, the next few years would be critical for BJP and for India.

Epilogue

*This is indeed India; the land of dreams and romance, of
fabulous wealth and fabulous poverty, of splendor and
rags, of palaces and hovels, of famine and pestilence,
of genii and giants and Aladdin lamps, of tigers and
elephants, the cobra and the jungle, the country
of a thousand nations and a hundred tongues, of a
thousand religions and two million gods, cradle of the
human race, birthplace of human speech, mother of
history, grandmother of legend, great-grandmother
of tradition, whose yesterdays bear date with the
moldering antiquities of the rest of the nations—the
one sole country under the sun that is endowed with an
imperishable interest for alien prince and alien peasant,
for lettered and ignorant, wise and fool, rich and poor,
bond and free, the one land that all men desire to see, and
having seen once, by even a glimpse, would not give that
glimpse for the shows of all the rest of the globe combined.*

—Mark Twain, *Following the Equator*

Will India Survive?

I t is still true what Mark Twain wrote about India way back in 1897. Not much has changed over so many years. Many people wonder about the identity of India. Some even say that India has never existed, and it was the British who created India from various tribes and kingdoms. Churchill thought of India as 'merely a geography's expression' that was 'no more a single country than the equator'. Even today, India struggles to find one single identity for itself. What defines India? Is it Chanakya's diplomacy, the Chola Kingdom's aggression, Akbar's secularism, Gandhi's nonviolence or RSS's Hindutva? Neither of them is the true answer. India is defined by its lack of identity, and that is what separates her from the bordering countries. Absence of identity meant that we never had an identity crisis. Contrasting cultures were never a threat. While the Islamic State today struggles and fights to hold on to their identity, India, instead of resisting the change, accepted and assimilated all the differences. India has always been a culture, a way of life, a concept that is not defined by its borders. It is the chaos of disorganized diversity and the extravaganza that defines India. The plethora of colors, sounds, and smells—the good, the bad, and the ugly—is an assault to the senses for an outsider. It can excite and exasperate a visitor both at the same time. No wonder India is called the mystical land of the East because outsiders can sense that uniqueness. That is exactly why foreign writers, since ancient times, described the whole of India as one identity. When Greeks wrote about Indians, they did not write about Mayurian Empire. They wrote about Indica (India). When Chinese writers came to India, they visited the whole of India.

When foreigners wrote about trading with Indians, they did not write about trading with Gujaratis or Bengalis or Kerealites; they traded with Indians. Arabs wrote about Hind (India) and not separate tribes and kingdoms of India. The idea of India is not a British creation; it has existed since ancient times.

Close to 70 years of freedom and India still has the problems of corruption, illiteracy, and poverty. Looking at India today, one can come to the conclusion that we have failed as a nation. But we often forget the condition of India when we achieved our independence. She was a fragile nation, and very few thought that she would survive. Our biggest achievement post-independence has been the story of our survival. We survived as a nation without breaking down to pieces despite the struggles, and today we can dream of becoming a global power. As Shekhar Gupta puts it, the concern of most Indians evolved from *roti, kapda aur makaan* (food, cloth, and shelter); through *bijli, sadak aur pani* (electricity, road, and water); to *padhai, sehat aur naukri* (education, health, and job) [190]. That itself speaks of growth. Though lots of concerns still remain, our once-biggest threat of surviving as one nation has been overcome.

Padhai (education) is one of India's biggest concerns. As high as 26 per cent of the Indian population is illiterate despite being a number that decreased substantially from 88 per cent when the British left. We have to find a way to educate our youth. Average number of years of formal education in India is just 4.4. That number should be 12 years in the least. For democracy to survive, we need the citizens to vote for the right candidates. Illiteracy leads to votes getting segregated along the lines of caste and religion. Wrong people in power also lead to corruption.

Teachers ought to help students develop not just knowledge but personality and free mind. Once the basic education is complete, people should be trained to develop specific skill sets. India has a huge number of unskilled labors. While the developed world has moved from agricultural sector, through manufacturing sector, to service sector, India skipped the middle part. That has made our framework weak. For a big country like India to grow, we need industries. That in turn requires skilled labors. Only by developing skilled labors can we hope to compete against the likes of China. A bit of investment on these people will actually work much better for the government.

Sehat (health) comes next in the list of worries. Most of the children born in India are underweight, and 7 per cent of them die before turning 5. Only 4 per cent of the GDP is spent on health care, much less than other developing countries. India cannot afford to spend the right amount of money because it is drained in subsidies. 80 per cent of the subsidy does not reach the poor because of corruption [190]. Instead of spending huge amounts on the subsidies, that money should be used on things that directly benefit the people. This includes not just education but also health care, social security, and sanitation. Private health care system in urban areas of India is quite good, but it is equally bad in the rural areas. Seventy per cent of Indians live in rural areas, of which 300 million are below poverty line [190]. The health insurance market is not prevalent in the rural areas where people cannot bear the cost of good treatment. The poor thus prefer cheap, and ineffective, alternate treatments. Ineffective treatment increases the concerns of diseases like HIV, malaria, tuberculosis, and diarrhoea. Sanitation is an important part of *sehat*. Greek writers once wrote about how clean the Indians were.

Oldest flushed toilets have been found from ISVC. Yet our cities are dirty, and majority of our population defecates in open. The dream of *Swatch Bharat* (clean India) can only be fulfilled by mass awareness and education.

We are a population of 1.2 billion people and growing, and 70 per cent of them are below 36 years of age. This huge youth population is both strength and weakness of India. Providing *naukri* (job) to the youths of India is a major challenge. Majority of Indians are farmers by occupation. The farmlands, whose yield is just half of that of China, become smaller with our ever-growing population. It makes the farmers poorer. We need to save the people who feed us. Though India's GDP has grown, just 14 per cent of that is spent on agriculture. Despite such low yield and 40 per cent of the food being wasted in storage and transport; the farmers provide sufficient food for the Indians. The government should collaborate with other countries and help improve our yields and also manage the storage of grains. Then our farmers would have the potential to feed the whole world. Majority of Indians will get out of poverty once the condition of farming improves. Until then, the farmers will keep moving to cities for a better life or commit suicide. The farmers are changing their profession to take up low-skilled informal services in cities like vegetable sellers, car washers, maids, and taxi drivers. Most of them live in slums, home to almost 70 million people. The growing population of the cities along with water and space shortage, increase in consumption of energy, increasing pollution, and unmanageable wastage is making our cities unstable. Smart cities that Indian government plan to build are going to provide shelter to the ever-growing young population moving from rural to urban areas. The construction is also going to provide jobs for them. Make in India campaign, if successful, would give employment to the skilled labors. If the initiatives from the government fail, then the large number of unemployed youths will take to antisocial activities. India will dive into further chaos.

If India did manage to provide *padhai*, *sehat*, and *naukri*, there will still be other issues that will need attention. In this vast-growing economy, the energy need is going to grow dramatically. We currently spend a lot of money importing hydrocarbons, increasing the trade deficit. The current government policies do not attract the investors in oil or mining sector. The government needs to make the policies more attractive in order to find more oil and mineral resource. An alternate solution might lie in the rich thorium deposits of South India. India has one of the largest thorium resources, and currently a lot of research is happening in Bhabha Atomic Research Center (BARC) that will help create a nuclear reactor that can burn thorium as its fuel core. Once these nuclear plants are up and running, it should take care of a lot of our energy needs. It is innovations like this that will take our nation forward. Despite the fact that less than 1 per cent of GDP is spent on research and development, we are able to produce nuclear weapons indigenously. We have sent satellite to Mars totally made in India. India also produces a lot of usable patents. Think of the amount of innovation Indians can do once we get right amount of funds to develop research and technology. Birla is Asia's biggest aluminum producer; Airtel has world's fourth biggest subscriber base; and Tata, Reliance, and Mahindra have made it big globally. Indian generic drugs are saving millions around the world [190]. Young Indians have led top companies like Google,

Pepsi, Motorola, HP, and Microsoft. Given the opportunity, Indians can excel in any field. That gives us hope.

There is an increasing trend of polarization amongst Indians that is evident in the social media. Internet has helped connect millions of Indians and given them a platform to raise their voice at the click of a button. The social media can easily spread misinformation. We need to be more responsible while interacting in social media. Calling others by names like '*feku*', '*bhakt*', '*sickular*', 'pseudo-liberal', '*aaptards*', 'anti-national' etc. reflects lack of maturity. There is a difference between 'nationalism' and 'patriotism'. The difference is brought out clearly by Sidney J. Harris in his quote: "The difference between patriotism and nationalism is that the patriot is proud of his country for what it does, and the nationalist is proud of his country no matter what it does; the first attitude creates a feeling of responsibility, but the second a feeling of blind arrogance that leads to war." While it is easy to be a nationalist and turn a blind eye to our problems, a true patriot recognizes the issues instead and tries to solve it. It is true that the media does blow out of proportion the amount of negative things in India. But we do have incidents of rape, honor killing, dowry, child labor, female infanticides etc. There is no point denying that. As long as there is even a single such medieval case happening, we cannot rest in peace because this goes against the idea of tolerant India.

For India to develop we need to respect each other. We have to re-kindle the faith in our countrymen, something that we lost over the hundreds of years of slavery. We have to get rid of our own conservatism and caste hierarchy and see all people as equals. Instead of blaming the Prime Minister for everything we need to blame ourselves for littering. Instead of wasting time in deciding whether we should chant 'Bharat mata ki jai', we should promise to attend the next meeting/appointment on time. Instead of shouting 'why some one did not stand-up while national anthem was played', we should shout against the rising crimes against women. We can then get rid of the problems of "dirt scattered around, the lack of public etiquette, the crazy driving, the bureaucracy and the hierarchy" that perplexed that British gentleman. We should wait neither for the government, nor for the judiciary that has a huge amount of pending cases that would take 300 years to solve [191]. We can turn India into a developed country if we take up the responsibility

Increasing intolerance is a worldwide problem. Religious conservatism is starting to gain ground once more. While ISIS carry out terrorist attacks and behead innocent people, such brutality is still not thinkable in India. But as intolerance rises the world over, India will not be left behind. We need to be very careful about the future we choose for ourselves. Intolerantly shouting and claiming that we are tolerant is not going to help us. While ISIS-like brutality is not expected in India, such brutality was not unheard of in this land either. Thousands were raped and brutally murdered during the partition. The Sikh and Gujarat riots were no different. Given an opportunity, we can be as brutal as any other community in the world. Let us not give ourselves the opportunity to become brutal. We have to start respecting our diversity and difference in opinion. Unity in diversity is our strength. Despite all odds, we can develop into a rich and happy nation in our own way. But for that, we need to free our mind as Tagore once wished. Instead of being hero worshippers, we have to become leaders. For long, our country has been known for its potential. It is now time for realization of that potential.

Will India survive? When people expect the worst to happen to her, she bounces back. She is a country of contradictions. While kids are murdered in our country because they are born as female and wives are killed because of dowry, goddesses find a special place in the hearts of Indians. People get killed for falling in love in a country that celebrates the illicit love between Krishna and Randha. While there will be cowards who turn blind eye to accident victims on the roads, there will be brave hearts who will die protecting the honor of the country. There are states in India where it is hard to get a house if you cook nonvegetarian food. But in the same locality, people flock to KFC or McDonald's to have a bite of chicken burger. While we are impatient and intolerant while driving our cars, we tolerate the erratic driving. Our tolerance of intolerance is perplexing. In the same country where Nirbhaya had received worldwide footage, media does not care about the rapes of Dalit girls as they are of low caste. Lower castes have been oppressed by the higher ones for generations, but there are also cases of lower castes becoming rich and powerful rulers like Nanda Empire and Gupta Empire. While there is a resistance against mingling of people of different castes, all castes exist in this land without destroying one another. In fact, they all need one another to survive. From personal experience, I can tell that most Hindu families in our society do not hire our Muslim maid because of her religion. While there have been cases of religious intolerance, Christian priests like Saint Thomas or a Muslim thieves like Kayam Kulam Kochunni have become Hindu deities. A mosque in Golconda is named after a Hindu courtesan. Indians have a unique character of coexisting without comingling. This uniqueness has helped different cultures survive. That exceptional journey has created the diversity of India. That has been our strength, as well as our weakness. While current superpowers will fade and new ones replace them, India will continue her journey through the chaos. The survivors will survive.

Summary Table of Important Events in Indian History

Dynasty	Important Rulers *Other Events*	Reign Start	Reign End	Important Battles / Rebellions / Incidents
Paleolithic		70,000 BCE	5000 BCE	
Great coastal migration	*Toba eruption*	7000 BCE		
Proto ISVC		7000 BCE	3000 BCE	
	First use of copper	4300 BCE		
ISVC		3000 BCE	2000 BCE	
	First use of bronze	2600 BCE		
Mahajanapadas		2000 BCE	500 BCE	Battle of Ten Kings
	First use of iron	1000 BCE		
	Buddha born *Sushruta wrote on surgery*	sixth-century BCE		
Haryanka Dynasty	Bimbisara	542 BCE	492 BCE	
	Ajatashatru Udayabhadra	492 BCE	460 BCE	
Sishunaga Dynasty	Sishunaga	412 BCE	395 BCE	
	Kakavarna Mahanandin	387 BCE	345 BCE	
Nanda Dynasty	Mahapadma Nanda	345 BCE	329 BCE	
	Dhana Nanda	329 BCE	321 BCE	Battle of Hydaspes (Alexander)
Mayuran Empire	Chandragupta *Megasthenes wrote on India*	322 BCE	298 BCE	Chandragupta versus Nanda, Chandragupta versus Selucid

	Bindusara *Chanakya's arthashastra*	298 BCE	272 BCE	
	Ashoka	274 BCE	232 BCE	Battle of Kalinga
	Dasaratha	232 BCE	224 BCE	
	Brihadratha	187 BCE	185 BCE	
Sunga Empire	Pusyamitra	185 BCE	149 BCE	
	Agnimitra	149 BCE	141 BCE	
	Devabhuti	83 BCE	73 BCE	
Mahameghavahana Dynasty	Kharavela	180 BCE	130 BCE	Kharavela versus Demetrius, Kharvela versus Sunga
	Heleodorous came to India	first-century BCE		
Indo-Greek Kingdom	Milinda	150 BCE	110 BCE	
	Saint Thomas landed in India	52		
Satavahana Dynasty	Shalivahana	78	102	Shalivahana versus Sakas
Kushan Dynasty	Kanishka	127	140	Kanishka versus Pan-cha
Gupta Empire	Sri Gupta	240	280	
	Ghatotkacha	280	319	
	Chandragupta I	320	335	
	Samudragupta	335	375	
	Chandragupta II *Faxian visited India*	380	415	Chandragupta II versus Rudrasimha
	Kumaragupta I	415	455	
	Skandagupta	455	467	
	Purugupta	467	473	
	Kumaragupta II *Aryabhata born*	473	476	

	Budhagupta	476	495	
	Narasimhagupta	495	510	
	Kumaragupta III	510	540	
	Vishnugupta	540	550	
Pushyabhuti Dynasty	Prabhakaravardhana	?	606	
	Harshavardhana *Xuanzang visited India*	606	647	Harsha versus Shashanka, Harsha versus Pulakeshin II
Karakota Empire	Lalitaditya Muktapida	724	760	Lalitaditya versus Arabs
Chalukya Dynasty	Pulakeshin I	543	566	
	Kirtivarman I	566	597	
	Mangalesha	597	609	
	Pulakeshin II	609	642	Pulakeshin II versus Mahendravarman
	Vikramaditya I	655	680	
	Vinayaditya	860	696	
	Vijayaditya	696	733	
	Vikramaditya II	733	746	
	Kirtivarman II	746	753	Dantidurga versus Kirtivarman II
Pallava Dynasty	Simhavishnu	575	600	
	Mahendravarman I	600	630	
	Narasimhavarman I	630	668	Narasimhavarman I versus Pulakeshin II
	Mahendravarman II	668	670	
	Paramesvaravarman I	670	695	
	Narasimhavarman II	700	728	

	Paramesvaravarman II	738	731	
	Nandivarman II	731	795	
	Aparajitavarman	880	897	
Gurjara Pratihara Dynasty	Nagabhata I	730	760	
	Indraraja	760?	780?	
	Vatsaraja	780	800	
	Nagabhata II	800	833	
Pala Empire	Gopala	?	?	
	Dharmapala	770	810	
	Devapala	810	850	
	Mahipala I	988	?	
Rashtrakuta Dynasty	Dantidurga	735	756	
	Dhruva	780	793	
	Govinda III	793	814	
	Amoghavarsha	814	878	
	Krishna II	878	914	
	Adi Sankaracharya	eighth– ninth century		
Chola Dynasty	Aditya I	891	907	
	Raja Raja Chola I	985	1014	Raja Raja versus Sri Lanka
	Rajendra Chola	1012	1044	Rajendra versus Sri Vijaya
	Rajadhiraja Chola	1018	1054	
Pandyan Dynasty	Sadayavarman	1251	1268	
Kabul Shahi Dynasty	Jayapal	964	1002	

	Anandpal	1002	1011	Battle of Chach (Mamud of Gazni)
	Trilochanpal	1011	1022	
Solanki Dynasty	Bhimdev I	1022	1063	
Paramara Dynasty	Raja Bhoja	1010	1055	
Chauhan Dynasty	Prithviraj Chauhan	1149	1192	Battle of Tarain I and II (Muhammad Ghori)
Slave Dynasty	Qutbu-i-Din Aibak	1206	1210	
	Iltutmish	1211	1234	
	Raiza Sultan	1236	1240	
	Balban	1266	1286	
Khilji Dynasty	Jalaal-ud-Khilji	1290	1296	
	Alauddin Khilji	1296	1316	
Tughlaq Dynasty	Khusro Khan	1320	1321	
	Ghiyas-ud-din	1321	1325	
	Muhammad bin	1325	1351	
	Firoz Shah	1351	1388	
	Guru Nanak born	1469		
Lodhi Dynasty	Sikander Vasco Da Gamma Lands in India in 1498	1489	1517	
	Ibrahim	1517	1526	Battle of Panipat I (Babur)
Mughal Empire	Babur	1526	1530	Battle of Khanwa (Rana Sanga)

	Humayun	1530	1540	
Sur Dynasty	Sher Shah Suri	1540	1545	
	Islam Shah Suri	1545	1554	
Mughal Empire	Humayun	1555	1556	
	Akbar	1556	1605	Battle of Panipath II (Hemu)
	Jahangir	1605	1627	
	Shah Jahan	1627	1658	
	Aurangzeb	1658	1707	
	Bahadur Shah II	1837	1857	
Maratha Kingdom	Shahaji			
	Shivaji	1674	1680	
East india Company		1757	1858	Battle of Plassey (Siraj-ud-Daulah), Revolt of 1857
	Warren Hastings	1774	1785	
	Lord Dalhousie	1848	1856	
British Raj				
	Lord Canning	1856	1862	
	Lord Chelmsford	1916	1921	World War I, Jalliwanwala Bagh Massacre, Non-Cooperation Movement
	Lord Irwin	1926	1931	Civil Disobidience Movement
	Lord Willingdon	1931	1936	
	Lord Linlithgow	1936	1943	World War II, INA and Japan versus British India
	Lord Wavell	1943	1947	
	Lord Mountbatten	1947		Partition of India

Dominion of India		1947	1950
Republic of India		1950	Present
	Republic of India declared by new constitution, Patel died, Liaquat-Nehru Pact	1950	
	Rajendra Prasad, president		
INC	*First Lok Sabha election, Congress elected* Nehru, prime minister	1951	
		1952	
		1953	*Potti Sreeramulu's fast-unto-death for Andhra*
	All French colonies to India	1954	
		1955	
	States Reorganisation Act	1956	
INC	*Second Lok Sabha election, Congress elected* Nehru, prime minister	1957	
	Controversial AFSPA	1958	
	Dalai Lama comes to India	1959	
		1960	
		1961	Invasion of Goa

INC	*Third Lok Sabha election, Congress elected* Sarvepalli Radhakrishnan, president Nehru Prime Minister	1962	Sino-Indian War
	Nagaland becomes part of India.	1963	
	Nehru died Lal bahadur Sastri came to power.	1964	
		1965	Second Indo-Pak War
	Sastri died.	1966	Tashkent ceasefire declaration
INC	*Fourth Lok Sabha election, Congress elected* Dr. Zakir Hussain President Indira, prime minister	1967	The Chola incident, Naxal bari incident
		1968	
	V V Giri President	1969	
		1970	
INC	*fifth Lok Sabha election, Congress elected* Indira, prime minister	1971	Third Indo-Pak War Operation Steeplechase
		1972	Simla Peace Agreement
		1973	
	JP movement against corruption Fakhruddin Ali Ahmed, president	1974	
	Emergency	1975	
	Emergency	1976	

Bharatya Lok Dal	*Sixth Lok Sabha election* Neelam Sanjiva Reddy, president Morarji Desai as the first non-Congress prime minister of India	1977	
		1978	
		1979	
INC (Indira)	*Seventh Lok Sabha election* Indira bounces back to power	1980	
	N R Narayana Murthy founds Infosys	1981	
	Zail Singh President	1982	
		1983	Nellie massacre
INC	*Assassination of Indira Gandhi, eighth Lok Sabha election, Congress wins* Rajiv Gandhi, prime minister	1984	Siachen war, Operation Blue Star, Anti-Sikh Riot
		1985	
	Muslim women protection bill	1986	
	R Venkataraman, president	1987	Sri Lanka mission
		1988	Sri Lanka mission, Operation Cactus
National Front	*Ninth Lok Sabha election* V P Singh, prime minister	1989	Sri Lanka mission
		1990	*Mandal Commission protests*, Sri Lanka mission
	Rajiv Gandhi assassinated, LK	1991	*Advani's Rath Yatra*

INC	*tenth Lok Sabha election* P V Narasimha Rao Prime Minister Shankar Dayal Sharma, president	1992	*Babri demolition*
		1993	Mumbai riots
		1994	
		1995	
BJP	*eleventh Lok Sabha election* Atal Bihari, prime minister	1996	
United Front	Deve Gowda and I K Gujral as prime minister in unstable phase K R Narayanan, president	1997	
BJP	*twelfth Lok Sabha election* Atal Bihari re-elected	1998	
NDA-I	*thirteenth Lok Sabha election* Atal Bihari re-elected	1999	Kargil War
		2000	
		2001	Attack on Indian Parliament
	Dr A P J Abdul Kalam, president	2002	Gujarat Riot
		2003	Marad massacre, twin bomb blast in Mumbai
UPA-I	*fourteenth Lok Sabha election* Manmohan Singh, the first Sikh prime minister of India	2004	
		2005	Delhi blasts
		2006	Mumbai train blast

	Pratibha Patil President	2007	
	Iron lady of India began fast	2008	Mumbai terrorist attack
UPA-II	*fifteenth Lok Sabha election* Manmohan Singh re-elected	2009	Pune bombing
		2010	Dantewada massacre
		2011	*Anna Hazare's fight for a strong Lokpal Bill*
	Pranab Mukherjee, president	2012	Nirbhaya incident
	Lokpal, Food Security, AAP popularity in Delhi,	2013	*Vapyam Scam*
BJP	*sixteenth Lok Sabha election* Narendra Modi, prime minister	2014	*Lalitgate*
	Swatch Bharat, Make in India	2015	Dadri lynching
	Peace talks with Pakistan	2016	Pathankot and Pampore terror attack, JNU row, Jat agitation for reservation

REFERENCES

[1] The Indian Genome Variation Consortium, *The Indian Genome Variation database (IGVdb): a project overview*, Springer-Verlag, 2005, http://imtech.res.in/raghava/reprints/igvdb.pdf, accessed 30 March 2016.

[2] Diamond J., *Guns, Germs, and Steel: The Fates of Human Societies*, W. W. Norton & Company, 1997.

[3] Gupta G., *Short essay on The Racial Classification of Indian People*, http://www.preservearticles.com/2011101115155/short-essay-on-the-racial-classification-of-indian-people.html, accessed 1 Apr. 2016.

[4] Anne H., *Direct Genetic Link between Australia and India Provides New Insight into the Origins of Australian Aborigines*, 23 and Me Blog, 24 Jul. 2009, http://spittoon.23andme.com/news/direct-genetic-link-between-australia-and-india-provides-new-insight-into-the-origins-of-australian-aborigines/, accessed 1 Apr. 2016.

[5] http://en.wikipedia.org/wiki/File:Neighbor-joining_Tree-2.png, accessed 5 Jan. 2016.

[6] http://www.thefreedictionary.com/Mongoloid, accessed 6 Jan. 2016.

[7] Patel S. S., *Stone Age India*, Archaeology, Volume 63 Number 1, January/February 2010 http://www.archaeology.org/1001/abstracts/stone_age_india.html, accessed 6 Jan. 2016.

[8] Chakrabarti P. K., *India-An Archaeological History* Second Edition, Oxford University Press, 2011.

[9] Bednarik R., Bhimbetka, *Auditorium Cave, Madhya Pradesh: Acheulian Petroglyph Site, c. 200,000 - 500,000 BP,* Rock Art Research, 13 Oct. 2016, http://www.originsnet.org/bimb1gallery/index.htm, accessed 16 Jan. 2016.

[10] ICOMOS, 2003, http://whc.unesco.org/archive/advisory_body_evaluation/925.pdf, accessed 23 Jan. 2016.

[11] Bose N. K., *Tribal Life of India*, National Book Trust India, 2002.

[12] Misra V. D., *Prelude to Agriculture in the North-Central India*, Paper presented in the International seminar on the "First Farmers in Global Perspective', Lucknow, India, 18-20 Jan. 2006.

[13] Lahiri N., *The Forgotten Cities*, Hachette India, 2005.

[14] Panel of authors, *How deep are the roots of Indian Civilization? An archaeological and Historical Perspective*, Draupadi Trust International Seminar, Vivekananda International Foundation, 2012.

[15] Danino M., *Genetics and the Aryan Debate*, Archaeology, http://archaeologyonline.net/artifacts/genetics-aryan-debate, accessed 16 Jan. 2016.

[16] *Building Göbekli Tepe,* National Geographic, 2011. http://science.nationalgeographic.com/science/archaeology/photos/gobekli-tepe/

[17] Kivisild T., Bamshad M.J., Kaldma K., Metspalu M., Metspalu E., Reidla M., Laos S., Parik J., Watkins W.S., DixonM.E., Papiha S.S., Mastana S.S., Mir M.R., Ferak V. and Villems R.", *Deep common ancestry of Indian and western-Eurasian mitochondrial DNA lineages*, Current Biology, Vol 9, No 22, 1999.

[18] Jarrige J. F., *Mehrgarh Neolithic*, Paper presented in the International Seminar on the 'First Farmers in Global Perspective', Lucknow, India, 18-20 January, 2006.

[19] Gupta A. K., *Origin of agriculture and domestication of plants and animals linked to early Holocene climate amelioration*, Current Science, Vol 87, No 1, 2004.

[20] Madella M., Fuller D.Q., *Palaeoecology and the Harappan Civilisation of South Asia: A reconsideration*, Quaternary Science Reviews 25, pp1283–1301, 2006.

[21] Osborn D., *Scientific Verification of Vedic Knowledge*, Archaeology Online http://www.archaeologyonline.net/artifacts/scientific-verif-vedas.html, accessed 27 Jan. 2016.

[22] http://www.sacred-texts.com/hin/rigveda/, accessed 29 Jan. 2016.

[23] Pattanaik D., *Jaya*, Penguin Books, 2010

[24] Thapar R., *The Penguin History of Early India from the Origins to AD 1300*, Penguin Books, 2003

[25] khttp://creationwiki.org/Chinese_characters_for_Noah's_ar, accessed 6 Feb. 2016.

[26] *Zoroaster*, BBC, Last Updated 2009-10-02 http://www.bbc.co.uk/religion/religions/zoroastrian/history/zoroaster_1.shtml, accessed 6 Feb. 2016.

[27] http://www.ejvs.laurasianacademy.com/ejvs1005/ejvs1005article.pdf, accessed 6 Mar. 2015.

[28] Radhakrishnan S., *The Principal Upanishads*, Indus / Harper Collins India, 1994.

[29] Swami Chinmayananda, *Kathopanishad*, Central Chinmaya Mission Trust, 2003

[30] http://en.wikipedia.org/wiki/C_rv_ka#Loss_of_original_works, accessed 8 Oct. 2015.

[31] Sen A., *The Argumentative Indian*, Allen Lane, 2005

[32] Shastri B. P., *The Ramayana of Valmiki*, Vol I, 1952, http://archive.org/stream/The.Ramayana.of.Valmiki.by.Hari.

Prasad.Shastri/The.Ramayana.of.Valmiki.by.Hari.Prasad.Shastri_djvu.txt, accessed 18 Dec. 2015.

[33] Charvaka: The Latest of the Three Eastern Atheists' Dogma, http://www.vjsingh.info/charvaka.html, accessed 4 Oct. 2015.

[34] Vergano D., *Oldest Buddhist Shrine Uncovered In Nepal May Push Back the Buddha's Birth Date*, National Geographic, 26 Nov. 2013, http://news.nationalgeographic.com/news/2013/11/131125-buddha-birth-nepal-archaeology-science-lumbini-religion-history/, accessed 14 Nov. 2015.

[35] Sharma C., *Critical Survey of Indian Philosophy*, Motilal Banarsidass Publishers Pvt. Ltd., 2009.

[36] http://en.wikipedia.org/wiki/Prince_Vijaya, accessed 14 Nov. 2015.

[37] http://en.wikipedia.org/wiki/Gangaridai, accessed 14 Nov. 2015.

[38] https://en.wikipedia.org/wiki/Alexander_the_Great, accessed 14 Nov. 2015.

[39] Simha R. K., *Marshal Zhukov on Alexander's failed India invasion*, Russia and India Report, 27 May 2013, http://indrus.in/blogs/2013/05/27/marshal_zhukov_on_alexanders_failed_india_invasion_25383.html, accessed 14 Feb. 2016.

[40] Allen C., *Ashoka: The search for India's lost emperor*, Abacus, 2012.

[41] Roger B., *Kautilya's Arthasastra on War and Diplomacy in Ancient India*, The Journal of Military History, Volume 67, Number 1, pp. 9-37 (Article), 2003.

[42] *Essence of Chanakya Sutras*, 1992, http://gurujinarayana.org/, accessed 1 Nov. 2015.

[43] Chanakya, Chanakyaniti.

[44] Nag K. and Dikshitar V. R. R., The Diplomatic Theories of Ancient India and the Arthashastra, Journal of Indian History 6, no. 1, pp. 15–35, 1927.

[45] Divyavandana.

[46] Dipavamsa Atthakatha.

[47] http://en.wikipedia.org/wiki/Kalinga_War, accessed 6 Dec. 2015.

[48] Dammika Ven S., *The Edicts of King Ashoka*, Buddhist Publication Society, 1993 http://www.cs.colostate.edu/~malaiya/ashoka.html, accessed 11 Jan. 2016.

[49] Mahavamsa by Mahanana.

[50] Jamil J., The case for changing Ashoka Road to VP Singh Raod, The Milli Gazette, Sep. 15 2015, http://www.milligazette.com/news/12979-the-case-for-changing-ashoka-road-to-vp-singh-raod, accessed 21 Nov. 2015.

[51] McCrindle J.W., *Ancient India: As described by Megasthenes and Arrian*, Thacker, Spink & Co (Bengal), Thacker & Co (Bombay), Trubner & Co (London), 1877.

[52] *Hathigumpha Inscription of Kharavela of Kalinga*, Epigraphia Indica, Vol. XX (1929-30), Delhi: Manager of Publications, pp 86-89, 1933. http://www.sdstate.edu/projectsouthasia/upload/HathigumphaInscription.pdf, accessed 1 Nov. 2015.

[53] Garuda (Heliodorus) Pillar of Besnagar, Archaeological Survey of India, Annual Report (1908-1909). Calcutta: Superintendent of Government Printing, pp129, 1912. http://www.sdstate.edu/projectsouthasia/upload/Garuda.pdf, accessed 1 Nov. 2015.

[54] http://www.worldmultimedia.biz/Culture/yuechih%20sakas%20kushans.pdf, accessed 1 Nov. 2015.

[55] https://en.wikipedia.org/wiki/Kanishka, accessed 1 Nov. 2015.

[56] Sanyal S., *Land of Seven Rivers*, Penguin Viking, 2012.

[57] Maddison A., *Contours of the World Economy, 1–2030 AD: Essays in Macro-Economic History*, Oxford University Press, 2007

[58] http://en.wikipedia.org/wiki/History_of_the_Jews_in_India, accessed 6 Apr. 2015.

[59] Gruber P., *St. Thomas' Arrival on the Coast of India*, 23 Jul. 2007, http://www.my-kerala.com/mb/messages/8/497.html?1307784092, 16 Apr. 2015.

[60] Saurabh, *The Guptas Part-1*, Indian History and Architecture, July 22, 2011, http://webcache.googleusercontent.com/search?q=cache:http://puratattva.in/2011/07/22/the-guptas-part-1-377.html, 24 Mar. 2015.

[61] Nehra R.K., *Hinduism and Its Military Ethos*, Lancer Publishers, 2010.

[62] Mookerji R.K., *The Gupta Empire*, Motilal Banarsidass, 2007.

[63] John F.F., *Corpus Inscriptionum Indicarum: Inscriptions of the Early Guptas*, Calcutta: Government of India, Central Publications Branch, Volume 3, pp. 10-17, 1888.

[64] Vincent S.A., The Conquests of Samudra Gupta, "Journal of the Royal Asiatic Society of Great Britain and Ireland, pp.859-910, 1897.

[65] Sen T., *The Travel Records of Chinese Pilgrims Faxian, Xuanzang, and Yijing*, Education about Asia, Volume 11, Number 3, 2006.

[66] Sharma K.V, *Aryabhata: His name time and Provenance*, Indian Journal of history of Science, 2001.

[67] Michel D., *Landmarks of Science in Early India*, 2009.

[68] Goonatilake S., *Toward a Global Science*, Indiana University Press., pp. 126, 1998.

[69] *Science of Ancient India*, Indian Culture and Heritage Secondary Course, Module-VI, 2002.

[70] Religious Movement of Gupta Period, 8 May 2012, http://www.indianetzone.com/22/religious_movements_gupta_period.htm, accessed 5 Jun. 2015.

[71] Banabhatta, The Harshacharita, http://books.google.co.in/books?id=91yI040vbT8C&printsec=frontcover#v=onepage&q&f=false, accessed 16 Apr. 2015.

[72] Yogesh, Complete biography of Emperor Harshavardhana – the greatest ruler of India, http://www.preservearticles.

com/2011081610838/complete-biography-of-emperor-harshavardhana-the-greatest-ruler-of-india.html, accessed 3 Jul. 2015.

[73] http://www.banglapedia.org/HT/S_0122.HTM, accessed 6 Sep. 2015.

[74] http://www.palikanon.com/namen/h/hiuen_tsang.htm, accessed 6 Sep. 2015.

[75] Sen S.N., *Ancient Indian History and Civilization*, 2nd edition, New Age International, 1999

[76] Armstrong K., *History of Religions*, Ballantine Books, 1993.

[77] Armstrong K., *Islam: A Short History*, Phonex, 2000.

[78] http://en.wikipedia.org/wiki/Muhammad_bin_Qasim, accessed 6 Sep. 2015.

[79] Agnihotri V.K., *Indian History*, Allied Publication, 26th Edition, 2010.

[80] Fotadar U., *Lalitaditya Muktapida: An Omnipotent Indian*, 2003, http://creative.sulekha.com/lalitaditya-muktapida-an-omnipotent-indian_101799_blog, accessed 6 Sep. 2015.

[81] Dhar K.N., *Glimpses of Kashmiri Culture*, Kashmir News Network, First Edition, 2002.

[82] Ashraf M., *Lalitaditya-Muktapida, Kashmir's Alexander*, 16 Ma7 2007, http://www.kashmirfirst.com/articles/history/070516_lalitaditya_muktapida.htm, accessed 8 Mar. 2015.

[83] Albinia A., *Empires of the Indus: The story of a river*, John Murray, 2009.

[84] http://en.wikipedia.org/wiki/Chalukya_dynasty, accessed 16 Oct. 2015.

[85] Mahadevan T.M.P., *Sankaracharya*, National Book Trust, India, 2011.

[86] Cronk G., *Ramanuja (1017-1137 [!]), Commentary on the Vedanta Sutras (Shri-Bhashya)*, 2005, www.bergen.edu/faculty/gcronk/ramanuja.ppt_, accessed 26 Nov. 2015.

[87] Verma S., Fernandes S., '*70 generations ago, caste stopped people inter-mixing*', Times of India, 5 Feb 2016. http://timesofindia.indiatimes.com/india/70-generations-ago-caste-stopped-people-inter-mixing/articleshow/50859632.cms, accessed 6 Feb. 2016.

[88] Chandra S., *History of Medieval India*, Orient BlackSwan, 2007.

[89] Liddle S., *Delhi: 14 Historic Walks*, Tranquebar Press, 2011.

[90] http://en.wikipedia.org/wiki/Rani_Padmini, accessed 26 Nov. 2015.

[91] http://www.factsninfo.com/2013/05/interesting-facts-history-of-alauddin-khilji.html, accessed 29 Nov. 2015.

[92] Daily Mail Reporter, Genghis Khan the GREEN: Invader killed so many people that carbon levels plummeted, 25 Jan. 2011, http://www.dailymail.co.uk/sciencetech/article-1350272/Genghis-Khan-killed-people-forests-grew-carbon-levels-dropped.html, accessed 28 Nov. 2015.

[93] Onon U., *Secret History of Mongols: The Life and Times of Chinggis Khan*, Routledge Curzon Press, 2005.

[94] http://www.independent.co.uk/travel/asia/uzbekistan-on-the-bloody-trail-of-tamerlane-407300.html, accessed 26 Dec, 2015.

[95] Moosvi S., *Episodes in the life of Akbar: Contemporary Records and Reminiscences*, National Book Trust, India, 2009.

[96] http://www.ias.ac.in/jbiosci/september1999/article2.htm, accessed 2 Jan. 2016.

[97] Pagadi, S.S., *Shivaji*, National Book Trust, India, 1983.

[98] Eaton M. R., *Temple desecration in pre-modern India*, Frontline, http://www.columbia.edu/itc/mealac/pritchett/00islamlinks/txt_eaton_temples1.pdf, 2000

[99] Armstrong K., *The Battle for God: Fundamentalism in Judaism, Christianity and Islam*, Knopf/HarperCollins, 2000.

[100] Bernstein P. L., Against the Gods: The Remarkable Story of Risk, John Wiley & Sons, 1996.

[101] Ferguson N., *The Ascent of Money: A Financial History of the World*, The Penguin Press HC, 2008.

[102] Landes D.S., *The Wealth and Poverty of Nations*, W.W. Norton and Company Ltd., 1999.

[103] Whipps H., How Sugar Changed the World, Livescience, 2 Jun. 2008, http://www.livescience.com/4949-sugar-changed-world.html, accessed 3 Jan. 2016.

[104] http://www.learner.org/courses/worldhistory/support/reading_14_1.pdf, accessed 26 Feb. 2015.

[105] http://www.westbengaltourism.gov.in/web/guest/little-europe, accessed 4 Feb. 2015.

[106] Jackson A., *The British Empire: A Very Short Introduction*, Oxford University Press, 2013

[107] Roy T., *The East India Company: The World's Most Powerful Corporation*, Penguin India, 2012

[108] Younger C., *Wicked Women of the Raj*, Harper Collins Publishers India, 2011

[109] Masters J., *Nightrunners of Bengal*, Rupa & Co., 2000.

[110] Chandra B., Mukherjee M., Mukherjee A., Mahajan S., and Panikkar K.N., *Struggle for Independence*, Penguin Books, 1989.

[111] http://www.banglapedia.org/HT/Z_0012.htm, accessed 26 Nov. 2015.

[112] Nehru J., *Glimpses of World History*, Penguin Books, 1934

[113] http://www.nndb.com/people/333/000102027/, accessed 16 Dec. 2015.

[114] *How we tax India- A lecture on the condition of India under British rule*, Leeds philosophical and literary society, Volume 17, 1858

[115] https://archive.org/stream/historyofbritish00kastrich/historyofbritish00kastrich_djvu.txt, accessed 13 Nov. 2015.

[116] Dash M., *Pass it on: The Secret that Preceded the Indian Rebellion of 1857*, Smithsonian, 24 May, 2012, http://www.smithsonianmag.com/history/pass-it-on-the-secret-that-preceded-the-indian-rebellion-of-1857-105066360/, accessed 26 Mar. 2015.

[117] Martineau H., *British Rule in India: A Historical Sketch*, Smith, Elder and Co., London, 1857.

[118] Ramesh R., *India's secret history: 'A holocaust, one where millions disappeared...'*, The Gurdian, 24 Aug. 2007, http://www.theguardian.com/world/2007/aug/24/india.randeepramesh, accessed 6 Feb. 2016.

[119] http://www.nios.ac.in/media/documents/SecSocSciCour/English/Lesson-07.pdf, accessed 6 Feb. 2016.

[120] http://en.wikipedia.org/wiki/Prostitution_in_colonial_India, accessed 6 Feb. 2016.

[121] http://satyameva-jayate.org/2006/02/04/economic-exploitation-drain-of-wealth/, accessed 7 Feb. 2016.

[122] Nehru. J., *The Discovery of India*, Oxford University Press, Fifth impression, 1986.

[123] Natarajan S., *A History of the Press in India*, Asia Publishing House, 1962, http://www.odia.org/books/A_Story_Of_The_Press_In_India.pdf, accessed 6 Feb. 2016.

[124] *History of Indian Press*, India Netzone, 22 Feb. 2014, http://www.indianetzone.com/42/history_indian_press.htm, accessed 16 Feb. 2016.

[125] http://rsf.org/index2014/en-index2014.php, accessed 14 Feb. 2016.

[126] Engdahl F.W., *'Oil and the origins of the 'War to make the world safe for Democracy'*, 2007.

[127] http://americanhistory.about.com/od/worldwari/tp/causes-of-world-war-1.htm, accessed 6 Feb. 2016.

[128] Omissi D., *"Indian Voices of the Great War: Soldiers' letters, 1914-18"*, Penguin Books Limited, 2014.

[129] http://en.wikipedia.org/wiki/World_War_I, accessed 16 Feb. 2016.

[130] Yergin D., *The Prize - The Epic Quest for Oil, Money and Power*, Simon & Schuster, 1992

[131] Gandhi M.K., *My Experiments with Truth*, Penguin Evergreen, 2011.

[132] Mail Foreign Service, *Was Gandhi gay? Letters between Indian leader and bodybuilding friend fuel speculation about true nature of relationship*, Mail Online, 3 Jan. 2013, http://www.dailymail.co.uk/news/article-2270778/Was-Gandhi-gay-Letters-Mahatma-Gandhi-bodybuilding-friend-fuel-speculation-true-nature-relationship.html#ixzz3EVp0ZuTW, accessed 9 Feb. 2016.

[133] Sen R., *Mahatma's attitude to sex continues to fascinate*, Times of India, 30 Mar. 2011, http://timesofindia.indiatimes.com/india/Mahatmas-attitude-to-sex-continues-to-fascinate/articleshow/7821432.cms, accessed 3 Jan. 2016.

[134] Mahurkar U., *Mahatma and Manuben*, India Today, 7 Jun. 2013, http://indiatoday.intoday.in/story/mahatma-gandhi-experiment-sexuality-manuben-discovered-diaries/1/278952.html, accessed 3 Jan. 2016.

[135] http://en.wikipedia.org/wiki/Reginald_Dyer, accessed 3 Jan. 2016.

[136] Roy K., Mazumdar M. K., *A Gandhi-Tagore Chronicle*, Visva Bharati Kolkata, Second Edition, 2008.

[137] Khimjee H., *Pakistan: A Legacy of the Indian Khilafat Movement*, iUniverse LLC, 2013.

[138] Garfield J.L., Bhushan N., *Gandhi and Tagore on Ethics, Development and Freedom*, http://www.smith.edu/philosophy/docs/garfield_swaraj.pdf, accessed 3 Jan. 2016.

[139] http://www.swaraj.org/tapan.htm, accessed 3 Jan. 2016.

[140] http://shodhganga.inflibnet.ac.in/bitstream/10603/558/8/11_chapter2.pdf, accessed 3 Jan. 2016.

[141] http://mukto-mona.net/Articles/mohammad_quayum/Tagore_Nationalism.pdf, accessed 3 Jan. 2016.

[142] Rabindranath T., *The English writings of Rabindranath Tagore*, A Miscellany Vol3 (The Cult of the Chakara, Modern Review, 1925), Sahitya Academy, 1996.

[143] *Selected letters of Gandhi (Poet and the Chakara)*, Young India, 1925.

[144] http://ijear.org/vol2issue2/2/sukhchain2.pdf, accessed 3 Jan. 2016.

[145] http://historypak.com/nehru-report/, accessed 3 Jan. 2016.

[146] http://www.columbia.edu/itc/mealac/pritchett/00ambedkar/ambedkar_partition/307c.html, accessed 3 Jan. 2016.

[147] http://en.wikipedia.org/wiki/Nehru_Report, accessed 15 Jan. 2016.

[148] http://en.wikipedia.org/wiki/Fourteen_Points_of_Jinnah, accessed 15 Jan. 2016.

[149] http://en.wikipedia.org/wiki/The_Lost_Leader_(poem), accessed 14 Jan. 2016.

[150] Bhagat Singh was a humanist - innately secular (Bhagat Singh was hanged March 23, 1931.), 22 Mar. 2014, http://news.oneindia.in/india/bhagat-singh-was-a-humanist-innately-secular-bhagat-singh-1416357.html, accessed 3 Jan. 2016.

[151] http://en.wikipedia.org/wiki/Surya_Sen, accessed 3 Jan. 2016.

[152] http://en.wikipedia.org/wiki/Gandhi%E2%80%93Irwin_Pact, accessed 3 Jan. 2016.

[153] Tunzelmann A.V., *Indian Summer: The Secret History of End of an Empire*, Pocket Books, 2007.

[154] http://www.telegraphindia.com/1110605/jsp/7days/story_14072487.jsp

[155] Bose S., *His Majesties Opponent*, The Belknap Press, 2011

[156] Das S., *Subhas: A Political Biography*, Rupa Publication India Pvt Ltd, 2001.

[157] West W.J., *Orwell: The War Commentaries*, http://www.oocities. org/vayujeet/netaji.html, accessed 13 Jan. 2016.

[158] http://en.wikipedia.org/wiki/Day_of_Deliverance (India), accessed 13 Jan. 2016.

[159] Ghosh S.K., *The Transfer of Power: Real or Formal?*, Jul. 2007, http://www.rupe-india.org/43/ghosh.html, accessed 13 Jan. 2016.

[160] Lazzaro J., *Bengal Famine Of 1943 - A Man-Made Holocaust*, I. B. Times, 22 Feb. 2013, http://www.ibtimes.com/bengal-famine-1943-man-made-holocaust-1100525, accessed 13 Jan. 2016.

[161] Simha R. K., *Remembering India's Forgotten Holocaust*, Tehelka, 13 Jun. 2014, http://www.tehelka.com/remembering-indias-forgotten-holocaust/, accessed 13 Jan. 2016.

[162] http://www.historylearningsite.co.uk/battle_imphal_1944. htm, accessed 23 Jan. 2016.

[163] http://www.battleofimphal.com/the-battle/imphal-and-ina, accessed 22 Jan. 2016.

[164] Dhar A., *India's Biggest Cover-up*, Vitasta Publishing Pvt. Ltd., 2014.

[165] Borra R., *Subhas Chandra Bose, The Indian National Army and The War of India's Liberation*, Institute of Historical Review, From The Journal of Historical Review, Winter 1982, Vol. 3, No. 4, pp 407-439, http://www.ihr.org/jhr/v03/v03p407_Borra.html, accessed 22 Jan. 2016.

[166] *Vignettes from the First independence Day Celebration*, Press Information Bureau,13 Aug. 2007, http://www.dadinani. com/images/pdf/firstindepdelhi/faujiakhbar1947.pdf, accessed 22 Jan. 2016.

[167] Ghosh P., *Partition Of India And Pakistan: The Rape Of Women On An Epic, Historic Scale, International Bussiness Times*, 16 Aug.

2013, http://www.ibtimes.com/partition-india-pakistan-rape-women-epic-historic-scale-1387601, accessed 23 Jan. 2016.

[168] Alexander H., *A Miracle in Calcutta*, Prospect, 1 Aug. 2007, http://www.prospectmagazine.co.uk/magazine/amiracleincalcutta, accessed 3 Jan. 2016.

[169] http://raghgavabharatiya.weebly.com/uploads/1/3/5/9/13590619/29637040-why-i-did-it-by-nathuram-godse-court-statement.pdf, accessed 3 Jan. 2016.

[170] Guha R., *India after Gandhi: History of the World's Largest Democracy*, Picador India, 2007.

[171] Davis M., *Late Victorian Holocausts: El Nino Famines and the Making of the Third World,* Verso, 2002.

[172] Malhotra R. and Neelakandan, A., <u>*Breaking India: Western Interventions in Dravidian and Dalit Faultlines*</u>, Amaryllis, 2012.

[173] Pirzada S. S., *Jinnah and Gandhi and the Indian Constitution*, Gandhi Topia, 12 Oct. 2013, http://www.gandhitopia.org/group/mgnd/forum/topics/jinnah-and-gandhi-and-the-indian-constitution, accessed 3 Jan. 2016.

[174] Megha, *The Original Constitution Writer*, I See India, 13 Aug. 2011, http://iseeindia.com/2011/08/13/the-original-constitution-writer/, accessed 19 Jan. 2016.

[175] Visvanathan, S., Poetics of a Nation: Remembering Nehru, The Hindu, 15 Nov. 2014, http://www.thehindu.com/opinion/lead/opinion-on-jawaharlal-nehru-125th-birth-anniversary/article6600161.ece?utm_source=vuukle&utm_medium=referral, accessed 17 Jan. 2016.

[176] Friedman G., *The Geopolitics of India: A Shifting, Self-Contained World*, Stratfor, 2008.

[177] Phelamei S., *Naga Movement: A Brief History and Peace Accord with the Indian government*, Zee News, 4 Aug. 2015, http://zeenews.india.com/exclusive/naga-movement-a-brief-history_2999.html, accessed 28 Jan. 2016.

[178] *Insults Fly on Nixon Tapes*, The Gurdian, 29 Jun. 2005, http://www.theguardian.com/world/2005/jun/29/india.usa, accessed 13 Jan. 2016.

[179] BSCAL, *The Nav-Nirman Movement*, Business Standard, 19 Feb. 2000, http://www.business-standard.com/article/specials/the-nav-nirman-movement-100021901024_1.html, accessed 9 Jan. 2016.

[180] Rajagopal K., *Debates Show Why Preamble's Original Text Left Out the Two Words*, The Hindu, 29 Jan. 2015, http://m.thehindu.com/news/national/debates-show-why-preambles-original-text-left-out-the-two-words/article6831694.ece/, accessed 5 Jan. 2016.

[181] http://guruprasad.net/posts/rajiv-gandhi-was-the-father-of-bjp/, accessed 5 Jan. 2016.

[182] http://www.bmhrc.org/Bhopal%20Gas%20Tragedy.htm, accessed 5 Jan. 2016.

[183] Nanda R., *Bhopal Gas Tragedy: How it Happened*, IBN Live, 8 Dec. 2014, http://ibnlive.in.com/news/bhopal-gas-tragedy-how-it-happened/517131-3-236.html, accessed 5 Jan. 2016.

[184] *What the Bofors Scandal is All About*, IBN Live, 26 Apr. 2012, http://ibnlive.in.com/news/what-the-bofors-scandal-is-all-about/252196-3.html, accessed 5 Jan. 2016.

[185] *Rajiv Gandhi Wanted Bofors Money to Run Congress: Ex-CBI Chief*, The Times of India, 14 Nov. 2013, http://timesofindia.indiatimes.com/india/Rajiv-Gandhi-wanted-Bofors-money-to-run-Congress-Ex-CBI-chief/articleshow/25720914.cms, accessed 7 Jan. 2016.

[186] Jha P. S., *Quiet Goes The Don*, Outlook India, 17 Jan 2005, http://www.outlookindia.com/article/Quiet-Goes-The-Don/226253, accessed 8 Jan. 2016.

[187] Baru S., *The Accidental Prime Minister: The Making and Unmaking of Manmohan Singh*, Viking by Penguin Books, 2014.

[188] Malik V.P., *Kargil: From Surprise to Victory*, Harper Collins Publishers India, 2010.

[189] Banerjee A., *Tales from Shining and Sinking India*, Amaryllis, 2013.

[190] Edited by McKinsey and Company, *Reimagining India : How to Unlock the Potential of Asia's Next Superpower*, Simon & Schuster, 2013.

[191] Luce E., *Inspite of Gods: The Strange Rise of Modern India*, London : Abacus, Originally published by Little, Brown Publisher, 2011

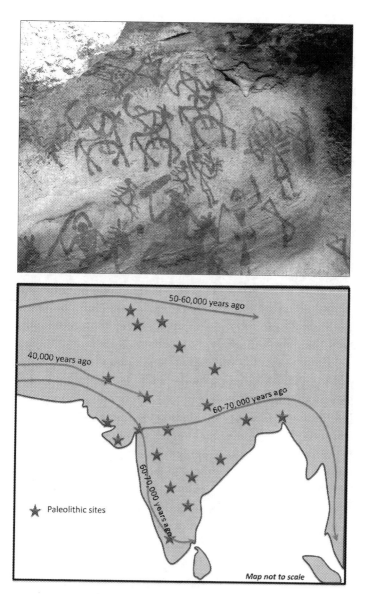

Figure 1 Map of paleolithic sites of India. Picture of hunters, Bhimbetka Cave paintings

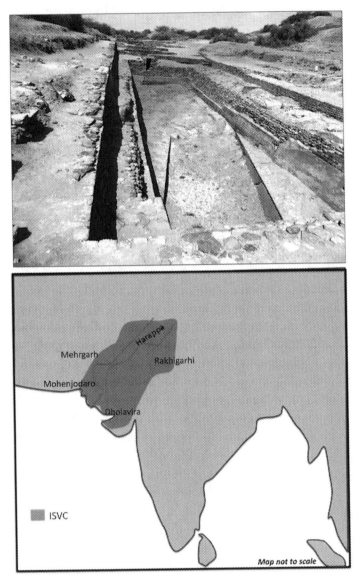

Figure 2: Map of ISVC, picture of a canal in Dholavira

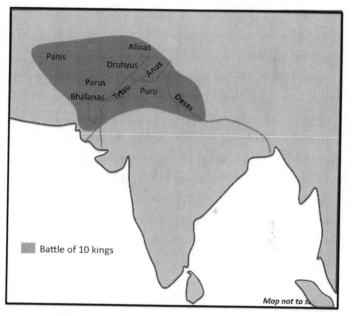

Figure 3: Battle of Ten Kings from Rig Veda

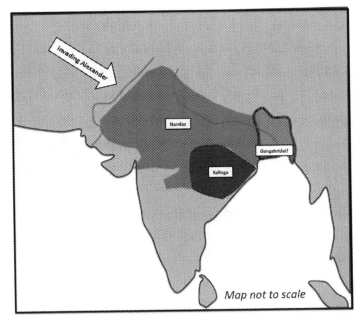

Figure 4: Nandas and Gangaridai Empires

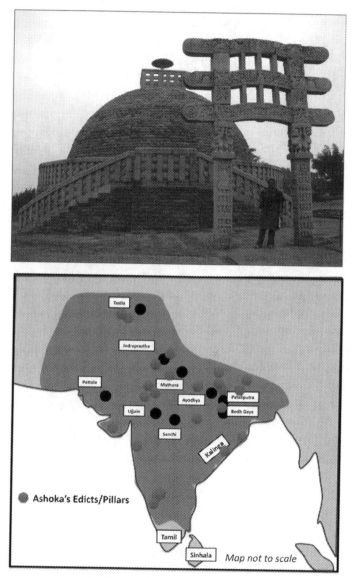

Figure 5: Map of pillars and inscriptions showing the extent of Ashoka's Empire. Picture of Sanchi Stupa near Bhopal.

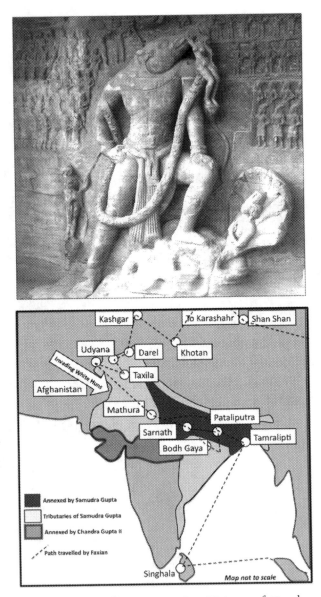

Figure 6: Map of Gupta Empire. Picture of Varaha Avatar in Udaigiri caves.

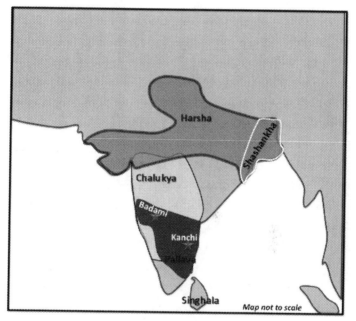

Figure 7: Map of seventh-century India

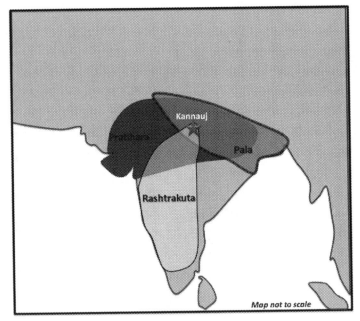

Figure 8: Kannauj Triangle

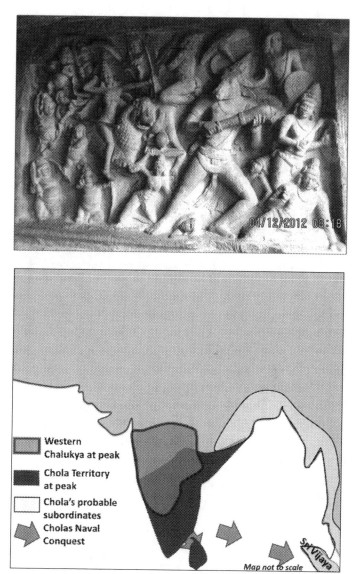

Figure 9: Rise of Chola Empire. Picture of Mahishasurimardini in Mahabalipuram

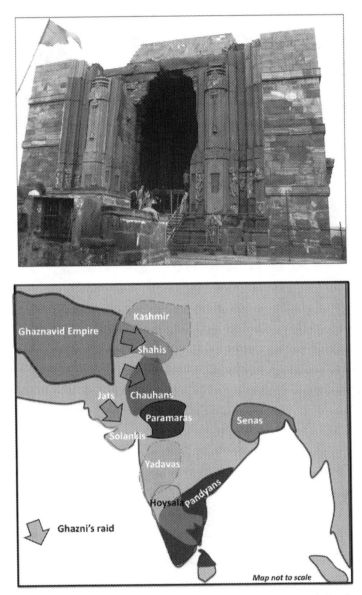

Figure 10: Attack of Ghazni. Picture of Bhojeshwar Temple built by Raja Bhoja

Figure 11: Slave Dynasty. Picture of Qutub Minar marking the victory and the beginning of Slave Dynasty.

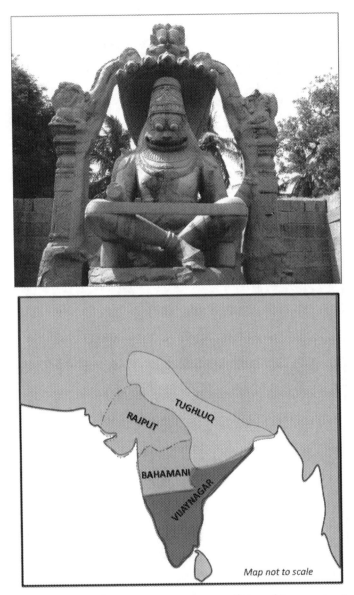

Figure 12: Rise of Vijayanagara. Picture of Narashima avatar in Hampi

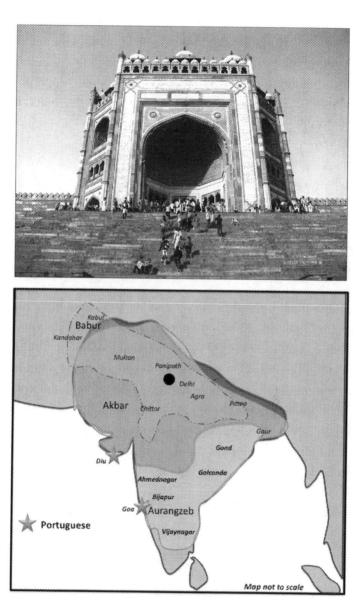

Figure 13: Map of Mughal Empire. Picture of Buland Darwaza built by Akbar

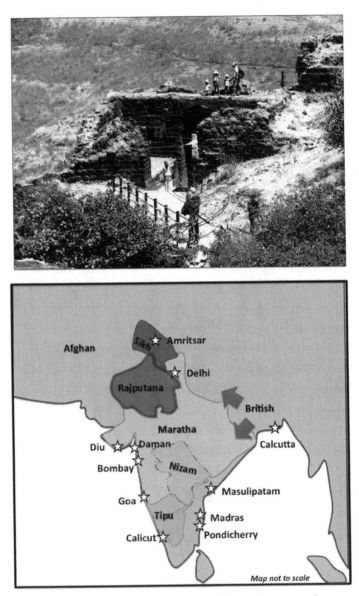

Figure 14: Rise of Marathas. Picture of Shivaji's Singagad Fort

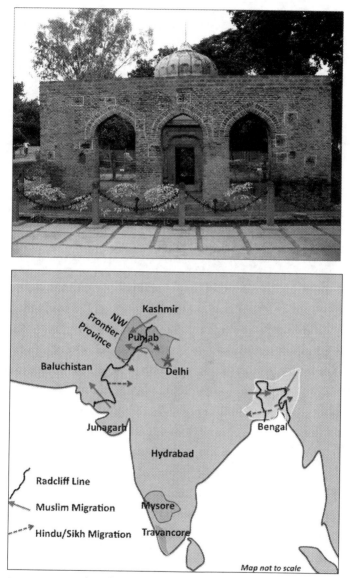

Figure 15: British India and Partition. Picture showing the bullet marks in Jallinwalabagh

ABOUT THE AUTHOR

Subhrashis Adhikari is a history enthusiast. He travels all around India, unraveling her glorious past, with his wife and little daughter as a companion. After completing his MTech from IIT Bombay, he now works as a geologist in a multinational oil and gas exploration and production company.

Printed in the United States
By Bookmasters